Systems Thinking: Managing Chaos and Complexity

A Platform for Designing Business Architecture

SECOND EDITION

Jamshid Gharajedaghi

AMSTERDAM • BOSTON • HEIDELBERG • LONDON
NEW YORK • OXFORD • PARIS • SAN DIEGO
SAN FRANCISCO • SINGAPORE • SYDNEY • TOKYO

Butterworth-Heinemann is an imprint of Elsevier

Butterworth-Heinemann is an imprint of Elsevier
30 Corporate Drive, Suite 400, Burlington, MA 01803, USA
525 B Street, Suite 1900, San Diego, California 92101-4495, USA
84 Theobald's Road, London WC1X 8RR, UK

This book is printed on acid-free paper. ∞

Library of Congress Cataloging-in-Publication Data
Gharajedaghi, Jamshid.
   Systems thinking : managing chaos and complexity : a platform for designing
   business architecture / Jamshid Gharajedaghi.
      p.   cm.
   Includes bibliographical references and index.
   ISBN-13: 978-0-7506-7973-2   ISBN-10: 0-7506-7163-5 (alk. paper)
   1. System analysis.   2. Chaotic behavior in systems.   3. Industrial management.
   4. Technological complexity.   I. Title.
   T57.6.G52 1999
   003—dc21

                                                                    98-55939

British Library Cataloguing-in-Publication Data
A catalogue record for this book is available from the British Library.

ISBN 13: 978-0-7506-7973-2
ISBN 10: 0-7506-7973-5

For information on all Academic Press publications
visit our Web site at www.books.elsevier.com

Printed in the United States of America
07   08   09   10   9   8   7   6   5   4   3

Working together to grow
libraries in developing countries

www.elsevier.com | www.bookaid.org | www.sabre.org

ELSEVIER   BOOK AID International   Sabre Foundation

*To Russ Ackoff, my mentor, colleaque and friend
of over thirty years who made it all possible.*

Contents

Foreword to Second Edition   xv
Preface   xvii
Acknowledgments   xix

PART I   **Systems Philosophy:**
            The Name of the Devil   1

Chapter 1   How the Game Is Evolving   3
            Imitation   4
            Inertia   5
            Suboptimization   6
            Change of the Game   6
            Shift of Paradigm   8
        Interdependency and Choice   9
        On the Nature of Organization: The First
            Paradigm Shift   10
            Mindless Systems: A Mechanistic View   10
            Uniminded Systems: A Biological View   11
            Multiminded Systems: A Sociocultural View   12
        On the Nature of Inquiry: The Second
            Paradigm Shift   13
        The Competitive Games   16
            Mass Production: Interchangeability
            of Parts and Labor   17
            Divisional Structure: Managing Growth
            and Diversity   18
            Participative Management: Self-Organizing
            Systems   20
            Operations Research: Joint Optimization   21
            Lean Production Systems: Flexibility
            and Control   22
            Interactive Management: The Design
            Approach   22

PART II   **Systems Theories:**
                The Nature of the Beast   25

Chapter 2   Systems Principles   29
                Openness   30
                Purposefulness   33
                Multidimensionality   38
                    Plurality of Function, Structure,
                        and Process   43
                Emergent Property   45
                Counterintuitiveness   49

Chapter 3   Systems Dimensions   56
                Throughput   59
                    Model of the Process   60
                    Critical Properties   63
                    Measurement and Diagnostic   64
                    Read-Only Memory   65
                    Target Costing   65
                Membership   66
                Conflict Management   67
                    From Lose/Lose to Win/Win
                        Environments   70
                    Changing Conflict to Competition   70
                Decision Systems   71
                    Duplication of Power   71
                    Decision Criteria   73
                Learning and Control Systems   75
                    Social Calculus   77

Chapter 4   The Sociocultural Model:
                Information-Bonded Systems   83
                Culture   84
                Social Learning   87
                Development   88
                    Schematic View of Theoretical
                        Traditions   89
                    Systems View of Development   92
                    Obstruction to Development   96
                    Recap   103

PART III   **Systems Methodology:**
               The Logic of the Madness   105

Chapter 5   Systems Methodology   107
               Foundation 1: Holistic Thinking   108
                   Structure, Function, Process, and Context   108
               Foundation 2: Operational Thinking   114
                   Understanding Chaos and Complexity   114
                   Understanding the Multi-loop Nonlinear
                       Feedback System   117
                   Mapping the Dynamic Behavior   118
               Foundation 3: Self-Organization   121
                   Socio-Cultural Model   121
               Foundation 4: Interactive Design   125
                   Defining Problems (Formulation of the Mess)   126
                   Designing a Solution (Idealization and
                       Realization)   128
               Conclusion   130

Chapter 6   Defining the Problem   131
               Formulating the Mess   131
                   Searching   132
                   Mapping the Mess   135
                   Telling the Story   140
               Mapping the Mess of XYZ Corporation, a Sample
                   Formulation   140

Chapter 7   Designing Business Architecture   152
               Multidimensional Modular Design   152
                   The System's Boundary and Business
                       Environment   153
                   Purpose   156
                   Functions   161
                   Structure   163
                   Outputs Dimension   165
                   Inputs Dimension   167
                   Markets Dimension   169
                   Internal Market Economy   170
               Processes   174
                   Planning, Learning and Control System   175
                   Measurement System   176

Realization: Successive Approximation   181
    Type I Constraints   181
    Type II Constraints   183
    Type III Constraints   183
Dissolving the Second-Order Machine   183
    Recap   184

PART IV   **Systems Practice: The Gutsy Few   185**

Chapter 8   The Oneida Nation   187

Desired Specifications   187
Systems Architecture   189
Governance   190
    Governing Body   192
    Chief of Staff   192
    Planning, Learning, and Control System   192
    Planning, Learning, and Control Board   194
Membership Systems   195
    Empowerment   195
    The Tie that Bonds   196
    Membership Network   196
    Consensus-Building Process   198
    Back to the Future   201
    Performance Criteria and Measures   202
Learning Systems   203
    Learning to Learn (Formal Education)   205
    Learning to Be (Cultural Education)   205
    Learning to Do (Professional Education)   206
    Support Functions   206
    Advocacy Functions   207
    Oneida Multiversity   207
    Performance Criteria and Measures   210
Business Systems   211
    Services Sector   212
    Industry Sector   213
    Leisure Sector   213
    Land and Agriculture Sector   213
    Marketing Sector   213
    Governance and Intersystems Relationships   214
Core Services   215
    Government Services Division   215
    Infrastructure Development Division   215
    Ordinance Division   216
    Performance Criteria and Measures   216
    Governance and Oversight   216

External Environment   217
Judicial System   218
  Contextual Analysis   218
  Contextual Challenge   219
  Democratic Challenge   220

Chapter 9   Butterworth Health Systems   222
Issues, Concerns, and Expectations   223
Design Specifications   225
The Architecture   226
Market Dimension   227
  Market Access   227
Care System   229
  Contextual Background   229
  Desired Specifications   229
  Common Features   231
  Preventive Care   233
  Interventional Care   234
  Viability Care   234
  Terminal Care   235
Output Dimension   237
  Health Delivery System Design: The Makeup   240
  Community-Based Health Delivery System   240
  Specialized Health Delivery System   242
  Shared Services   243
Core Knowledge   245
Shared Services   249
  Need for Centralization   250
  Control versus Service   251
  Customer Orientation   251
*Health Delivery System, Core Knowledge, and Care Systems
  Interactions*   253
The Executive Office   257
Recap   258

Chapter 10   The Marriott Corporation   260
The Environment: How the Game Is Evolving   261
  Bases for Competition   261
Purpose   262
  Principles and Desired Characteristics   262
The Architecture   263
  Product/Market Mix   264
  Region/Market Operation   264
  Brand Management   266
  Core Components   266

Core Knowledge   267
Critical Processes   268
Recap   269

Chapter 11   Commonwealth Energy Systems   270

Stakeholders' Expectations   271
   Shareholders' Expectations   271
   Regulators' Expectations   272
   Employees' Expectations   272
   Customers' Expectations   272
   Suppliers' Expectations   273
   Public's Expectations   273
Business Environment   273
   The Changing Game: The Energy Industry   273
   The Changing Game: COM/Energy   275
Design   276
   Purpose and Strategic Intent   276
   Core Values and Desired Specifications   278
General Architecture   279
Core Business Units: Gas and Electricity Distribution   282
   Customer-Oriented Business Units: Energy Supply
     Systems and Management Services   283
   Cogeneration and Packages of Energy Supply (Industrial
     and Commercial)   283
   Energy Efficiency and Electrotechnologies (Residential
     and Commercial)   285
Technology/Supply-Oriented Business Units: Energy
  Generation and Supply   286
   Energy Generation (Canal)   286
   Gas Storage (LNG)   287
   Steam Services   288
Energy Brokerage and International Operations   288
   Energy Brokerage   288
   International Operations   289
Shared Services (Performance Centers)   290
   Service Company   291
   Financial Systems   292
Executive Office   292
   Core Knowledge Pool   293
   Learning and Control System   294

Chapter 12   Carrier Corporation   297

Expectations, Assumptions, and Specifications   298
   The Changing Game: In General   298
   The Changing Game: The HVAC Industry   299

Drivers for Change 299
Bases for Competition 299
Core Values 300
Products and Services 300
Core Technology and Know-How 301
Sales and Distribution System 302
Systems Architecture 303
Desired Characteristics 303
A Multidimensional Framework 304
Markets 304
Regional Units 305
Area Units 307
Output Units 307
Components 309
Inputs 310
The Technology 310
Operational Support (Process Design) 310
Management Support Services 311
Business Processes 312
Decision System 312
Performance Measurement and Reward System 312
Target Costing and Variable Budgeting System 312

Conclusion 315
Bibliography 319
Index 325

Foreword to Second Edition

Professor Thomas Lee of MIT was a dear friend. I met him in the early 1980s when he was the Secretary General of the International Institute for Applied Systems Analysis (IIASA). Tom was obsessed with the notion that two distinct traditions of systems thinking—Ackoff's interactive design and Forrester's systems dynamics—are complementary. For years he insisted that we should work together to merge the two prominent systems methodologies into a single unified one. But at the time I was preoccupied with two other exciting conceptions. The first one was consideration of culture as an operating system that guides social organizations toward a predefined order. The second was a hunch that iteration is the key for understanding complexity.

Sadly, Tom passed away, but managed to get a promise from me to work on his favorite project. To fulfill my promise I tried several different approaches, all in vain, before realizing that I had the solution all along. In fact I had used it in the first edition of the present work to combine my version of holistic thinking—iteration of structure, function, and process—with Interactive design. Suddenly it became clear that Interactive Design is not just a simple methodology. It is also a platform that could be used to integrate the iterative approach, systems dynamics, and the challenge of self-organization of sociocultural systems (neg-entropic process) into a comprehensive systems methodology.

I prepared a draft of my thinking and showed it to my mentor Russ Ackoff. He liked it very much and insisted that I should publish it in a new book.

Coincidentally, at that time, Dean Thomas Manahan of Villanova University and Niel Sicherman, Associate Dean of Executive Education, asked me to help them design a distinctive Executive MBA program that would use systems thinking as a platform to integrate the relevant subjects into a unified whole. I was ready for this assignment. The systems methodology I had developed was uniquely qualified to deal with the challenge that most MBA programs have not been able to deliver. Four successful classes of Villanova Executive MBA graduates are testimony for the effectiveness of this approach.

When Dennis McGonagle, my editor from Elsevier, called to see whether I was ready for a new edition, I welcomed the opportunity to revise chapters 4, 5, 6, and 7 of the present work to incorporate this exciting concept.

But, in the end, it was the remarkable support of my valued partner Susan Leddick that got the job done. Susan not only edited the revised chapters with utmost attention but also had many invaluable suggestions that improved the outcome significantly.

Here it is, my new version of a comprehensive systems methodology. I sincerely believe that the beauty of interactive design and the magic of the iteration of structure, function, and process—when combined with the power of operational thinking, and genuine understanding of neg-entropic processes—create a competent and exciting systems methodology that goes a long way in dealing with emerging challenges of seemingly complex and chaotic sociocultural systems.

Jamshid Gharajedaghi

Preface

This is an unconventional book for an unconventional reader. It is intended for those professionals who, in addition to their specialized knowledge, would like to get a handle on life so they may put their special text into its proper context. It speaks to those thinkers and practitioners who have come to realize that *learning to be* is as much a necessary part of a successful professional life as is the *learning to do*; and that to remain unidimensional is to become boringly predictable.

This book is about a new mode of seeing, doing, and being *in the world*; a way of thinking through chaos and complexity. It is not another *"how to"* book, nor an alternative to what is already available. It is not a variation on the tired theme of offering the latest version of the common characteristics of the winners.

It also violates the golden rule of best sellers. I am told the experience of dealing with too many ideas in a single book is way out of the comfort zone of most readers, but given the choice between breaking the message or breaking the norm, it was obvious which one had to go. If that meant being a minority of one, so be it. The ideas in this book, although many, converge and create a whole that is profoundly more beautiful than any one concept in isolation. The real beauty, therefore, lies in experiencing the whole, seeing the concepts all fuse into one.

The book, nevertheless, speaks to everyone for whom the joy of thinking is still alive and kicking and whose enthusiasm to entertain exciting but unfamiliar conceptions is not yet exhausted.

In a nutshell, the book is about systems. The imperatives of interdependency, the necessity of reducing endless complexities, and the need to produce manageable simplicities require a workable systems methodology and a holistic frame of reference that will allow us to focus on the relevant issues and avoid the endless search for more details while drowning in proliferating useless information.

Contrary to widely held belief, the popular notion of a multidisciplinary approach is not a systems approach. The ability to synthesize separate findings into a coherent whole seems far more critical than the ability to generate information from different perspectives. This book, with a practical orientation and yet a profound theoretical depth, goes beyond the simple declaration of the desirability of systems thinking. It deals with the challenges of interdependency, chaos, and choice using an elaborate scheme called *iterative design*.

The iterative design explicitly recognizes that choice is at the heart of human development. Development is the capacity to choose; design is a vehicle for enhancement of choice and holistic thinking. Designers, in this book, seek to choose rather than predict the future. They try to understand rational, emotional, and cultural dimensions of choice and to produce a design that satisfies a multitude of functions. They learn how to use what they already know, how to realize what they do not know, and how to learn what they need to know.

The book is divided into four parts. Part I identifies where systems thinking fits into the overall scheme of things. It provides an overview, a total picture of major theoretical traditions in management and systems thinking and their relationship.

Parts II and III are the guts of the book. Part II discusses the five systems principles as the building blocks of the mental model used to generate the initial set of assumptions about the system. It also identifies the comprehensive set of variables that collectively describe the organization in its totality. Part III deals extensively with the development of iterative design and its practical implications in defining problems and designing solutions.

Part IV reviews five actual cases of designing a business architecture. The Oneida Nation, Butterworth Health Systems, the Marriott Corporation, Commonwealth Energy Systems, and Carrier Corporation represent a diverse group of challenging social organizations. I call them "the gutsy few" because they were willing to experiment with unconventional solutions without worrying about who had done it first. I am grateful for their trust and permission to share synopses of their designs with others.

Acknowledgments

A lifetime of teaching and consulting involves indebtedness to innumerable sources of wisdom. I have learned from my students and clients far more than I ever taught them. Looking back, I can hardly even begin to recall the fires by which I was warmed, the lights by which I found my way. And yet there are faces that vividly stand out. To them, thankful acknowledgment is in order.

First and foremost is Bijan Khorram. It is almost impossible to separate him from so much that is here. As a friend and colleague of over three decades, the effect of his thinking on me knows no bounds. He acted as the sounding board to examine the soundness of ideas and the potency of their configurations. He directly collaborated in the redesigns and write-ups of the cases presented under Systems Practice. Stylistically, his influence permeated the entire exercise.

Russell L. Ackoff has been my mentor, partner, and a great friend. He was there, as always, with his infinite wisdom and uncompromising critique to examine every line and dissect every concept of the manuscript. I welcomed his measured views and took most of his recommendations.

Johnny Pourdehnad's insatiable love of searching was a blessing. With him around, access to valuable resources was fun rather than an obstruction. Jason Magidson helped with graphics. Pat Brandt and Tina Fellenbaum provided the logistical support. Pat Egner did the editing; the Anglicized version is indebted to her efforts.

There were, of course, those who discovered the pony in what I had to say. Professors Gerry Wilson and Tommy Lee, Dean Pat Stocker, Kathy Dannemiller, Martine Dodds, Carol and David Schwinn, Susan Leddick, Bill Roth, and March Jacques just kept cheering me on.

Then there were the special clients whose patronage, courage, and intellectual challenge in bringing the conceptual ideas to concrete fruition proved invaluable indeed. Charlie Ligon, Karl J. Krapek, Len Devanna and Artley Skenandore, with their unfailing trust, turned out to be the difference that made the difference.

Last but not least is Karen Speerstra, Publishing Director of Butterworth-Heinemann, who, with remarkable decisiveness, got the project rolling. March Jacques proved to be a fantastic matchmaker.

My gratitude to them all will remain a debt I can never repay.

PART I

Systems Philosophy
The Name of the Devil

1

How the Game Is Evolving

The most stubborn habits which resist change with the greatest tenacity are those which worked well for a space of time and led to the practitioner being rewarded for those behaviors. If you suddenly tell such persons that their recipe for success is no longer viable, their personal experience belies your diagnosis. The road to convincing them is hard. It is the stuff of classic tragedy.[1]

In 1996, the Dow Jones Industrial Average marked its 100th anniversary. Of the original companies listed in 1896, only General Electric had survived to join in the celebration.

In the mid-1960s, Jean Jacques Schreiber, in his best-selling book, *American Challenge*, told his fellow Europeans: "Swallow your pride, imitate America, or accept her dominance forever." But in the late 1970s, it was "Japan Inc." that somehow posed the greatest competitive challenge to corporate America. It took a 300 percent devaluation of the dollar to ward off this challenge

Fourteen of the 47 companies featured in Tom Peters' much-acclaimed book of the 1980s, *In Search of Excellence*, lost their luster in less than four years, at least in the sense that they had suffered serious profit erosion.

The collapse of savings and loans and real estate, along with the fall of the defense industry in the late 1980s, could have led to a disastrous 1990s. But counterintuitively, these phenomena resulted in a restructuring of the financial and intellectual resources in America, which may very well have been a co-producer of one of the longest periods of economic expansion and prosperity in America. Ironically, in mid-1998, worries about Japan's economy were the nagging concerns of American investors.

What is going on? The game, obviously, keeps changing. But this is hardly news. By now it is a well-known and even a tired secret that what underlies the fall of so many great enterprises is that somehow their recipe for

---

[1]Charles Hampden-Turner and Linda Arc, *The Raveled Knot: An Examination of the Time-to-Market Issue at Analog's Semi-conductor Division*, unpublished internal report.

3

success becomes ineffective. There seems to be a devil at work here, and the name of this devil is success.

Each one of us can recall cases of great powers, nations, organizations, or personalities rising and falling. The phenomenon occurs all too frequently to be dismissed as coincidental. So what underlying forces convert success to failure? Let's start with the following observation. The forces that make a failure out of success form a five-level hierarchy. (See Figure 1.1.) Each level represents a distinct tendency, but together they form an interactive whole in which higher levels provide the context for the lower levels. At each level, success plays a critical but different role.

Imitation

Operating at the first level, imitation is the most basic force. Competitive advantage is by definition a distinction. Successful distinctions, in time, are eroded by imitation. At that point, exceptions become norms and lose their advantage.

Although imitation has always been present, its current significance for American business has changed by an order of magnitude. Advances in information technology, communication, and reverse engineering have increased product technology's vulnerability to imitation. Any technological distinction in a given product is now fair game for potential imitators, who can learn, copy, and reproduce it in practically no time. Such easy imitation has been significant for American industry. While product technology has traditionally

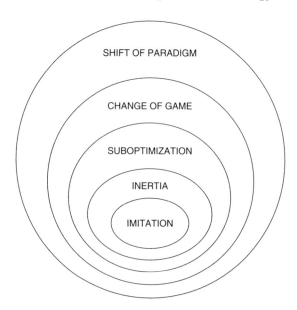

FIGURE 1.1   Hierarchy of Forces that Erode Competitive Advantage

been the cornerstone of the American competitive game, countries with an advantage in process technology have gained a dual advantage.

First, it is difficult to copy a distinction in process technology because its critical elements are knowledge workers. Second, competency in a process technology makes it simpler to transfer knowledge from one context to another, facilitating the operationalization of new knowledge. The results are dramatic: much faster time-to-market performance, a lower break-even point, better product variety, and faster response to change.

In the late 1970s, a well-known equipment company in America realized it had a 40 percent cost disadvantage in comparison with its direct Japanese competitor. The company, ironically, was the technological leader in the lift truck industry. Its cost structure was 40 percent raw material, 15 percent direct labor, and 45 percent overhead. Overhead (transformation cost) was simply calculated as 300 percent of direct labor.

The company had decided to reduce its costs by 20 percent. It was assumed that a 5 percent reduction in direct labor would automatically reduce overhead by another 15 percent, resulting in a 20 percent cost reduction. After a whole year of struggle, direct labor was reduced to 10 percent without any reduction in overhead. When we were asked to deal with the situation, our first reaction was: Why would anyone want to reduce their cost by 20 percent when there was a 40 percent cost disadvantage? Where did the competitor's 40 percent cost advantage come from? It was obvious that even if the workers gave up all of their wages, the company would not survive.

When we realized that the competitive product used only 1,800 parts, while our product employed 2,800, the difference in the number of the parts perfectly explained the difference in cost. The surprising element in all of this was that a lower number of parts was achieved by utilizing technologies that had been developed by our client in the last ten years. The problem was that our client had patched each one of its newly developed technologies into an old platform, resulting in a complex and inefficient product, whereas the competition started with a clean slate and took full advantage of the potentials each technology offered. The moral of this story is that once in a while one should pause and reflect on oneself and begin anew.

Inertia

Inertia is responsible for all the second-level tendencies and behaviors that delay reactions to technological breakthroughs. For example, sheer inertia by the Continental Can Company provided the opportunity for two-piece can technology to replace three-piece can technology and destroy the once-mighty Continental Can. Five hundred factories all over the United States and a 45 percent share of the three-piece can market couldn't prevent a delayed reaction to two-piece technology from destroying Continental Can in less than three years.

Ironically, the likelihood that an organization will fail to respond to a critical technological breakthrough is directly proportional to the level of success it had achieved in a previously dominant technology. Stated another way, the more success an organization has with a particular technology, the higher is its resistance to the prospect of change. The initial reaction is always denial! (We do have an amazing capacity for denial in the face of undeniable events.) But the real danger arises when the organization finally decides to patch things up. Patching wastes critical time. It provides the competition with a window of opportunity to disseminate the new technology and dominate the market. Patching, moreover, increases the cost of the operation and reduces the quality of the output, producing a double jeopardy.

Suboptimization

Exaggeration, the fallacy that if *X* is good more *X* is even better, is at the core of the third-level processes that effectively destroy a proven competitive advantage. A tendency to push one's strength to its limits transforms the strength into a destructive weakness. Unfortunately, many stories follow the same line: a winning formula gains adulation, and the heroes or heroines who shaped it become the sole authorities. One right answer prevails. An increasingly monolithic culture produces an ever-decreasing set of alternatives and a narrow path to victory. This limited set redefines the corporate culture, the assumptions, the premises, and the common wisdom that bounds or frames a company's understanding of itself and its industry and drive its competitive strategy.

An interesting treatment of this phenomenon can be found in Danny Miller's book, *The Icarus Paradox* (1990). Miller refers to Icarus of Greek mythology, who became emboldened to fly higher and higher until he came so close to the sun that his wax wings melted and he plunged to his death. Miller explains how craftsmanship and productive attention to detail by Digital Equipment Corporation, turned into an obsession with minutia and technical tinkering. Exaggeration was also at work when the innovative capability of Control Data Corporation (CDC) and Polaroid escalated into high-tech escapism and technical utopia. Miller's list of firms that have been trapped by this phenomenon includes IBM, Texas Instruments, Apple Computer, General Motors, Sears, and many more of the most acclaimed American corporations.

Change of the Game

Change of the game, or transformation of the problem, is at the heart of a counterintuitive process that converts success into failure. In other words, the act of playing a game successfully changes the game itself. Failure to appreciate the consequences of one's success and tenacity in playing the good old game are what tragedies are made of. Once success is achieved or a problem is effectively dissolved, the concerns associated with that problem are irreversibly affected. Dissolving a problem transforms it and generates a whole new set of concerns. That is why the basis for competition changes and a new competitive game emerges as soon as a competitive challenge is met.

The role of success is quite different in the third- and fourth-level processes. When it is exaggerated (third level), success works against the nature of the solution and diminishes its effectiveness. By contrast, success in handling a challenge (fourth level) transforms the nature of the problem; in other words, it changes the game. Henry Ford's success in creating a mass-production machine effectively dissolved the production problem. A familiar concern for production was replaced with an unfamiliar concern for markets. The once-unique ability to mass-produce lost its advantage through widespread imitation. This event changed the competitive game from concern for production to concern for markets, which required an ability to manage diversity and growth.

Henry Ford's refusal to appreciate the implication of his own success and his unwillingness to play the new game ("They can have any color as long as it is black") gave Alfred Sloan of GM the opportunity to dominate the automotive industry. Sloan's concept of product-based divisional structure turned out to be an effective design for managing growth and diversity. The new game, artfully learned and played by corporate America, became the benchmark for the rest of the world to copy.[2]

In an attempt to duplicate the American system, Ohno, the chief engineer of Toyota, came up with yet another new design. His introduction of the lean production system changed the performance measures by more than an order of magnitude. While it took the American auto industry three days to change a die, Toyota could do it in only three minutes. Once again, success transformed the game. This time the differentiating factors were flexibility and control.

But corporate America was too overwhelmed and overjoyed by its own success to even notice the emergence of the new game. This inattentiveness provided Japan with an opportunity to launch a slow but effective challenge. The insidious manner in which the new game evolved underscores another important principle of systems dynamics, exemplified by the story of the frog that boiled to death, sitting happily in water that gradually grew hotter.

Examples of the change of the game can also be found in politics. Although the success of the Persian Gulf War of 1991 boosted the approval rating of then

---

[2]See *The Machine That Changed the World* (Womack, Jones, Ross, 1990).

President Bush to an unprecedented level, it inadvertently cost him the election. The triumph of his foreign policy caused the nation to shift its concern from national security to domestic economy. Failure to understand the implication of this change converted the success to failure.

Recognizing that success changes the game, think about what the phenomenal success of information technology means. Success marks the beginning of the end of the Information Era. Competitive advantage is increasingly shifting away from having access to information toward generating knowledge and, finally, toward gaining understanding.

Shift of Paradigm

The cumulative effects of imitation, inertia, suboptimization, and change of the game ultimately manifest themselves in the fifth force, a shift of paradigm.

A shift of paradigm can happen purposefully, by an active process of learning and unlearning. More commonly, however, it is a reaction to frustration produced by a march of events that nullify conventional wisdom. Faced with a series of contradictions that can no longer be ignored or denied, and/or an increasing number of dilemmas for which prevailing mental models can no longer provide convincing explanations, most people accept that the prevailing paradigm has ceased to be valid and that it has exhausted its potential capacity.

This is a twilight zone where Stafford Beer's aphorism rings true (1975): "Acceptable ideas are competent no more and competent ideas are not yet acceptable." It is where powerful threats and opportunities emerge, where great organizations rise and fall. Eventually, the exceptional courage of a few leads to questioning the conventional wisdom and pointing to the first crack in it. Thus begins a painful struggle whose end result is reconceptualization of critical variables into a new ensemble with a new logic of its own.

Shifts of paradigm can happen in two categories: a change in the nature of reality or a change in the method of inquiry. Also possible, however, is a dual shift involving both dimensions. The significance and impact of any paradigm shift cannot be overestimated, but facing a dual shift is an even more formidable challenge. It tests the outer limits of human capacity to comprehend, communicate, and confront the problematic. For example, the shift of paradigm from a mechanical to a biological model, despite its huge impacts, represented a unidimensional shift in our understanding of the nature of organization. It happened in the context of analytical inquiry (Figure 1.2).

We are now facing the challenge of a dual shift. Not only has there been a shift of paradigm in our understanding of the nature of the beast—i.e., from our conception of an organization as a biological model to a sociocultural model— but there has also been a profound shift in our assumptions regarding the

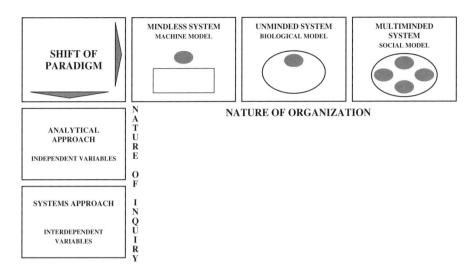

FIGURE 1.2   Shifts of Paradigm

method of inquiry, the means of knowing, from *analytical thinking* (the science of dealing with *independent* sets of variables) to *holistic thinking* (the art and science of handling *interdependent* sets of variables). The complementary nature of these two dimensions is at the core of both understanding how the game is evolving and identifying the drivers for change.

INTERDEPENDENCY AND CHOICE

While the organization as a whole is becoming more and more *interdependent*, its parts increasingly display choice and behave *independently*. The resolution of this dilemma requires a dual shift of paradigm. The first shift will result in the ability to see the organization as a multiminded, sociocultural system, a voluntary association of purposeful members who have come together to serve themselves by serving a need in the environment.

The second shift will help us see through chaos and complexity and learn how to deal with an interdependent set of variables. Failure to appreciate the significance of this dual change results in excessive structural conflict, anxiety, a feeling of impotency, and resistance to change. Unfortunately, prevailing organizational structures, despite all the rhetoric to the contrary, are designed to prevent change. Dominant cultures, by default, keep reproducing the same nonsolutions all over again. This is why the experience with corporate transformation is so fraught with frustration. The implicitness of the organizing assumptions, residing at the core of the organization's collective memory, is overpowering. Accepted on faith, these assumptions are transformed into unquestioned practices that may obstruct the future. Unless the content and implications of these implicit, cultural codes are made explicit and dismantled, the nature of the beast will outlive the temporary effects of interventions, no matter how well intended.

ON THE NATURE OF ORGANIZATION: THE FIRST PARADIGM SHIFT

To think about anything requires an image or a concept of it. To think about a thing as complex as an organization requires models of something similar, something simpler, and something more familiar. The three models represent the successive shift in our understanding of the nature of the organization, from a mindless mechanical tool to a uniminded biological being and, finally, to a multi-minded organized complexity.

Mindless Systems: A Mechanistic View

The mechanistic view of the world that evolved in France after the Renaissance maintains that the universe is a machine that works with a regularity dictated by its internal structure and the causal laws of nature. This worldview provided the basis not only for the Industrial Revolution but also for the development of the machine mode of organization.[3]

In the early stages of industrialization, machines replaced agricultural workers by the thousands. The reservoir of an unemployable army of unskilled agricultural workers threatened the fabric of Western societies. Then came a miracle, an ingenious notion of *organizations*. It was argued that in the same way a complicated tractor is built by parts, each performing only a simple task of horizontal, vertical, and circular motions, an organization could be created in such a manner that each person performed only a simple task. The mechanistic mode of organization was born as a logical extension of this conception and became instrumental in converting the army of unskilled agricultural laborers to semiskilled industrial workers.

The impact of this simple notion of organizations was so great that in one generation it created a capacity for the production of goods and services that surpassed the previous cumulative capacity of mankind. The essence of the machine mode of organization is simple and elegant: an organization is a mindless system—it has no purpose of its own. It is a tool with a function defined by the user, an instrument for the owner to use to achieve his goal of making profit. The important attribute of this tool is its reliability, and its performance

---

[3]See "Mechanisms, Organisms and Social Systems" (Gharajedaghi, Ackoff, 1984).

criterion is simply efficiency. The principle that parts should not deviate is at the core of the glamour of tidiness, efficiency, controllability, and predictability of its operation. The parts of a mindless mechanical system, just like the whole, have no choice. Its structure is designed into it, leaving it with no ability to restructure itself. The system functions reactively and can operate effectively only if its environment remains stable or has little effect on it.

Uniminded Systems: A Biological View

The biological thinking, or living systems paradigm, which led to the concept of the organization as a uniminded system, emerged mainly in Germany and Britain, but then caught fire in the United States. The underlying assumptions and principles of the biological mode of organization are also simple and elegant: an organization is considered a uniminded living system, just like a human being, with a purpose of its own. This purpose, in view of the inherent vulnerability and unstable structure of open systems, is survival. To survive, according to conventional wisdom, biological beings have to grow. To do so, they should exploit their environment to achieve a positive metabolism.

In organizational language, this means that growth is the measure of success, the single most important performance criterion, and that profit is the means to achieve it. Therefore, in contrast to the machine mode, in which profit is an end in itself, profit, for the biological mode, is only a means to an end. The association of profit with growth, considered a social good, gives profit the much needed social acceptability and status compatible with the American way of life.

Although uniminded systems have a choice, their parts do not. They operate based on cybernetics principles as a homeostatic system, reacting to information in the same way as a thermostat. As a matter of fact, the beauty of a uniminded system is that the parts do not have a choice and react only in a predefined manner to the events in their environment. For example, my heart cannot decide on its own that it doesn't want to work for me. My stomach will not get suspicious, thinking "the liver is out to get me." No consciousness, no choice, no conflict. The operation of a uniminded system is totally under the control of a single brain, the executive function, which, by means of a communication network, receives information from a variety of sensing parts and issues directions that activate relevant parts of the system. It is assumed that a malfunctioning of any normal uniminded system is due to a lack of information or noise in the communication channel. Therefore, the perceived answer for most of the problems is more information and better communication. However, if parts of a system develop consciousness and display choice, the system will be in real trouble. Imagine for a moment that the thermostat in your room suddenly develops a mind of its own—when it receives information about the temperature in the room it decides it doesn't like it and wants to sleep on it. The undeniable result is a chaotic air conditioning system.

When parts display choice, the central issues become conflict and the ability to deal with it. However, as long as paternalism is the dominant culture, the imperatives of "father knows best" or "give the apple to your sister" become an effective way to handle conflict. Paternalism best approximates the essential characteristics of a uniminded system, and it creates powerful organizations. Corporate giants such as Ford, Du Pont, General Motors, and IBM owe much to their paternalistic founding fathers.

Multiminded Systems: A Sociocultural View

Multiminded systems are exemplified by social organizations. A sociocultural view considers the organization a voluntary association of purposeful members who themselves manifest a choice of both ends and means. This is a whole new ball game. Behavior of a system whose parts display a choice cannot be explained by mechanical or biological models. A social system has to be understood on its own terms.

The critical variable here is *purpose*. According to Ackoff (1972), an entity is purposeful if it can produce 1) the same outcome in different ways in the same environment and 2) different outcomes in the same or different environment. Although the ability to make a choice is necessary for purposefulness, it is not sufficient. An entity that can behave differently but produce only one outcome in all environments is goal-seeking, not purposeful. Servomechanisms are goal-seeking, but people are purposeful. As a purposeful system, an organization is part of a larger purposeful whole, the society. At the same time, it has purposeful individuals as its own members. The result is a hierarchy of purposeful systems of three distinct levels. These three levels are so interconnected that an optimal solution cannot be found at one level independent of the other two. Aligning the interest of the purposeful parts with each other and that of the whole is the main challenge of the system.

In contrast to machines, in which integrating of the parts into a cohesive whole is a one-time proposition, for social organizations the problem of integration is a constant struggle and a continuous process. Effective integration of multilevel purposeful systems requires that the fulfillment of a purposeful part's desires depend on fulfillment of the larger system's requirements, and vice versa. In this context, the purpose of an organization is to serve the purposes of its members while also serving the purposes of its environment.

The elements of mechanical systems are energy-bonded, but those of sociocultural systems are information-bonded. In *energy-bonded systems*, laws of classical physics govern the relationships among the elements. Passive and predictable functioning of parts is a must, until a part breaks down. An automobile yields to its driver regardless of the driver's expertise and dexterity. If a driver decides to run a car into a solid wall, the car will hit the wall without objection. Riding a horse, however, presents a different perspective. It matters to the horse who the rider is, and a proper ride can be achieved only after a series of information exchanges between the horse and the rider. Horse and rider form an *information-bonded system*, in which guidance and control are achieved by a second-degree agreement (agreement based on a common perception) preceded by a psychological contract.

The members of a sociocultural organization are held together by one or more common objectives and collectively acceptable ways of pursuing them. The members share values that are embedded in their culture. The culture is the cement that integrates the parts into a cohesive whole. Nevertheless, since the parts have a lot to say about the organization of the whole, consensus is essential to the alignment of a multiminded system.

ON THE NATURE OF INQUIRY: THE SECOND PARADIGM SHIFT

Classical science is preoccupied with *independent variables*. It assumes that the whole is nothing but the sum of the parts. Accordingly, to understand the behavior of a system we need only to address the impact that each independent variable has on that system. (See Figure 1.3.)

Handling independent variables is the essence of analytical thinking, which has remained intact in all three contexts—physical, biological, and social. As a matter of fact, in order to share in the glory of classical science, both biological and social sciences opted to use the analytical method with no deviation. This might help explain why a whole set of phenomena, known as type II (emergent) properties, has been conveniently ignored. Properties like love, success, and happiness do not yield to analytical treatment.

However, increasingly we are finding out that our independent variables are no longer independent and that the neat and simple construct that served us so beautifully in the past is no longer effective. The following experience illustrates this point.

Ford Motor Company was one of the first American corporations to embark on the quality movement. "Quality is Job One" was the theme, and the

$$Y = F(x1, x2, x3, x4,)$$

FIGURE 1.3   Independent Variables

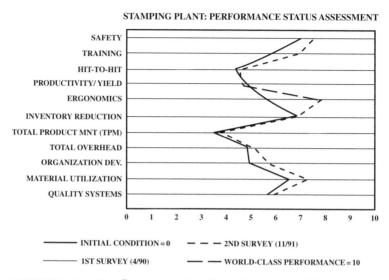

FIGURE 1.4   Woodhaven Stamping Plant's Quality Variables

operating units were encouraged to use continuous improvement to achieve world-class performance. Following the lead was Ford's Woodhaven Stamping operations, which identified eleven areas of improvement (see Figure 1.4). Initial (or baseline) measures in each area were designated as zero and world-class performance as 10. The company established a detailed and comprehensive program to go from zero to 10 in three years. Initially, significant improvement was recorded, but the operation reached a plateau after only 18 months.

Even doubling the efforts to improve the selected variables' performance failed to produce any further change. After 36 months of intense effort, the operation remained at the midway point of its goals, well short of the benchmark, world-class performance. At the time, I was teaching in the Ford Executive Development Program. Mr. Vic Leo, Program Director, introduced me to Mr. E. C. Galinis, Plant Manager of the Woodhaven Operation, who shared his frustration with me. After spending a few days in the plant, I concluded that the Woodhaven Operation had used up all of its slack and was now faced with a set of interdependent variables that could be improved only with a redesign of the total operation.

As Figure 1.5 demonstrates, a given design may contain some slack between variables. This permits us to deal with each variable separately as though it were an independent variable. The performance of each variable can be improved independently until the slack among them is used up. Then the perceived set of independent variables changes to a formidable set of interdependent variables. Improvement in one variable would come only at the expense of the others.

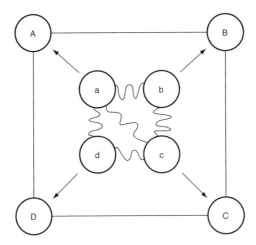

FIGURE 1.5   Using Up the Slack Among Interdependent Variables

Using the conventional approach to deal with this type of situation would be like running on a treadmill: one needs to keep running faster and faster to stay in the same place. In Ford's case, the existing design of Woodhaven operations had reached its highest potential, unfortunately far below the world-class performance level. To reach their performance goals, the operation would have to be redesigned, and this was done. A new design helped the operation to reach their target goals in six months.

An independent set of variables is, therefore, a special case of a more general scheme of *interdependency*. As systems become more and more sophisticated, the reality of interdependency becomes more and more pronounced (see Figure 1.6).

Understanding interdependency requires a way of thinking different from analysis; it requires systems thinking. And analytical thinking and systems thinking are quite distinct. Analysis is a three-step thought process. First, it takes apart that which it seeks to understand. Then it attempts to explain the behavior of the parts taken separately. Finally, it tries to aggregate understanding of the

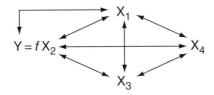

FIGURE 1.6   Interdependent Variables

parts into an explanation of the whole. Systems thinking uses a different process. It puts the system in the context of the larger environment of which it is a part and studies the role it plays in the larger whole.

The analytical approach has remained essentially intact for nearly four hundred years, but systems thinking has already gone through three distinct generations of change. The first generation of systems thinking (operations research) dealt with the challenge of interdependency in the context of mechanical (deterministic) systems. The second generation of systems thinking (cybernetics and open systems) dealt with the dual challenges of interdependency and self-organization (neg-entropy)[4] in the context of living systems. The third generation of systems thinking (design) responds to the triple challenge of interdependency, self-organization, and choice in the context of sociocultural systems.

In addition to being purposeful, social organizations are living systems; therefore, like all living systems, they are neg-entropic and capable of self-organization. They create order out of chaos. Biological systems primarily self-organize through genetic codes, and social systems self-organize through cultural codes. The DNA of social systems is their culture.

Social systems, however, can be organized either by default or by design. In default, the beliefs, assumptions, and expectations that underlie the system go unexamined. In design, the beliefs, assumptions, and expectations are made explicit, being constantly examined and monitored. The third generation of system thinking therefore has to deal not only with the challenge of interdependency and choice, but also with the implications of cultural prints reproducing the mess, or the existing order, all over again by default. This is why design, along with participation, iteration, and second-order learning, is at the core of the emerging concept of systems methodology.

Details of this exciting concept are explored in Part III of this book, which develops an operational definition of systems thinking. The remainder of this chapter explores implications of the dual paradigm shift in the context of six distinct competitive games.

THE COMPETITIVE GAMES

Each of the competitive games discussed below corresponds to a given paradigm in the following matrix (Figure 1.7). Together, these games have dominated the management scene for the better part of the past century. Each has

---

[4]Entropy is the measure of randomness and disorder in the universe. According to the Second Law of Thermodynamics, "close-systems" move toward increasing disorder or higher levels of entropy. However, "open-living systems" display an opposite tendency; they move toward order, thus generating negative entropy (neg-entropy).

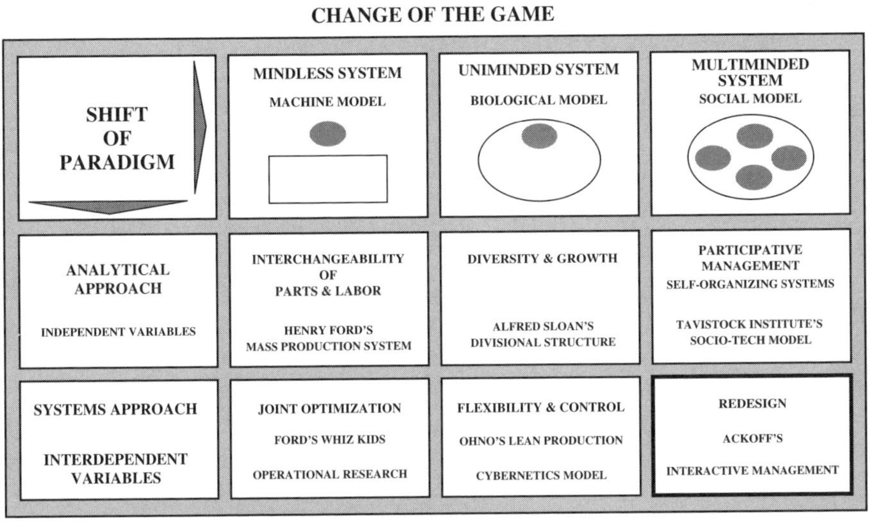

CHANGE OF THE GAME

SHIFT OF PARADIGM	MINDLESS SYSTEM MACHINE MODEL	UNIMINDED SYSTEM BIOLOGICAL MODEL	MULTIMINDED SYSTEM SOCIAL MODEL
ANALYTICAL APPROACH INDEPENDENT VARIABLES	INTERCHANGEABILITY OF PARTS & LABOR HENRY FORD'S MASS PRODUCTION SYSTEM	DIVERSITY & GROWTH ALFRED SLOAN'S DIVISIONAL STRUCTURE	PARTICIPATIVE MANAGEMENT SELF-ORGANIZING SYSTEMS TAVISTOCK INSTITUTE'S SOCIO-TECH MODEL
SYSTEMS APPROACH INTERDEPENDENT VARIABLES	JOINT OPTIMIZATION FORD'S WHIZ KIDS OPERATIONAL RESEARCH	FLEXIBILITY & CONTROL OHNO'S LEAN PRODUCTION CYBERNETICS MODEL	REDESIGN ACKOFF'S INTERACTIVE MANAGEMENT

FIGURE 1.7   Six Competitive Games

produced an order-of-magnitude change in performance measures, and each has had a profound effect on our lives.

Of course, each paradigm has its own unique mode of organization, and every mode of organization, by virtue of its requirement for specific talents, creates its own clique and privileged members. These members often translate their privileges into power and influence. The higher the level of success, the greater the stake in the continuing of an existing order and the higher the resistance to change. Unfortunately, the inability to change an out-dated mode of organization is as tragic for the viability of a corporation as the consequence of missing a technological breakthrough is for the viability of a product line.

Mass Production: Interchangeability of Parts and Labor

Mass production resulted directly from the machine mode of organization. Henry Ford's success in designing a production machine by making both parts and labor interchangeable led to a mass-production system and a whole new competitive game. He could produce 6,000 cars a day, while his closest competitor in France could muster only 700 cars a year. The ability to produce increased by more than an order of magnitude. In one generation we produced goods and services that surpassed the previous cumulative capacity of mankind.

The effectiveness of this mode of organization in producing goods and services created not just a quantitative change but a qualitative change in the nature of the problem itself. The question was no longer how to produce, but how to sell. And so dawned the marketing era. What emerged was an environment with an entirely new set of challenges. Foremost among them was how to respond to increasing demand for variety and diversity, and how to manage growth in size and complexity.

This challenge was too great for even the best that a machine mode of organization could offer. The requirement for no deviation, in view of the assumption that human nature is essentially deviant, places high emphasis on tight supervision to ensure conformity, predictability, and reliability of individual behavior within the organization. This emphasis undermines the organization's creative ability and limits its response to meeting the increasing demand for variety and diversity. A defensive reaction to consumer dissatisfaction calls for greater adherence to the rules and more rigidity, resulting in a vicious circle.

On the other hand, growth in size tends to reduce efficiency and organizational effectiveness. Because of an inverse relationship between an organization's size and the effectiveness of its control system, large organizations are forced toward decentralization. But this result is inconsistent with the principle of no deviation and unity of command. No driver in his or her right mind would drive a car with decentralized front wheels. In an organization that demands a passive functioning of parts with a high degree of compatibility and predictability, decentralization leads to chaos and suboptimization. The best answer for production may be in conflict with the best answer for marketing, and may not necessarily agree with the best answer for finance or personnel. Could this be why most large organizations constantly oscillate between centralization and decentralization?

Divisional Structure: Managing Growth and Diversity

Unlike Ford, Sloan recognized that the basis for competition had changed from an ability to produce to an ability to manage growth and diversity. He not only used public financing to generate the necessary capital to sustain growth, but also capitalized on the emerging biological model to provide a structural vehicle for control that made it possible to manage growth and diversity.

Sloan's is the model that, with small variations, constitutes the foundation of the MBA programs being taught in all prominent schools of management, including Harvard, Wharton, Stanford, and MIT. Operationally, this model is built around two concepts: *divisional structure* and *predict-and-prepare mode of planning*. (See Figure 1.8.)

Corporations, in their simplest form, are divided into two distinct parts: corporate office and operating unit. A corporate office with a traditional functional structure is the "brain of the firm," with an algorithm, a procedure for producing a desired outcome and for monitoring its implementation. The operating unit, on the other hand, is the body, which, despite a semiautonomous

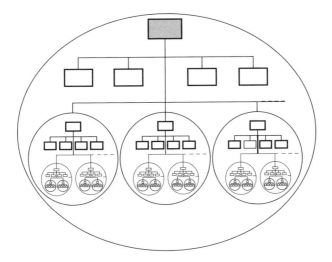

FIGURE 1.8 The Divisional Structure

structure, has no choice and no consciousness. It can only react to the command signal from the brain and/or events in its environment. Ideally, an operating unit is a robot programmed to carry out, with no deviation, a set of procedures predefined by the functional units of the corporate office.

Replicas of this operating model—product divisions—are created as needed, to produce a given product and/or service and sell it in a specified market. Operating product divisions are usually not authorized to redesign their products or redefine their markets. The main responsibility of the groups is to "stay the course." However, they are required to forecast the demand for their product and adjust their capacity to produce it accordingly. Therefore, the core concept of "predict and prepare" dominates the management process and complements the divisional structure in the pursuit of the essential functions: growth and viability.

The post–World War II environment, with its stability and predictability, provided ideal conditions for product-based divisional organizations. However, their very success in playing the game once again changed the game. The divisional mode of organization, despite its unquestionable successes, found itself up against two unprecedented challenges:

1. The operationalization of new knowledge, in response to an overall shortening of product life cycles.
2. The reality of multimindedness, or understanding the implication of choice, and thus conflict, among the organization's members.

As a result of the R&D era, knowledge was being generated at a faster rate, which called for periodically redesigning the product and redefining the markets. This capability, however, was incompatible with the mode of organization artfully designed to prevent change and stay the course. Successful divisional structure had tied the fate of product divisions to the life cycle of a single, predefined product. The division, then, like the product, experienced periods of uncertainty, growth, maturity, and decline. A popular solution for this concern, called strategic planning, dominated the practice of management in the United States for more than a decade. It simply called for identifying and assigning product divisions such designations as "Question Mark," "Star," "Cash Cow," or "Dog," and issuing imperatives to "drop the Dog," "milk the Cow," watch the "Question Mark," and "invest in the Star." By default, it created the strategy of giving up on difficult challenges by simply tagging them "Dogs."

The divisional structure, finally, was challenged from two different directions: participative management and the lean production system. Both were emerging in tandem as alternative bases for new competitive games.

Participative Management: Self-Organizing Systems

The unprecedented generation and distribution of wealth and knowledge resulted in ever higher levels of choice, which changed the nature of social settings and individual behavior in America. But the enhancement of choice, which resulted in higher levels of sophistication in social interactions, proved a double jeopardy for the biological mode of thinking. Not only did organizations conceived as uniminded systems become more difficult to manage, but they also became more vulnerable to the actions of a few. Members of an organization, unlike the parts of a biological being, do not react passively to the information they receive.

In this regard, advances in information technology and communication as a means of control did not produce the panacea once expected. Even the ultimate in this mode of thinking, Stafford Beer's famous *Brain of the Firm* (1972), despite its elegance, in my experience, is unable to deal with the complexities of emerging social interactions. Nevertheless, the model was successful in the context of paternalistic cultures, where loyalty, conformity, and commitment are considered core virtues. These virtues are reinforced by the security of belonging to a group, which in turn protects and provides for its members. For example, Japan, an industrialized society, with a relatively strong paternalistic culture, closely approximates a uniminded system. Therefore, it has been able to capitalize more effectively on the strength of the biological mode of organization.

In a strong paternalistic culture, conflict can be resolved by the intervention of a strong father figure. But the realities of highly developed multiminded social systems are fundamentally different. Members of societies that have outgrown the secure, unifying web of a paternalistic culture display real choice. But a price must be paid for this transformation, especially in terms of insecurity and the level of conflict. The purposeful actors, individually or in groups, generate unprecedented levels of conflict by disagreeing with each other on the compatibility of their chosen ends and means.

Corporate America, ill-equipped to deal effectively with the consequences of its members' purposeful behavior, is finding itself increasingly paralyzed. It is not surprising that a significant part of its energy is lost to the conflict. Frustration associated with excessive levels of conflict reinforces the organizational inability to change. Members increasingly behave independently, and management, on the pretext of empowerment, abdicates its authority and responsibility. Nobody seems to have a handle on integration. Feelings of impotency and alienation are commonplace.

Pursuing the ideal of a conflict-free organization has proved problematic. Creating a conflict-free organization means less choice, reducing members to the level of robots. Such a situation, even if feasible, may not be desirable.

Unable to uncook eggs already half cooked, we have rejected the paternalistic culture, but have not yet found an effective replacement for it. Unfortunately, QWL, participative management, multifunctional teams, chaos theory, self-organizing teams, and the other concepts that socio-tech had to offer have yet to show us how to manage a multiminded complexity and effectively dissolve conflict. We are still vascillating between centralization and decentralization, collectivity and individuality, and integration and differentiation, without appreciating the complementary nature of these tendencies. We will deal with these issues, in more detail, in Part II of this book.

The next three games represent the other dimension of the dual paradigm shift: dealing with the challenge of interdependency. They actually map the evolution of systems thinking in the context of mechanical, biological, and socio-cultural models of organization.

Operations Research: Joint Optimization

The success of the first Operations Research (OR) group, created by Ackoff and Churchman at the Case Institute of Technology, which dealt with the challenge of interdependency, resulted in the spread of OR programs to most American universities. But the first full application of OR in corporate America came with Ford's whiz kids, when McNamara and his associates moved from the Defense Department to the Ford Corporation.

The essence of this effort was to use models, basically mathematical, to find optimal solutions to a series of interdependent variables. However, the assumptions regarding the nature of the organization remained mechanical. The other significant contribution to this version of systems thinking was the concept of systems dynamics developed by J. Forrester of MIT.

Operations research dominated the field of systems thinking for the better part of the 1960s until it was challenged, ironically, by one of its founding fathers. In a famous article (1979), Ackoff declared, "The future of Operations Research is past." Instantaneously, he converted an army of devoted followers into staunch enemies. He blasted his own creation on the grounds that operations research assumes passive or reactive parts and does not appreciate the vital implications of parts having choice.

By the assertion that parts in a social system have a choice, he left his contemporaries behind by a quarter of a century. His concept of multiminded purposeful systems effectively bypassed the next generation of the systems models, most importantly Stafford Beer's *viable systems*, which in its own right is a masterful thinking in the biological context.

Lean Production Systems: Flexibility and Control

Effective commercial use of organized research, which evolved during World War II, accelerated the role of product development, giving rise to a new era marked by rapid change. Unpredictability associated with the high rate of change undermined the usefulness of the core concept of *predict and prepare.* Both the Chase and Wharton Econometric models, which had brought fame and fortune to their respective organizations, even a Nobel Prize for the Wharton School, were sold quietly.

The research and development era had generated explosions of new knowledge. This knowledge, when successfully operationalized, radically changed the competitive game. The new generation of winners was comprised of those players with the ability to create their own futures by interactively influencing their environment. The name of the game became flexibility and control, which shortened the time to market of a new product, increased product/market differentiation, and improved price/quality performance of the outputs, doing more and more with less and less.

This game emerged slowly but effectively in Japan, when Ohno, chief engineer of Toyota, created the Lean Production System by applying systems thinking in the biological context. Using cybernetics principles, he was able to lower the break-even point by an order of magnitude and elevated the competitive game to an incredibly higher level. In this game, flexibility and control became the basis for competition.

Interactive Management: The Design Approach

Design is the operational manifestation of the purposeful systems paradigm developed by Ackoff (1972) in response to the challenge of managing interactions between purposeful members of a highly interdependent social organization.

Systems design, at present, represents the latest chapter of the evolution of systems thinking. In *Redesigning the Future* (1974), Ackoff argues that purposeful social systems are capable of recreating their future; they do so by redesigning themselves. Ackoff then proposes a design methodology by which stakeholders of a multiminded system participatively design a future they collectively desire and realize it though successive approximation.

In *The Design of Inquiring Systems* (1971), Churchman demonstrated that the best way to learn a system is to design it. Later, in *A Prologue to National Development Planning* (1985), Gharajedaghi and Ackoff use design as the main vehicle of social development. The design model explicitly recognized that choice is at the heart of human development. Development is the enhancement of the capacity to choose; design is a vehicle for enhancement of choice and holistic thinking.

Designers seek to choose rather than predict the future. They try to understand rational, emotional, and cultural dimensions of choice and to produce a design that satisfies a multitude of functions. The design methodology requires that designers learn how to use what they already know, learn how to realize what they do not know, and learn how to learn what they need to know. Finally, producing a design requires an awareness of how activities of one part of a system affect and are affected by other parts. This awareness requires understanding the nature of interactions among the parts.

The remainder of this work attempts to explore this exciting conception by introducing the interactive management model. The template (Figure 1.9) captures the basis of this model and provides a roadmap that we will follow.

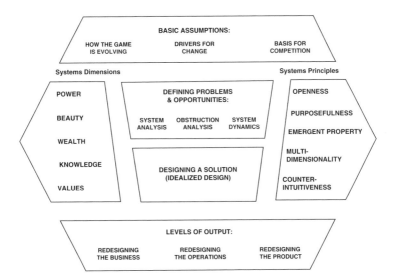

FIGURE 1.9   Interactive Management

PART II

Systems Theories
The Nature of the Beast

"God is dead," says graffiti on a notice board in Oxford University, England. "No!," it says underneath, "He is just working on a less ambitious project."

Maybe God has given up the idea of an orderly and deterministic world. Maybe he/she has playfully decided to mix it up with some degree of randomness and choice. Or maybe this has been the state of affairs all along. Zoroaster, the ancient Persian prophet, proclaimed some 3,000 years ago: "There are elements of *chance, choice,* and *certainty* in every aspect of our lives." Maybe having choice is not an illusion, after all. Nevertheless, choice is but one of the three elements. The interaction of choice with chance (randomness) and certainty (laws of nature) can indeed produce some counterintuitive outcomes.

Natural science has discovered "chaos." Social science has encountered "complexity." But chaos and complexity are not characteristics of our new reality; they are features of our perceptions and understanding. We see the world as increasingly more complex and chaotic because we use inadequate concepts to explain it. When we understand something, we no longer see it as chaotic or complex.

Maybe playing the new game requires learning a new language. We have used a multitude of languages to express the different ways in which we exist in the world. We first told the story of our lives as myth. We sang it, danced it, and expressed it in rituals that defined the parameters of our cultures and so gave us a degree of security in a threatening environment. As our proficiency increased, so did our learning and creative capacity. We started writing in the languages of poetry, mathematics, philosophy, and science. There were times when music, along with literature and art, produced our most beautiful texts.

But during the past century, we increasingly specialized in one language, the language of analytical science. As we emphasized one language to the exclusion of all others, we became unidimensional—and boringly predictable.

Today the analytical language has penetrated every facet of our lives. Our system of production, organization, interaction, communication—even our choice of recreation, sport, and foods—is done in terms of the assumptions and applications of analytical tools. Finding a correlation is the order of the day. Best sellers, in all areas, are those that simply identify a few common attributes of the winners. No one can deny the success of this language, but it has acquired an importance disproportionate to its position as only one method of inquiry. When one game states the rules for all games, it doesn't matter how many new games you create, they're all the same kind. History, unfortunately, has not been too kind to those who have capitalized so extensively on a single winning strategy. The price on selecting only one pattern of existence has been very high.

Alienation, lust for power, frustration, insecurity, and boredom are only a few symptoms of the emerging culture, where ready-made intellectual goods are making the formation of mass opinion a matter of mass production.

The tendency to simplify everything to a level not requiring serious thinking has turned the political system into a voting industry, which assumes that people are ensured choice over their lives when they elect the decision-makers. We have let the default values of an analytical culture define what is good, proper, and beautiful.

But, somehow, something is missing with the way we think about our lives. What has become the dominant language of our time produces only a partial understanding of our reality and relates only to parts of our being, not the whole of it. We need a holistic language, a language of systems, which will enable us to see through chaos and understand complexity. A language of interaction and design will help us learn a new mode of living by considering various ways of seeing, doing, and being in the world. We can then design new methods of inquiry, new modes of organization, and a way of life that will allow the rational, emotional, and ethical choices for interdependent yet autonomous social beings.

This systems language, by necessity, will have two dimensions. The first will be a framework for understanding the nature of the beast, the behavioral characteristics of multiminded systems. The second will be an operational systems methodology, which goes beyond simply declaring the desirability of the systems approach and provides a practical way to define problems and design solutions.

To build the first dimension of this language, we need to develop a system of systems concepts. In this context, Ackoff's *On Purposeful Systems* (1972) is a Herculean work, a must-read book, which cannot be reproduced here. What I intend to do is share the principles and concepts that I believe are critical for developing a system view of sociocultural systems. These principles have evolved with me during years of struggling to get a handle on systems.

Details of these exciting concepts, which have been tested in a variety of contexts and cultures, are so rich that each could be the subject of a separate book. To fit my purpose here they had to be simplified at the risk of considerable distortion.

Five systems principles will be discussed in Chapter 2. Chapter 3 shows how power, knowledge, wealth, beauty, and values form a mutually exclusive and collectively exhaustive set for a holistic investigation of a social system. Finally, Chapter 4 discusses the essence of the sociocultural model, theory of development, and organizational implications of systems thinking. These concepts (the subject of Part II), combined with systems methodology (the subject of Part III), constitute an interactive whole that, in my view, defines the essence of systems thinking.

A note of caution to those readers with a strong background in Total Quality Management (TQM). There is a fundamental difference between TQM and systems thinking. TQM operates within an existing paradigm; it can be learned and applied as an independent set of tools and methods. But systems methodology cannot be separated from systems principles. Systems tools and methods are impotent if isolated from the paradigm of which they are an integral part.

2

Systems Principles

The five principles of *openness, purposefulness, multidimensionality, emergent property*, and *counterintuitiveness*, acting together as an interactive whole, define the essential characteristics and assumptions about the behavior of an organization viewed as a purposeful, multiminded system (see Figure 2.1).

These principles are an integral part of the third-generation systems view. Their implications will be present in every aspect and in all of the subsequent parts of this work, from defining problems to designing solutions. Please read them carefully, more than once. Make them your own. Use them in different contexts so you can internalize them. They are the building blocks of the mental model you will need to construct in order to become a systems thinker and systems designer.

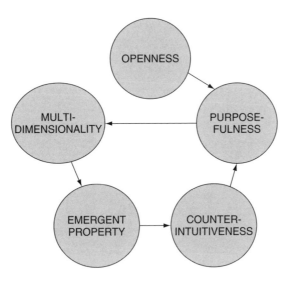

FIGURE 2.1 Systems Principles

OPENNESS

Openness means that the behavior of living (open) systems can be understood only in the context of their environment (see Figure 2.2). The world is, indeed, a complex whole in interaction. Therefore, even genuine inquiries regarding the nature of man, such as the love of liberty, lust for power, and search for happiness, are abstractions that cannot be meaningfully entertained when separated from the context, the culture of which they are a part.

We can observe, somewhat helplessly, that "everything" depends on "everything else," concluding that we should not mess around with "the natural order of things" and that we may be better off leaving everything in the hands of the "One" who has control over all. But if there are elements of chance, choice, and certainty in everything we do, we need to know which elements are certain and which ones offer the opportunity for choice. And how do we deal with the randomness of chance? Remember that appreciation of *drag*, a law of nature, as a certainty made it possible to convert that so-called obstruction into an opportunity and use it as an instrument of flying.

Our first break came by recognizing that although everything depends on everything else, this "everything" can be grouped into two categories: those elements that somehow can be controlled and those that cannot. This distinction gave us an operational definition of the system, environment, and system boundary. The system therefore consists of all the interactive sets of variables that could be controlled by participating actors. Meanwhile, the environment consists of all those variables that, although affecting the system's behavior, could not be controlled by it. The system boundary thus becomes an arbitrary,

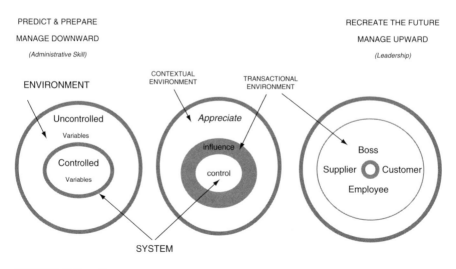

FIGURE 2.2 Openness

subjective construct defined by the interest and the level of the ability and/or authority of the participating actors.

Then a second break came along. We discovered that the behavior of the variables in the environment, although uncontrollable, is more or less predictable. In fact, in most cases, the less controllable a contextual variable, the more predictable it becomes. This led to the formulation of the first rule for getting a handle on open systems: the imperatives of *predict* and *prepare*. Predicting the environment and preparing the system for it became the foundation of the neoclassical school of management. Developing the econometric model and winning the Nobel Prize brought fame and fortune to Wharton. Chase followed suit with its own model, and soon thousands of organizations were each specializing in forecasting different industries. The new game was learned and played artfully by almost all entities—large and small, business and governmental.

But success somehow changed the game. Something went wrong. In the last sixteen years we have observed, with much apprehension, that all the predictions made by our prize-winning models were wrong. So much so that those who never used them were much better off than those who did. We were back to the drawing board again and this time rediscovered a whole new category of variables that we had missed the first time: those variables that we do not control, but only *influence*. To *control* means that an action is both necessary and sufficient to produce the intended outcome. To *influence* means that the action is not sufficient; it is only a coproducer.

As our knowledge about the environment increased, however, so did our ability to convert the uncontrollable variables to those that could be influenced. As we increased our ability to influence a variable, we decreased our ability to predict it. If a rain dance had any influence on the weather, we would not be able to predict the weather. Ironically, the extent to which we are able to predict the weather is an indication that we might not be performing the rain dance properly.

The new category of variables, those that could be influenced, form a new region called the *transactional environment*. The transactional environment is becoming significant to understanding the behavior of an open purposeful system. It includes all the critical stakeholders of a system: customers, suppliers, owners, the boss, and, ironically, the members themselves.

Customers used to be predictable, but uncontrollable. We were told they were always right. Increasingly, they are becoming more and more susceptible to influence, and therefore are less and less predictable. It seems that the nerds are taking over. The boss has become weird and unpredictable as well.

Suppliers used to be the most agreeable group. They did what they were told. Nowadays they claim to house the core technology. Who's in control of the computer industry? It's not the big system houses like IBM or Digital that are in charge; it's the component builders, the Microsofts and Intels of the world, that have much more to say and are, in all likelihood, the ones in control.

Slowly, we are realizing that we do not actually control much of anything, but do have the ability to influence many things. I don't really know how much of me is me and how much is those whom I love. Managing a system is, therefore, more and more about managing its transactional environment, that is, managing upward. *Leadership* is, therefore, defined as the ability to influence those whom we do not control.

Open (living) systems display certain characteristics that are most significant to our understanding of their behavior. Open (living) systems not only preserve their common properties but jealously guard their individualities. At the biological level, living systems achieve this durability through *genetic coding* (DNA), a blueprint for self-reproduction. Unless their genetic coding is altered, living systems go on replicating themselves almost indefinitely. The continuity of the individual and collective identities owes itself to a similar phenomenon—a tendency to create a predefined order based on an internal blueprint.

As open (living) systems, social groups such as organizations exhibit the same tendency, a movement toward a predefined order. Therefore, the cultural code becomes the social equivalent of biological DNA, those hidden assumptions deeply anchored at the very core of our collective memory. Left to be self-organized, these internal codes, by default, act as organizing principles that invariably reproduce the existing order.

In an earlier work, *Theory and Management of Systems* (1972), I devoted a whole chapter to the subject of chaos and order, articulating how living systems are able to reverse the formidable second law of thermodynamics and move toward complexity and order.

The second law states that a general tendency in the universe (as a closed system) is toward elimination of all differences. Thus, the ultimate state is sameness and randomness, a *chaotic simplicity*. Entropy (S), the measure of randomness, will therefore always increase. However, we know that living systems are neg-entropic (–S). They are able not only to negate this formidable process by differentiation, but also to move toward a predefined order, an *organized complexity*. Using the formula $I = -S$, which indicates that a neg-entropic system must have information, one might conclude that movement toward complexity and order is possible only if the system has a means of knowing and an internal image of what it wants to be. This result provided the first clue for constructing the sociocultural model, the subject of Chapter 4.

To summarize the major points, I have argued the following:

- Open systems can be understood only in the *context* of their environments.
- Leadership is managing upward; it is about influencing what one cannot control and appreciating what one cannot influence.
- Open systems, by default, are guided by an internal code of conduct (DNA or culture). If left alone, open systems tend to reproduce themselves.

PURPOSEFULNESS

To influence the actors in our transactional environment we have to understand *why they do what they do*. Understanding is different from both *information* and *knowledge*. Information deals with the *what* questions, knowledge with the *how* question, and understanding with the *why* questions (Figure 2.3). If there once was a time when having information about clients was a competitive advantage, it isn't so nowadays. To maintain competitive position one must move to a new plateau, the knowledge level, and learn how clients do what they do. Thereafter, to be an effective player, one has to move yet higher, to the level of understanding, and learn *why they do what they do*.

The *why* question is the matter of purpose, that of choice. And the choice is the product of the interactions among the three dimensions: rational, emotional, and cultural (Figure 2.4). *Rational* choice is the domain of self-interest, or the interest of the decisionmaker, not the observer. A rational choice is not necessarily a wise choice. It reflects only the perceived interest of the decisionmaker at the time. Meanwhile, wisdom has ethical implications and considers the consequences of an action in the context of a collectivity.

The following examples explain rational choice with much more clarity. My daughter Jeyran was only five and jumping up and down on our bed. I said to her, "Jeyran, I would not do that if I were you." Giving me an innocent look, she replied, "No, I don't think so. If you were me, you would be doing exactly what I'm doing. You don't know how exciting this is."

When I worked for IBM, we were told, "The customer is right, *always* right. If you don't believe this, you will not work here. We know he's right even if we don't know why; your job is to find his rationale, and learn why he's doing what he's doing." Actually, in trying to find this rationale, I learned the most important lesson of my professional life: market economies, like democracies, make only rational choices. The winners are not necessarily the best, but those who are most compatible with the existing order. Being ahead of your time is sometimes more tragic than falling behind.

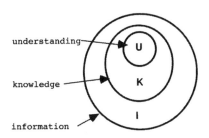

FIGURE 2.3 Hierarchy of Influence

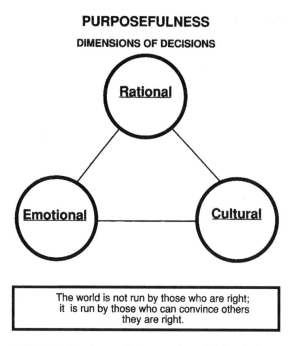

PURPOSEFULNESS

DIMENSIONS OF DECISIONS

Rational

Emotional

Cultural

The world is not run by those who are right;
it is run by those who can convince others
they are right.

FIGURE 2.4   Rational, Emotional, and Cultural Choice

The story of the Ford Foundation's birth-control project in India was another eye-opener for me. During a working visit to India, my senior partner, Russ Ackoff, met a number of Americans trying to teach family planning and birth control to natives. They were not succeeding and were frustrated over the program's failure to produce any results. "Indians are irrational," the project manager told Russ. "They know population is their number-one enemy, and here we are teaching them control, giving them all the contraceptives they need, plus a transistor radio as a reward. But look what happens. They go home, turn the radio on, and with music make a new baby." Russ suggested that they simply could not dismiss this behavior as irrational and should be looking for other explanations. He then produced a newspaper clipping from the *New York Times* in which it was reported that a Brazilian woman had given birth to her 42nd child. To this report, the project manager reacted, "If this isn't irrational then I don't know what irrational is!"

Russ then posed the following: "If a woman can have 42 children, then why do Indians, on average, have only 4.6? This means they know how to practice control, but aren't willing to do so. Maybe you are solving the wrong problem." Now the issue was put in a different context. Later on, we discovered that at that time there was no social security, no retirement, and no unemployment benefits. Therefore *three sons*, by default, was considered the retirement system. The first priority for each couple was to put their retirement in place. Statistically, to have three sons requires an average of 4.6 children. Not surprisingly, those who had three sons had stopped having children. Now who was irrational? The Indian couple who got a free transistor radio by attending a lecture? Or the Ford Foundation guy who thought he could get a couple to give up their retirement by giving them a transistor radio?

The *emotional* choice is the domain of beauty and excitement. We do lots of things because they are exciting or, more precisely, because they are challenging. If you happen to beat me ten times in a tennis game, I don't think you will look forward to playing me again. Probably you will want to play someone who can challenge you—the one, ironically, who might have a chance of beating you.

A colleague and friend at the Wharton School, Professor Aron Katselenenboigen, likes to use episodes in chess to explain interesting social phenomena. I once asked him why a majority of chess players like to play with those who are much better at the game than themselves. "It's the challenge," he replied. "Winning is fun if it's associated with a real challenge." I tested this theory with ten of my graduate students at Wharton. We had a computer program that could play chess at nine different levels. Level one was very simple. Anyone with a basic knowledge of chess could win with no difficulty. However, the higher levels posed a much greater challenge. Winning at level six, for example, required considerable mastery. Each student was told that he/she could play ten games at any level he/she wanted; for every game won, he/she would receive a dollar, and for every game lost, he/she would have to give back a dollar. All the students started at level one, but after winning a few dollars all moved to higher levels. By the finishing time most were playing at level five, and two were even at level six.

If the excitement of a good challenge were not part of our decision criteria, life would be a bore. In other words, setting and seeking attainable goals is a banal existence. This may come as a surprise to many "human resource managers," but for sure it explains the boredom and meaninglessness associated with huge segments of corporate life.

In contrast to rational choice, which reflects on instrumental (extrinsic) values, the emotional dimension deals with stylistic (intrinsic) values. It is the enjoyment and satisfaction derived from the emotional state in and of itself. While rational choice is risk aversive, emotional choice is not. Risk is an important attribute of excitement and challenge.

Culture defines the ethical norms of the collective, of which the decision-maker is a member. The ethical values are the constraining elements of the decision process. However, by dictating the default values, culture has a profound impact on the decision process. Just like a high-level computer language that provides default parameters when the programmer fails to choose one, the culture provides default values when actors fail to choose one explicitly.

Purposeful systems are value-guided systems; in other words, values are what purposeful behaviors strive to achieve. More often than not, these values are implicit in the culture, and the decisionmaker is not even aware that she or he has a choice. Default values are usually treated as realities out there; and they will remain out there as long as no one is willing to challenge them.

Finally, the essence of purposefulness can be appreciated only by understanding the distinctions that Ackoff makes among the three types of system behavior: reaction, response, and action. A *reaction* is a system behavior for which an event in the environment is both necessary and sufficient. Thus, a reaction is an event that is (deterministically) caused by another event. A *response* is a system behavior for which an event in the environment is necessary but not sufficient. Thus a response is an event of which the system itself is a coproducer. An *action* is a system behavior for which a change in the environment is neither necessary nor sufficient. Actions, therefore, are self-determined events, or autonomous behavior.

Reactive, responsive, and active systems are, in turn, correlated with *state-maintaining*, *goal-seeking*, and *purposeful* systems (Table 2.1).

A *state-maintaining system* is one that reacts to changes in order to maintain its state under different environmental conditions. Such a system can react (not respond) because what is done is determined entirely by the change in its environment, given the structure of the system. Nevertheless, it performs an intrinsic function by being able to maintain its state in a different way under different conditions. For example, many heating systems

TABLE 2.1   Behavioral Classification of Systems

BEHAVIOR (process)	MEANS (structure)	ENDS (function)
PASSIVE Tools	FIX One structure in all environments No choice	FIX One function in all environments No choice

REACTIVE
Self-maintaining
  systems
	Variable and Determined
	Different structures in
	  different environments
	No choice of means
		FIX
		One function in all
		environments
		No choice of ends

RESPONSIVE
Goal-seeking systems
	Variable and Chosen
	Different structures in
	  same environment
	Choice of means
		Variable Determined
		Different functions in
		  different environments
		No choice of ends

ACTIVE
Purposeful systems
	Variable and Chosen
	Different structure in the
	  same environment
	Choice of means
		Variable and Chosen
		Different function in same
		  environment
		Choice of ends

are state-maintaining. An internal controller turns the system on when the room temperature goes below a desired level, then turns it off when the temperature goes above this level. The state being maintained is the room temperature. Such a system is able to adapt to change but is not capable of learning because it cannot choose its behavior. It cannot improve with experience.

A *goal-seeking system* is one that can respond differently to different events in the same or a different environment until it produces a particular outcome (state). Production of this state is its goal. Such a system has a choice of means but not of the end; hence it is responsive rather than reactive. Response is voluntary; reaction is not. For example, lower-level animals can seek food in different ways in the same or a different environment. If a goal-seeking system has memory it can learn to pursue its goal more efficiently over time.

A *purposeful system* is one that can produce not only the same outcomes in different ways in the same environment but different outcomes in both the same and different environments. It can change its ends under constant conditions. This ability to change ends under constant conditions is what exemplifies free will. Such systems not only learn and adapt; they can also create. Human beings are examples of such systems.

Purposeful systems have all the capabilities of goal-seeking and state-maintaining systems. Meanwhile, goal-seeking systems have the capabilities of state-maintaining systems, though the converse is not true.

Finally, it is reasonable to assume that decision implies *power*, and power is a concept of many meanings and dimensions. However, according to Boulding, it may be defined as the amount of change created in a future state by a decision. Since doing nothing is always an option, the power of a decisionmaker can be measured by the difference in the future state between doing something and doing nothing.

A concept closely related to that of power is *freedom*, which also has many meanings and dimensions. One meaning is that of an alternative, or a range of choices. If I have no alternatives, I am clearly not free to choose; therefore I have no power to change the future state.

Recap

- The world is not run by those who are right. It is run by those who can convince others that they are right.
- Choice has three aspects: rational (self-interest), emotional (excitement), and cultural (default).
- While rational choice is risk averse, emotional choice is not. Risk is an important attribute of excitement and challenge.

- Realities out there will remain out there as long as no one is willing to challenge them.
- Choice is a matter of competence; it implies power-to-do. Liberty without competence is an empty proposition.

This brings us to the next discussion: the principle of multidimensionality.

MULTIDIMENSIONALITY

Multidimensionality[1] is probably one of the most potent principles of systems thinking. It is the ability to see complementary relations in opposing tendencies and to create feasible wholes with unfeasible parts.

For the majority of cultures, a fallacy has dominated the treatment of opposing tendencies as a duality in a zero-sum game. Everything seems to come in a pair of opposites: security/freedom; order/complexity; collectivity/individuality; modernity/tradition; art/science; and so on. They are cast in such a way that a win for one is invariably associated with a loss for the other.

In the context of a zero-sum game, opposing tendencies are formulated in two distinct ways: First, conflicting tendencies are conceptualized as two mutually exclusive, discrete entities. The conflicts are treated as dichotomies that are usually expressed as *X* or *Not X* (Figure 2.5). If *X* is right, then *Not X* has to be wrong. This represents an *or* relationship, a win/lose struggle with a moral obligation to win. The loser, usually declared wrong, is eliminated.

Second, opposing tendencies are formulated in such a way that they can be represented by a continuum (Figure 2.6). Between black and white are 1,000 shades of gray. This calls for a compromise, or resolution of the conflict. Compromise is a frustration point, a give-and-take struggle. Depending on the relative strength of the poles of tension, the power game will come to a temporary halt. The compromise point is an unstable mixture, usually containing elements of two extremes. As the power structure changes, so does the compromised position.

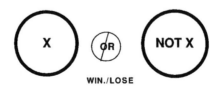

FIGURE 2.5   Dichotomy

---

[1]Throughout this book I use *dimensions* to identify quantifiable variables and also to reflect aspects and facets of a system.

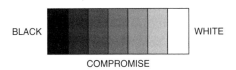

FIGURE 2.6 Continuum

The constant struggle between groups of people who see different "clear and urgent" necessities when dealing with social realities—the urgency of production versus that of distribution; the desire to protect the rights of victims versus the rights of the accused; the need to protect the environment versus the individual right to make a living—is the manifestation of a need to develop new frameworks. Churchman's concern with the "environmental fallacy" (1979), Boulding's rejection of suboptimization (1968), and Ackoff's concept of "separately infeasible parts making a feasible whole" (1978) are reflections of the same concern.

It seems as though we live in an age of paradoxes. Even time-honored values such as freedom and justice are not spared. Boulding (1953) acknowledges the dilemma with the observation that some are afraid of freedom, seeing always behind it the specter of anarchy. Whereas some others are afraid of justice, seeing always behind it the specter of tyranny. Furthermore, consider the relationship between security and freedom. One cannot be free if one is not secure; one will not be secure if one is not free. Maybe freedom, justice, and security are three aspects of the same thing and were not meant to be separated in the first place. Certainly, treating them in isolation has been problematic.

A complement is that which fills out or completes a whole. The principle of *multidimensionality* maintains that the opposing tendencies not only coexist and interact, but also form a complementary relationship. The complementary relationship is not confined to pairs. More than two variables may form complementary relationships, as the trio of freedom, justice, and security demonstrates. (See Figure 2.7.)

The mutual interdependence of opposing tendencies is characterized by an *and* instead of an *or* relationship. This means that each tendency is represented by a separate dimension, resulting in a multidimensional scheme where a low/low and a high/high, in addition to low/high and high/low, are strong possibilities. This is a non-zero-sum formulation, in which a loss for one side is not necessarily a gain for the other. On the contrary, both opposing tendencies can increase or decrease simultaneously.

Using a multidimensional representation, one can see how the tendencies previously considered as dichotomies can interact and be integrated into something quite new. The addition of new dimensions makes it possible to discover new frames of reference in which opposing sets of tendencies can be interpreted

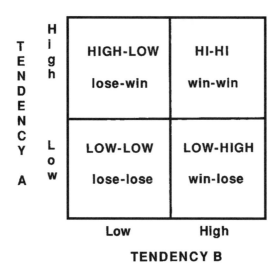

FIGURE 2.7 Complementary Relationships

in a new ensemble with a new logic of its own. Says Churchman: "The usual dichotomy of X or *Not X* never seems to display the general, because neither of the above is always so prominent an aspect of social systems" (1979).

Note that in classical logic, contradictions are relative to a domain; adding a new dimension expands the domain and converts the contradictions to complementaries. To explain this further, let us look at a related concept: *typology.*

A proper way of developing typologies, which corresponds with my intentions here, requires that the relevant variables, which together define the state of the phenomenon under study, be identified and each conceptualized as a separate dimension.

A dimension represented by an arrow is used to reflect a quantification of a variable on a given scale. It measures a characteristic specified by the operational definition of the variable involved. Segmentation of this scale into two regions of *low* and *high* is usually based on an assumption that the low or high value assigned to the variable will have a significant impact on the behavior of the system that is coproduced by the variable.

In this context, the point of distinction between low and high is not arbitrary (Figure 2.8). It signifies the level at which the behavior of the dependent

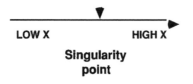

FIGURE 2.8 Change of Phase

system is qualitatively affected. This is a change that corresponds to the singularity or inflection point (change of phase) in physical phenomena. In other words, if the variable *income* has an impact on an individual's behavior, there seems to be a critical level of income at which a change in lifestyle occurs, qualitatively affecting that behavior.

If I make $10 a week, I may eat one hamburger; with $20 I may have two; and with $30 I will try three. However, if I make $1,000 a week, I will not eat 100 hamburgers. I may not eat hamburgers at all. Therefore, a quantitative change in my income at some point has produced a qualitative change in my way of life. That is the point of distinction between the low and the high level of income.

Provided one is aware of their underlying assumptions and limitations, typologies can show how behavior of a multidimensional system differs significantly according to the emphasis on one or the other dimension.

For example, the interaction of a high concern for change with a high concern for stability produces a completely different mode of behavior than the one produced either by a high concern for change coupled with a low concern for stability or the one produced by a high concern for stability coupled with a low concern for change (see Figure 2.9).

The high/high represents the behavior of a mature system, searching for stability through change. While the low/high reflects a radical system interested in change at any price, it can be reactionary or progressive, depending on the direction of the change sought. The high/low, on the other hand, represents

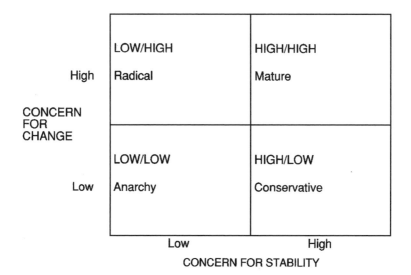

FIGURE 2.9   Behavior of a Multidimensional System

a conservative state, preferring the status quo and, therefore, a tendency for regulation and compromise. But the low/low is anarchy with a low concern for change and a low concern for stability, opposed to government in any form. Therefore, with different combinations of the levels of concern (low or high), different modes of behavior will emerge. Each mode represents a new system whose character can be understood only in its own right.

The typology of the management style developed by Blake and Mouton (1964) underscores the same point by demonstrating that although the 1,9 and 9,9 styles both reflect a high concern (9) for people, the manifestations of these concerns are different in both cases (Figure 2.10).

The 1,9 is a paternalistic, populist leader, whose concern for people is basically a concern for their weakness. Therefore, he/she assumes a protective role. Meanwhile, the 9,9 is a leader whose main concern for people stems from a respect for their ability and individuality. He/she assumes a different role— that of a motivator.

In the work of Gerald Gordon and his colleagues (1974), which studies the factors conducive to innovation, we see the following two abilities as complementary to an individual's propensity to innovate: the ability to differentiate between objects that seem similar and the ability to find similarities between seemingly unrelated matters (Figure 2.11).

Similarly, we can show how seemingly contradictory requirements for order and complexity are simultaneously achieved by an organization, and the requirement for stability and change is achieved with adaptation. In each case, the desired characteristic would not be a compromise, but a new totality with characteristics of its own.

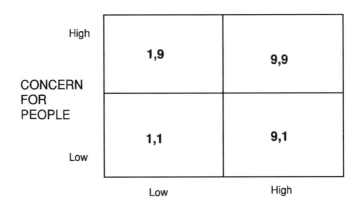

FIGURE 2.10   *Style of Management*

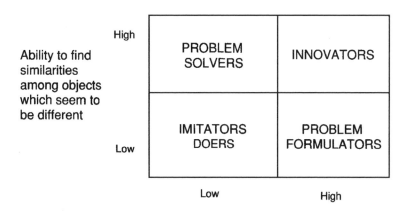

FIGURE 2.11 Innovative Abilities

Plurality of Function, Structure, and Process

Complementary to the principle of multidimensionality and parallel to it is the concept of plurality. Plurality of function, structure, and process, as we will see later on, is at the core of systems theory of development. It makes the high/high a possibility and choice a reality. Plurality simply maintains that systems can have multiple structures and multiple functions and be governed by multiple processes (Figure 2.12); it denies the classical view of a single structure with a single function in a single cause-and-effect relationship.

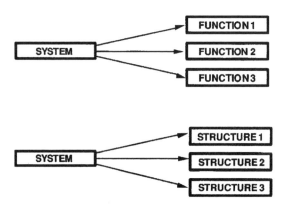

FIGURE 2.12 Plurality of Functions and Structures

Plurality of Function

A system can have multiple functions, both implicit and explicit. A car, for example, in addition to having the explicit function of transportation, might have an implicit function of, say, an identification tag. For many, a car defines the lifestyle of its owner and can have considerable snob value.

Furthermore, an investor might consider a car company a money-making machine, while union leaders see it as a job-producing system. For an entrepreneur, the organization may present a lifetime challenge to create a winning system; however, for a professional corporate citizen it might be the platform for an internal power game. Indeed, organizations have multiple functions, generating and disseminating wealth, power, and beauty. Still, corporate actors, depending on their mindsets or the roles assigned to them, consider only one of these functions as primary. This is the fallacy that results in successful operations but dead patients.

Plurality of Structure

Earlier, we proposed that the system's structure defines the components and their relationships. Plurality of the structure, therefore, means that the components and the relationships among them are multiple and variable. Consider, for example, salt (NaCl). Its components—chlorine (Cl) and sodium (Na)—form a single type of relationship in all environments; therefore, salt is said to have a singular structure. But the same cannot be said about hydrocarbons. Hydrogen and carbon enter into various combinations and relationships, resulting in multiple structures. Carbon's ability to combine with itself gave rise to a whole new branch of evolution, the biological systems, creating unstable but steady-state structures.

Human beings display a similar tendency. They form varying relations with each other, creating an interactive type of structure, a social system. Interactions between purposeful actors in a group take many forms. Social actors may cooperate on one pair of tendencies, compete over others, and be in conflict over different sets, all at the same time. In addition, members of a social system learn and mature over time and are therefore variable and subject to change. The result is an interactive network of variable members with multiple relationships, recreating itself continuously. This is what is meant by the plurality of structure.

Acceptance of plurality of structure, unlike that of functions, is a difficult proposition, since it goes against the traditional concept of structure as something that endures. However, a reconceptualization of this traditional concept is necessary to appreciate the principle of purposefulness and multidimensionality.

Plurality of Process

The classical principle of causality maintained that similar initial conditions produce similar results, and consequently, that dissimilar results are due to dissimilar initial conditions. Therefore, for a given structure, behavior of the system is completely predictable and its future states invariably depend on its initial conditions and the laws that govern its transformation (determinism).

Bertalanffy (1968), in analyzing the self-regulating or morphostatic features of open biological systems, loosened this classical belief by introducing the concept of *equifinality*: a final state may be reached by any number of different developmental routes. Buckley (1967), in his discussion of morphogenetic processes in sociocultural systems, goes even further and suggests an opposite principle, *multifinality*: similar initial conditions may lead to dissimilar end states. So the process, rather than the initial conditions, is responsible for future states. Accordingly, a social phenomenon can also be studied as the end result of a set of interactive processes. This adds a new dimension to the process of inquiry, which is key for understanding a powerful concept: the emergent property.

Recap

"With infeasible parts you can create a feasible whole."[2]

- In a multidimensional scheme, differences in degrees are differences in kind. A "high-high" concern represents a different behavior from a "low-high" concern. Each mode has its own distinct interpretation for the meaning of the variables involved.
- Freedom, justice, and security, in my belief, are three aspects of the same thing. They should not be separated, treating them in isolation has always been problematic.

EMERGENT PROPERTY

I can love, but none of my parts can love. If you take me apart, the phenomenon of love will be lost. Furthermore, love does not yield itself to any one of the five senses. It doesn't have a color, a sound, or an aroma. It can't be touched or tasted. Then how does one measure love? Of course one may always measure the manifestation of love. "If you love me why don't you call me?" someone may say.

Something doesn't seem quite right. The phenomenon of love doesn't fit the classical description of a property. Furthermore, it doesn't seem to be alone in this distinction. Similar phenomena, such as success, failure, and happiness, display the same type of characteristics. So let's give them a name, *emergent properties*, and put them in a category of their own: *type II properties*, as distinct from the more classical type, which we will call *type I properties* (Figure 2.13).

---

[2]For demonstration of this beautiful concept see *The Art of Problem Solving*, Ackoff, 1978.

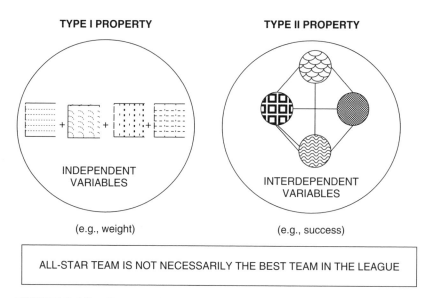

FIGURE 2.13   Emergent Properties

Emergent, or type II, properties are the property of the whole, not the property of the parts, and cannot be deduced from properties of the parts. However, they are a product of the interactions, not a sum of the actions of the parts, and therefore have to be understood on their own terms. Furthermore, they don't yield to any one of the five senses and cannot be measured directly. If measurement is necessary, then one can measure only their manifestation.

Emergent properties, by their nature, cannot be analyzed, they cannot be manipulated by analytical tools, and they do not yield to causal explanations. Consider the phenomenon of *life*, the most significant emergent property. No one has yet been able to identify a single cause for life. Falling into the trap of trying to find correlation, we could probably find one between life and almost everything. Unfortunately, these correlations do not explain much about the essence of life. Relying exclusively on an analytical approach, not surprisingly, fails to produce a basic understanding about emergent properties.

I have suggested that emergent properties are the product of interactions among several elements. The mere notion of interaction signifies a dynamic process producing a time-dependent state. In other words, the emergent phenomenon is being reproduced continuously *online* and in *real time*. Therefore, life, love, happiness, and success are not one-time propositions; they have to be reproduced continuously. If the processes that generate them come to an end, the phenomena cease to exist as well. They cannot even be stored or saved for future use. And for sure, none can be taken for granted. Life, love, and happiness can be there for a moment and gone in a moment. The same is true of success; it is just as vulnerable as love and happiness.

If emergent properties are the spontaneous outcome of ongoing processes, then to understand them one has to understand the processes that generate them. Dying is very natural; staying alive is the miracle. It takes simultaneous interactions among hundreds of processes to keep someone alive. Those who try to explain the phenomenon of life as a single accident don't know what they are talking about.

If success is an emergent property, then it has to be about managing interactions rather than actions. An all-star team is not necessarily the best team in the league, and it might even lose to an average team in the same league. What characterizes a winning team is not only the quality of its players but also the quality of the interactions among them. A few years ago the New Orleans Saints football team had four defensive players in the Pro Bowl. But that didn't mean the Saints had the best defense in the league. The same year, the Dallas Cowboys won the Super Bowl, without having any defensive players in the Pro Bowl.

The compatibility between the parts and their reinforcing mutual interactions create a resonance, a force, which will be an order of magnitude higher than the sum of the forces generated by the separate parts. On the other hand, incompatibility among the parts will result in a less potent force than what the aggregate would have been able to produce. In the same way, an organization, depending on the nature of the interactions among its members, can be a value-adding or value-reducing system.

I have argued elsewhere that an organization's success is the product of the interactions among the five basic processes of throughput, decisionmaking, learning and control, membership, and conflict management. These processes correspond with generating and disseminating wealth, power, knowledge, beauty, and values. For example, to understand the success of GE, one cannot simply look at its earnings and market shares. At any given time, one might win or lose for the wrong reasons. Understanding GE's organizational processes (specifically, decision, learning, and measurement systems) may provide a better explanation for its continuous success.

We have said that emergent properties cannot be measured directly; one can measure only their manifestations. However, measuring the manifestation of a phenomenon has proven very problematic. For example, if the number of phone calls is the measure of love, then one can fake it. People can call people without necessarily loving them. In fact, since most of the behavioral characteristics of living systems are type II properties, the art of faking has been the major preoccupation of behavioral sciences in recent decades. How one can pretend to be something that one is not has been the money-making question of our times. Consider the huge market for how-to books, which give advice on a multitude of topics, such as how to come across as a caring person when one doesn't care at all. Remember when one could pretend to be powerful simply by wearing a red tie?

Measuring the success of an organization hasn't been an easy proposition, either. As the manifestation of success, growth has been considered an important performance measure of an organization. If an organization is successful, most probably it will grow; however, if an organization is growing this does not necessarily mean that it is successful. One can easily grow by "faking," or making lousy acquisitions. But unfortunately, two turkeys will not make an eagle. And that is exactly how many organizations have grown, only to destroy themselves.

To avoid pitfalls in measuring an emergent property, one has to measure more than one manifestation. In this context, EVA (economic value added) is a much more reliable measure of past success than simple growth.

$$EVA = \text{Investment (rate of return} - \text{cost of capital)}$$

EVA is based on two important manifestations of success. It is the product of both growth and value generation over and above the cost of capital. A positive EVA indicates a value-adding growth, while a negative EVA shows a value-reducing one.

Finally, manifestation of a phenomenon in its totality can be assessed only by picturing the future implicit in its present behavior. To map this future, we need a handle on social dynamics.

Recap

- Instead of trying to describe a property only in terms of *being*, we can also try to understand it as a process of *becoming*.
- An all-star team is not necessarily the best team in the league, and it might even lose to an average team in the same league. What characterizes a winning team is not only the quality of its players but the quality of the interactions among them.
- The compatibility between the parts and their reinforcing mutual interactions create a resonance, or force, which may be an order of magnitude higher than the sum of the forces generated by the parts separately.
- Emergent properties are the spontaneous outcome of ongoing processes. Life, love, happiness, and success are not one-time propositions; they have to be reproduced continuously. If the processes that generate them end, the phenomena will also cease to exist.

COUNTERINTUITIVENESS

Social dynamics are fraught with counterintuitive behavior. They stand on a level of complexity beyond the reach of the analytical approach. *Counterintuitiveness* means that actions intended to produce a desired outcome may, in fact, generate opposite results. It has been said that the path to hell is paved with good intentions. Things can get worse before getting better, or vice versa. One can win or lose for the wrong reason.

Making drugs illegal, while costing the nation a fortune, was meant to curb abuse and save the society from its ills. Counterintuitively, it has produced a multi-billion-dollar crime industry, higher consumption, and an overburdened criminal justice system.

To appreciate the nature of counterintuitiveness, one needs to understand the practical consequences of the following assertions:

- Cause and effect may be separated in time and space. An event happening at a given time and place may have a delayed effect, producing an impact at a different time and a different place.
- Cause and effect can replace one another, displaying circular relations.
- An event may have multiple effects. The order of importance may shift in time.
- A set of variables that initially played a key role in producing an effect may be replaced by a different set of variables at a different time. Removing the initial cause will not necessarily remove the effect.

Expanding the welfare system to reduce the number of poor families in a community may, counterintuitively, increase their numbers. Improvement of welfare usually requires additional resources, which means an increase in taxes. Excessive taxation may push the wealthy and many businesses to move out of the region, diluting the tax base and reducing revenues. Moreover, a more attractive welfare system will attract higher numbers of the needy to the region. It may also reduce the incentive to work, adding the burden of unemployment to an already overloaded system. Increased cost, coupled with reduced revenue, becomes a recipe for disaster (Figure 2.14).

To see how an event can produce multiple effects, consider the habit of smoking. In the short term smoking may reduce anxiety and, therefore, be good for the heart. Smoking also helps keep body weight in check, which is also good for the heart. However, in the long run, smoking will harden the arteries and damage the lungs, which may very well destroy the heart (Figure 2.15).

We have said that multifinality negates the classical principle of causality, suggesting that process, using different combinations of certainty, chance, and

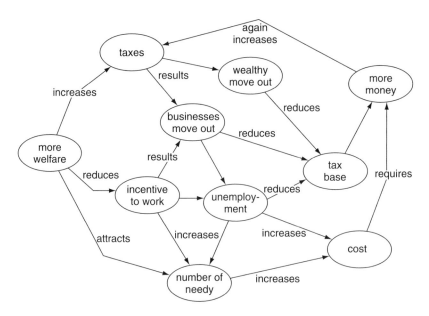

FIGURE 2.14   Dynamics of a Welfare System

choice rather than the initial condition, is mostly responsible for future states. All this means that understanding the short- and long-term consequences of an action, in its totality, requires building a dynamic model to simulate the multi-loop, nonlinear nature of the system. The model should capture the critical time lags and relevant interactions among major variables. This approach is distinctly different from the conventional one, where the fallacy of generating simple correlation is responsible for proliferating misinformation that is floated around continuously. Considering the level of confusion that exists around

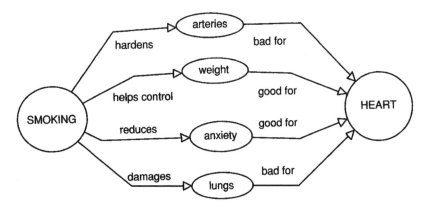

FIGURE 2.15   Effects of Smoking

counterintuitive outcomes, it is not difficult to see how one might attribute them to the chaotic nature of the universe.

Ironically, an interesting formulation known as chaos theory (Gleick, 1987) provides an alternative insight into the nature of this phenomenon. In fact, unpredictability of nonlinear systems parallels counterintuitive behavior in a social context. *Chaos theory* was advanced by a group of scientists[3] with different backgrounds (in physics, chemistry, and mathematics) working on the dynamics of complex physical phenomena. It seemed, at first, that chaos theory is but a systems theory of fluid dynamics. But I found it to be very relevant to the problems of social dynamics and a welcome addition to the realm of systems thinking. It adds a new, somehow twisted perspective to the notion of complexity and holistic thinking.

Chaos theory, using a different perspective, reconfirms the significance of the Herculean work done by Ackoff, some 46 years ago, in explaining the behavioral characteristics of purposeful systems. The work essentially provides the basic tools and concepts needed to understand choice and why social systems do what they do. There is, of course, another reason for my interest in chaos theory; recognition of the fundamental role *iteration* plays in the discovery of complex patterns is very compatible with my long-held belief that iteration is the essence of the holistic approach—and the core element of the design methodology. (For details, see Part III of this book.)

The following is my take on the relevant and interesting points of chaos theory:

- Analyzing the behavior of a nonlinear system is like walking through a maze whose walls rearrange themselves with each step you take (in other words, playing the game changes the game).
- Systems too complex for traditional mathematics could yet obey simple laws, e.g., fractal geometry[4] and fuzzy logic.[5]
- Laws of complexity hold universally across hierarchical scales (scalar, self-similarity) and are not influenced by the detailed behavior of constituent parts
- We are less likely to be able to explain the behavior of a complex whole by studying the behavior of the parts; contrarily, we are more likely to be able to explain the behavior of the parts by studying the behavior of the whole.

---

[3]Famous among them were: Edward Lorenz, Benoit Mandelbrot, William M. Schaffer, and James A. Yorke.

[4]For anyone interested, the original, indispensable source is Benoit Mendelbrot, *Fractal Geometry of Nature*, 1977.

[5]For definition and description see Zadeh, et al., 1987.

- A new understanding of time brings the realization that time is not really defined by the clock but by rhythms and iterations.[6]
- "Nature forms patterns, some orderly in space but disorderly in time, others orderly in time but disorderly in space. Some patterns are fractal, exhibiting structures self-similar in scale, while others oscillate."[7]

Four kinds of attractors determine the nature of the patterns:

1. *Point attractor* (drawn to or repelled from a particular activity).
2. *Cycle attractor* (oscillation between two or more activities).
3. *Torus attractor* (organized complexity repeating itself).
4. *Strange attractor* (unpredictable complex patterns emerging over time).

If one is tempted to use chaos terminology in the social context, the four attractors, viewed from a systems perspective, can be explained as follows:

- The point attractors (dichotomy/unidirectional) represent the behavior of social beings in pursuit of their natural instincts—fear, love, hate, desire to share, or self-interest.
- The cycle attractors (dialectic/self-maintaining) would correspond to our principle of multidimensionality, pursuit of seemingly opposite but complementary tendencies: stability and change, security and freedom, and, in general, differentiation and integration. Cyclicality, or periodic shift of emphasis from one orientation to another, is the result of sub-optimization.
- Torus attractors (equifinal/neg-entropic/goal-seeking) exemplify the behavior of open systems. These systems are guided by the image (DNA) of what they ought to be, as growth patterns of biological systems.
- Strange attractors (multifinal/self-organizing/purposeful) reflect the behavior of sociocultural systems with choice of ends and means; unpredictable patterns emerge out of stylistic preferences of purposeful actors.

Self-organization is not always a conscious act. More often than not, it happens by default or through a random iterative process of deviation amplification (evolution). Therefore, self-organization, if it happens by default using implicit cultural codes, would be more like the patterns produced by the Torus attractor. However, redesign would be the type self-organization created by a strange attractor.

---

[6]This also corresponds with the old Persian concept of time.
[7]James E. Lovelock in Gleick, *Chaos: Making a New Science*, 1987, p. 308.

Ackoff's description of passive, reactive, responsive, and active systems corresponds beautifully to the behavioral patterns attributed to the four attractors described above. (See the section on purposefulness, earlier in this chapter.)

With attractors, it is the iteration that makes it possible for order to appear from chaos. Nature automatically creates the iteration. But social beings can return to zero only by choice in order to start a new iteration. Designing from a clean slate is a reflection of this imperative.

Counterintuitive behavior of social systems is further exemplified by the following observations:

- Social systems display a tendency to repeat themselves and reproduce the same set of nonsolutions all over again.

One can never overestimate the resistance to change. "Conventional wisdom is like an old guard; it would rather die than surrender." A level of comfort with the familiar, combined with fear of the unknown, creates a formidable force that may even override potential self-interest. People may genuinely become excited by a beautiful idea and even support it wholeheartedly. But as the idea moves closer to implementation, insecurity and self-doubt set in. The supporters of the idea may then subconsciously sabotage their own efforts and prevent the change. Along with this comes pathological behavior, which is produced when those in charge of removing an obstruction benefit from it. Absent the support of a courageous, charismatic leader who enjoys the confidence of his or her people, any suggestions for a fundamental change become potentially self-destructive propositions. The fool who chooses to take on this role should be aware of his/her eventual loneliness.

- A difference in degree may become a difference in kind.

A commonly accepted principle of systems dynamics is that a quantitative change, beyond a critical point, results in a qualitative change. Accordingly, a difference in degree may become a difference in kind. This doesn't mean that an increased quantity of a given variable will bring a qualitative change in the variable itself. However, when the state of a system depends on a set of variables, a quantitative change in one variable beyond the inflection point will result in a *change of phase* in the *state of the system*. This change is a qualitative one, representing a whole new set of relationships among the variables involved. Suppose my style of life (state of a system) depends on my income. If my income were to suddenly change from $1,000 a month to $100,000 a month, it would certainly change my style of life. The change, of course, would be a qualitative one, representing a new mode of being. The income level that brings a qualitative change in lifestyle may be different for different people; however, it defines a critical juncture called the "inflection point."

Catastrophe theory (Zeeman, 1976), which deals with the same phenomena but in a physical context, reveals that at the inflection point, systems display catastrophic behavior (a cusp). In the social context, an inflection point will usually occur when one of the critical variables changes by an order of magnitude—i.e., when something can be done ten times faster, cheaper, and/or better than would have been possible before.

In his book (*Only the Paranoid Survive*, 1996), Andrew S. Grove, president and CEO of Intel Corporation, has dealt beautifully with the change of phase in a modern, technology-driven corporation. He explains, with great insight, how a "10×" change in certain variables (such as technology, markets, and regulations) resulted in a "strategic inflection point" and a change in the nature of the business, where the known facts of the business become invalid and a whole new set of emotions, including denial, fear, insecurity, and feeling of betrayal, sets in.

Market economies, like democracies, do not usually select the best solutions. They choose the most compatible, *satisfying* solution. Being ahead of your time is sometimes more tragic than falling behind.

The following episode, used by Grove to indicate the impact of a 10× change in the marketplace, demonstrates, in my opinion, the essence of market economies' counterintuitive behavior as well.

> Steve Jobs, co-founder of Apple, is arguably the founding genius of the personal computing industry. He left Apple in 1985 to create the "next" generation of superbly engineered hardware, a graphical user interface that was even better than Apple's Macintosh interface, and an operating system much more advanced than Mac. The software would be built in such a way that customers could tailor applications to their own uses by rearranging chunks of existing software rather than having to write it from the ground up. He wanted to create a computing system that would be in a class by itself. Jobs did not like PCs. He thought them inelegant and poorly engineered. The irony is that he was right. It took him a few years, but the Next computer and operating system delivered basically on all its objectives.
>
> Yet while Jobs was working on his "insanely great computer," Microsoft Windows had come on the market. Windows wasn't even as good as the Mac, let alone the Next interface, and it wasn't seamlessly integrated with computers or applications. But it was cheap and it worked, most importantly on the inexpensive personal computers that by the late 1980s were available anywhere in the world from hundreds of PC manufacturers.[8]

---

[8] *Only the Paranoid Survive*, Grove, 1996, pp. 59–60.

The Next machine, even with all its beauty, never took off. In fact, despite an ongoing infusion of cash, a state-of-the-art software operation, and a fully automated factory built to produce a large volume of Next computers, Jobs could not overcome the widespread momentum generated by the combination of Microsoft Windows and Intel Pentium chips, known figuratively as "Win-Tel." Ironically, Microsoft owes as much of its success to Intel as Intel owes to Microsoft. Each one, by default, created a 10× market for the other.

- Passive adaptation to a deteriorating environment is a road to disaster.

It's been said that if a frog is suddenly dropped into boiling water it will immediately jump out. However, if you put the same frog in warm water that is heated gradually, the frog will boil to death with no objection. The same is true of social systems. The capacity to adapt gradually to a changing environment can lead to a disaster if the adaptation is to a deteriorating environment. That only one of the original companies in the Dow Jones index participated in its centennial celebration is an indication that death, even among successful organizations, is more common than we like to believe. In fact, gradual deaths are more common than sudden deaths. In what is called the "Pan Am Syndrome," organizations bleed to death by adapting to an imperceptible gradual change, always doing too little too late. Ironically, sudden change of phase with all of its ramifications is less dangerous than imperceptible, gradual change. An organization facing a sudden change may still have enough organizational strength left in it to cope. But in the case of passive adaptation, by the time an organization recognizes the severity of the problem, it may already have lost most of its strength and be unable to do anything about it.

Recap

- Success in playing the game changes the game, and tenacity in playing the old game converts success to failure.
- Market economies, like democracies, make only rational choices. The winners are not necessarily the best, but those most compatible with the existing order. Being ahead of your time is sometimes more tragic than falling behind.
- Cause and effect display circular relations. Events have multiple effects, each with a different time lag, and independent life of its own.
- Removing the cause will not necessarily remove the effect.
- Nature's tendency for iteration, pattern formation, and creation of order out of chaos creates expectations of predictability. It seems, however, that nature, because of varying degrees of interaction between chance and choice, and the nonlinearity of systems, escapes the boredom of predictability.

3

Systems Dimensions

In discussing systems principles, I identified success, development, and happiness as emergent properties. I also asserted that, to get a handle on emergent properties, we need to understand the processes that produce them. I said that *choice* implies an ability and desire to create the future and that *ability* is the potential means of controlling, influencing, and appreciating the parameters affecting the system's existence.

However, the parameters that coproduce the future are found in the interactions of five dimensions of a social system. These five dimensions, in my experience, form a comprehensive set of variables that collectively describe the organization in its totality.

- The generation and distribution of *wealth*, or the production of necessary goods and services and their equitable distribution.
- The generation and dissemination of *truth*, or information, knowledge, and understanding.
- The creation and dissemination of *beauty*, the emotional aspect of being, the meaningfulness and excitement of what is done in and of itself.
- Formation and institutionalization of *values* for the purpose of regulating and maintaining interpersonal relationships: cooperation, coalition, competition, and conflict.
- Development and duplication of *power*, the questions of legitimacy, authority, and responsibility or, in general, the notion of governance.

Historically, the identification of social system dimensions has been both reactive (reacting to certain problems in social life) and proactive (reaching for the ultimate good). Reactively, the five dimensions of social systems correspond to the following major problem areas historically faced by all human societies: economics, scientifics, aesthetics, ethics, and politics.

Although some prominent social thinkers have implicitly considered more than one dimension in their analysis, most have chosen a *single* and, not surprisingly, different function as the *prime cause* of all social phenomena. Marx, for example, considered the *economy*, the mode of production, as the underlying cause of social realities. For Weber, *power*, supported by notions of authority and legitimacy, seemed the prime concern. Bagdanov used *knowledge* as the organizing principle of society. Meanwhile, religious thinkers place *values* at the core of everything.

On the proactive side, Ackoff, in his discussion of ideal-seeking systems, identifies four classes of societal activity individually necessary and collectively sufficient for progress toward the ideal of omnicompetence: the pursuits of *truth* (scientific function), *plenty* (economic function), *good* (ethical-moral function), and *beauty* (aesthetic function).

Coming from a different culture, I had a different point of view. In addition to knowledge, wealth, and values I included *power*, more specifically power-to-do (freedom and ability to choose) as a critical function of social systems. Surprisingly, I had missed the notion of beauty as a separate dimension. When I met Ackoff, some 31 years ago, we argued over this for days, until he decided that I needed a good lecture on the subject. That lecture was beautiful, and I realized that I had missed the notion of beauty for exactly the same reason that Ackoff had missed the notion of power.

Thinking with my heart, I considered beauty to be the liveliness that defined life. Beauty for me was the whole, or the emergent property. On the other hand, the phenomenon of choice has been a major preoccupation of Ackoff's. He saw ability to satisfy needs and desires as being equivalent to competence. Competence for Ackoff is a matter of *power-to-do* (as distinct from *power-over*, which is about dominance) and the emergent property of the whole. Maybe it's true that fish don't realize that something called water exists.

Revisiting Aristotle's concept of the "good life," the pursuit of happiness, and his elaborate scheme defining the elements necessary to achieve a good life (Adler, 1978), confirms my earlier assertion that the above dimensions may form a complete set and collectively define the whole.

Paralleling our five dimensions of power, wealth, knowledge, beauty, and values are Aristotle's association of liberty with choice and the willfulness to carry the choices out; his discussion of health, vitality, and vigor under the heading of wealth; the profound argument about the need to know and the skill of thinking; the assertion that a loveless life may not be worth living; and, finally, the magnificent notion of moral virtues (the good habits of choosing correctly).

In a different context, about 2,000 years later, John Dewey (1989), the great American philosopher, in discussing freedom and culture, explicitly refers to the states of politics, economics, science, art, and morality as the elements of the culture that determine the state of the society. Of course, his notion of art includes the sphere of emotionality. And in this context he argues convincingly that emotions are much more potent than reason in shaping public perception.

Recognizing these five dimensions as a complete set, unlike those of conventional practice, is not meant to isolate each dimension so it can be analyzed separately. Rather, it is to emphasize their interactions. It is quite feasible to use any four of the above dimensions to partly explain the characteristics of the fifth. For example, power, as the ability to do, can be defined in terms of wealth, knowledge, beauty (charisma), and values (tradition). Each dimension could be the source of power. However, we also need to recognize the significance of power in the decision process and as the organizing element of society in its own right.

Our main purpose here, however, is to explore the practical implications of these five dimensions in designing business processes. The following diagram (Figure 3.1) shows the relationships between power, knowledge, beauty, and values (the organizational processes) with throughput (the generation and dissemination of wealth).

The main function of a business, of course, is to produce a throughput— that is, in the most general terms, to generate and disseminate wealth. In this context, throughputs define how the organization's output is to be produced. It is the effectiveness of this process that ultimately results in a business concern's success or failure. However, an effective throughput cannot be designed

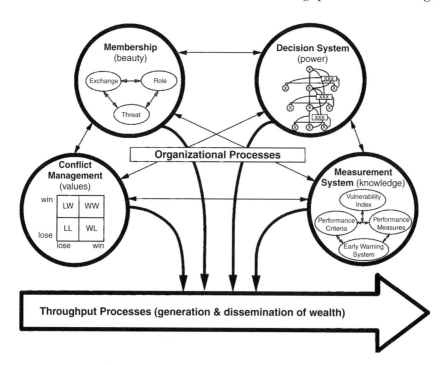

FIGURE 3.1   Throughput and Organizational Processes

independent of organizational processes that provide the platform and infra-structure for its operation.

The holistic approach requires that designers explicitly define the parameters of these subsystems and understand the behavioral implication of different designs. Systems theory of organizations maintains that major obstructions in developing multiminded systems are the results of a malfunction in one or all of the five dimensions of social systems.

Design parameters and characteristics of organizational processes are basically defined by assumptions and imperatives of the dominant culture or the paradigm in use for each organization. The four organizational processes are very much interdependent and value driven. Together, they define critical attributes of the organizational culture. More often than not, these attributes are produced by default rather than design. Once in place, however, they remain intact during the ups and downs of technological change.

Throughput processes, on the other hand, are technologically driven. They explicitly define how the output of an organization is to be produced in the context of a given technology. Uniquely designed for each output, throughput processes are subject to continuous change and improvement.

Since throughputs are redesigned more frequently, there is always a good chance that new generations of throughput designs will become incompatible with more traditional organizational processes already in place. This has been the major cause of the failures, already witnessed, in most reengineering efforts of recent times. A redesigned throughput process cannot be effectively implemented without proper concern for its compatibility with the existing order, the organizational processes already in place.

The rest of this chapter explores the operating rules and basic elements of a throughput system, then discusses the basics of organizational processes in the following order:

1. Membership
2. Decision system
3. Conflict management
4. Learning and control

THROUGHPUT

We have defined throughput as the process of generating and disseminating wealth. It contains all the activities necessary to obtain required inputs, convert inputs to outputs, and then take the final products to market. Therefore, marketing, selling, order processing, purchasing, producing, shipping, billing, and accounting—in addition to cash management, quality, time, and cost—are among the activities of a throughput chain.

Of course, the list of activities for a service function might be slightly different. For example, throughput of an education system will include activities for selecting and registering students, scheduling the courses, teaching, giving exams, and issuing certifications. Meanwhile, the throughput of a health-care system may include access to patients, access to health-care providers, interface with third-party payers, delivery of health care, delivery of patient care, and management of the reimbursement system.

Nevertheless, it is obvious that even a simple throughput consists of a chain of events and activities that need to be integrated. Since these activities are usually carried out by different groups in different departments of an organization, strong interface and effective coupling among them are a must for a competitive throughput. Actually, to design a throughput system, we need to:

- Know the state of the art, as well as the availability and feasibility of alternative technologies and their relevance to the emerging competitive game.
- Understand the *flow*, the interface between active elements, and how the coupling function works.
- Appreciate the dynamics of the system—the time cycle, buffers, delays, queues, bottlenecks, and feedback loops.
- Handle the interdependencies among critical variables, plus deal with open and closed loops, structural imperatives, and system constraints.
- Have an operational knowledge of throughput accounting, target costing, and variable budgeting.

Figure 3.2 describes elements of a holistic approach to designing a throughput. The four basic elements of this scheme are the model, the critical properties of the process, the measurement and diagnostic system, and the read-only memory.

Model of the Process

The central element of this scheme is the model of the process. The model is a set of interrelated activities designed to produce an explicit output. Different ways and several levels of sophistication can be used to model a process. The most common is a simple flow chart. However, to get a handle on interdependencies and the dynamics of the system, we can use the new software programs such as Extend[1] or ithink[2] to build a more helpful simulation model.

---

[1] Extend is a software from Imagine That, Inc., San Jose, CA.
[2] Ithink is a software from High Performance Systems, Hanover, NH.

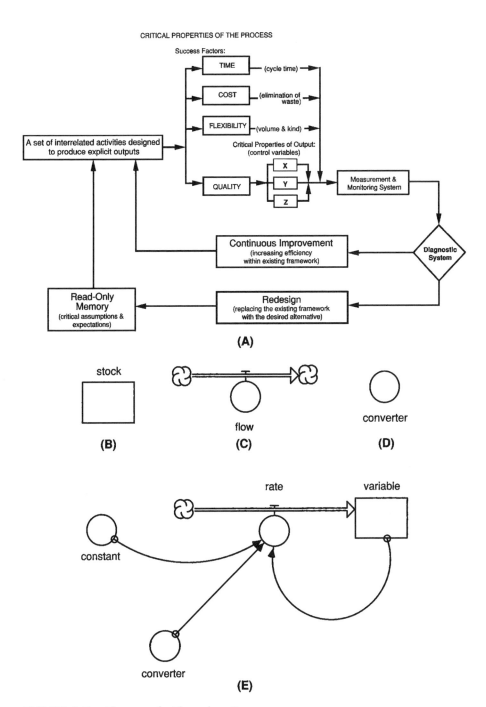

FIGURE 3.2   Elements of a Throughput Process

Extend is simpler and, for those familiar with conventional flow-charting techniques, provides an effective way to handle the dynamics of the process. Critical elements of a process, such as buffers, queues, and time lags, can easily be simulated with this program. Still, the ithink model, though more difficult to use, provides a better handle on interdependencies.

To model the dynamics of a throughput process, we need to identify and map the behavior of the relevant throughput variables. We do this by looking at the state of the variables, the manner in which the variables change, and the way they relate to one another. Using a simplified version of the conventions and icons provided by the ithink program—stocks, flows, converters, and connectors—we can map the behavior of each variable separately and then put them all together in a web of interdependencies.

Stocks, symbolized by a rectangle, reflect a level, condition, or attribute of a variable at a given time. They can also be used to represent buffers and conveyors to define transit times, and/or delays.

Flows, symbolized by a pipe, an arrow, and a flow regulator, are used to represent activities or things in motion. In modeling a throughput process we use them to capture the rate of change in the state of the variables under consideration.

Converters, signified by circles, represent constants, conversion tables, conditions, or any significant factors and/or variables that have an influence on the behavior of a flow.

Connectors, signified by pointers, reflect the relationships and interdependencies among the variables. They explicitly define the assumptions about what depends on what.

For example, assume that relevant throughput variables for the operation of a telephone company are customer base, installations, repairs, preventive maintenance, and plant capacity. First, we map the behavior of each of the above variables separately, as shown in lines one to five of the following ithink model, using stocks, flows, and converters. Then we identify and capture the interdependencies among them with the help of connectors (Figure 3.3).

Usefulness of this or any such model depends, of course, on the validity of the underlying assumptions used to develop the operating formulas behind the icons. Therefore, it is imperative that the model be simulated first using actual data for the last three years. That way we can compare the behavior of the model's variables with those in actual settings in known environments and then make the necessary adjustments. The following is a sample simulation run (Table 3.1). It shows only limited variables for a period of two years.

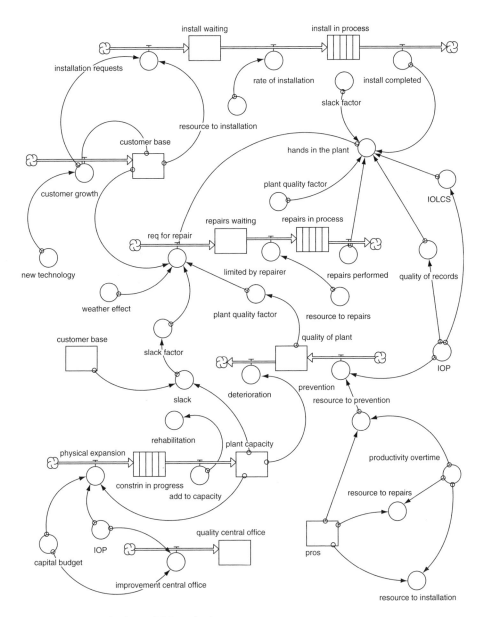

FIGURE 3.3 Ithink Model for Telephone Operation

Critical Properties

The second element in the above scheme is identification of critical properties of the process. Time cost, flexibility, and quality are usually among the major factors that determine the success of a throughput process. The challenge is to reduce cycle time, eliminate waste, ensure availability of the output (in kind,

TABLE 3.1   Sample Simulation Run

Month	Repairs	Installation	Customer Base	Number of Pros	Repairs Queue	Install Queue
1.	251,458	125,117	12.5	8,000	120,000	270,000
2.	219,186	125,430	12.5	7,967	139,946	287,743
3.	220,957	125,744	12.6	7,934	160,642	274,187
4.	222,759	126,059	12.6	7,901	182,088	263,370
5.	224,592	126,374	12.6	7,868	204,282	255,319
6.	226,457	126,691	12.7	7,835	227,224	250,062
7.	228,356	127,008	12.7	7,802	250,913	247,626
8.	230,289	127,325	12.7	7,770	275,347	248,041
9.	232,256	127,644	12.8	7,738	300,526	251,337
10.	234,259	127,963	12.8	7,705	326,448	257,544
11.	236,298	128,284	12.8	7,673	353,112	266,695
12.	238,404	131,832	12.8	7,641	380,519	278,821
13.	240,575	132,195	12.9	7,610	411,893	293,986
14.	257,775	132,559	12.9	9,094	429,212	279,279
15.	265,462	132,924	13.0	9,089	442,057	271,025
16.	268,230	133,290	13.0	9,084	455,334	270,606
17.	271,044	133,657	13.0	9,078	469,046	273,106
18.	273,903	134,025	13.1	9,073	483.193	278,575
19.	276,810	134,394	13.1	9,068	497,780	287,061
20.	279,766	134,764	13.1	9,062	512,809	298,615
21.	282,771	135,134	13.2	9,056	528,281	313,290
22.	285,828	135,506	13.2	9,050	544,200	331,138
23.	288,937	135,880	13.2	9,045	560,568	352,213
24.	292,100	136,254	13.3	9,039	577,387	376,572

volume, space, and time), and finally, manage the process in such a way that it is "competent and in control" with regard to selected properties of the output (control variables). Because of the interdependencies among success factors, performance of any one variable can be improved at the expense of the others. To avoid suboptimization and subsequent structural conflict, the process should be manipulated in a way that achieves all four objectives at the same time.

Measurement and Diagnostic

The third element of our scheme is the measurement and diagnostic system. The simulation model should provide an online capability to monitor all of the interdependent success factors in the same frame, at the same time, so their relationship can be monitored. This condition is necessary for an effective diagnostic system. The diagnostic system should be able to recognize when the improvement process hits a plateau, because this indicates that the system has used up the slacks and that the existing design has exhausted its maximum potential. To achieve an order-of-magnitude change in the system's performance, we need to replace the existing framework and redesign the process.

Read-Only Memory

Read-only memory is the fourth element of our scheme. We need to incorporate a learning system so that all of our assumptions, expectations, and changes in the design process are recorded in a read-only memory. These entries, which cannot be altered, will be kept intact for learning purposes and future reference.

Target Costing

Final consideration in designing a throughput system is the concept of *target costing*. Since 70 percent of an operation's cost is design driven, the designers of a throughput system must have cost responsibility. Without a target cost, every fool is a designer. Incorporation of target costing and *variable budgeting* in operating a throughput system is often the difference between success and failure.

Pricing, in the conventional cost-accounting system, is based on a cost-plus formula. The assumption is that costs are uncontrollable and that the producers are entitled to recover their costs plus a reasonable margin for profit. Therefore, the prices are set by the cost of the least efficient producer, who still manages to remain in the competitive game. Higher profits are achieved by targeting higher price levels if one commands a dominant share of the market. Thus, in this context, price is a controllable variable.

By contrast, with target costing prices are assumed to be set by the market on a competitive basis. In a market economy, values are defined by the users. As we move toward a global economy, prices increasingly become uncontrollable variables, while costs, because of technological advances, increasingly become controllable variables. This is a whole new ball game.

After deciding to enter the luxury car market and compete head-on with Mercedes-Benz, Toyota had to use target costing in designing and producing the Lexus. Toyota had discovered that $20,000 of a Mercedes' $65,000 price tag is *snob value*. Customers, at the time, were willing to pay $20,000 more just for the name Mercedes-Benz. This meant that Lexus had to be, at a minimum, a car of the same quality but one that sold for less than $45,000. Toyota targeted the car to be priced at $40,000. But Lexus was a new entry, requiring a whole new distribution channel. The cost of selling was estimated to be nearly 25 percent, or about $10,000 per car. With a 10 percent return on sales also put aside, the design team was given a $26,000 target cost to produce the car. The charge was, "Produce it within the target cost or get the hell out of the way."

Target costing requires a variable budgeting scheme. With variable budgeting, every active element in the process becomes a performance center. None will get a fixed budget, but everyone will have a working capital and a monthly income. This income will be a percentage of monthly throughput, which in turn will determine the level of the expenditure of the activity.

MEMBERSHIP

In contrast to machines, in which integration of the parts into a cohesive whole is a one-time proposition, for organizations the problem of integration is a constant struggle and a continuous concern. Despite a desire for individuality and uniqueness, we, as emotionally vulnerable social beings, display a strong tendency to be members of a collectivity. Most of us have a burning desire to identify with others, to be accepted by others, and to conform to the norms of a group of our choice.

This integrative phenomenon seems rooted in the emotional dimension of our beings. An exciting book, an object of beauty, a heroic or a tragic encounter, all generate an urge to share. So much so, that the boundary between individuality and collectivity, the question of how much of me is me and how much is those to whom I am bonded, remains at the heart of the manifestation of beauty. Beauty is, therefore, the ultimate agent of social integration. The level of integration that an organization achieves depends on the level of excitement and commitment it generates among its members.

The significance of membership in sociocultural systems (families, groups, organizations, nations) lies in the fact that the units of these systems are not so much the individuals, but the roles imparted to them. Under different circumstances and in different social settings, individuals display different behaviors. A good friend is not necessarily a good employee. A successful vice president might make a lousy president. The nature of these roles is influenced by expectations and the limitations imposed by the social structure, the culture, and various environmental realities mapped by the actors.

Effective membership in a multiminded system requires a role, a sense of belonging, and a commitment to participate in creating the group's future, so much so that rolelessness is the major obstruction to integrating a social system. When an individual feels that his or her contributions to the group's achievements are insignificant, or when he or she feels powerless to play an effective role in the system's performance, a feeling of indifference sets in and the individual gradually becomes alienated from the very system in which he or she is supposed to be an active member.

In this context, inability to carry out the responsibilities of a specific role (incompetence) results in anxiety and frustration. To fulfill the role of a physician or carpenter requires certain levels of expertise and mastery. Otherwise, the individual to whom the role is entrusted will be alienated. As the strength of a chain is determined by its weakest link, incompatibility among the members often causes the more dynamic ones to retrogress to the level of the weakest, spreading a general feeling of ineffectualness and impotency.

Of course, conflicting values within a social system also contribute to alienating its members. The extent to which an individual's value image coincides with that of the community determines the degree of that individual's membership in that community.

A multiminded organization is a voluntary association of purposeful members. The purpose of an organization, in addition to its own viability, is to serve the purposes of its members while serving the purposes of its containing whole. Members join an organization to serve themselves. Unless the organization serves them, they will not serve it well.

Although it is possible to persuade purposeful members of a purposeful social system to engage in a sacrifice for a limited period of time, it is highly improbable that they will accept this condition as a way of life. There needs to be an *exchange system* so that the individual's struggle for his or her own gain is enhanced by the degree of contribution he or she makes toward satisfying the needs of the higher system and those of the other members.

Nevertheless, proper functioning of a multiminded organization also requires an implicit *threat system*. In other words, continued membership in a system should depend on avoiding a certain set of behaviors considered antagonistic to the survival of the whole. For an elaborate treatment of role, exchange, and threat see Boulding (1968).

CONFLICT MANAGEMENT

To integrate a multiminded system is to design an organization whose members can operate as independent parts with individual choices, while acting as responsible members of a coherent whole with a collective choice. The effectiveness of an organization, therefore, depends not so much on managing the actions of individuals, but on managing the *interactions* among its members.

The interactions among members of an organization take many forms (Figure 3.4). Members may cooperate with regard to one pair of tendencies, compete over others, and be in conflict with respect to different sets at the same time. In general, actors (individually or in groups), by agreeing or disagreeing with each other on compatibility of their ends, means, or both, can create four types of relationships: conflict, cooperation, competition, and coalition.[3]

---

[3]Definitions for *cooperation, conflict, coalition,* and *competition*, as well as those for *solving, resolving, dissolving,* and *absolving*, are from *On Purposeful Systems* (Ackoff, 1972).

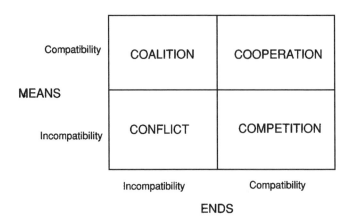

FIGURE 3.4   Four Types of Relationship

In *conflict*, each party reduces the expected value of the outcomes for the others. The opposite is true of *cooperation*. *Competition* represents a situation in which a lower-level conflict serves the attainment of a commonly held higher-level objective for both parties. It is a conflict of means, not ends. *Coalitions* are formed when actors with conflicting ends agree to remove a perceived common obstruction. In this unstable situation, conflict is temporarily converted to cooperation, only to be succeeded by possibly more severe conflict at a higher level.

If organizations are to serve their members as well as their environments, they must be able to deal with conflict. Creating a conflict-free organization may not be possible, but creating one capable of dealing with conflict is. Conflict can be addressed in four different ways: solve, resolve, absolve, or dissolve.

- To *solve* a conflict is to select a course of action believed to yield the best possible outcome for one side at the cost of the other—in other words, a win/lose struggle.
- To *resolve* a conflict is to select a course of action that yields an outcome good enough and minimally satisfactory to both the opposing tendencies—in other words, a compromise.
- To *absolve* a conflict is to wait it out, hoping that, if ignored, it will go away—in other words, benign neglect.
- To *dissolve* a conflict is to change the nature and/or the environment of the entity in which it is embedded, thus removing the conflict.

Selecting any one of these courses of action depends on how the relationships between opposing tendencies are formulated. As discussed before (under the principle of multidimensionality), these relationships are conceived in at least three ways: dichotomy, continuum, or multidimensional scheme.

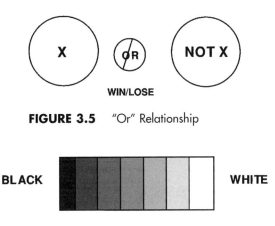

FIGURE 3.5   "Or" Relationship

BLACK   WHITE

FIGURE 3.6   Compromise

Dichotomy represents an "or" relationship, a win/lose struggle (Figure 3.5). This way calls for a solution to the conflict. The loser, usually declared wrong, is eliminated.

Continuum calls for a compromise, or resolution of the conflict (Figure 3.6).

For multidimensional concepts, however, interaction between opposing tendencies is characterized by an "and" relationship (Figure 3.7). This formulation permits a dissolving of the conflict.

When the conflict situation is formulated as a zero-sum game, gain for one player is invariably associated with a loss for the other. But in the multidimensional concept, lose/lose as well as win/win, in addition to win/lose struggles, are strong possibilities. Therefore, a loss for one side is not always a

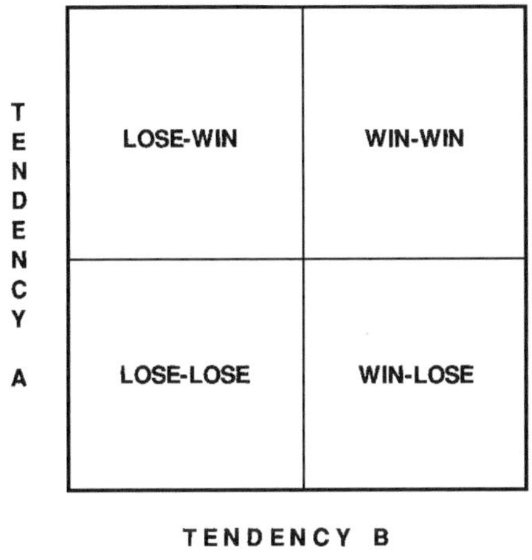

	TENDENCY A	
	LOSE-WIN	WIN-WIN
	LOSE-LOSE	WIN-LOSE

TENDENCY B

FIGURE 3.7   "And" Relationship

gain for the other. On the contrary, both opposing tendencies can increase or decrease simultaneously.

To dissolve a conflict is to discover new frames of reference in which opposing tendencies are treated as complementary in a new ensemble with a new logic of its own. It requires reformulation or, more precisely, reconceptualization of the variables involved. Finally, to dissolve a conflict is to redesign the system, which contains the conflict, in its totality, creating "a feasible whole from infeasible parts."

From Lose/Lose to Win/Win Environments

An important characteristic of a win/lose struggle is the possibility of converting it to either a lose/lose or a win/win environment. In the present complex and highly differentiated social systems, emergence of a lose/lose environment is not only highly probable, but an increasingly dominant reality.

Nowadays, winning requires much greater ability than ever before. It is easier for groups to prevent others from winning than to win themselves. Increasing numbers of small special interest groups are diluting the strength of the traditional power centers. Even many disadvantaged minorities have been forced to learn how to keep the opposing sides from winning. But the illusion that increased losses for the other side is equivalent to winning is what prolongs the struggle and forces the game to be played to a lose/lose end.

Ironically, it is awareness of this high probability for lose/lose that becomes instrumental in converting a win/lose to a win/win. This is easily confirmed by understanding the reason why the players in the famous prisoners' dilemma[4] chose the win/win strategy to avoid a lose/lose end. Dynamic interaction of the players, combined with awareness of a possible lose/lose situation, creates a metagame leading to selection of a win/win strategy.

Changing Conflict to Competition

Ends and means are interchangeable concepts; an end is a means for further ends. Changing conflict to competition requires finding higher-level objectives shared by lower-level conflicting tendencies. The lower-level opposing ends are converted into conflicting means with a shared higher-level objective, becoming part of a competition.

---

[4]See *Prisoner's Dilemma* (Rapoport, 1965).

The search for a shared higher-level end can continue up to and include the ideal, when ends and means converge and become the same. The probability of finding a shared objective increases by moving to higher and higher levels, becoming maximized at the ideal level. Now, if even the ideal level cannot produce a common end for conflicting tendencies, then the conflict is considered nondissolvable within the context of existing worldviews. In this situation, dissolving the conflicts requires a change of worldviews. This change can be a reaction to frustrations with the existing assumptions' failure to deal with the challenges of a new era, a march of events nullifying conventional wisdom. Or it can happen by an active learning and unlearning process of purposeful transformation.

DECISION SYSTEMS
Duplication of Power

To deal effectively with multiminded systems requires understanding choice, and choice is a matter of freedom and power-to-do. We have argued that while the parts of a multiminded system increasingly display choice and behave independently, the whole becomes more and more interdependent. This represents a dilemma: a dichotomy of centralization (a concern for the interest of the whole) or decentralization (a concern for the interest of the parts). This dichotomy leads either to suffocation (concentration of power) or chaos (abdication of power). On the other hand, a compromise based on "sharing the power" produces frustration and gridlock.

The answer lies in the fact that centralization and decentralization are two sides of the same coin. Both must happen at the same time. This phenomenon is possible because power is like knowledge. It can be duplicated. The conceptualization of power as a non-zero-sum entity is the critical step toward understanding the essence of empowerment and the management of multiminded systems. Significantly, empowerment is not abdication of power, nor is it sharing of power. It is duplication of power. The following episode illustrates this point.

Suppose you have just started to work for a no-nonsense management-by-objective guy, who has promised you that he will manage in a decentralized manner and will judge you only on the results. You look forward to this opportunity to try a few exciting ideas that require a degree of autonomy in order to be realized. After a few weeks, you run into your new boss and decide to share with him some of the exciting things you have been doing. Although he attempts a poker face, you somehow sense he doesn't like what he's hearing. Maybe he isn't in the right mood. You tell yourself, "When he sees the final results, he'll like it."

A few weeks later, at a cocktail party, he seems very upbeat and you assume this might be a good time to share your new ideas with him. But he doesn't like them! Maybe you should leave him alone for a while, you think. But it's too late; he's already nervous. A few days later, he shows up in your office and asks a few questions about some things you have proposed. When he leaves, you know he's not happy. Decentralization has gone out the window. You cannot risk being found incapable by the man who controls your future! So what do you do? You call him every time you need to make a decision to ask him what he wants you to do. You both become increasingly frustrated, and finally you decide to quit.

At this point, a manager from another department reminds you that you have two kids in college and a mortgage to pay. She offers you a job if you are willing to forget the nonsense about decentralization and autonomy and do exactly what she tells you. Having no other choice, you reluctantly accept the offer. Your new boss, however, has a funny style. Not only does she tell you what to do, but she tells you why her way is best. For a while you think she wants to brainwash you. Or maybe she is insecure and wants to prove something. You try to reassure her of your loyalty. "Just tell me what to do and I'll do it," you tell her. But she won't give up. Apparently, she loves to talk. During these interactions, somehow, you find out how she makes decisions, you learn her decision criteria, and you begin to understand her value system. One day, when she's thinking out loud trying to tell you what to do, you ask her, "How about this?" She says, "Fantastic." Decentralization happens.

The message of this brief story is that it's the *sharing of decision criteria*, not abdication of power, that results in empowerment and makes centralization and decentralization happen at the same time. Achieving a higher order of decentralized decisionmaking requires a higher order of centralized agreement on decision criteria. However, to produce a shared understanding of decision criteria among all members of an organization individually is an impossible task. The process of empowerment must be institutionalized. An effective means of duplication of power, in my experience, has been the creation of a nested network of "learning and design cells" that engage members in an interactive design process, described below.

Every manager in the organization forms a design cell. The membership of the cell will be the manager, his or her boss, and all the direct reports (see Figure 3.8). Since every cell includes three levels of membership, a nested network is created. This provides an opportunity for everyone to interact with at least three levels in the organization (with peers on the same level, with the boss and boss's boss, and finally with the direct reports and their subordinates). The main function of these cells is to create a shared understanding of why the organization does what it does, to develop an awareness of the default values of the culture, and to take collective ownership of the decision criteria.

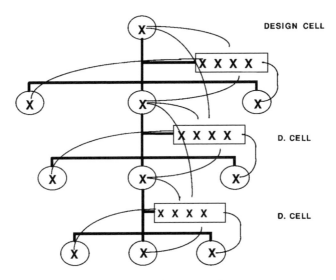

FIGURE 3.8   Learning and Design Cells

The above scheme, which is known as *circular organization*, was first published by Ackoff in 1981. It is a design for participation that has been used effectively in different contexts.[5]

Decision Criteria

Decision criteria define the rules of decisionmaking; whereas, decisions themselves are applications of the decision rule to specific situations. What operationally distinguishes decision criteria from decisions per se is the existence of some degree of freedom in decision criteria. The absence of at least one degree of freedom virtually converts the decision criteria to decisions.

Decision criteria can be grouped into two categories: policies and procedures. A *policy* is a decision criteria at a higher level of abstraction. Policy essentially deals with choice dimensions (variables involved), "why" questions, underlying assumptions, and expected outcomes. Policy decisions are value-loaded choices that should be explicit about their implications for human, financial, and technical domains. *Procedures*, on the other hand, are derived from policies. They deal with "how" questions. They should specify the method or the model to be used for applying policies to specific situations.

Each design cell should make its own rules and procedures on how to conduct its business (how often to meet, how to reach decisions, and so on). However, for its operation to be effective, each should have the following four attributes.

---

[5]See *Democratic Corporation* (Ackoff, 1994).

Degree of Freedom

Each cell may formulate two kinds of policies: 1) policies for the lower level and 2) policies for itself, provided they are compatible with the policies handed down to it by the higher cell. The development of procedures for executing policies is done exclusively by the level responsible for executing those policies. In other words, no cell should formulate procedures for any cell other than itself.

Policies should leave a healthy degree of freedom for the executing cell. They should be specific enough to ensure consistency of action, as well as constancy of purpose and direction. At the same time, they should be broad enough to avoid straitjacketing by allowing room for flexibility and learning. Responsibility for formulating procedure is given to the same level responsible for its execution to reinforce this degree of freedom. Although derived from policies, procedures should be developed with regard to specific circumstances known only to the those who deal with them directly.

Consistency

Each design cell should ensure that the policies it sets are internally consistent and that they do not create structural conflicts by introducing contradictory performance criteria. Examples: conflicts between input-based compensation and output-oriented performance; or between cost centers (such as production units) and revenue centers (such as sales units).

Explicitness

Policy decisions ought to be explicit. They should reveal the assumptions on which the policies are made and spell out the expected outcome. The expectations should reflect at least these three areas: financial (financial performance), people (human system), and customer (quality of output).

Consensus

The effectiveness of any decision depends on the degree of consensus generated for it. The understanding and consensus reached in adopting a particular policy decision determine the level of collective commitment to that policy's implementation. Generating consensus is purely a matter of leadership. Here, as in many other issues involving rational, emotional, or cultural dimensions of behavior, the role of leadership is indispensable. It cannot be reduced to a magic formula. Ultimately, consensus will stand or fall on the quality of leadership.

Consensus is not majority rule; it does not even imply unanimity. It is an agreement to act. No one should be allowed to take the process hostage. Nor should the group as a whole be allowed to absolve the challenge and hope against hope that benign neglect will eventually take care of the problem. A "no decision" *is* a decision for the status quo, and it should therefore be acknowledged as such.

Situations that defy consensus call for leadership in its highest form. The absence of consensus would be a judgment call on the leader to ensure that the process is not hung up. He or she would then have to formulate an explicit working synthesis of the different positions. The emergent working synthesis should be adopted as the default decision.

For a working synthesis to be effective, the participants, at a minimum, must feel that they:

- Have been heard and given a chance to influence the outcome
- Have understood why the default decision has been taken, even though they might disagree with it
- Are willing to live by the decision and support it with commitment

When the above conditions for default decision cannot be met and the group remains seriously polarized, the alternative is for the opposing parties to agree on an experiment, the results of which will produce the decision. The group should not only agree on the design of the experiment, but should specify its performance criteria. It is also very useful for the opposing parties to specify, up front, what will prove them wrong.

LEARNING AND CONTROL SYSTEMS

The other side of a decision system is learning and control. In my experience, Ackoff's management system (1981) provides one of the best frameworks to design a learning system.[6] The following diagram (Figure 3.9) is a simplified version of this rich and elaborate scheme. It has been modified to fit my intention to relate learning to control, and underline the importance of "social calculus."

Learning results from being surprised: detecting a mismatch between what was expected to happen and what actually did happen. If one understands why the mismatch occurred (diagnosis) and is able to do things in a way that avoids a mismatch in the future (prescription), one has learned.

---

[6]Ackoff's "Management System," *Creating the Corporate Future* (Ackoff, 1981, Ch. 6) is currently being deployed at GM as a conceptual framework to link strategic decision making with knowledge networking.

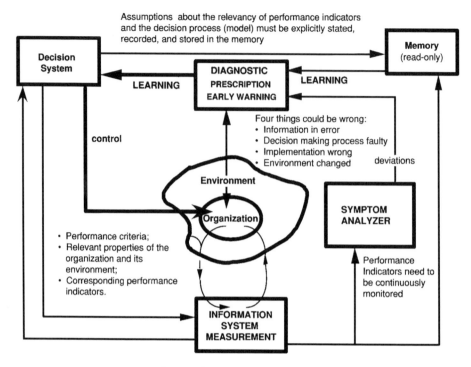

FIGURE 3.9 Learning and Control System

To detect a mismatch in the first place, a formal process is needed to record expected outcomes. This system will be used only for major decisions and will record the following information:

- The assumptions on which the decision was made.
- The information used to make the decision.
- The process used to arrive at a conclusion.
- The expected outcome(s).

Although reasons for mismatches are infinite, they fall into one of the following four categories:

1. The information (input) was wrong.
2. The implementation was wrong.
3. The decision was wrong.
4. The environment has changed.

Therefore, during a diagnosis, all four categories must be checked: the data, the decision, the implementation, and the environmental conditions.

A learning system will be most effective if it includes an early warning system that calls for corrective action before the problem has occurred. Such a system will continuously monitor the validity of the assumptions on which the decision was made, as well as the implementation process and intermediate results.

An integral part of a learning and control function is a measurement system. Winning is fun. To win we have to keep score, and the way we keep the score defines the game.

To the extent that membership in a group is desired, the criteria by which the group evaluates the behavior of its members have a profound effect on the manner in which individuals conduct themselves. But we know all too well how to play a zero-sum game. We know how one can win here at the expense of there, or succeed today at the cost of tomorrow. In the context of biological thinking, we have all learned how to exploit our environment by undermining our collective viability.

Social Calculus

Controlling the behavior of purposeful individuals in a multiminded system by using supervision is no longer feasible or even desirable. To manage a multiminded system with self-controlling members, we need a new *social calculus*. This calculus should provide a new framework for creating vertical, horizontal, and temporal compatibility among the members of an organization. Vertical compatibility deals with the extent of compatibility between members at different levels; horizontal compatibility is concerned with members at the same levels; and temporal compatibility is concerned with the compatibility of the interests among past, present, and future members in the system.

Vertical Compatibility

We have argued that effective integration of multilevel purposeful systems cannot be achieved without performance criteria that make fulfillment of a member's needs and desires dependent on fulfillment of the larger system's needs, and vice versa. In other words, individuals' efforts for their own gain should be enhanced by the degree of contribution they make toward the needs of the higher system, of which they are willing members. This would change the measure of success and relative advantage of various activities for the actors in favor of those activities that satisfy the requirement of both levels.

Consider the following simple exchange system: A productive unit consumes the scarce resources of its environment; in return, it produces outputs (goods or services) that partially fulfill the needs of that environment. The assumption is that the unit will survive as long as the total value of the outputs produced is greater than or equal to the total value of the inputs it consumes.

The pricing system determined by "dollar votes" is supposed to be a reliable and sufficient criterion for determining production and distribution priorities.

This supposition might be tenable if 1) dollar votes were distributed more equitably, and 2) end prices were not manipulated. However, factors such as price control or government protection make the actual cost of service much higher than perceived. In other words, inputs are purchased from the environment at a lower price, and outputs (measured by the classical accounting method) are made to look more valuable than they really are.

Furthermore, even though creating a productive employment opportunity for all members of a social system is an effective means of simultaneous production and distribution of wealth, existing social calculus considers employment only as a cost and, not surprisingly, tries to minimize it. To remedy the situation we need a new framework, one that will use employment on both sides of the equation, input as well as output. We also need performance criteria that, in addition to efficient production of wealth, explicitly consider its proper distribution as a social service to be adequately rewarded. Of course, without a proper concern about production, a sole obsession with distribution will result in nothing but equitable distribution of poverty.

The following scheme is a simplified version of an attempt to measure the actual costs and benefits of each major economic activity as perceived on the national level. It complements the productive strength of a market economy by enhancing its allocation function. The model registers the needs of those members who lack the dollar vote to register their needs. It also explicitly values the distribution of wealth (salaries paid) as social service.

For simplicity, let us limit inputs to the two categories of 1) raw materials and 2) human resources, and the outputs to the two corresponding categories of 1) finished goods produced and 2) employment opportunity created. Assigning a "scarcity coefficient" to each set of inputs obtained from the environment, and a "need coefficient" to each set of outputs (goods/services) yielded to the environment, we can compute the relative contribution of each major economic activity using Table 3.2.

Once the contribution ratio is calculated, the idea of a new social calculus would be to reward activities with higher social contributions.

Suppose a certain productive unit produces bread with a contribution ratio of 2, but with a low rate of return on investment of 8 percent (because of the weak purchasing power of the consuming class). On the other hand, suppose another unit produces yo-yos with a contribution ratio of 1, but with a rate of return on investment of 18 percent. Accordingly, our incentive system ought to be able to change the relative rates of return on investment in favor of bread.

TABLE 3.2   Calculating the Contribution Ratio for Each Economic Activity

Inputs Consumed	*Outputs Produced*
Raw Materials	**Goods Produced**
Raw Material A: Quantity A × Price A × Scarcity Ratio A	Output D: Quantity D × Price D × Need Ratio D
Raw Material B: Quantity B × Price B × Scarcity Ratio B	Output E: Quantity E × Price E × Need Ratio E
Raw Material C: Quantity C × Price C × Scarcity Ratio C	Output F: Quantity F × Price F × Need Ratio F
Human Resources Utilized	**Employment Opportunity Created**
No. of Highly Skilled Employees × (Training Cost ÷ Productive Years) × Scarcity Ratio	No. of Highly Skilled Employees × Salary Paid × Need Ratio for Employment
No. of Skilled Employees × (Training Cost ÷ Productive Years) × Scarcity Ratio	No. of Skilled Employees × Salary Paid × Need Ratio for Employment
No. of Unskilled Employees × (Training Cost ÷ Productive Years) × Scarcity Ratio	No. of Unskilled Employees × Salary Paid × Need Ratio for Employment

Total Value Consumed:———   Total Value Produced:———

Total Value Produced ÷ Total Value Consumed = Contribution Ratio

The problem can be overcome with an integrated and coordinated application of well-known tools such as 1) a differentiated loan structure, 2) a differentiated interest rate structure, and 3) a differentiated tax structure. Depending on the contribution ratios (computed from the previous table), a different loan equity ratio, a different interest rate, and a different tax rate can be assigned to each major economic activity. The method of determining scarcity and need coefficients is based on successive approximation. The initial raw coefficients, however, are revised and updated regularly to reflect further learning.

As demonstrated by Table 3.3, this scheme will increase the rate of return on investment for bread to 18 percent and decrease that of yo-yos to 10 percent. Such a scheme has the advantage of minimizing the bureaucratic dangers associated with centralized planning, while enhancing the market economy's strength by promoting a more equitable allocation and distribution system.

Horizontal Compatibility

Major organizational theories have implicitly assumed that perfectly rational microdecisions would automatically produce perfectly rational macroconditions. This might have been acceptable if there were not a whole range of incompatible performance criteria, such as a cost center, a revenue center, and an overhead center, producing structural conflicts among peer units in the organization.

TABLE 3.3   Changing Relative Rate of Return on Investment Based on Contribution Ratio

Product	Bread	Candy	Yo-yo
→ Contribution ratio	2	1.5	1
Current return on investment	8%	12%	18%
Initial equity	$1,000,000	$1,000,000	$1,000,000
→ Equity/loan ratio	1/4	1/2	1/1
Total loan	$4,000,000	$2,000,000	$1,000,000
→ Interest rate	5%	9%	16%
Cost of loan	$200,000	$180,000	$160,000
Total capital employed	$5,000,000	$3,000,000	$2,000,000
Income	$400,000	$360,000	$360,000
(Income-cost of loan)	$200,000	$180,000	$280,000
→ Tax coefficient	10%	25%	50%
Net income after taxes	$180,000	$135,000	$100,000
Final return on investment	18%	13.5%	10%

Consider, for example, a typical setup within a corporation. The performance criterion for manufacturing units is the minimization of cost of production for a specified output. The performance criterion of the marketing units is to maximize sales revenue. (These units are often referred to as *cost centers* and *revenue centers*.) Intuitively, we would expect the interaction between the two centers to be complementary and result in maximum efficiency. Unfortunately, this is not the case. In fact, in most organizations the relationship between marketing and production is one of constant friction.

The reason is simple: this design violates a basic systemic principle. Suboptimization of each part of an interdependent set of variables in isolation will not lead to optimization of the system as a whole. The two objectives of cost minimization and revenue maximization, taken independently, lead to a basic contradiction within the system. To maximize revenue, sales would prefer to increase the variety of products, add customized features, change delivery schedules on short notice, and so on. Minimization of cost of production, on the other hand, can be achieved more easily by standardizing the production process, reducing the number of products, and making long-run production schedules. Thus, the basic contradiction emerges: the best answer for marketing comes at the expense of manufacturing, and vice versa.

Ironically, the only reason this setup works at all in present-day organizations is that the performance criteria are not taken seriously. (This is the major advantage that systems with purposeful parts have over mechanistic and organismic systems. Such incompatibility could never be tolerated in a mechanistic system.)

The usual solution that most corporations adopt for this problem is one of compromise. The higher-level authority over both centers determines which set of criteria should dominate the other at any particular time. Of course, the possible gain in one area might be more than offset by the loss in the other.

A totally different approach to this problem is to aim for compatibility of performance criteria rather than seek a compromise between incompatible sets. One way is to change the performance criteria for marketing and for manufacturing so that they both try to maximize the *difference* between cost and revenue.

This means that both complementary units can be profit or performance centers where the relationship between marketing and manufacturing is based on *exchange*, much like that of a customer and a supplier. Both units are now expected to be value-adding operations.

Consider the difference in how the two designs handle flexibility of delivery schedules. Flexibility is a value to some users, who are willing to pay a certain premium. For a cost center, this premium has no value whatsoever. The only thing important to the cost center is that a change in production schedules will increase the cost. Since it is not concerned with revenues, the cost center will resist flexibility even when it results in positive net value to the corporation as a whole. Furthermore, since transfer of costs is based on average cost rather than marginal cost, there can be no distinction between users who demand flexibility (or various degrees of it) and those who do not; average cost is the same for both.

A profit center, on the other hand, examines each opportunity on a marginal cost versus marginal revenue basis. The price that the customer is willing to pay for the additional service is balanced against the marginal cost that the supplier will have to incur. While a cost center is instinctively resistant to any change of operations requested by marketing, a profit center looks forward to opportunities to increase its net contribution to the system.

Note that in a profit-center design it may still be possible for one unit to benefit at the cost of another. But the critical difference is that a win/win situation is now a possibility. Both production and marketing can benefit from meeting customer demands, and, more significantly, the performance criteria are compatible. Note that uniformity of performance criteria, although desirable, is not necessary; the important point is compatibility. In other words, the performance criteria must be designed such that the success of one part does not imply failure of another.

Temporal Compatibility

Concern for compatibility over time in a social system is concern for its continuity. Among stakeholders of an organization are those who were members in the past and those who will be its members in the future. The argument for compatibility between the interest of past, present, and future members, especially on ethical grounds, is so rich that it is beyond the scope of the present work; our concern here is essentially pragmatic.

It is not difficult to appreciate that a social system can succeed today at the expense of its future, or suffer today for the creation of a better future. It can also be demonstrated that past members of a social system can have a profound (negative or positive) influence in shaping its present, although a need for compatibility between the interests of present and future members is more or less appreciated in the notion that decisions made today should not limit the options available to future members. However, the same recognition is not extended to the need for compatibility between the interests of present and past members.

In some cultures, the interests of past members continue to dominate the present, while in other cultures there is no concern for the interests of those who are gone—out of sight, out of mind. Nevertheless, rejecting the interests of past members is as undesirable as accepting their dominance. The effectiveness of an organization, as a voluntary association of purposeful members, depends on the degree of their commitment and sense of belonging. In this context, alienation is a serious obstruction to an organization's development. Incompatibility between the interests of past, present, and future members is a main source of its present members' alienation. This is because a constant threat to the organization's long-term viability is a continuous coproducer of anxiety and insecurity among members who identify with the future.

But members identify themselves with the past as well. They can see the image of their own future in the fate of those who had once been effective members of the system and served it well. An undesirable and unfortunate image is a serious source of insecurity that is at the core of alienation, corruption, and lust for power. This is why concern for the interests of past members, minimally in the form of an acceptable retirement system, is essential. In this respect the notion of gradual retirement, with all of its ramifications, should be considered more seriously than it has been.

In summary, to manage a throughput in a multiminded system, we need to:

- Align the interest of purposeful members and generate excitement and commitment to the purpose of the whole and vice versa.
- Let empowerment happen by duplicating power, not abdicating it.
- Separate control from service and convert it to a learning function.
- Prevent a win/lose struggle and dissolve paralyzing conflicts.

4

The Sociocultural Model
Information-Bonded Systems

"Many things about the behavior of a social system refer to the interaction of its members rather than the individuality of its members. Each social system manifests certain characteristics that it may retain even if all its individual members are replaced." (Ervin Lazlo, 1972)

What characterizes a social system are not only its members, but also the relationship of its members to one another and to the whole. This is, of course, implicit in the definition of a system. Some kind of linkage between the elements is presupposed if the aggregate is to be considered a system. The point of emphasis, then, is not the existence of a relationship, but the assumptions regarding the nature of the relationship.

These relationships, which in our conception denote the structure of a system, in turn depend on the nature of the bonds that link and hold the components of the system together. In this context, there are fundamental differences between the nature of the bond in mechanical systems and those in sociocultural systems.

While the elements of mechanical systems are "energy-bonded," those of sociocultural systems are "information-bonded." In energy-bonded systems, laws of classical physics govern the relationship existing among the elements. Therefore, passive and predictable functioning of parts is a must, until a part breaks down. However, the behavior of active parts of an information-bonded system and their integration into a cohesive whole is a different proposition. Organization of a multi-minded sociocultural system is considered a voluntary association of purposeful members in which the bonding is achieved by a second-degree agreement, which is an agreement based on a common perception. In first degree agreements actors may agree on a course of action for completely different reasons. One even might vote for a candidate A because he thinks candidate A will end the war but others may vote for the same candidate on the perception that he would win the war. Second-degree agreement, on the other hand, requires an agreement on the why question. Therefore, even agreeing to disagree is considered a second-degree agreement.

Buckley (1967) explains the structural characteristic of sociocultural systems by focusing on the organization and its dynamics based on the effect of information, as opposed to energy transmission. The sociocultural system is viewed as a set of elements linked almost entirely by intercommunication of information. It is an organization of meanings emerging from a network of interactions among individuals.

To clarify the meaning of information bondedness, we need to examine the concepts of culture and that of social learning in more detail.

CULTURE

Image building and abstraction are among the most significant characteristics of human beings, allowing them not only to form and interpret images of real things, but also to use these images to imagine things that may not exist (for a beautiful and in-depth discussion of image, see Kenneth Boulding, 1956). For example, man feels hunger, observes the fleeing prey, and realizes his inability to capture it. After discovering other related objective realities (wood, stones, etc.), he/she thinks about and eventually creates a subjective image of a tool, one yet to be, which would help him secure food. Transformation of this subjective image into an objective reality results in the bow and arrow, which in turn will be a producer of yet another image, and so on. This dialectic interaction between objective and subjective realities lies at the core of a process responsible for the dynamic development of human societies.

As a prerequisite to survival it has always been necessary for man to observe and understand events that are constantly occurring in his environment. He/she does so in order to use favorable opportunities and be prepared for antagonistic events. But understanding scattered phenomena in isolation, although necessary, is not sufficient for man to relate to his environment. Therefore, an additional struggle to find a logical relationship among these isolated findings impels him to synthesize this fragmented information into a unified, meaningful mental image[1] and eventually into a worldview.

Coproduced by the environment and man's unique process of creativity, the image establishes a link between man and his environment. It consists of a system of assumptions (possibly unconscious) on the nature of spatio-temporal-causal realities, in addition to a concept of values, aesthetics, and finally his perceived role in the environment.

---

[1]For an elaborate discussion of *image* see Kenneth Boulding (1956)

A considerable part of this image or mental model of the universe is shared with others who live in the same social setting. The rest remains private and personal. It is the shared image that constitutes the principal bond among members of a human community and provides the necessary conditions for any meaningful communication. The extent to which the image of an individual coincides with the "shared image" of a community determines the degree of his membership in that community. It is the "shared image" that we refer to as the culture of a people. Incorporating their experiences, beliefs, attitudes, and ideals, it is the ultimate product and reflection of their history and the manifestation of their identity—man creates his culture and his culture creates him.

Although culture pre-exists for individuals, it can be transformed and reproduced by their purposeful actions. It is here that the key obstacles and opportunities for development are found, the collective ability and desire of a people to transform their culture and recreate the future they want.

Human culture with all its complexity, ambiguity, and manifold potentialities, stands at the center of the process of change. This process of change cannot be understood except against the background of the culture of which it is a part, which it builds upon and reacts against. So much is this so that the success of individual actions invariably depends on the degree to which they penetrate and modify the "shared image."

Operational implications of culture lie in the fact that cultures act as default decision systems. For example, if you do not decide explicitly what kind of parent you want to be, the culture decides for you. Actors, by repeated use of default values, tend to forget that they have a choice and treat such values as "realities out there," undermining the fact that those "realities" will remain "out there" as long as no one is willing to challenge them. The problem is that the implicitness of the underlying assumptions prevents actors from questioning their validity; therefore, the defaults usually remain unchallenged and become obsolete.

The potentiality and vitality of the culture lies in its creative ability to meet the challenges of continuously emerging desires and ideals. This process demands conscious and active adaptation, not a passive acceptance of events. It is a struggle for the creation of new dimensions, appreciation of new realities, and, finally, enrichment of the common image. It is a learning process that entails coordinated changes in motivation, knowledge, and understanding throughout the social system.

Although social systems learn through the members who adjust their worldviews or mapping of reality by observing the actual or potential results of their actions, social learning is not the sum of each member's learning. Sociocultural systems manifest greater inertia and resistance to change than do their individual members.

The inertia of a culture is manifested by public and private images acting as filters, developing a selective mode of reception. This tunes the receptors for particular messages. Those consistent with the image are absorbed and reinforced, while contradictory and antagonistic ones have no significant effect. This phenomenon, although an impediment to change, acts as a defense mechanism and structure-maintaining function.

Furthermore, since truth is commonly identified with simplicity and comprehensibility, what one does not understand is simply rejected as false. A high level of specialization in science moves it further away from the common image, creating a small, isolated subculture. Creation of a scientific subculture that fails to communicate its insights reduces the needed influence of science on the behavior of the public at large. As systems become more sophisticated and problems become more profound, the increasing disconnection between science and the public image becomes the dilemma of the democratic process and remains its main challenge.

Recently involved with a community development project aimed at creating a shared vision of a desired future for all the stakeholders, I was confronted with the following statement: "Common people don't understand these fancy concepts. They would be better off sticking with tangible and familiar things they understand." My answer was as follows: "Understanding among common people is usually the end result of a developmental process, not its beginning. If understanding among common people becomes a prerequisite for introducing a 'fancy' concept, I assure you that we will fast fall to the lowest level of banality. Life would proceed with setting and seeking attainable goals that would rarely escape the limits of the familiar."

As a matter of fact, the greatest obstacle, in most developmental processes, is not so much lack of understanding among common people as a lack of common understanding among the so-called experts. It has always been easier to generate required levels of understanding among common people than among experts, not only because they do not have an ego problem but more so because learning is much simpler than unlearning. The patronizing myth of protecting common people from fancy concepts now borders on the art of demagoguery.

Finally, fear of rejection and a strong tendency toward conformity among members of a social system are other obstructions to social change. An example is the experience of a dry county whose constituents were to vote on the alcohol ban. A pre-vote survey indicated that 75% of the voters favored abolishing the ban. However, the individual voters thought the majority wanted a dry county. When the results were tabulated, 60% of the voters had voted to keep the county dry. Not surprisingly, after the survey results were published, the next vote on the issue produced a 65% majority in favor of abolishing the ban.

SOCIAL LEARNING

Social learning is not the sum of the isolated learning of each member. It is the members' shared learning as manifested in a notion of shared image and culture.

Recall that the role of knowledge in social systems is analogous to that of energy in physical systems. But unlike energy, knowledge is not subject to the "law of conservation." One does not lose knowledge by sharing it with others. The ability to learn and share knowledge enables sociocultural systems to continuously increase their capacity for higher levels of organization. This is what social development is all about. It is this collective and shared learning that enables societies to redesign themselves by successively creating new modes of organization at higher levels of order and complexity. However, creating a new mode of organization involves a cultural transformation. More specifically, it requires changing the default values of the organizing principles.

But challenging the conventional wisdom is a painful process. It demands questioning the sacred assumptions and developing a collective ability to reconceptualize the relevant variables into a new ensemble with a new characterization of its own. This is a learning process of the second order, which must be distinguished from first-order learning. Ackoff makes this distinction lucid: "Consider a choice model in which actors choose from among several courses of action. This choice model is formed by what actors collectively believe are the possible courses of action available to them. Inclusion or exclusion of alternatives in the choice model is not arbitrary. The choices in the set usually share one or more properties based on an explicit or implicit set of assumptions or constraints produced by the actors' previous experience with similar situations.

In this context, first-order learning represents a quantitative change. It revises the probabilities of choice, modifying parameters in a fixed structure. The underlying assumptions governing the selection of alternatives remain unchallenged.

Second-order learning, on the other hand, involves challenging the assumptions. It represents a qualitative change that identifies a new set of alternatives and objectives. Second-order learning redefines the rules for first-order learning and provides for orderly transformation and development of sociocultural systems."

Further in social learning context, ideologies (not to be mistaken for a vision), in any form or type, represent a profound obstruction to second-order learning. The significant and common characteristic of all ideologies is a claim of ultimate truth with a predefined set of ends and means. Underlying assumptions are not to be questioned by true believers. This is incompatible with second-order learning, which requires questioning the sacred assumptions and challenging the implicit set of default values.

Second-order learning is a participative process of redesigning the future and inventing the means to bring it about.

DEVELOPMENT

Development is a core concept of the systems view of the world. In contrast to the mechanistic and biological views concerned respectively with efficiency and growth, the systems view is basically concerned with development.

A critical review of major traditional views of development suggests that they are generally characterized by problems of 1) ethnocentrism 2) uni-dimensionality and 3) deterministic perspective.

In the first place, most developmental theories have built-in ethnocentric biases. The models, as ideal types of developed societies, bear unmistakable signs of the western historical experience.

Furthermore, the fragmentation of developmental theory into competing disciplinary perspectives results in a uni-dimensional view of development. Each discipline tends to exclude the other variables from its own unique domain of analysis—material quantities in economics, power in political science, and order in sociology.

Perhaps the most serious problem lies in the fact that most developmental theories begin with a preconceived law of social transformation. Assumed to be true at all times and in all environments, the path is charted beforehand.

But development plays a central role in the systems view of the world. Therefore, it is important to clarify any misconceptions that exist about the nature of development and the properties usually identified with it.

Although it is risky to lump developmental theories together, we need for practical purposes some kind of classification scheme. Still, important differences and some significant continuity exist among them. Further, these theories do not necessarily refute each other. In most cases, they either complement or supersede one another.

The typology presented here (Figure 4.1) categorizes developmental theories into eight types depending on their underlying assumptions (explicit

	Singularity of Function		Plurality of Function	
	Singularity of Process	Plurality of Process	Singularity of Process	Plurality of Process
Singularity of Structure	Classical Neo-classical	Behaviorism	Structural Functionalism	General Systems
Plurality of Structure	Orthodox Marxism	Radical Humanism	New-Left	Purposeful Systems

FIGURE 4.1   Typology of Development Theories

or implicit) with regard to the singularity or plurality they attribute to function, structure, and process.

Singularity refers to theories in which a particular structure, function, or process is considered fixed and/or primary in all environments.

Plurality refers to theories that consider structure, function, or process to be multiple and/or variable in the same or different environments.

Note that the theories in Category 1 (singularity of function, structure, and process) are descriptive and do not deal with any means of intervention. Other categories, by assuming plurality in at least one dimension, provide for some means of intervention. Category 8 (purposeful systems) assumes plurality in all three dimensions: function, structure, and process. Therefore, category 8, systems view of development, is an inclusive theory. It provides a framework to explain other seven categories as special cases. The following scheme summarizes the assumptions and the main features of each type and their perspectives on development.

Schematic View of Theoretical Traditions

Singularity of Function, Structure, and Process

Model: Determined, mechanistic, and descriptive model of man in a state of nature, homo-economicus; forms social contract to increase wealth through increasing productivity and division of labor.

Theoretical Tradition: Classical and neo-classical, as exemplified by the writings of Smith, Ricardo, Malthus, Mill, Marshall, Keynes, Schumpeter, and Rostow.

Development Process: Stability and growth against major constraints of capital accumulation, population growth, and limited natural resources; automatic mechanism of adjustment. Keynes introduces the principles of conscious manipulation of productive forces (neo-classical) to maintain stability and growth. Rostow considers a stage theory, traditional, pre-take-off, take-off, self-sustaining growth and high mass consumption.

Singularity of Function and Process with Plurality of Structure

Model: Deterministic and mechanistic model based on linear cause-and-effect relationships. Conflict, the prime producer of change, results in a stage theory and formation of a new social structure.

Theoretical Tradition: Orthodox Marxism and radical Weberianism, as exemplified by the writings of Engels, Lenin, Kautsky and Plekhanov, Weber, Dahrendorf, and Rex.

Development Process: In orthodox Marxism: economy is the prime function, and class struggle is the prime process. Historical determinism, moving from primitive communism to ancient slave societies, feudalism, capitalism, socialism, and finally the ideal of communism (classless society) through class conflict and progressive system transformation. In radical Weberianism, power is the prime function, legitimization is the prime process; varying structures are defined by authority and classified into three pure types to correspond with different types of society: traditional, charismatic, and rational-legal. Increasing rationalization of authority from patriarchal to patrimonial to feudal and modern society moving toward an ideal type of bureaucracy (frictionless machine). Dahrendorf sees the interest of the power holder as so clearly distinct from the interest of the powerless that conflict becomes the permanent feature of social life, with varying degrees of effect, ranging from revolution to small-scale reform.

Singularity of Function and Structure with Plurality of Process

Model: Input/output (stimulus-response) model of human and social behavior (environmentalism). An organic model that uses deviation amplification or positive and negative feedback loops to change.

Theoretical Tradition: Behavioral, as exemplified by the writings of Watson, Skinner, Erikson, and Lasswell.

Development Process: Increasing order through induced motivational and behavioral change. Sublimation of destructive instincts into creative work, and finally formation of a world culture shaped by "behavioral technology," which is needed for survival. Watson places the central emphasis on controlling behavior through learning, which, he believes, could be achieved by the principle of "conditioning." Skinner suggests that freedom is an illusion that man can no longer afford. He claims that behavior can be predicted and shaped exactly as if it were a chemical reaction. But for Erikson, physical, social, cultural, and ideational environments are partners to biological and psychological innate processes.

Singularity of Function with Plurality of Structure and Process

Model: There is no absolute above man that could recreate the social order in which he/she lives. Emancipation of man is the prime function, whereas process and structure are seen as multiple and variable.

Theoretical Tradition: Radical humanism, as exemplified in the early writings of Marx, Marcuse, Lukacs, Sartre, Fromm, Gramsci, and the Frankfurt School.

Development Process: Changing the social order through a change in mode of cognition and consciousness. Release from the constraints the existing social structure places on human development. The emphasis is on modes of domination, emancipation, deprivation, and potentiality.

Singularity of Structure and Process with Plurality of Function

Model: Biological, integrated, and dynamic equilibrium model; multiple functions to maintain an unstable but fixed structure (steady state) through the prime process of homeostasis; representing analytical, positivistic, and empirical view of the world.

Theoretical Tradition: Structural functionalism, as exemplified by the writings of Comte, Spencer, Durkheim, Parsons, and Eisenstadt.

Development Process: Integration, adaptation, goal attainment, and pattern maintenance are regarded as the four functional imperatives for a social system's continuing existence and evolution toward maturity and growth.

Plurality of Function and Structure with Singularity of Process

Model: Multi-functional, organic, and nonlinear cause-and-effect relationships. Conflict is considered to be the prime producer of change. Varying structure "over-determined" by interaction of economic, political, ideological, and theoretical subsystems of totality.

Theoretical Tradition: New-left, as exemplified in the writings of Althusser, Poulantzas, Della-Volpe, and Colletti.

Development Process: Increased integration, through law of "uneven and combined development," "method of successive approximation," "fact of conquest," and increased accumulative knowledge of mankind with regard to nature.

Plurality of Function and Process with Singularity of Structure

Model: Holistic, open, multi-loop feedback and input/output model of social systems. Biological analogy is used to search for the underlying regularities and structural uniformity.

Theoretical Tradition: General systems theory and cybernetics, as exemplified by the writings of Bertalanffy, Ashby, Miller, Beer, and Bogdanov.

Development Process: Equifinal, neg-entropic processes moving toward organized complexity. System change through learning, adaptation, and induced motivational and behavioral change.

Plurality of Structure, Function, and Process

Model: Purposeful, sociocultural, information-bonded systems. Capable of redesigning themselves by new functions, structures and processes creating new modes of organization at the higher levels of order and complexity.

Theoretical Tradition: Systems view (third generation), as exemplified by the writings of Ackoff, Boulding, Buckley, and Churchman.

Development Process: Multifinal, interactive, and purposeful movement toward increased differentiation and integration. A learning and creative process to increase ability and desire to recreate the future. An ideal-seeking mode of organization to resolve conflicts at higher levels. Systemic view of development, by accepting plurality in all three dimensions of function, structure, and process; considers the other seven categories as special cases. From the systems perspective, development is not only a multi-functional phenomenon, but involves multiple and varying concepts of structure and process as well.

Systems View of Development

Development of an organization is a purposeful transformation toward higher levels of integration and differentiation at the same time (as represented in Figure 4.2). It is a collective learning process by which a social system increases its ability and desire to serve both its members and its environment.

Differentiation represents an artistic orientation (looking for differences among things that are apparently similar) emphasizing stylistic values and signifying tendencies toward increased complexity, variety, autonomy, and morphogenesis (creation of a new structure).

Integration, on the other hand, represents a scientific orientation (looking for similarities among things that are apparently different) emphasizing instrumental values and signifying tendencies toward increased order, uniformity, conformity, collectivity, and morphostasis (maintenance of structure).

Depending on the characteristics of a given culture, a social system can move from a state of chaotic simplicity toward organized simplicity, which is produced by emphasizing integration at the cost of differentiation. It can also move toward chaotic complexity produced by increased differentiation at the cost of integration. Or, it can move toward organized complexity, signifying a higher level of organization achieved by a movement toward complexity and

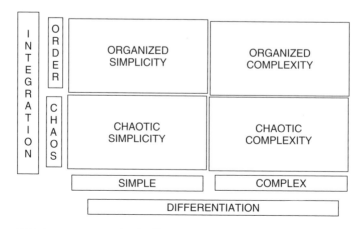

FIGURE 4.2   Levels of Differentiation and Integration

order concurrently. This means that for every level of differentiation there exists a minimum level of integration below which the system would disintegrate into chaos. Conversely, higher levels of integration require higher degrees of differentiation in order to avoid impotency.

Within the boundaries of a given culture, a variety of different orientations exist. The presence of a "left" and a "right" in every social group and political party is the manifestation of this phenomenon. (Figure 4.3)

In a flexible social setting, oscillations of low amplitude occur within the cultural boundaries without disruption, as demonstrated by periodic shifts of government between the Labor and Conservative parties in the United Kingdom or the Democrats and Republicans in the United States. However, if an orientation tries to cross the limits of the cultural line, a powerful reaction will move it back to the other extreme, producing further oscillations and cusping into a change of phase. Unfortunately, in societies polarized by antagonistic and rigid ideologies, social transformation takes place by a violent change of phase (a cusp). Retrieval from such a situation is often extremely problematic, since the relationship between members is irreparably damaged, as happens in societies that are thrown into a perpetual state of civil disorder.

Development of social systems is a transformation into successive modes of organization. Each mode is a whole, characterized by higher degrees of both integration and differentiation, and is potentially capable of dissolving lower level contradictions by converting them into contraries. In contrast to physical systems, whose energy level determines their mode of organization, in social systems the knowledge level defines the mode. The role of knowledge in social

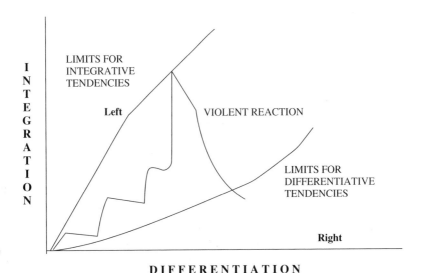

FIGURE 4.3 Cultural Boundaries

systems, therefore, can be said to be analogous to that of energy in physical systems. The significant point is that knowledge, unlike energy, is not subject to the first law of thermodynamics (the law of conservation of energy). One does not lose knowledge by sharing it with others. On the contrary, its dissemination increases the knowledge level of the social system and helps the creation of new knowledge. It is this capability that enables a social system of its own accord to constantly recreate its structure and redefine its functions.

In defining development, we identify two active agents: desire and ability.

Desire is produced by an exciting vision of a future enhanced by the inter-action of creative and recreative processes. The creative capacity of man, along with his/her desire to share, results in a shared image of a desired future. This generates dissatisfaction with the present and motivates pursuit of more chal-lenging and more desirable ends. Otherwise, life proceeds simply by setting and seeking attainable goals, which rarely escape the limits of the familiar.

Unfortunately, for some religions, the fundamentalist interpretation regards creation as a sole prerogative of God. Human beings are not allowed to engage in any act of creation. Art in almost any form—whether painting, sculpture, music, or drama—is prohibited. Recreation is also considered sinful. This antagonistic attitude toward aesthetics militates against development, in that it does not pro-vide much opportunity to articulate and expand one's horizon beyond the imme-diate needs of mere existence. This self-limitation provides one explanation for cases of underdevelopment despite the availability of vast resources.

Dissatisfaction with the present, although a necessary condition for change, is not sufficient to ensure development. What seems to be necessary as well is a faith in one's ability to partly control the march of events. Those who are awed by their environment and place the shaping forces of their future out-side of themselves do not think of voluntary or conscious change, no matter how miserable and frustrated they are.

Ability, therefore, is the potential for controlling, influencing, and appreci-ating the parameters that affect the system's existence. But ability alone cannot ensure development. Without a shared image of a more desirable future, the frustration of the powerful masses can easily be converted into a unifying agent of change—hatred—which in turn will successfully destroy the present but will not necessarily be a step toward creating a better future.

To understand the process of development of a social system, we have to deal with structures and the processes that help or limit the creation of collective desire and ability for the pursuit of its ends. We have said that the parameters that co-produce the future are found in the interaction of five dimensions: Wealth, Knowledge, Beauty, Power, and Values. Compatibility among these five dimensions of social system defines the effectiveness of the emerging mode of organization. It also determines the level of integration, and the collective ability of the members to create the future they want. This means that a minimum level of integration is required if the aggregate of individuals is to function as an effective system. Ironically, the prime concern of every organization theory has been to define the criteria by which the whole is to be divided into parts. Major theories have implicitly assumed that the whole is nothing but the sum of its parts and have conveniently ignored the fact that effective differentiation requires incorporation of a means that would integrate the differentiated parts into a cohesive whole. In this regard, the classical school of management depends solely on the unity of command and the imperative of no deviation. At the opposite end, advocates of self-organizing systems rely on the assumption that perfectly rational micro-decisions would automatically produce perfectly rational macro-conditions. Both approaches fall short because they fail to recognize that effective social integration requires that compatibility among the members be continuously and actively re-created. Ultimately, the level of integration and development that an organization will achieve depends on the means by which it deals with interaction among its members.

Differentiation poses little challenge because it is the very nature of social systems to become different from each other. From families to cities and nations, groups of people can usually describe with ease how "we're different or unique." Integration, however, requires skill to accomplish. To integrate, one must appreciate the systemic nature of the interactions between opposing tendencies. For example, security and freedom, usually considered dichotomous, are actually two aspects of the same phenomenon. Freedom is not possible without security, and security makes no sense without freedom. But if we choose to deal with each one of these aspects separately, then we should not be surprised to find them in conflict. The easiest solution to security, if treated in isolation, would be to limit freedom, and that of freedom would be to undermine security. Despite seemingly contradictory requirements for pursuit of opposing ends, there are processes that would make the attainment of both ends feasible. For instance, both freedom and security are attainable by a process called participation, stability and change by adaptation, and order and complexity by organization. Similarly, production and distribution of wealth form a complementary pair. Without an effective production system, there can never be an effective distribution system. To fail to note this important interdependency is to leave out the most important challenge of the problem. An obsession with distribution without a proper concern about production will result in nothing but an equitable distribution of poverty. Preoccupation with production without a similar concern for an equitable distribution will lead to an alienated society.

The emerging tendencies—innovation, learning and adaptation, socialization (parity), participation and organization—cannot stand alone. Together, they form the whole, and coproduce a process called development. The holistic view of societal development requires that all of the five social functions—the generation and dissemination of knowledge, power, wealth, value and beauty—develop interdependently, utilizing all of the five complementary processes outlined above.

Central to this notion of development is its distinction from growth. According to Ackoff:

> "They are not the same thing and are not even necessarily associated. Growth can take place with or without development, and development can take place with or without growth. A cemetery can grow without developing. On the other hand, a person may continue to develop long after he or she has stopped growing, and vice versa. A person can build a better house with good tools and materials than he/she can without them. On the other hand, a developed person can build a better house with whatever tools and materials he/she has than a less-developed person with the same resources. Put another way: a developed person with limited resources is likely to be able to improve his quality of life and that of others more than a less-developed person with unlimited resources. Constraints on a system's growth are found primarily in its environment, but the principal constraints on a system's development are found within the system itself." (Gharajedaghi and Ackoff, 1982)

Obstruction to Development

Obstructions to development of a social system can be viewed as malfunctioning in any one of the five dimensions. Scarcity, maldistribution and insecurity in any one of the five social functions—generation and dissemination of knowledge, power, wealth, values and beauty—are considered primary or first-order obstructions. Alienation, polarization, corruption and terrorism are among social phenomena that represent second-order obstructions.

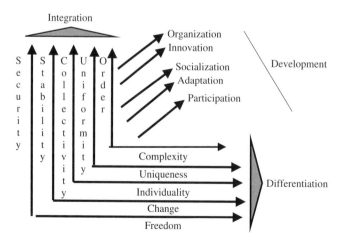

FIGURE 4.4   Developmental Processes

TABLE 4.1 Obstructions to development

Dimensions of Social Systems	Expected Yield	Scarcity	Primary Obstructions Mal-distribution	Insecurity	Second Order Obstructions
Wealth (Economics)	Plenty	Poverty	Disparity	Deprivation	Alienation
Knowledge (Scientific)	Truth	Ignorance	Elitism/illiteracy	Obsolescence	Polarization
Power (Politics)	Potency	Power-lessness	Autocracy	Illegitimacy	Corruption
Values (Ethical moral)	Peace Good	Norm-lessness	Discrimination	Fanaticism	Terrorism
Beauty (Aesthetics)	Excitement Belonging	Hopelessness	Hatred	Loss of identity	

Second-order obstructions are coproduced by the interaction of primary obstructions. Dealing with primary obstructions is beyond the scope of the present work. Interested readers will find a full discussion of these concepts in *A Prologue to National Development Planning* (Gharajedaghi and Ackoff, 1986). However, since the second-order obstructions—alienation, polarization, corruption, and terrorism—are very much part of our present reality, a brief discussion of these four phenomena may be in order.

Alienation

A social system in its ideal form is a voluntary association of purposeful members, so that emigration of a member from the system is considered to be the highest manifestation of his/her protest. But because of a series of self-imposed or external constraints, a dissatisfied member is not able to leave the system. He/She therefore becomes alienated from the very system of which he/she is supposed to be a voluntary member.

The underlying causes of alienation can be found in the interactions of following primary obstructions.

- Powerlessness. Powerlessness is equivalent to ineffectualness and impotency. When an individual feels that her/his contributions to the group's achievements are insignificant or she/he cannot influence the behavior of the group of which she/he is a member, a feeling of indifference gradually sets in and the individual loses interest in the group.
- Rolelessness. Incompetence or lack of the necessary knowledge to carry out responsibilities of one's accepted role results in excessive anxiety and frustration.

- Meaninglessness. Lack of excitement in life, and insensitivity toward the creative and recreational aspect of being most probably will result in feeling of meaninglessness.
- Exploitation. When individuals or a group feel that they have been deprived of their fair share of system's achievements, feelings of injustice will set in and harmful hostilities will result.
- Conflicting value system. As mentioned before, the extent to which an individual's value image coincides with the shared image of her/his community determines the degree of his/her membership in that community. An extreme difficulty arises when an individual needs to be a member of two communities with conflicting value systems. The level of integration that a society will achieve depends on the means by which it dissolves the value conflict among all of its diverse membership groups. Certainly, this challenge cannot be met by merely a legalistic approach as the following example demonstrates.

In a recent study, a group of my graduate students observed that young black Americans are caught in an impossible dilemma. To be accepted as a member by their community and peers, they must demonstrate that they are not playing the white man's game. However, "not playing the game" or deviation from the norm, has a huge price tag. It is usually punished harshly and disproportionately to the degree of harm it has caused society. Unfortunately, the likes of Colin Powell, Condoleezza Rice, Oprah Winfrey, Bill Cosby, and many more success stories do not seem to be the role models for young black Americans. Accused of playing the white man's game, they might not even be considered a true member of the black community. This unfortunate second-order obstruction has resulted in a vicious circle which undermines the development of otherwise talented black communities. Appreciating this conflict can help us understand why a phenomenal basketball player with all the apparent success and popularity, sometimes has to come across as a "bad boy" to keep his membership in his own community as well.

Polarization

The formation of highly polarized groups around conflicting ideologies is perhaps one of the most destructive obstructions to development. Polarization usually takes the form of religious versus secular tendencies, with each further divided into left and right orientations. This polarization is further reinforced by ethnic conflicts and "divide and rule" strategies of politicians. In their struggle for fame and power, self-serving, and cynical intellectuals manipulate the masses with demagoguery—pulling them from one extreme to the other like a pendulum. The problem is that none of the so-called opposing groups is strong enough to govern without the cooperation of the others, and yet each one is powerful enough to disrupt and undermine the effectiveness of the ruling group. This is partly due to increased complexity in the system, making it more vulnerable to sabotage on the one hand and difficult to manage on the other. Hatred of the ruling group usually becomes the unifying agent of change. Another cycles begins with opposing forces regrouping. The oscillation will not end until opposing ideologies learn to modify their dogmatic positions, give up their monopolistic claim on power, and work towards creating a shared image of a desired future through processes of integration, not at the expense of differentiation, but alongside it.

Corruption

Corruption is not just malfunctioning of the value system, but a second-order obstruction. It is the result of structural defects in more than one dimension of social systems including generation and distribution of power, wealth, and knowledge. To carry out its vital functions, a social system, must be organized. The way a social system is organized determines its ability to overcome the obstructions it faces. In this context a social-pathology is produced when an obstruction to development benefits those who are responsible to remove it. Unfortunately, bureaucracy represents a pathological mode of organization where an organized interest group benefits from the obstructions it has created. For instance, the more complex a bureaucratic process can be made, the more staff is required to manage it, and the larger and more controlling the administering agency becomes. In addition, the present level of interdependence and complexity demand a higher level of sophistication that far surpasses the known capabilities of the present bureaucratic system. Under these conditions, only a source of power outside the bureaucracy can create movement within the system. Therefore, individuals will seek out and support these external power sources. In time, the hierarchy of powerful patrons demands certain rewards in exchange for their valuable support. This reward structure enables corruption to spread throughout the entire system, ultimately becoming a justifiable way of life.

Charles Handy, in an interesting article, *What is a Business For* (*Harvard Business Review*, 2002) makes a serious observation regarding recent corporate practices. "The current disease is not just a matter of dubious personal ethics or of some rogue companies fudging the odd billion. The whole business culture of our current Anglo-American version of stock market capitalism may have become distorted. We can see, with hindsight, that in the boom years of the 1990s America had often been creating value where none existed, bidding up the market capitalization of companies to 64 times earning, or more." If one took this argument to its logical conclusion, it would reveal that corporate America is facing two critical challenges. The first challenge concerns the effectiveness of corporate governance. The absentee shareholders that Charles

Handy calls "gamblers" or investors are supposed to elect the members of the board of directors. Most of these gamblers do not have any long-term commitment to the entity in which they hold shares. Today, his or her interest might be in X Corporation, but no one knows where it will be tomorrow. It might even find its way in the Y Corporation that is a direct competitor of X. In reality, the boards are virtually appointed by the management they are supposed to control. They usually re-elect the CEO who has placed them on the board in the first place.

The second challenge is produced by the tremendous pressure to manage for short term. Unless the reports of the next quarter meet the expectation of the stock market for another double-digit growth performance, the over-rated stock price would tremble and the gamblers would start to sell off the stock. Under this kind of pressure, devious behavior will be the norm rather than the exception.

Terrorism

Terrorism is perhaps the single most critical obstruction to development of a peaceful international order. It is a second-order obstruction that has most of the primary obstructions—poverty, disparity, deprivation, powerlessness, hopelessness, discrimination, ignorance, hatred, and fanaticism—as its co-producers. Yet, there is no agreement on its operational definition. One person's terrorist is another person's freedom fighter.

However, irrespective of where one comes from, there is no question that terrorism is based on a false assumption of the "zero-sum-game." In a zero-sum game, the total sum of winnings and losses adds up to zero. If you lose, I will win, and vice versa. As systems get more sophisticated, they become increasingly vulnerable to the actions of the few. Making the other side lose becomes easier than trying to win oneself. This is why terrorism becomes the favorite means of weaker sides when confronting stronger enemies. Therefore, to get a handle on terrorism, I propose to look at it as means toward an end.

The ends in this context, seem to fall into one of three categories: revenge, cry for help, or ideological battle.

The tragedy of Oklahoma City is an example of terror as a means of revenge. Revenge is a random act difficult to detect.

A cry for help, on the other hand, represents the struggle of desperate people trapped in an unfortunate, unjust politico-economic mess. This type of terrorism is a reflection of the sustained frustration of a people who are not able to deal with their humiliating powerlessness through normal channels. The most effective way to stop this type of terror is to dissolve the paralyzing impasse.

The bombing of abortion clinics is an example of terrorism in an ideological battle. Ideological terrorism, in all of its manifestations—secular left or religious fundamentalism—has used intimidation and random terror to impose its value systems or preferred way of life on the population at large. The strategy is based on the assumption that in order to paralyze people, one should make them feel guilty and insecure. This type of terrorism usually needs a powerful enemy to hate. Hate, converted to need, becomes a way of life. It is used to produce goal-seeking robots. These robotic, true believers are capable of brutality that is incomprehensible to normal human beings. Unfortunately, the first and second types of terrorists become foot soldiers for the third type.

In light of the ideological vacuum created by the collapse of communism, various forms of fundamentalism have gained momentum and are growing noticeably all over the globe. Among these groups, the one that generates the most concern is religious fundamentalism with its unshakable faith that a secular style of life is "corruption on the earth." This bunch is against beauty, happiness, choice, pluralism, and freedom. They oppose all of the values that have made the world a better place to live.

Unfortunately, in the late 1970's, religious fundamentalism got a tremendous boost from American policy in the Middle East. After World War II, despite winning the war, America found herself losing the ideological battle. For years, leftist ideology had become synonymous with intellectualism. In most of the third world, the youth, were lost to the leftist movement. The US administration at the time, working on the assumption that the only way to combat an ideology is with another potent one, decided to engage Islam in the ideological battle with communism. America created the Mojahedin to counter the Soviet Union's invasion of Afghanistan and supported the Islamic fundamentalists in the Iranian revolution. The United States Ambassador to the United Nations called Khomeini a saint. Ironically, after sensing strong anti-American sentiments in the Middle East, and with a Machiavellian move, Khomeini decided to identify his Islamic revolution with anti-Americanism. He took and held more than fifty Americans hostage for 444 days and called America the great Satan. This anti-American tag was needed to promote his version of Islam in the vulnerable countries of the region. He called the hostage-taking the second revolution, even more important than toppling the Shah. Figure 4.5 illustrates the interaction of two reinforcing feedback loops. Note how the first loop generates radical Islamists, and the second one converts them to terrorists.

The network of nation-less fundamentalists, unhappy about the progress of women toward equality and freedom, poses a dangerous threat to all of humanity. These true believers are ready to use any kind of intimidation and brutality to keep their women subordinated and under control. To dissolve this mess is a human rights obligation. It should be treated above partisan politics and competing economic interests. Nothing short of the uncompromising commitment and determination of the whole international community to support the development and formation of civil societies will do the trick. Acceptance as a member of the

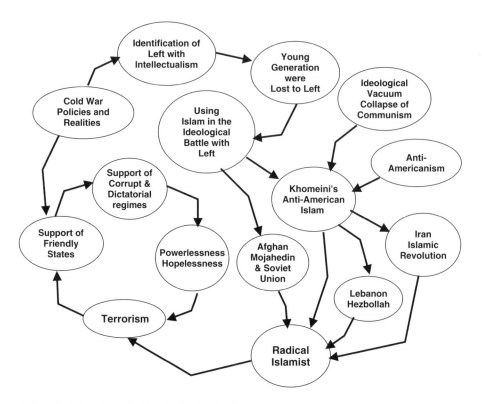

FIGURE 4.5   Islam in the Ideological Battle

world community must be contingent upon accepting and forming a civil society. In the age of globalization, no nation can afford to be left out of the world community. This fact is the most practical means of dissolving the mess we now face. It provides the strongest motive for development of civil societies.

The civil society is a secular state that cannot endorse any religion or ideology. The basis for its authority is in man-made law, not in religious doctrine, divine revelation or a secular deity. Freedom of religion—including freedom from religion—and the freedom not to believe in any deity, are the preconditions to formation of a pluralistic order, where majorities that are not capable of protecting the rights of minorities do not deserve to govern.

Dire as the current world situation may be, this chapter ends not in desperation, but in the belief that interactive design of sociocultural systems offers practical and positive solutions to most of these difficult problems. The conceptual framework of creating successive modes of organization at higher levels of complexity and order has significant practical implications in shaping the systems theory of organization. We will deal with this exciting conception in Chapter 7—Designing Business Architecture.

Recap

- Each social system manifests certain characteristics and may retain these even if all of its individual members are replaced. What characterizes a social system is not only its members, but also the relationship of its members to one another and to the whole.
- The culture of a people is the ultimate product of their history and the manifestation of their identity; man creates his culture and his culture creates him.
- Truth is commonly identified with simplicity and comprehensibility; what one does not understand is simply rejected as false.
- Fear of rejection and a strong tendency toward conformity among members of a social system are important obstructions to social change.
- Development of an organization is a purposeful transformation toward higher levels of integration and differentiation. It is a collective learning process by which a social system increases its ability and desire to serve itself, its members and its environment.
- For every level of differentiation, there exists a minimum level of integration below which the system would disintegrate into chaos. Conversely, higher levels of integration require higher degrees of differentiation in order to avoid sterility.
- Unless an organization effectively serves the purposes of its containing systems and its purposeful parts, they will not serve it well. This requires that the organization be designed in such a way as to enable the parts to operate as independent systems with the ability to be relatively self-controlling while acting as responsible parts of a coherent whole that has the right to make collective choices.

PART III

Systems Methodology
The Logic of the Madness

5

Systems Methodology

The version of systems methodology presented in this chapter is a holistic language of interaction and design. It is developed to see through chaos and understand complexities. It is also intended to face the dilemma of systems where the whole is becoming more and more interdependent while the parts display choice and behave independently.

We said that we see the world as increasingly more complex and chaotic because we use inadequate concepts to explain it. When we understand something, we no longer see it as chaotic or complex. An effective systems methodology would deal not only with the imperative of interdependency and the complexities of self-organizing systems, but also with the question of purposeful behavior of multi-minded systems. Unless we understand the implications of self-organizing purposeful behavior, the multi-minded beast will out-maneuver any attempt to tame it.

This chapter attempts to explicitly and operationally define the systems methodology as we practice it at INTERACT. Although this definition has its origin in the rich and colorful tradition of Ackoff, in its present form it has been greatly influenced by the works of Stafford Beer, Kenneth Boulding, Jay Forrester, and my own fascination with the complexities and engaging potency of the phenomenon known as culture. Years of struggle to get a handle on the whole and real-life experimentation with different systems at different levels, have led me to believe that effective systems methodology lies at the interaction of the following four foundations of systems thinking:

- Holistic Thinking (iteration of structure, function and process)
- Operational Thinking (dynamics of multi-loop feedback systems; chaos and complexity)
- Self-organization, movement toward a predefined order (socio-cultural model)
- Interactive Design (redesigning the future and inventing ways to bring it about)

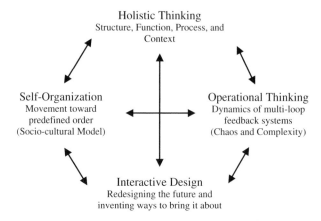

FIGURE 5.1   The Four Foundations of Systems Methodology

In my experience, the beauty of interactive design and the magic of the iteration of structure, function, and process, when combined with the power of operational thinking, and an understanding of the implications of self-organizing behavior, create a competent and exciting methodology that goes a long way in dealing with emerging challenges of seemingly complex and chaotic social systems.

FOUNDATION 1: HOLISTIC THINKING
Structure, Function, Process and Context

The distinction of systems thinking is its focus on the whole. But in most cases, this claim has been a simple declaration of intent without an explicit, workable methodology. What is systems methodology and how can we get a handle on the whole? There seems to be more agreement on the desirability of systems thinking than on its operational definition.

Contrary to a widely held belief, the popular notion of a multi-disciplinary approach is not a systems approach. In fact, the ability to synthesize separate findings into a coherent whole is far more critical than the ability to generate information from different perspectives. Without a well-defined synthesizing method, however, the process of discovery using a multi-discipline approach would be an experience as frustrating as that of the blind men trying to identify an elephant. Positioned at a different part of the elephant, each of the blind men reported his findings from his respective position, as "It's a snake;" "It's a pillar;" "It's a fan;" "It's a spear!"

Consider the futility of trying to make sense of the whole by using the above story without the prior conception of "elephant." But I am sure you experienced no frustration in sorting out the distorted information and putting it in perspective, because the storyteller had already told us that the subject is an elephant. It seems we need a preconceived notion of the whole before we can glean order out of chaos.

A different version of the same story, found in Persian literature and narrated by Molana Jalaledin Molavi (Rumi) captures the level of complexity produced when we have no preconceived notion of the subject. The story is about a group of men who encounter a strange object in complete darkness. Since the storyteller is in the dark himself, he cannot provide a clue about the object. Here, all efforts to identify the object by touching its different parts prove fruitless until someone arrives with a light. The light, which in this context is a metaphor for methodology, enables them all to see the whole at last.

Rumi's version of the story means that the ability to see the whole somehow requires an enabling light in the form of an operational systems methodology. In his mystical wisdom Rumi proposed that to get the enabling light, one needed to tune oneself with the universe. For our purpose here, the operational meaning of tuning is that one should be able to make one's underlying assumptions about the nature of the socio-cultural systems explicitly known and verifiable to oneself.

Whatever the nature of the enabling light, my contention is that it must have two dimensions. The first dimension is a framework for reality, a system of systems concepts to help generate the initial set of working assumptions about the subject. The second dimension is an iterative search process to 1) generate the initial working assumptions, 2) verify and/or modify initial assumptions, and 3) expand and evolve the emerging notions, until a satisfactory vision of the whole is produced. As Singer put it "Truth lies at the end, not at the beginning of the holistic inquiry (Singer, 1959).

Despite their success, three well known inquiring systems (analytical thinking, synthetic thinking, and behavioral science), have yet to agree on the method to see the whole.

- Analysis has been the essence of classical science. The scientific method assumes that the whole is nothing but the sum of the parts, and thus understanding the structure is both necessary and sufficient to understanding the whole.
- Synthesis has been the main instrument of the functional approach. By defining a system by its outcome, synthesis puts the subject in the context of the larger system of which it is a part, and then studies the effects it produces in its environment.
- Process orientation, on the other hand, has long been the focus of behavioral science, It looks to the how question, for the necessary answer to define the whole

However, I contend that seeing the whole requires understanding structure, function, and process at the same time. They represent three aspects of the same thing and, with the containing environment, form a complementary set. Therefore, structure, function, and process with the context, define the whole or make the understanding of the whole possible. Structure defines components and their relationships; function defines the outcomes or results produced; process explicitly defines the sequence of activities and the know-how required to produce the outcome; content defines the unique environment in which the system is situated.

Use of all three perspectives of structure, function, and process as the foundation of a holistic methodology can be justified on both practical and theoretical grounds, as this chapter will demonstrate.

On more familiar and practical territory, we could observe that the classical school of management, with its input orientation, deals with structure. The neo-classical school, with its notion of management by objective, is concerned with functions. And the total quality movement, with its concern for control, is preoccupied with the process. Analysis, synthesis, and process orientation, each in its own right, have produced a great deal of information and knowledge. However, if we looked at the same phenomenon from all three perspectives of structure, function, and process, at the same time, no doubt we could develop a more complete understanding of the whole. So it is reasonable to conclude that a holistic approach must include all three notions of structure, function, and process.

On theoretical grounds, we can reach the same conclusion with the following arguments. In a classical concept of reality, a specific structure (S) causes a particular function (F), and different structures cause different functions (Figure 5.2).

Therefore, it is assumed that to understand a system, we need to know only its structure. This is why analysis, understanding structure, is the dominant method for classical science.

But according to Ackoff:

1. A given structure can produce several functions in the same environment (Figure 5.3). For example, the structure of the existing education system produces the functions of babysitting and buffer, in addition to the explicit function of transferring knowledge:
2. Different structures can also produce a given function (Figure 5.4). For example, the transportation function can be achieved by different means such as a train, plane, or car:

The classical notion of causality—where cause is both necessary and sufficient for its effect—proves inadequate to explain this phenomenon. In

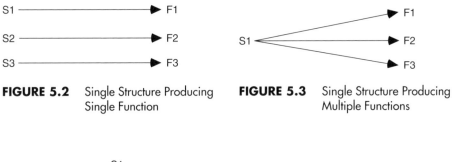

FIGURE 5.2   Single Structure Producing Single Function

FIGURE 5.3   Single Structure Producing Multiple Functions

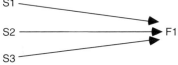

FIGURE 5.4   Multiple Structures Producing the Same Function

fact, production of different functions by a single structure in the same environment can be explained only by the assertion that different processes were involved with the same structure in producing different functions. A simplistic example illustrates the point: a screwdriver can be used as a gouge, a chisel, a hammer, or a variety of other tools, depending on how it is applied.

This idea is compatible with the systemic notion of producers and product (Singer, 1959), which claims that a producer is necessary but not sufficient for its product. That is why a structure cannot completely explain its outcome and why we need the additional concept of an environment as a co-producer. However, when several outcomes are produced in the same environment by a given structure, then knowledge of the process becomes as necessary to understand the whole as the knowledge of environment, structure and function is to understanding the whole. Structure, function, and process, along with the environment or context, form an interdependent set of mutually exclusive and collectively exhaustive variables. Together, these four perspectives define the whole or make possible the understanding of the whole.

A set of interdependent variables forms a circular relationship. Each variable co-produces the others and in turn is co-produced by the others. Which one comes first is irrelevant because none can exist without the others. They must happen at the same time. Failure to see the significance of these interdependencies is to leave out the most important aspect of the challenge of seeing the whole. Therefore, to handle them holistically requires

Iterative Process of Inquiry

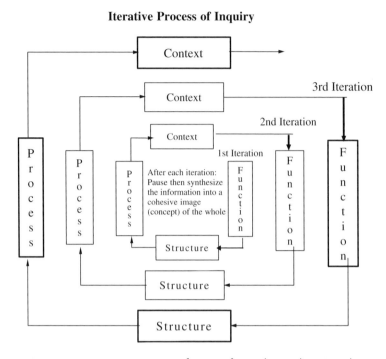

FIGURE 5.5   Iterative Process of Inquiry for Understanding Complexity

understanding each variable in relation to the others in the set at the same time. This demands an iterative inquiry.

Iteration is the key for understanding complexity. Stephen Wolfram (2002) demonstrates how an iterative process of applying simple rules is at the core of nature's mysterious ability to produce complex phenomena so effortlessly.

Iterations of structure, function, and process in a given context would examine assumptions and properties of each element in its own right, then in relationship with other members of the set. Subsequent iterations would establish validity of the assumptions, then compatibilities and/or conflicts are identified and dissolved. Dissolving conflicts may require re-conceptualization of the variables involved. Finally, successive iterations will produce an integrated design. (See Figure 5.5, above.)

For example, to appreciate the heart holistically, we must understand its function, structure, and process. Starting with the function, we simply note that the output of the system is circulation of the blood. Therefore, its function must be that of a pump. Structure of this pump consists of four muscular chambers and a set of valves, arteries, and veins. And the process, which must explain how the structure produces the function, simply uses alternative cycles of contractions and expansions of the chambers to push the blood through arteries and then pull it back into the chambers through the veins by suction.

Now we need to pause and relate our understanding of function, structure, and process together to appreciate why the heart does what it does. By placing the heart in the context of the larger system of which it is a part, we might conclude that the heart is at the core of a circulatory system. The purpose of the circulatory system is to exchange matter and energy between the body and its environment. This closely links the heart with Autopoiesis, the self-generation of living systems. (See Figure 5.6)

The principle of iterative inquiry is reinforced by Singerian experimentalism: "There is no fundamental truth; realities first have to be assumed in order to be learned." (Singer, 1959), Successive iterations would yield a greater understanding and more closely approximate the nature of the whole. These iterations, then, are like a reverse zoom lens through which we see the system we are trying to understand as a working part of successively bigger and bigger pictures. We stop enlarging the view when we no longer gain useful insights as we "go around."

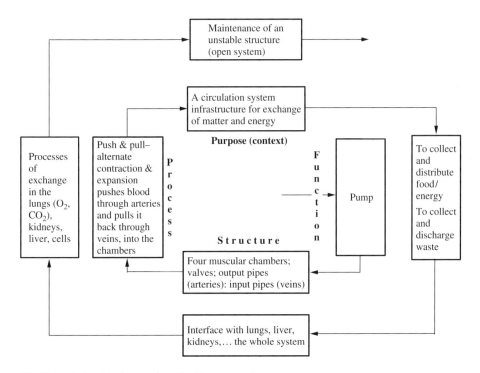

FIGURE 5.6 Understanding the Heart as a System

FOUNDATION 2: OPERATIONAL THINKING: THE DYNAMICS OF MULTI-LOOP FEEDBACK SYSTEMS

Understanding Chaos and Complexity

Complexity is a relative term. It depends on the number and the nature of interactions among the variables involved. Open loop systems with linear, independent variables are considered simpler than interdependent variables forming non-linear closed loops with a delayed response. Key words in the above statement are open or closed loop, linear or nonlinear, and delayed response.

Open or Closed Loop System

The first step for understanding complexity is to appreciate the iterative and thus dynamic nature of closed loop systems and their counterintuitive behavior. Consider the following two simple examples:

1. A savings account in a bank earning simple 10% interest reflects an open loop behavior. Both yearly earnings and the amount of principal ($10,000) remain constant, and the total sum (principal plus interest) would increase at a slow pace. (See Figure 5.7.) After 56 years, $66,000 would accumulate in this account.

2. However, if the savings in the bank were to earn 10% compound interest, it would represent a closed loop behavior, and the money in the savings account would grow exponentially, doubling every seven years. The initial principal of $10,000 would grow to $1,280,000 in 56 years. (See Figure 5.8.) Compare this amount with the $66,000 that would accrue in the simple interest example to understand the dramatic difference in behavior.

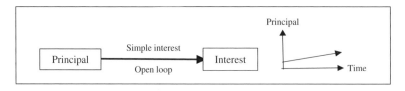

FIGURE 5.7   Open Loop System

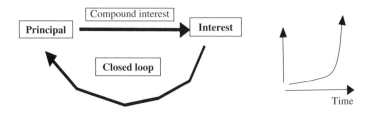

FIGURE: 5.8   Closed Loop System

Linear or Nonlinear Systems

Now, if the interest rate in the previous example varied according to market conditions, then we would be facing a nonlinear system. Please note that in closed loop thinking, linear and nonlinear refer to the rate of change, not the state of a system. (See Figure 5.9.)

It is worthwhile to note that most of our mathematical tools are based on the assumption of linearity rather than nonlinearity. In a linear system, a value for the whole can be arrived at by adding the value of its parts (type I property). Nonlinearity, by contrast, is characteristic of an emergent property where the whole is the product of interactions of the parts.

In his pioneering work on dynamic behavior of systems, J.W. Forrester observed that simple reinforcing (positive) or counteracting (negative) feedback loops are responsible for creating counter-intuitive behavior. Let us first look at the dynamic behavior of a simple negative feedback loop (which we will call goal seeking). A thermostat best describes this. Room temperature is set to a desired degree (goal). Periodically, discrepancies between the current state of the system (room temperature) and the goal are measured and used to initiate corrective actions to bring the state of the system closer to the goal. (See Figure 5.10)

Effects of a Delayed Response

Introducing a delay function to our simple negative feedback loop will produce an unexpected oscillation (a counter-intuitive behavior). For example, a delay

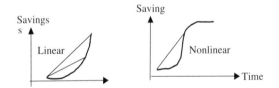

FIGURE 5.9   Linear vs. Nonlinear System

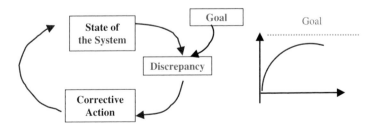

FIGURE 5.10   Goal-Seeking Behavior

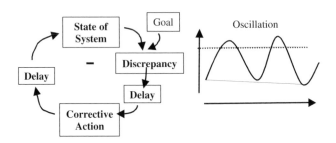

FIGURE 5.11 Counterintuitive Impact of Delay (Oscillation)

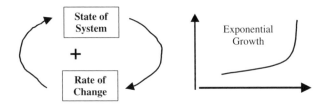

FIGURE 5.12 Positive Feedback Loop Producing
Exponential Growth Curve

between the times a discrepancy is observed and when a corrective action is taken will produce oscillation in the room temperature (See Figure 5.11.)

Second, we will consider the common phenomenon known as positive feedback loop—a bank account earning a compound interest, or a company growing annually at a fixed rate. We said that it would result in an exponential growth curve. (See Figure 5.12.)

The exponential growth curve resulting from a positive feedback loop, of course, assumes unlimited resources. But in reality, resource is a universal constraint and all exponential growth curves will eventually be influenced by carrying capacity and will, therefore, ultimately convert to an S-shaped curve.

Impact of Carrying Capacity

Now, if we just add the impact of carrying capacity to our simple positive feedback loop, we create a counteracting double loop system, producing an S-shaped curve. Superimposing a delay function, another unavoidable reality, will produce the same type of oscillation as we experienced in the previous example. The overshoot and collapse scenario reflects the cases where the growth strategy has an additional negative impact on the carrying capacity of the system. This phenomenon explains the collapse of Dotcoms, the fiasco of Enron, and the faith of thousands of corporations that pursue a blind short-term growth strategy with no regard for the limitations imposed by the carrying capacity of the system and/or its environment. (See Figure 5.13.)

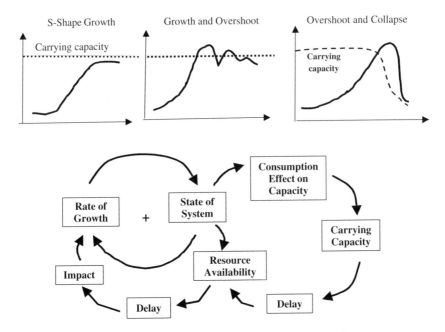

FIGURE 5.13 Impact of Carrying Capacity on the Behavior of a System

Understanding the Multi-loop Nonlinear Feedback System

Please note that by combining a few simple and ordinary phenomena we have managed to create a "multi-loop nonlinear feedback system." This is the infamous monster that, according to Chaos Theory, produces chaotic behavior. Unfortunately, as you see, the monster is not an unusual phenomenon, and it is much more common than we have been led to believe.

The point to emphasize is that the interaction of counteracting feedback loops—the prime source for generating chaos and complexity—is a common phenomenon in our daily life. Understanding these dynamics is the key to getting a handle on the notion of complexity, interdependency and counter-intuitive behavior of social systems. For an in-depth discussion of dynamic behaviors of feedback loops see Business Dynamics (John D. Sterman 2000).

Unfortunately, our cognitive ability has evolved around assumptions of unidirectional causality or open loop thinking. Therefore, we experience extreme difficulties in visualizing the outcome of closed loop systems or the behavior of interdependent variables.

The late Barry Richmond, creator of the i-think model, believed that "The way we think is outdated. As a result, the way we act creates problems, and we are ill-equipped to address them because of the way we think." (B. Richmond, Stela-software, 2001). He further defines thinking as two activities: constructing mental models and simulating them in order to draw conclusions and make decisions. We certainly need help on both accounts.

Apparently our highly regarded mathematical tools are not doing the job. Otherwise, how can we explain the sorry fact that we have been applying the same set of non-solutions to crucial social problems such as drugs, poverty, crime, illiteracy and maldistribution of wealth for most of the last fifty years?

Stephen Wolfram in New Kind of Science (2002) makes an important observation:

> "The idea of describing behavior in terms of mathematical equations works well where the behavior is fairly simple. It almost inevitably fails whenever the behavior is more complex. Indeed, there are many common phenomena about which theoretical science has had remarkably very little to say. Degree of difficulty encountered in mathematical representation of a phenomenon increases exponentially by the degree of its complexity."

Wolfram then goes on to demonstrate how systems too complex for traditional mathematics could yet obey simple operational rules. He also shows how remarkably simple iterative computer programs capture the essential characteristics of complex phenomena.

Operational Thinking is an ingenious way to overcome the difficulties encountered in constructing and simulating complex mental models. Relying solely on mathematical representation for dealing with complex phenomena has been a practical nightmare. Combining operational thinking with more manageable forms of mathematical representation, programs such as i-think software have made it practical to get a grasp of the increasingly relevant phenomena of multi-loop nonlinear feedback systems.

It is important to note that although multi-loop nonlinear feedback systems exhibit chaotic behavior, there is an order in this chaos. Such systems seem to be attracted to particular patterns of behavior. By operational thinking, we can discover this pattern and recognize the "Second Order Machine" (the attractor in action) that locks the system to its existing pattern. In this context, recognizing the *rhythm*, or the iterative cycle, of a closed loop system is the first step to understanding the dynamics of change and emergence of organized complexities.

Mapping the Dynamic Behavior

Remember that to map the dynamic behavior of a system is to capture the interaction of positive and negative feedback loops. These interactions, in essence, define the interdependencies, which in turn are responsible for nonlinearity in the system. It is the interdependency that poses a major challenge

Stock Flow Converter **Connector**

FIGURE 5.14 Four Symbols in a Universal Modeling Language

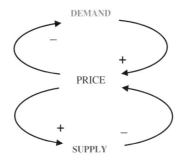

DEMAND

PRICE

SUPPLY

FIGURE 5.15 Adam Smith Invisible Hand

to our cognitive abilities. It is this challenge that we need to overcome by using an operational modeling.

As we mentioned earlier (Chapter 3 page 62) the four symbols: stock, flow, converter, and connector form a complete set for a context free universal modeling language.

Together they can capture the state of variables, feedback loops, interdependencies, and nonlinearity for building an operational model of a dynamic phenomenon. Examples can help to explain how this modeling language works.

First, the following two simple feedback loops capture the essence of Adam Smith's famous "invisible hand."

I-think software representation of this phenomenon is shown in Figures 5.16A and B. Notice that inventory (stock) is increased by supply (flow) and reduced by demand (flow). But both supply and demand are determined by price (defined by the connectors and converters). However, the price itself is in turn determined by the supply and demand (the dotted connector). This model is a simple, but beautiful classic example of interdependency.

Following is the computer-generated simulation of above I-think model (See Figure 16B).

Pattern recognition is critical for understanding and changing undesirable behavior. This leads us to the third foundation of systems thinking: implication and the role of mental models in the behavior of socio-cultural systems.

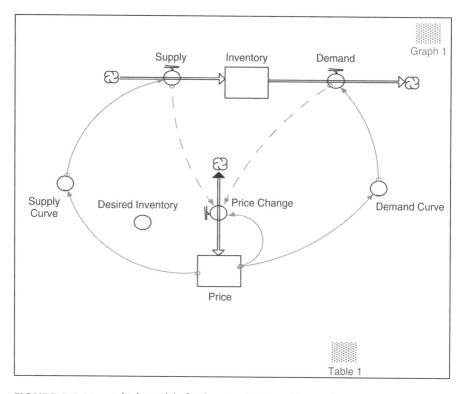

FIGURE 5.16A I-think Model of Adam Smith's "Invisible Hand"

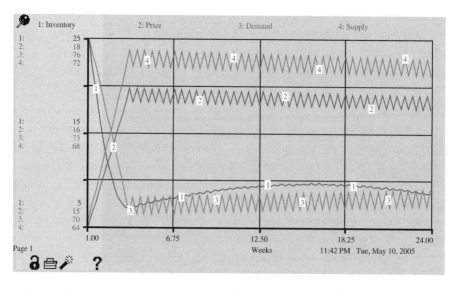

FIGURE 5.16B Computer Generated Simulation of I-think Model

FOUNDATION 3: SELF-ORGANIZATION: MOVEMENT TOWARD A PREDEFINED ORDER

Socio-Cultural Model

To think about anything requires a mental model or an image of it. The explicitness and the richness of the mental model we use to generate an initial set of assumptions about the phenomenon under study are at the core of effective systems methodology. Therefore, systems principles (openness, purposefulness, multidimensionality, emergent property, and counter-intuitiveness), and systems dimensions (wealth, power, knowledge, beauty, and values), developed in the previous chapters are integral parts of systems thinking. However, in order to appreciate the operational meaning of socio-cultural systems and the critical role implicit cultural-codes play in the process of learning, change, and dynamics of social systems, we ought to reiterate and enrich our understanding of the essential functions of shared image.

Shared Image

We have argued extensively in the previous chapter that image building and abstraction are among the most significant characteristics of human beings. We are not only able to form and interpret images of real things, but also to synthesize them into a unified, meaningful mental model and eventually into a worldview. A considerable part of this image, our mental model of the universe, is shared with others who live in the same social setting. The rest remains private and personal (K. Boulding 1952). It is this shared image that is known as the culture of a people. It forms the principal bonds among members of a social system, incorporating their experiences, beliefs, attitudes, and ideals. Finally, culture is the ultimate product and reflection of their history and the manifestation of their identity.

The systems methodology proposed in this work is presented with full appreciation of the challenges posed by the critical functions of the shared image.

Perhaps the most significant function of the shared image—in addition to acting as a filter and providing default values for the decision that we discussed in the previous chapter—is a blueprint for production of a predefined order. The formidable second law of thermodynamics states that the universe, as a closed system, has a tendency toward elimination of all distinctions. Thus, the ultimate state is sameness and randomness, (a chaotic simplicity). Entropy (S), the measure of randomness and sameness, will therefore always increase.

But, living systems are open and neg-entropic (–S). They exhibit a tenacity to move toward a predefined order (organized complexity). It seems as though open living systems have an image of what they ought be. They continuously reposition themselves to move closer to their pre-defined order.

To move toward order and complexity, a neg-entropic system must possess information or an internal image of what it wants to be (a blueprint). For biological systems, DNA provides this required information or blueprint. For socio-cultural systems, on the other hand, shared image (culture) is the source of the desired future. Living systems not only move toward a prede-fined order, but also jealously guard their individualities. Unless their stored shared image is altered, living systems go on to replicate themselves almost indefinitely.

The shared image, therefore, stands at the center of the process of change in a socio-cultural system. So the success of any action invariably depends on the degree to which it penetrates and modifies the "shared image." That is why experience with corporate transformation is fraught with frustration. The triumphant resurgence of old patterns of behavior, despite the concerted efforts of change agents, is an uninterrupted saga of despair. What seems to make this stubborn insurgency so overpowering is the fact that a set of implicit organizing principles (cultural codes) make the system to be what it is and behave the way it does.

The subset of cultural codes responsible for regenerating the existing order is what we metaphorically refer to as the "second-order-machine." The second-order-machine is equivalent to the notion of attractor in chaos theory. To produce a change in the behavioral pattern of a social system, its underlying assumptions need to be challenged. A new set of alternatives must be gener-ated and the attractor in action must be modified.

With open, neg-entropic systems, changes do not occur randomly. They are always consistent with what has gone on before, with the history, and identity of the system. This phenomenon, known as self-reference, is what facilitates orderly change toward organized complexity. Self-reference and iterative process together provide a more exciting explanation for the beauty and the magic of the evolutionary process than random mutation.

Finally, the function of culture most relevant to systems thinking is similar to that of the operating system of a computer. Without an operating system, a computer is simply a useless box. Without a viable and dynamic culture, a social system is doomed.

It has been said that our most critical survival ability can only be learned socially. And this socially learned ability—culture—has two dimensions:

1. Cognitive: Language, Meaning, Ways of Thinking & Reasoning
2. Normative: Values, Beliefs, and Social Contracts

In his recent book, *The Hidden Connections* (2002, page 34) Capra makes a key observation: "The central insight of Santiago Theory is the identification of cognition, the process of knowing, with the process of life. Cognition, according Maturana and Varela, is the activity involved in the self-generation and self-perpetuation of living systems. In other words, cognition is the very process of life. The organizing activity of living systems, at all levels of life, is a mental activity. The interactions of a living system with its environment are cognitive interactions."

Self-organizing, purposeful, socio-cultural systems must be self-evolving in order to be viable. They cannot passively adapt to their environments but should co-evolve with them. They should be able to change the rules of interaction as they evolve over time.

To meet the viability test, a culture must be capable of actively adapting to emerging realities. Active adaptation is an iterative, learning process of the second order which demands freedom to question the sacred assumptions. Unfortunately, it is here that major obstructions to development of socio-cultural systems are found. Many of the traditional societies lack the freedom to question any one of their sacred cultural codes. Most are subject to enormous intimidation by traditional forces. Questioning a sacred practice is often treated as an insult and is punishable by death. But, the ability to question sacred assumptions, without fear of repercussion, is not only an individual right but also a necessary social good that must be preserved at any price. Sometimes, intimidating forces present such a monumental obstruction to development that paying any price to remove them might be justified. So true is this that even the tragic intervention of outside power, if it results in dissolving the entrenched intimidating forces, may prove to be a tipping point for potent cultural evolution (Japan and Turkey provide sobering examples for this arguments).

On the other hand, chaotic orders, representing a form of seemingly stable, less developed but frustrated social systems may experience sudden, unexpected change. This phenomenon—known as butterfly effect—is produced when a small disturbance is fed back on itself to create a monumental impact. Of course, disturbance to any system will be resisted when it first appears. But if it survives the first attempts at suppression, and resonates with pre-existing frustrations within the system, an iterative process of deviation amplification begins. This is how a small group of strongly bonded individuals can produce a phenomenal change in the structure of a less developed social system. But, unfortunately, this change may not always produce transformation to a self-evolving purposeful socio-cultural system. The reality of highly developed socio-cultural systems that have outgrown the secure web of paternalistic culture is fundamentally different from that of less developed ones. Unless paternalistic cultural codes are properly challenged and modified, the repeated pattern of chaotic order with alienated people and authoritarian ruler will continue to emerge. (The Islamic revolution of Iran and the collapse of the Soviet Union are recent anecdotal evidence.) Emancipation, according to Habermas, takes place whenever people are able to overcome past restrictions that resulted from ideological distortions. According to Kenneth Boulding (1981), "The systemic vision of social dynamics is unfriendly to any monistic view of human history that seeks to explain it by a single factor, whether this is a materialistic interpretation as in the case of [classical] Marxism, a simple theistic interpretation, as in biblical Judaism, or an eschatological interpretation in terms of some simple denouncement. The simple rhetoric of class struggle and revolution, therefore, must be regarded as an essentially minor element in the ongoing process of human and societal evolution, although it is sometimes important as a special case under particular circumstances."

At this point, a reference to Margaret J. Wheatley's interesting book, *Leadership and New Science* (1994) would be in order. With simple and understandable language, Wheatley reviews relevant and intriguing concepts from the quantum world and chaos theory, bringing additional insights to understanding socio-cultural systems.

In this context, appreciation of Field Theory as a field of vision permeating the organizational space adds a new dimension for the role of culture in development of social systems.

The following quotations from Rupert Sheldrake are meant to highlight the essential message contained in this interesting conception.

- "Something strange has happened to space in the quantum world. No longer is there a lonely void. Space everywhere is now thought to be filled with invisible, intangible, inaudible, tasteless, odorless fields that are unapproachable through our five senses." (Page 50)
- "Some of what we know how to do comes not from our own acquired learning, but from knowledge that has been accumulated in the human species field to which we have access. (Page 10)
- Whole populations of species can shift their behavior because the content of their field has changed, not because they individually have taken the time to learn new behavior." (Page 10)

To recreate the future by way of influencing the shared image and bringing about a more desired pattern of behavior is what interactive design is all about. This brings us to the fourth and the most exciting foundation of systems methodology.

FOUNDATION 4: INTERACTIVE DESIGN

Redesigning the Future and Inventing Ways to Bring it About

Interactive design is essentially identified with Russell Ackoff. It is the core of his famous purposeful systems methodology. For Ackoff, "choice" is at the heart of human development. "Development is the capacity to choose; design is a vehicle for enhancement of choice and holistic thinking." Not surprisingly, I found interactive design to be a perfect framework to incorporate the other three elements of iterative inquiry, operational thinking, and neg-entropic behavior to form a comprehensive systems methodology. The truth is that after a lifetime association with Ackoff, I wonder where in the following formulation does Ackoff end and where do I actually begin?

We have said that self-organizing, purposeful, socio-cultural systems are self-evolving. They do not simply adapt to their environments but co-evolve with them. They can change the rules of interaction as they evolve over time. However, like all open systems, they exhibit a tendency toward a predefined order. Their behavior is guided by an implicit, shared image. They tend to approximate and reproduce their pattern of existence very closely. To change this pattern of behavior the implicit shared image or (the organizing attractor) needs to be changed.

The ultimate aim of interactive design is to replace the existing "shared image" responsible for regenerating a pattern of malfunctioning order with a shared image of a more desirable future.

We strongly believe that a participative design process is the most effective way to produce a desirable change in the behavioral pattern of a social system. This pretentious (daring) optimism, however, is based on the following assumptions:

1. "The future is not contained in the past; much of it is yet to be written." (Ackoff, 1982)
2. The best way to learn and understand a system is to redesign it.
3. People are more likely to accept an idea when they have had a hand in shaping it.
4. Performance of a system is essentially design-driven. An order of magnitude improvement requires a redesign.
5. "With unfeasible parts, one can create a feasible whole." (Ackoff, 1982)
6. Opposing tendencies form an "and" not "or" relationship. Both win/win as well as lose/lose are strong possibilities.

We further believe that penetrating the shared image is more a question of excitement than logic. An exciting vision of the future with a desire to share is a powerful instrument of change. This is why active participation of members (stakeholders) in producing a design is the fundamental, uncompromising operating principle of interactive design.

Interactive design is both the art of finding differences among things that seem similar and the science of finding similarities among things that seem different. Designers seek to choose rather than predict the future. They try to understand rational, emotional, and cultural dimensions of choice and produce a design that satisfies a multitude of functions.

Two distinct outputs of interactive design are defining problems (Formulation of the Mess), and designing solutions (Idealization). Each one adds a unique characteristic to this captivating process, and each requires further explanation.

Defining Problems (Formulation of the Mess)

The separation of defining problems from designing solutions is a unique characteristic of interactive design. According to Ackoff, "We fail more often not because we fail to solve the problems we face, but because we fail to face the right problem." We have been taught how to solve problems, but never how to define one.

Traditionally, there are three ways to define a problem. The most common approach defines a problem as deviation from the norm. The major shortcoming of this approach, besides the difficulty in defining the "norm" in a sociocultural system, is to reinforce the existing order. This is usually done despite strong suspicion that the existing order might be the source of the problem itself. A simple example is the "back to basics" movement in education.

A lack of resources is the next popular way to define a problem. It seems that somehow we cannot get enough information, money, and most certainly we do not have enough time, to deal with most situations. This should hardly be a surprise, because time, information, and money are universal constraints. We will never have enough money; we will never have enough time; we will never have enough information. The more we know, the more we know that we don't know. A minister of economy in my native country once asked me to help him assess the impact of a certain decision on three important factors he was concerned with. I told him it would take me a month to develop the proper model. He replied, "The decision is going to be made without you. If you want to have any influence on this one, be in my office with your model at 7:00 a.m. Monday morning. Otherwise, get the hell out of the way."

The third, and perhaps the most obstructive, way to define a problem is the tendency to define it in terms of the solution we already have. Existing solutions conveniently shield us from seeing the reality, so we accept the problem on face value. Not surprisingly, an operations researcher may see a situation as an allocation problem, while an accountant may consider it a cash-flow problem.

Those of us trained as professionals—engineers, doctors, and lawyers—come with a tool bag. In each instance, we have been exposed to a series of classic cases, which supposedly resemble the problem set we are expected to encounter in our professional lives. We learn the solutions to these problems at professional schools and store them in our tool bag for future use. What we have to do, in real-life situations, is find similarities between the situation we face and one of those cases, and then simply apply the proposed solution in the case to the problem at hand.

This approach is so ingrained in the way we do things that we are not even willing to entertain a question if we don't already have the answer. A valued client once protested, "Why are you pressuring me to face this problem when you know very well that I don't have a solution for it?" It was not easy to convince him that today's problems no longer yield ready-made solutions and that his job had changed from a tool user to a toolmaker. I had to remind him that he was paying me quite handsomely to help him do so. Unfortunately, even if we have a potent and innovative solution at hand, most of the time we lack the confidence to use it. We need to know who has done it before. It is as if, despite all claims to the contrary, we don't dare to be the first. Stafford Beer has expressed this phenomenon elegantly: "Acceptable ideas are competent no more, but competent ideas are not yet acceptable. This is a dilemma of our time." (Beer, 1967)

Recall the openness principle. It means that neither problems nor solutions can be entertained free of context. A phenomenon that can be a problem in one context may not be one in another. Likewise, a solution that may prove effective in a given context may not work in another. However, the tendency to define the problem in terms of the solution, and a strong preference for the context-free solution that is tried and true, create a closed loop. The process keeps on regenerating the past, leaving us wondering why history repeats itself as if no lesson had ever been learned.

To separate the process of defining a problem from the process of designing a solution, interactive designers usually form three different teams, so that each can deal with the trio of context, problem, and solution independently. This practice is to ensure that the problem is defined within the proper context without the undue influence of solutions at hand.

Further, interactive design methodology defines the problem as a "mess," the future implicit in the present operation.

A mess is neither an aberration nor a prediction, It is, instead, an early-warning system reminding the actors of unintended consequences of the present operation; It is an exaggeration intended to highlight the critical issues that may become the seed of a system's destruction in the future. More often than not, the mess is the result of success rather than failure, the consequence of a belief based on the fallacy that if X is good, more X is even better.

To formulate a "mess" is to capture the interaction of feedback loops, discover repeated patterns of behaviors and finally identify the culprit (second order machine) responsible for regenerating the existing order. Perhaps the best example of mess formulation is *Das Capital*. Ironically, the most important contribution of Karl Marx was not the solution he proposed but the problem he defined.

A good formulation of the mess makes a convincing case for fundamental change and sets the stage for effective redesign. A detailed discussion of how to formulate a mess, is the subject matter of our next chapter.

Designing a Solution (Idealization and Realization)

Interactive design is a process for operationalizing the most exciting vision of the future that the designers are capable of producing. It is the design of the next generation of their system to replace the existing order. Design process consists of two distinct phases—idealization and realization.

Idealization

The basic idea of idealization is the notion of backward planning. It starts with the assumption that the system has been destroyed overnight and that the designers have been given the opportunity to recreate the system from a clean slate. The new design is subject to only three constraints:

1. Technological feasibility
2. Operational viability
3. Learning and adaptation

Although idealizing, we are not dealing with science fiction; our idealized system is designed to be self-sustaining in the current environment. We are not forecasting the future and do not have a crystal ball. The idealized design will have sufficient sources of variety to learn and adapt to possible emerging environments. Systems design is as much an art as a science. A system designer should have the capacity for abstraction, and sensitivity to be moved by the power of an idea.

Design is an iterative process. All three aspects of function, structure, and process are addressed in each iteration.

The first iteration concentrates on developing the specification of the system's desired properties. Designers will try to understand and define the interdependencies among desired specifications. They will find out which specifications are complementary, which are compatible, and which are in conflict. They will also try to reconceptualize any conflicting requirements in order to dissolve them. In the second iteration, designers produce an initial sketch of alternative designs to show how desired properties could be realized. They explore the state of the art and develop alternative design elements that could produce one or many of the required functions. In the third iteration, they select and integrate different elements of a design to produce a single design that satisfies all concerned. Then, they elaborate on the initial design and achieve consensus. In successive iterations, after testing for operational viability, more detail and specificity are incorporated into the design.

Realization

Just as the idealization phase of interactive design is iterative, so is the realization phase. Successive approximation is at the core of realizing an ideal design. Realization takes place in a real-world environment. Therefore, designers must identify all the constraints that might interfere with proper implementation of the design. These constraints usually fall into the following three distinct categories.

Type I constraints

Type I constraints cannot be removed within the existing framework. Such constraints would require revisions and improvisations of the design in order to create a target design capable of being implemented. Target I would be the first approximation of the unconstrained design. If necessary, subsequent approximations will identify Target II and Target III generations of the desired design. It is critical that Type I constraints be continuously monitored so that the target design can further approximate the idealized design as soon as these constraints are removed. Clearly, the realization effort will not be a one-time proposition. Successive approximations of the desired state make up the evolutionary process by which the transformation from current reality to desired future is affected. It may take a number of attempts before the desired design is implemented.

Type II Constraints

Type II is essentially concerned with universal constraints whose removal will require extensive preparations. They consist of activities that consume time and resources, as well as knowledge and management talent. These activities usually involve redesign of the products (if necessary), redesign of through-put, and redesign of organizational processes. Design of the measurement and reward system with variable budgeting and target costing seems to be an integral part of all successful realization efforts. This is usually the most resource-intensive part of the change effort. For control purposes, all critical assumptions and expectations about the selected course of actions must be explicitly recorded and continuously monitored.

Type III Constraints

Type III constraints are essentially behavioral in nature. These are the constraints that can be removed if designers so desire. Selling the idea, removing resistance to change, ensuring acceptance, cultivating support, and providing training are among the efforts targeted at constraints that are basically self-imposed. These constraints, taken together, represent the cultural default of the organization, and their function is to reinforce the status quo. Without a prior foundation of trust and commitment, the system would simply refuse to undergo the planned transformation irreversibly. When confronting Type III constraints dissolving the "second-order machine" is the most critical phase of realizing the design. We will revisit process of idealization and realization in more detail in Chapter 7, Designing Business Architecture.

CONCLUSION

Interactive design, if done with active participation of the critical actors, is an irreversible process of redesigning mental images. Its impact is long-term and far exceeds the value of immediate implementation of the design document. One of the important outcomes of an idealized design is to see the light at the end of the tunnel. This light acts as a guide and defines the direction for future interventions as soon as opportunities arise. However, if even a design with no constraints cannot produce a desired outcome, then, most probably, the problems lie in the environment and the focus of change should be directed outward.

6

Defining the Problem

FORMULATING THE MESS[1]

Misconceptions about reality display self-fulfilling qualities. Unless uncovered and dismantled, they outmaneuver and outlive assaults aimed at uprooting them.

The obstructions that prevent a system from facing its current reality are self-imposed. Hidden and out of reach, they reside at the core of our perceptions and find expression in mental models, assumptions, and images. These obstructions essentially set us up, shape our world, and chart our future. They are responsible for preserving the system as it is and frustrate its efforts to become what it can be.

Mess is a system of problems. It is the future implicit in the present behavior of the system, the consequence of the system's current state of affairs. The essence of the mess is the systemic nature of the situation; it is not an aggregate representing the sum of the parts. The elements of a mess are highly interrelated. No part can be touched without touching the other parts. As such, it is an emergent phenomenon produced by the interactions among the parts. Formulation of the mess, therefore, requires understanding the essence of the behavioral characteristics of social phenomena. Mess is the natural consequence of the existing order. It is based on a false assumption that nothing will change. Messes are very resilient; they have a way of regenerating themselves. It is this quality that makes a mess an intractable phenomenon. The prevalent powerlessness and impotency in dealing with the mess lead to the inevitable denial on which messes thrive. Finally, the mess is not defined in terms of 1) deviations from a norm, 2) lack of resources (time, money, and information), or 3) an improper application of a known solution.

---

[1]"Formulating the Mess" and "Idealized Design" are synonymous with the name Ackoff. However, those of us who associated with him long enough, have been formulating messes and producing idealized designs so many times that each has, inevitably, come to develop an unique version of her/his own.

The mess is formulated to achieve the following aims:

- Provide a perspective that sets the relevant host of problems in the proper context;
- Develop a shared understanding of why the system behaves the way it does and generate a shared understanding about the nature of the current reality among the major actors;
- Minimize the resistance to change and maximize the courage to act by making the real enemy explicitly visible and believable; and
- Identify the areas of greatest leverage, vulnerability, and/or possible seeds of the system's destruction.

Formulation of the mess is a three-phase process of:

1. Searching.
2. Mapping.
3. Telling the story.[2]

Searching

"Searching" is the iterative examination that generates information, knowledge, and understanding about the system and its environment. The searching phase of mess formulation involves three kinds of inquiry (Figure 6.1):

Systems Analysis: To develop a snapshot of the current system and its environment that describes their structural, functional, and behavioral aspects without making a value judgment.

Obstruction Analysis: To identify the malfunctioning in the power, knowledge, wealth, beauty, and value dimensions of a social system.

System Dynamics: To understand the nature of multi-loop feedback systems and interactions of interdependent variables in the context of time.

The three inquiries—systems analysis, obstruction analysis, and system dynamics—evolve iteratively. With each successive cycle of iterations, we try to achieve a higher level of specificity. In the first iteration, we try to get a feel for the whole; define the system boundary; identify important variables; note areas of consensus and conflict; and identify gaps in information, knowledge, and understanding. Between iterations, we try to fill in the gaps. In subsequent iterations, we verify the assertions made in the previous iteration; obtain agreement on significant issues; and develop models to understand the behavior of the system.

---

[2]I have adopted this classification on the suggestion of my old friend and colleague John Pourdehnad. Look for a more elaborate classification in J. Pourdehnad (1994).

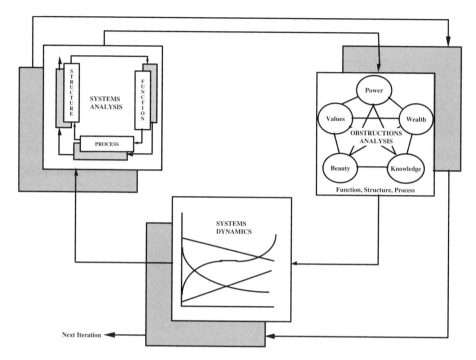

FIGURE 6.1   Iterative Process of Inquiry

In a search process, time is the most important consideration. A group might have just a day, a week, a month, or a full year to formulate the mess. The available time defines the level of generality and the degree of specificity that can be achieved. However, the available time should be allocated to each part of the inquiry to permit a pass through the cycle at least twice to understand, at a minimum, the holistic nature of the situation and identify the significant elements of the mess.

Having completed the first iteration of systems analysis, obstruction analysis, and systems dynamics, we must pause to make sense of what we've already learned. We need assumptions to be able to develop a tentative picture of the whole. Subsequent iterations will clarify, verify, and/or modify this picture. But we use this picture initially to develop a guideline of what we need to know in more detail in following iterations.

Systems analysis, obstruction analysis, and system dynamics tables (Tables 6.1 to 6.3) are to be used only as guides, or examples of the types of questions that may be examined in the search process. Use them, but do not let the forms take over the content. Remember, this is an iterative process. Avoid getting lost in the jungle of information. Generate enough information so you can establish the relevancy of each variable under consideration.

TABLE 6.1   Systems Analysis

	System	*Environment*

STRUCTURE (input)
Who are the actors, what
  is their interest, how much
  influence or stake do they
  have, and how are they
  organized?
	Members
	
	Major components and
	  their relationships
		Stakeholder analysis
		  customers, consumers,
		  suppliers, creditors,
		  government, regulators,
		  other interest groups

FUNCTION (output)
What is being produced,
  for whom, and why?
  Implicit, explicit, and
  latent requirements
	Products/markets
	Basis for differentiation
	Basis for competition
	Market access
		Market potential
		Competitive analysis
		Intensity of competition

PROCESS (knowledge)
How we do what we do
	Core technology
	Throughput processes
	Organizational processes
		Industry standard
		  (minimum requirement
		  to be a player)
		Benchmark (the best
		  player in the game)
		cost of selling
		cost of producing
		  (goods)
		cost of developing (R&D)
		cost of membership
		  (overhead)

TABLE 6.2   Obstruction Analysis

	Function	*Structure*	*Process*

Power	Potency of the
	  output in meeting
	  the explicit,
	  implicit, and latent
	  requirements
		Source of power
		Authority &
		  responsibility
		Coupling (nodes
		  of intervention)
			Decision process
			Discrepancies in existing
			  policies and procedures

Knowledge	Explicitness of the
	  assumptions
	  about the
	  working
	  paradigm
		Measurement
		  system
		Compatibility of
		  performance
		  criteria, measures,
		  and rewards
			Learning and control
			Early-warning system
			Feedback loop (time lag)

Wealth	Viability of the
	  market niche
	Reliability of
	  demand
		Source of money
		Relationships
		  within the
		  value chain
			Operational viability
			How demand for output
			  is rationalized

Beauty	Vision of a desired
	  future
		Alienation,
		  insecurities,
		  boredom
			Integration &
			  differentiation

Values	Risk and
	  vulnerability
		Default values
		  of the culture
			Conflict management

TABLE 6.3   System Dynamics

	Past	*Future*	*Pattern Recognition*
March of events	Identify critical events of the last 10 years or more that have had significant impact on your immediate environ. (e.g., industry, profession, community, family)	Identify plausible events in the near future (next 10 years or more) that you suspect would either put you in a significant disadvantage or advantage	Is there a pattern or a trend? (positive or negative) Identify periodic and/or random events
Drivers for change	Changing from?	Changing to?	Identify conflicting, competing, collaborating, or reinforcing (cooperating) behaviors
Basis for competition (success factors)	Changing from?	Changing to?	
Behavioral patterns or practices of critical actors	Identify the dimensions	• Rational • Emotional • Cultural	Identify causal and/or feedback loops

Mapping the Mess

The search phase usually identifies a large number of obstructions. To make sense of these obstructions, we have to synthesize them into a few categories so we can examine their interactions and understand the essence of the mess.

The process involves grouping various phenomena into categories or subsets, then identifying themes, each of which is the emergent property of its constituent elements (members of subsets).

Generation of these themes usually requires an interactive discussion to achieve a shared understanding of the grouping criteria. Each theme should be 1) defined clearly so there is no confusion about what it represents, and 2) substantiated in terms of its prevalence. Themes should not reflect isolated occurrences. A litmus test for the validity of the themes is that, when presented to relevant stakeholders, a clear sign of recognition results (an "aha" experience).

Finally, after all relevant themes are identified and substantiated, the relationships (interactions) among the elements must be addressed.

Each theme is normally a mini-mess in its own right; however, for the purpose of studying the interactions, we would initially treat each theme as a self-containing whole. In subsequent iterations, if a theme emerges as the central concern, we would break it down further into smaller components so

their interactions with the other elements of the mess can be properly represented. Developing pictorial representations of the interactions among themes
is often helpful.[3] Figure 6.2 is an example of such a representation, one in
which four themes have been identified: viability of market niche, product
division culture, product potency, and operational effectiveness.

This type of diagram can be read by tracing the lines of interactions as
follows: As a substitute product gradually gains acceptance, a gradual loss of
product potency results in decreased market demand. In a divisional culture,
the identity of any division is defined by the viability of its market niche. Any
threat to this niche constitutes a threat to that division. Therefore, the first
reaction to this unpleasant reality is denial.

The division, to protect itself, repeatedly issues exaggerated forecasts,
which prove false and damage its credibility. This increases the pressure to
improve sales by reducing cost at any price. But the change in the marketplace
demands a redesign to improve product potency. Meanwhile, pressure to produce immediate results encourages short-term remedies. An ineffective operational system, under this pressure, is not capable of redesigning the product,
so it patches minor changes onto the existing product. This further increases
the cost, reducing the sales and, most unfortunately, granting precious time to
the competition to solidify its position. The vicious circle thus continues.

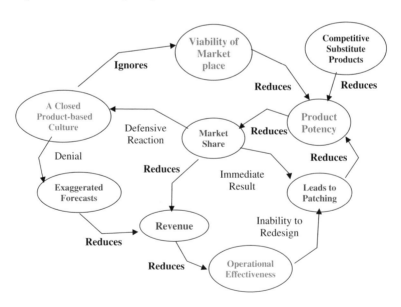

FIGURE 6.2   Mapping the Mess

---

[3]Peter Checkland (1981) uses a similar method of mapping to capture "the shape of systems
movement."

To map the mess, we need to underscore the nature of interdependency and the dynamics of the situation. This requires remembering the assertion we made regarding the counterintuitive behavior of social systems. Recall the following:

1. An event (cause) might have more than a single outcome (effect).
2. Cause and effect are separated in time and space (time lag).
3. Cause and effect can replace one another (circularity).
4. Effects, once produced, might have an independent life of their own. Removing the cause will not necessarily remove the effects.

For example, to examine the total effects of smoking on the heart, we should consider its multiple outcomes. Smoking might reduce anxiety and therefore, in the short term, be beneficial to the heart. In addition, smoking, by reducing excessive desire to eat, helps maintain body weight, also helping the heart. But the pleasure associated with reduced anxiety is habit-forming and results in a desire to repeat the act.

However, in the long run, smoking has a negative effect on the arteries. Combined with genetic dispositions and/or other oxidizing processes, smoking results in rigidity, roughness, and hardening of the heart's arteries. The natural defenses of the body react with multiple layers of cholesterol coatings to smooth things out, which ultimately result in a blockage and heart attacks.

Furthermore, smoking negatively affects the functioning of the lungs, resulting in a less-than-optimum supply of oxygen to the heart (Figure 6.3). In this context, it seems that developing a simple correlation between variables doesn't mean much; it might even be misleading. Is cholesterol the real villain or just the element of an overprotective defensive mechanism?

Once the elements of the mess and their interactions are mapped, we need to know why and how the current mess has evolved. Assuming that the system has been rational and was acting in its own best interest, we need to understand why a system behaves the way it does and why it reproduces the mess all over again.

Mapping the mess is the heuristic process of defining essential characteristics and the emergent property of the mess. It involves finding the "second-order machine" residing within the system. This unanticipated consequence of the existing order produces paralyzing "Type II" properties that create inertia, prevent change, and frustrate attempts to make significant improvements. To achieve an order-of-magnitude improvement in any system's performance, the second-order machine has to be recognized and dismantled. Exaggeration of the winning formula, combined with a possible change of game, more often than not will point to a set of seemingly innocent, simple, but deep-rooted assumptions that are at the core of the second-order machine.

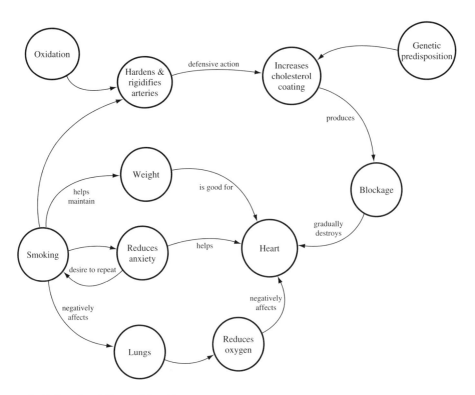

FIGURE 6.3 Effects of Smoking

Figure 6.4 attempts to map the mess of the education system. Although produced specifically for a given state, it captures the generality of how the system has been uncoupled from both market and government control—and how it has been able to convert its undeniable failure into success by exploiting the false assumption that money can solve all shortcomings in education.

In a different context, Figure 6.5 represents a supermarket operation. It underscores the significance of location for a retail business. Two different locations for the operation of a retail store are examined by using two scenarios. The decision is on the dollar amount to be spent on prime locations. Scenario one is based on the strategy of getting the best available location irrespective of the cost.

High rent for a prime location, however, increases the absolute amount of the cost, but counterintuitively reduces both occupancy cost and labor cost ratios by increasing the throughput (sales volume). This leads to better profitability, increased market share, and higher rate of growth. Growth improves the labor-mix ratio (senior/junior) and significantly reduces the labor cost, making money available for more prime locations. A positive feedback loop

Educational System: Dynamics

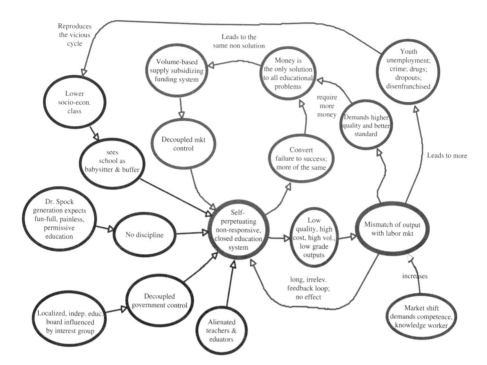

FIGURE 6.4 Education System

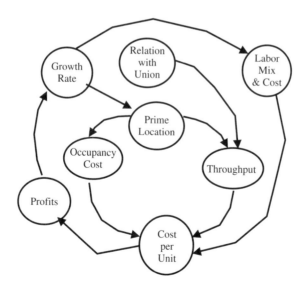

FIGURE 6.5 Supermarkets Dynamics

is created. Scenario two follows a penny-wise-and-pound-foolish strategy of constraining the occupancy cost, which reduces volume and throughput. This negatively affects profitability, growth of market share, and the labor-mix ratio, creating a negative feedback loop, or a vicious circle.

Telling the Story

Mess is not a prediction; it is an early-warning system. Proper packaging and communication of the message is as important as the content of the message itself. Formulating and disseminating the mess is as significant a step as solving it. More often than not, knowledge of the mess helps dissolve it. A believable and compelling story that reveals the undesirable future implicit in the current state has to be developed. Assume that things will go wrong, if they can, all at the same time. Try to produce a resonance and show how a system breakdown can occur. The challenge is to create a shared understanding of the current reality and its undesirable consequences, thus creating a desire for change. The story should consider the stake, influence, and interest of the relevant stakeholders. It should not assess blame or make people defensive. The mess should be presented as a consequence of past success, not as a result of failure. Remember, the world is not run by those who are right; it is run by those who can convince others that they are right.

Generally, there seems to be reluctance on management's part to share the mess with other stakeholders, especially the members, under the pretext that this might discourage them. But this practice not only defeats the purpose of formulating the mess, but also is counterintuitive. It has been my experience that members of an organization, more often than not, are aware of the nature of the mess; in most cases they are simply not allowed to talk about it, or they might not be able to articulate it as completely as during the formulation of the mess. What they really don't know is whether or not management is aware of the mess. Usually, sharing the mess brings a sigh of relief and a willingness to confront it.

MAPPING THE MESS OF XYZ CORPORATION, A SAMPLE FORMULATION

This document is a sample of a real mess formulation. It represents the mess of the utility industry in general. It is given a fictitious name of *XYZ Corporation* to reflect the fact that it does not refer to any one company specifically. However, it is so typical of the majority of the utility companies of the time (early 1990s) that I am sure most of them will easily identify with it.

You will recall that the essence of the mess is the interactive set of co-producers, here referred to metaphorically as the second order machine, which makes the *XYZ* Corporation behave the way it does.

Mapping the mess followed an iterative search process. It involved systems analysis and obstructions analysis. Systems analysis provided a non-judgmental picture of the system as it is. Obstructions analysis identified sets of internal and external obstructions that co-produced the mess. The search process categorized the obstructions around major themes. Generation of the themes involved extensive discussions so that a shared understanding of the grouping criteria was achieved. Each theme, therefore, is a symbolic representation of a complex set of obstructions reflecting the collective subjectivity of the mess team.

The critical elements of the mess are:

1. The monopolistic, cost-plus environment,
2. The non-competitive culture,
3. The input-based personnel policy,
4. Mediocrity, tolerance of incompetence,
5. Absence of strategic thinking,
6. Uncertainty about the future,
7. Structural conflict, and
8. Problems specific to the region in which *XYZ* operates.

Each individual theme is defined, so there is no confusion as to what it represents. Then, the pattern of interactions among the themes is developed and pictorially represented (refer to Figure 6.6). A deliberate effort was made to provide in-depth explanations as to why the system behaves the way it does and what was responsible for this behavior.

The initial investigation indicated that the source of *XYZ's* mess is not significantly separate from the overall mess of the industry to which it belongs. It also became equally apparent that the emergent mess is so profound and overpowering enough to warrant an in-depth understanding of it. Any mess, as was pointed out, is highly interrelated. It is a system-wide phenomenon. No part of a mess can be dealt with independently of other elements. Messes, therefore, cannot be dissolved partially or locally. No sooner would an element of a mess be removed than the remaining parts would regenerate it. This explains why, despite recent management's best efforts, the mess has not gone away. Mess is an exaggeration. It is a deliberate concentration on major obstructions that intensifies the system's rigid lock into a specific context. The idea is that awareness of the mess is the precondition to its dissolution. Once we know where the long-term consequences of our actions are taking us, we are likely to make the commitment to take the necessary measures and act preventively. The systemic properties of the mess are the unintended consequence of the past success. Mess is the legacy of the old game. Given the general context of the regulated utilities, it is only natural that the mess is more or less typical of the industry as a whole. The mess is *XYZ*'s long-term adaptation to a long-secured context. Had the advent of deregulation not rendered the erstwhile context of utilities obsolete, the mess would not have been considered a mess. It would still be regarded as an adequate adaptive response to an uncontrollable dominant environment. In fact it is the mismatch between the existing culture and the new challenges that is fraught with unintended (read catastrophic) consequences. Therein lies the age-old lesson behind the rise and fall of man-made institutions: success changes the game and converts, by default, the very secrets of success to the ultimate seeds of destruction.

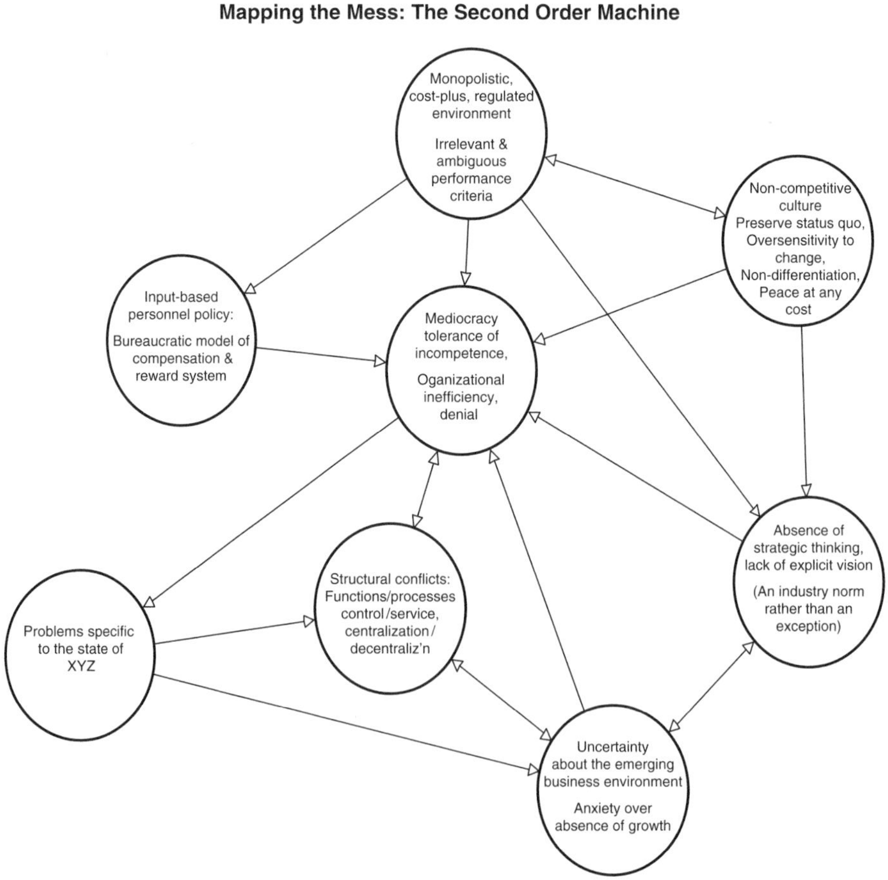

Mapping the Mess: The Second Order Machine

FIGURE 6.6   Interrelated System of Problems of XYZ

The mess of XYZ is the product of an exaggerated imbalance: excessive attention to a particular aspect of the system (cost-plus, input-based, friction-free, variety-reducing, and stability-oriented characteristics) and extreme neglect of the others (performance-based, entrepreneurial, market-driven, change-oriented, and variety-amplifying characteristics). Sub-optimization, given enough time, has made virtual evils out of proven virtues. Under the circumstances, to achieve an order-of-magnitude improvement in the performance of XYZ requires that this second order machine be recognized and dismantled. Understanding the mess, therefore, provides XYZ with a powerful tool to realize its transformation effort.

Element 1 – Monopolistic, Cost-plus, Regulated Environment

The nature of XYZ is defined by its exclusive franchise operating in a cost-plus regulated environment. No other single factor has been more responsible for influencing the nature of XYZ, being what it is, and behaving the way it does.

Utility regulations were originally established to correct the utility industry's abusive business practices, restore public confidence in the monopolistic system, and serve as a proxy for competition. Once the industry's abuses were curbed, rate-making evolved into the validation process in a "cost-plus" system. The cost-plus environment performed reasonably well in the post-war era, and even more so in the 1960s, as new, less expensive energy sources were developed and rate decreases became the industry norm. Price decreases fueled an expanding economy, stimulated customer demand, and elevated the industry's stature, adding value to shareholder investments. However, the decade of the 1970s ushered in shortages, embargoes, high inflation, record interest rates, environmental regulations and the "China Syndrome," all of which propelled costs and the industry into a more contentious relationship with customers and environmentalists. In response to higher prices, environmental concerns and public pressures, regulators implemented "social justice" into rate design and regulation. During the 1980s, environmentalists and self-interest groups used the regulatory arena to promote conservation programs, force even further "social justice" into rate designs, and promulgate rules designed to displace the electric industry from its traditional role of plant builder, owner and operator. In the cost-plus regulated environment, the regulator looms omnipotent. What it does overrides almost every other source of influence in the operation of a utility company. The necessity to cope with the regulated environment has led to a bureaucratic competency in the form of an ability to manage costs and allocation techniques to the best advantage of the system. The cost allocation skills, perfected to an art form, then shape all operating policies, procedures, and processes. This context leads to ambiguous and irrelevant performance criteria. Typical business measures are usually disregarded in lieu of cost-plus regulatory environment. For example, the ill-defined social and economic agenda defy the establishment of meaningful performance measures. In a sound competitive environment, for example, it would simply be dismissed as facetious to expect that a company not only reduce the demand for its output but also at the same time pick up the tab for it. Once the survival of the system becomes independent of its performance, the luxury of operating in a cost-plus third-party payer environment leads to the emergence of a totally new game with its own unique ground rules and motivational consequences. People realize over time that they can afford to ignore early warnings and look up to the regulator as the main source of their viability with a limited concern for the effectiveness of organization and the discipline of a real marketplace.

The cost-plus system is terminally ill! The customer base resents it, and the political machine will surely demand its demise. While the future model for rate regulation and the industry as a whole has yet to be designed, it is clear that a new industry leader or set of standards will emerge for others to follow. Any new performance standards will probably draw heavily from the competitive model and will, at least initially, favor cost efficiency initiatives and reward creative entrepreneurial efforts.

Element 2 – The Non-Competitive Culture
Organizational culture of XYZ, influenced by cost-plus regulatory environment, is characterized by the following attributes:

- Non-competitively regulated environment conducive to peaceful co-existence of peers.
- Mutual respect of players for well-established and sacrosanct territories.
- A mainstream tendency to comply with the law of averages; a bias toward being similar and non-threatening among like-minded peers as opposed to being differentiated and distinct from the other utilities.
- A time-honored respect for such communal values as stability, harmony, and camaraderie over competency.
- A habitual expectation of taking for granted guaranteed earnings and continued growth.
- An unspoken assumption that the survival of the system is independent of the efficiency of its operation.
- Looking up to 'regulators' as the single source of change, albeit a benign one.
- Considering the regulator as the real customer, who determines the future, instead of the end user who has no choice.
- Determining the inputs (size of personnel, years of education, length of seniority, etc.) rather than the outputs (innovations, productivity,

performance, etc.) as the basis of status and benefits. Change is perceived as a threat to hard-won security and status.

- A much greater sensitivity to errors of commission as opposed to errors of omission; an implicit denial of the fact that organizations fail more often, not because of what they do but because of what they do not do.
- The need for power overriding the need for achievement: status and membership are enhanced more by patronage and loyalty than competitive behavior. (Whom you know is as important as what you produce).
- Not recognizing the significance of vital talent and relevant technology.
- Formation of identities around closely-guarded turfs, rather than the whole, which is conveniently ignored.
- The unity of command being the overriding vehicle to manage conflict, remove confusion, create alignment, and correct deviation.
- Considering the superior-subordinate relationship as the only building block of the organization, leading to hierarchical one-dimensional structure.

Element 3 – The Input-Based Personal Policy

The compensation and reward system of *XYZ* is based on a mechanistic model. This model was originally created in response to strong unions' demands for social justice, fairness, and security for workers in large industrial concerns.

The conventional model is still dominant in a majority of manufacturing environments. Notwithstanding the obvious flaws of the conventional model, the competitive nature of these industries produces a somewhat balancing effect, which makes the model workable despite its vital shortcomings. Unfortunately, however, in cost-plus non-competitive environments, the model brings out the worst of protected bureaucracies. At *XYZ* the model's absence of clear performance measures has become a major obstruction. It has become an integral part of the second order machine that determines the essential character of *XYZ* and makes it behave the way it does. For instance, marginal performers can receive favorable reviews and remain with *XYZ* for many years. To compensate for the consequential under-performance, additional personnel are then utilized to accomplish the designated work assignments. Personnel policy systems, once in place, take on a life of their own. In fact, no aspect of organization is so hypersensitive to redesign. It is, therefore, no accident that the conventional compensation system has long endured as a default value, despite its crippling effects. The following summarizes the characteristics of the conventional compensation system of *XYZ*. As pointed out, these manifestations are not unique. They are shared by many organizations that have adopted the traditional model. The existing system is characterized by "job" evaluation. It is the job and not the occupant that is the focus of evaluation. Fixed or base pay is determined by the job content and the qualifications derived from it. Different people having the same job get essentially the same pay. The system reflects the motto that constitutes this mechanical notion of fairness, i.e., "equal pay for equal job." The system avoids differentiating people based on the differences that make a difference. The overriding concern seems to be with stability and ease of measurement. Since average performers constitute the commanding majority of employees, it is therefore believed that compensation based on the typical average performer produces less dissatisfaction, and results in a more stable work environment. The system is selectively geared to the features that are common to all jobs. The real occupant is deliberately ignored. It is implied that considering the occupant's unique talents, skills, and interests as well as performance and contributions would involve personalities, intangibles, complexities and subjective judgments. It is, therefore, imperative to deliberately insulate the process of evaluation from individual judgment "no matter how good it is." Such job evaluation systems are products of machine age thinking. They assume that organizations are machines consisting of structurally defined tasks whose outputs are determined by their structures. All inputs are, therefore, limited to job statements. The relevant human elements, be it the personal judgment of the manager or the characteristics of the occupants, are conveniently eliminated from the process in the name of objectivity. There is an overriding concern with the ease of accuracy and measurement. In the name of objectivity, the process gets linked to the easily measurable dimensions such as years of experience, levels of formal education, number of employees, size of budgets, etc. This reconfirms the fact, widely ignored in human systems, that 'the wrong criteria accurately measured' produces unintended and self-defeating consequences. The following summarizes some of the conventional system consequences, which are widespread in organizations driven by such a model:

- Encourages empire building (inflates budget and staff to achieve salary-earning status).
- Encourages bureaucratization and resistance to change.
- Rewards mediocrity and discourages differentiation based on talent and performance.
- Encourages promotions to higher levels of incompetence as a means of salary increase.
- Creates inflated (top- and bottom-heavy) organizations.
- Generates indifference and alienation.
- Raises the entire pay base by averaging the whole system rather than selectively differentiating the occupants in terms of their performance.
- Replaces the need for achievement by the need for power.

Element 4 – Mediocrity, Tolerance of Incompetence

XYZ operates in a force field that drives everything toward average. The gravitation toward normalcy comes from three separate and yet interrelated areas:

- A cost-plus regulatory environment and irrelevancy of performance criteria.
- Commitment to a noncompetitive culture.
- An input-based personnel policy.

The convergence point of these reinforcing drivers generates an entropic process, a systemic gravitation to non-differentiation and uniformity. The welfare of the system, therefore, requires maintenance of a state of predictability, harmony and conformity. Risk and tension are anathema. Motivation to achieve competitive advantage and desire to excel are invitations to disruption and a serious threat to peace and healthy balance. Differential tendencies away from the established norms are discouraged. Innovation and entrepreneurial tendencies are treated as social pathologies, discordant deviations from the state of normalcy. To maintain this desirable state of uniformity and equality, the system has to develop a capacity to tolerate incompetence. Success is defined by being average, maintaining a low profile, and making no noise. Consequently, the system, under inertia, slips into a downward spiral of organizational ineffectiveness. Vitality suffers; banality sets in. When competence becomes irrelevant, then nobody is indispensable. Therefore, maintaining proper relationship with the source of power becomes the ultimate criteria for success. If left unchecked, this process will ultimately result in an unacceptable level of non-performance. In order to counter this and produce the necessary levels of output, the system has some degrees of differentiation. Unfortunately the only feasible means for differentiation, under the circumstances, is creation of multilayer hierarchies. Proliferation and subdivision of real tasks into insignificant jobs allows successive cycles of promotions to the levels of incompetence. The by-products of an overpopulated workforce further obstruct the workflow. Since the strength of a bureaucratic chain is determined by its weakest element, the organization became increasingly self-absorbed. Inflated workforce took a life of its own and created enough internal work to keep it busy. Redundancy proliferates. Process becomes an end in itself. Need for duplication is never ending, since those who want to do something realize that they could hardly rely on others for effective and timely support. This context is responsible for the experience of the following paradoxical duality. An implicit appreciation and desire to preserve the system that produces these opportune levels of generous benefits, security, and peace of mind militates against the natural human desire for a rational alternative that promotes earned distinction, legitimate authority, and recognition through superior performance. Witnessing the wasteland, therefore, pains the social conscience. Widespread expressions of frustration and criticism are reflections of experiencing this on-going tension. The frustrating struggle of trying to resolve this dilemma gives rise to the prevalence of a denial syndrome: a tendency to blame the actors for the shortcomings of the system rather than the system itself.

Element 5 – Absence of Strategic Thinking

The utility system of America, despite whatever self-criticism is leveled at it, is still the envy of the world. To have covered and provided for the insatiable energy needs of a vast continent in a span of a few decades could not have been achieved without gigantic vision, phenomenal leadership and Herculean effort. Even today, a comparable achievement would be a daunting challenge to other industrial societies, even in terms of internal technical consistency and operational reliability, let alone the sheer scale. In fact, in America, the utilities used to be looked up to as icons of modern management. They were not waiting for rate increases to be granted. Efficiencies kept pushing costs down. With success came complacency. The system stopped developing because it was pointless to improve a system that was already perfect. Therefore, feeling no need for any new sources of variety, utilities closed their gene pool, exclusively dealing with the insiders to the industry.

As a consequence, strategic thinking has become a casualty of:

- A retroactive pride in the past.
- A shift of focus from new discoveries and frontiers to safeguarding what has already been achieved.
- Crisis management, the organization operating in a reactive mode, responding only to problems as they emerge.
- Erosion of core competence.

An annual planning process identified as strategic planning is performed. The plans generated are, in effect, operating plans which evolve into "to do" lists for the upcoming year. Lack of an articulated strategy has caused XYZ to forego new business opportunities. In the absence of a new vision for a more exciting future, the system engages in a constant struggle to preserve the old, a nostalgic preoccupation with the rearview mirror.

Element 6 – Uncertainty about the Future

XYZ, like other members of the energy industry, is entering uncharted waters. Once characterized by the stability of a publicly regulated environment, the industry has suddenly found itself in the throes of unpredictable change. The familiar and closely-knit environment is being thrown open. Deregulation is ushering in the market and competitive forces which will reshape the industry beyond recognition. The future, if anything, is uncertain. No one knows, with any degree of certainty, what it will look like. What is certain, however, is that the future of the utility industry is not going to be what it used to be. The only certainty will be uncertainty. The challenge is to excel in an environment where the competition defines the opportunities and the end-user picks the winners. Great Britain and Canada are already in the throes of total utility restructuring. Washington and Wisconsin are leading the United States and began experimenting with new forms and relationships for doing the same things differently. Connecticut has taken a "wait and see" approach and others, such as Massachusetts, are bracing for the turbulence that lies ahead.

As to what directions the future of the utility industry may take, there are speculations; amongst them are:

- Opening up of the energy industry to market-driven competition and management.
- Emergence of the independent producer as a major player.
- Rise of brokerage: wholesale traders and, in particular, retail wheelers.
- Prospects of a change in cost equation by inclusion of the environmental costs.
- Rates differentiation.
- Introduction of mergers and acquisitions.
- The prospect of limited growth opportunity in the traditional energy business.

The emerging new reality, whatever shape it takes, will be pregnant with an array of new threats and opportunities. In light of the possible impact of the emerging reality, different stakeholders have already begun reassessing their expectations. Most importantly, the prospect of the limited growth of energy is a source of anxiety not only for the stockholders but all the other stakeholders of the organization. This is so because the viability of the system is growth-based. Insufficient growth will have two disturbing effects: Internally, it will upset the built-in cost increase system; and externally, the emerging new game will disrupt the peaceful coexistence of the peer utility companies. The game will become essentially zero-sum; some will win at the expense of others. Anxiety seems to be the order of the day.

Element 7 – Structural Conflict
XYZ is faced with a series of incompatibilities in its architecture (structure, function, and process) that arise from the requirements of new realities in its

environment. The present structure of *XYZ* is consistent with an organizational legacy that proved extremely successful in an era when the system was operating in a stable and growing environment. It is a typical organizational structure, a dominant form of organization in corporate America today. The model was initially developed (by Alfred Sloan of GM) to meet the increasing challenges of managing growth in diversified markets.

The basic architecture of this model is comprised of a series of semi-autonomous divisions operating under the central control of a powerful headquarters (The Brain of the Firm). Each division is a miniature of the whole and is responsible for operating in a predefined product/market niche. The assigned niche defines the identity, viability, and scope of the operation of each division. The required competency of each division is prediction of the demand and preparation for it. Otherwise, they are expected to follow a preestablished mode of operation with no deviation. The administrative functions are the essential means of central control. These functions are duplicated throughout the organization. Conversely, technical competencies are diffused and differentiated across product divisions in the form of local technologies. Since each division is to operate with a predefined product, technology, and a given market territory, interactions between them are minimized. This reduces conflict and complexity and increases focus and accountability. Success is achieved by staying the same and cloning the product divisions in several markets, a perfect model for a stable and growing and predictable business environment. This perfect structure, however, becomes grossly dysfunctional in an unstable and unpredictable environment laden with new sets of obstructions and opportunities. To be viable in this environment requires *flexibility* and *core competency*. Note that state-of-the-art capabilities, which are specific to a particular operation and cannot be successfully duplicated in different contexts, are not considered to be core competencies. Incompatibility of control and service functions at the corporate level produces unnecessary confusion, making both functions ineffective. Service providers are expected to perform a control function while simultaneously providing a service. As a means to avoid the control/service conflict, services which could be easily and effectively shared, are duplicated. This chimerical quality results in continuous boundary disputes and loss of accountability. On the other hand, control functions, by being part of a service company, lose their proper legitimacy to be taken seriously. This, especially in a context of a culture that avoids bad news and conflicts in exchange for peace, does not provide a proper setting for an effective learning and early warning system. It reduces the control function to a minimum, mostly a bureaucratic form, i.e. supervision. Finally, determination of the attributes and capabilities that are to be common to all parts of the organization and those that are unique to specific parts of an operation is of paramount importance. The critical question, then, is the process (how) by which these objectives are to be achieved. Ironically, both centralization and decentralization, as two complementary processes, can be instrumental in this regard. So the question is not whether to have a centralized or decentralized operation, but to distinguish between what should or should not be centralized/decentralized. Of course, this question cannot be resolved free of context. For example, as long as a business is operating under a regulated environment, it makes a lot of sense to centralize the administrative functions. This will easily produce the internal consistency and uniformity that are so essential to regulatory oversight. But if it becomes necessary to operate in a non-regulatory environment as well, then *centralized* administrative functions, in their present form, will surely stifle the new businesses. They should, therefore, be decentralized in order to keep them confined to the regulated business

Element 8 – Problems Specific to the Region in Which XYZ Operates
The following problems specific to the region in which XYZ operates further aggravate the system of problems by adding a political dimension.

Parts of XYZ service territory have been in economic decline. Lack of growth and relative poverty constrains the rate of consumption. In an industry that is capital-intensive, limited consumption means higher per unit energy cost. This has led the system into a vicious spiral of decline where higher unit cost drives overall consumption even lower.

The problem is aggravated by the conditions in another part of the region that is, ironically, quite well off. It is an internationally known upscale resort. The luxury vacation homes, however, are used only seasonally. For most of the year, they are left unused. The seasonal owners pay only for what they actually use, leaving their huge share of fixed cost to be picked up by the less fortunate year-round customers who are outside the resort area. It is only fair to say that, insofar as energy is concerned, the vacation residents effectively live off the subsidies that are imposed by default on year-round residents.

7

Designing Business Architecture

MULTIDIMENSIONAL MODULAR DESIGN

In a global market economy with ever-increasing levels of disturbance, a viable business can no longer be locked into a single form or function. Success comes from a self-renewing capability to spontaneously create structures and functions that fit the moment. In this context, proper functioning of self-reference would certainly prevent the vacillations and the random search for new products/markets that have, over the past years, destroyed so many businesses.

In fact, the ability to continuously match the portfolio of internal competencies with the portfolio of emerging market opportunities is the foundation of the emerging concept of new business architecture (Figure 7.1).

Business Architecture is a general description of a system. It identifies its purpose, vital functions, active elements, and critical processes and defines the nature of the interaction among them. Business architecture consists of a set of distinct but interrelated platforms, creating a multidimensional modular system. Each platform represents a dimension of the system, signifying a unique mode of behavior with a predefined set of performance criteria and measures. Designing business architecture follows the general rules of iterative idealized design described in chapter 5. It therefore starts by assuming that the system to be redesigned has been destroyed overnight, but that everything else in the environment remains unchanged. The designers have been given the opportunity to design the system from scratch.

The schematic (Figure 7.2) outlines the process of designing business architecture.

FIGURE 7.1   Matching Internal and External Competencies

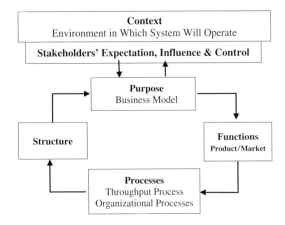

FIGURE 7.2 Schematic Outline of a Design Process

The System's Boundary and Business Environment

The first step in designing system architecture is to define the system's boundary and appreciate the environment in which system intends to operate.

To define the system's boundary, we need to understand the behavior of its stakeholders. A stakeholder of an organization is any individual or group who is directly affected by what the organization does, and consequently, has a stake in its performance. Therefore, we need to know the following: Who are the major stakeholders? What are their expectations? What are the desired properties of the system from their perspective? What is their influence? Which critical variables do they control (or influence)?

For example, in a market economy the customer provides the operating income, the boss defines the membership, stockholders pay the capital, suppliers are the source of complementary technologies, and distributors provide access to customers. However, stake and influence do not necessarily go hand in hand. On the contrary, a high stake is often coupled with low influence, and vice versa. For example, customers with the highest level of influence (refusing their patronage) show very low levels of stake in the system. On the other hand, employees with a very high stake in the system often have low levels of influence. Shareholders with very high influence have least at stake. If unhappy, they would simply take their money out.

As we alluded before, the systems boundary is a subjective construct defined by the interest and level of influence and/or authority of the participating actors. The system, therefore, consists of all variables that could be sufficiently influenced or controlled by the participating actors. Meanwhile, the environment in which the system must remain viable consists of all those variables that, although affecting the system's behavior, could not be directly influenced or controlled by the participating designers.

Because in this formulation the business environment is to remain intact, it is critical to gain an appreciation of its behavior by understanding: How is the game evolving? What are the drivers for change? What are the bases for competition?

Figure 7.3 is a schematic representation of how the game is evolving and the drivers for change in the energy business. Note how a single event, the oil crisis of 1979, by producing an unrealistic forecast for energy prices, triggered a chain of events to reduce consumption. But, in a fixed-cost and price-regulated environment, it counterintuitively resulted in higher prices, and ultimately restructured the whole industry.

Figure 7.4 captures the drama of the health-care system. The game is still evolving. The industry has yet to find alternatives for the three villains of third-party payer, cost plus reimbursement, and fee-for-service, which are assumed to be responsible for creating insatiable demand. Note how a counterintuitive event, General Motors' agreement with the labor union to cover the health care cost of workers in exchange for a one-time concession on wages, combined with President Johnson's Medicare and Medicaid programs, led to the "Health Care Bonanza" and dynamics to which no one has yet found a satisfactory solution.

As for changes in the bases of competition, consider the fact that the past was the age of mass production based on the interchangeability of parts and labor. We have since entered the mass customization era, where success is defined by producing smaller batches of customized products at lower break-even points. Honda's break-even point for a given model is two thousand cars; whereas Ford Motor Company requires five hundred thousand units of the same model car to break even. Mastery of a simple procedure was the cornerstone of mass production, but the multi-skilled knowledge worker is now the core requirement of mass customization. Globalization means that price is set in the global marketplace, and is therefore considered to be an uncontrollable variable. This fact makes cost the controllable variable (target costing), just the opposite of the "Cost Plus Economy" in which cost is considered to be the uncontrollable and price the controllable variable (target pricing). Efficiency in performing a routine used to be a virtue when the cost of automation outweighed the cost of labor. The digital revolution has reversed the equation. Increasingly cheaper computers have rendered the "narrow skill" and "simple procedure" approach obsolete. In fact, when it comes to performing a specific procedure, the computer is the ideal actor.

But computers cannot answer the call for knowledge work. Knowledge workers of today are capable of putting together whatever pieces of know-how it takes to produce an integrated solution.

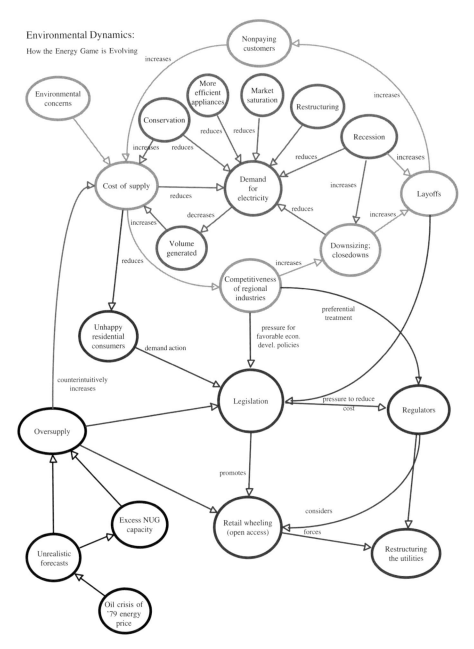

FIGURE 7.3   How the Energy Business Environment is Evolving

There was a time when problems could be neatly formulated and conveniently solved within the confines of a single discipline or department. Modern problems, however, are increasingly complex and interrelated. These problems

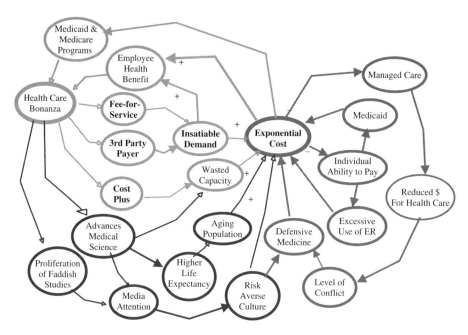

FIGURE 7.4 How the Game is Evolving in the Health Care Industry

are messy; they come in bundles and require a different approach. Knowledge workers of today are required to be competent not only in their own vocation, but are expected to be intimately aware of the total context and overall process within which they are to collaborate.

Purpose

Many commonsense statements invoked in the process of developing organizations prove counterintuitive. The surprise element does not occur because people are knowingly disingenuous. Emerging consequences contradict expectations because the operating principles are rooted in assumptions that belong to different paradigms. Such surprises are inevitable unless the underlying premises are surfaced and their eventual consequences are mapped out. In fact the purpose of business enterprise is essentially defined by its implicit paradigm. If the organization in question operates in a mechanistic mode, then it is considered to be a tool of its owner. Its purpose, therefore, would be to serve the purpose of its owner. Performance criteria of a tool, of course, would be efficiency and reliability. The purpose of an organization in the biological mode of operation is survival, and thus its performance criterion would be growth at any cost. Profit as the means of growth finds additional social value and overcomes the negative stigma of the mechanistic era. However, since an organization in a sociocultural mode of operation is considered to be a voluntary association of purposeful members, its purpose would be to serve its members and its environment by doing more and more with less and less.

But, as stated so elegantly by Milton Friedman, ultimately "the business of a business is business." For designers of business architecture, understanding the vision of the desired future of the enterprise and its business model are, therefore, of the utmost importance.

The initial sketches of a vision of the desired future can usually be put together after the first iteration of idealized design. Although we are told that visions are escape mechanisms of daydreamers, we must recognize that without a vision there will be no sense of direction. Without a vision, all possibilities would have equal value; there would be no basis to judge the relevancy of the emerging opportunities.

The business model, on the other hand, defines the way a business generates value, creates a deliverable package and exchanges it for money. Nowadays, amazing originalities shown in developing new business models are radically influencing traditional business concepts. Consider, for example, the case of the search engine, Google, which, by providing free service to a group of consumers, can make enough money from advertisers to exceed the value of giants such as General Motors. Creating a multibillion-dollar business to create, package and sell operating systems independently from computer hardware, as is done by Microsoft, was inconceivable for those of us who worked for IBM during the 1960s. In the early 1990s, I was involved with a Fortune 100 Company as a consultant in the acquisition of a $10 billion business. The total sum of money that all service providers—legal, financial and management—charged the client was less than $500,000. It was based on actual time spent multiplied by an hourly rate. Today, the same task would cost over $200 million in commission, based on a business model that works on percentage.

In general, business is usually defined in terms of three dimensions: know-how, or technology that is transformed into a set of tangible products or services and delivered via an access mechanism to its target customers or markets. Business architecture defines the nature of relationships among the three dimensions of technology, product, and market.

Traditionally, one of these dimensions has been designated as primary, forcing the other two into subordinate roles.

When the product defines the business, technological requirements and the markets to be served are determined by product characteristics. Alternative technologies are sought for making the product, and different markets are sought for selling the product (Figure 7.5).

The success of a product-based business is usually measured by the success of its product divisions. That is why everything is easily compromised and subordinated to the product. However, when the potential value of a given

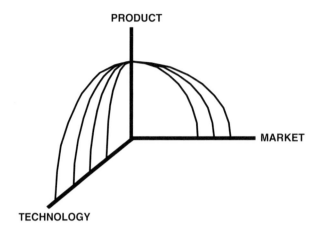

FIGURE 7.5 Business Defined by Product

technology somehow becomes more than the value of the product it supports, the business faces a dilemma.

Unfortunately, experience shows that, in these cases, technology has always been compromised. In a product-based business, the product manager is the boss. Technology is seen only as a competitive advantage for their product; therefore, technology will never get the chance to realize its potential in the context of a product-based business. Quite a few cases support this assertion, but the most conspicuous is the fate of the Apple operating system (the famous graphic interface). This phenomenal operating system had been used exclusively to sell Apple computers, when its potential all along had been much higher than the maximum potential of the products it supported. This was proven by Microsoft, whose claim to fame, Windows 95, is the best imitation of the Apple operating system open to be used by all. A second illustration comes from IBM.

It is reported that IBM spent billions to lay off about 200,000 people (some say the best available knowledge workers) but did not consider capitalizing on its advanced "digital technology" and state-of-the-art "electronic packaging" to become the major player in the most potentially explosive markets of the future.

When the market is used as the basis for defining the business, the characteristics of the market determine the product mix and the types of skills and technologies required to produce it (Figure 7.6). Procter and Gamble, for example, provides as many of the products sold in supermarkets as it can profitably make. Pharmaceutical companies make a variety of different products for the same market segment.

However, the trauma of the defense industry, when its market collapsed overnight, was another confirmation that the price tag on selecting a single pattern of existence is very high. The industry's inability to take advantage of its access to and knowledge of emerging Internet technology was not

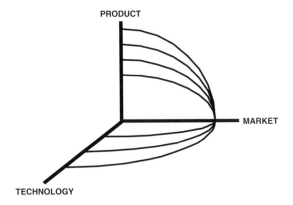

FIGURE 7.6   Business Defined by Markets

surprising. Managing technology requires a different set of criteria than those necessary to manage products and/or markets.

Finally, when the business is technologically defined, a variety of products are developed around a given core technology, using the same base of know-how, and sold in different markets (Figure 7.7). For example, 3-M defines itself as being in the "sticking" business. The company evolves around technologies used to bind different things together (from Scotch tape and composite structures to electronic packaging). Using its materials science and processing technology, it continually searches for new products that it can produce and offer in different markets. Managing a technology-based business not only requires broader planning vision, but also the ability to use the same knowledge in different contexts.

The success or failure of each approach depends on its compatibility with the emerging competitive challenge at the time. Because competitive games

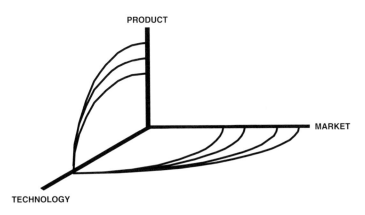

FIGURE 7.7   Business Defined by Technology

change over time, they force companies to switch their strategic emphasis from one dimension to another. Since each strategy has organizational implications in terms of authority and responsibility, changes in strategy require changes in organizational structure and the dominant culture of the business. As competition intensifies and the changes become more frequent, the uni-dimensional approach of product or market or technology becomes even more ineffective. Shifts from one dimension to another in search of an effective competitive base cause organizational turmoil and strategic confusion. The waste and frustration associated with periodic restructuring have necessitated a search for alternative solutions.

The interactive systems architecture uses product, market, and technology in an interactive mode. It recognizes the necessity for achieving competitive advantage in all three dimensions of market, product, and technology (Figure 7.8).

The objective is to capitalize on the totality of the value chain and actively generate synergy among the three dimensions. An interactive architecture is based on managing the interactions among technology, product, and markets.

The emerging multidimensional structure and multiple business cultures dissolve the need for subordination or sub-optimization around any one business dimension, eliminate periodic restructuring, and shift from one dimension to another in search of an effective competitive base.

In an unpredictable, turbulent environment, the viability of any design will depend on its capability to explore and exploit emerging opportunities all along the value chain. These opportunities, which emerge out of interactions among technology, product, and markets, remain inaccessible to unidimensional cultures and architecture. A platform that identifies the basic dimensions of multicultural architecture is the starting point from which the initial elements of the value chain will evolve. Of course, as the business gains maturity and stability, new elements will be added.

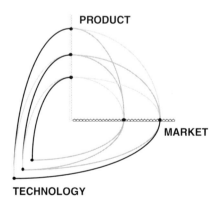

FIGURE 7.8   Business Defined by All Three Dimensions

In formulating the strategic intent of an enterprise, we must remember that competitive advantage is a dynamic and relative phenomenon, different in different contexts and in reference to different classes of users. For example, the element of time, as a basis for competition, is not the same for supermarket shoppers at 10 a.m. and those at 5 p.m. Often the former are spending time, whereas the latter are interested in saving time. What might be an advantage in one context could be a disadvantage in another.

Now recall the concept of "experience curve," which is volume-based learning. An important outcome of learning through an experience curve is process control. This type of control takes considerable time and resources to achieve in a given context. When this context is changed or even modified, the whole body of knowledge that was gained in controlling that particular process is lost. Now assume that, somehow, we have gained the ability to make this know-how context-free and are able to transfer it to different applications, without having to go through the time and resource-consuming notion of the experience curve each time. If we can really do this, then we have created a core competency, an unmatched opportunity for competitive advantage. Formulating and developing state-of-the-art knowledge that can be operationalized in different contexts is, in my opinion, a much more profound way of formulating a competitive strategy. For example, adding digital technology to miniaturization has provided Sony with a whole new dimension in its competitive strategy.

Strategic intent can be formulated as a core competency. In this context, a core competency is the attribute of the organization as a whole; it cannot be housed in a single division. Creation of context-free transferable knowledge requires multiple sources of learning and application.

Functions

To serve its own interest in an exchange, a purposeful system ought to have something to give back to its environment. Therefore, it requires access to a group of potential users with adequate purchasing power who have a need or desire for the product or service it can produce. A true customer, in reality, is a pain in the neck. He/she has something you want; and his/her satisfaction, in competition with other sources of supply, is the price you have to pay in order to get it. Selecting a product-market niche is the first step in defining an enterprise's function and designing its architecture. We must answer the following questions: Whose problem are we trying to solve? What solutions are we offering? How will we access the target customers? And, finally, will the target customers have sufficient purchasing power to pay for this solution?

Competitive advantage is an attribute of outputs produced by an enterprise. It is a difference that makes a difference, for a given class of users, in affecting their choice. And it must be transferable to a value for the provider. To select a desired product-market niche, it is necessary to differentiate the customer base. There are many different ways to segment a market. Each segment reveals something new about the nature of the market and the behavior of the target customers. Use as many criteria as you can to differentiate user characteristics and identify their purchasing habits. The most useful segmentation is the one that identifies:

1. The group of customers for whom the desired properties of the product are more compatible with the organization's potential capabilities, and
2. Those potential customers who have a lower stake in the old product system and who, therefore, display less inertia and offer easier access.

Using the traditional bell-shaped distribution curve to differentiate the customer base assumes that the majority in the big category alone defines the market (Figure 7.9). The behavior of this single group, considered normal, is used to determine the desired properties of outputs, while behavior of the smaller groups, considered nerds, are conveniently ignored as insignificant.

Struggle for a share of this monolithic market leads to a game of intense competition among big, powerful players. Increasingly, however, it seems that the nerds are taking over. And the bell-shaped curve is somehow flattening out (Figure 7.10). Targeting and understanding behaviors of the smaller groups that are rapidly emerging provides the best, and sometimes only,

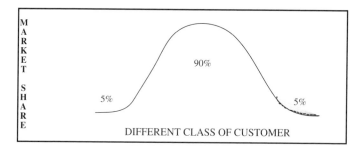

FIGURE 7.9   Traditional Assumptions on Distribution of Customer Base

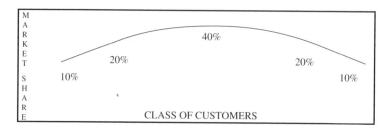

FIGURE 7.10   Emerging Distribution of Customer Base

window of opportunity for a new player to successfully enter the game and skillfully avoid the intense competition.

Structure

Traditionally, organizational theory deals with two types of relationships: 1) responsibility (who is responsible for what), and 2) authority (who reports to whom).

Structure, so conceived, can be represented by a two-dimensional chart in which boxes represent responsibilities and levels and lines represent the loci and flow of authority. (Figure 7.11)

The criteria used for dividing the whole into areas of responsibility, and for determining their relative importance (line of authority), represent the major differences among organization theories. These criteria, not surprisingly, have evolved primarily around three components of a system: input (technology), output (products), and environment (markets).

Depending on the nature of the competitive game at any given time, a priorities scheme is used to designate one component as primary and the other two as subordinates. For example, when ability to produce was the defining factor of competition, input became the primary concern, rendering market and product subordinate to manufacturing. The marketing era saw the shift of emphasis from production to market, and thus subordination of manufacturing to marketing. It seems that a self-imposed unidimensional concept of organization has prevented realization of a multidimensional alternative.

For a majority of designers, the unidimensional mode of organization based on structurally defined tasks, segmentation, and hierarchical coordination of functions seems to be the only acceptable way of organizing work. A predominant management culture continues to value command and control very dearly, and considers any form of variety in the organizational structure unacceptable, wasteful, and at best, impractical.

The multidimensional structure assumes that the three common criteria—input (technology), output (products), and environment (markets)—

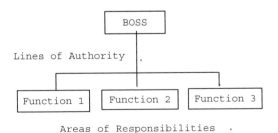

FIGURE 7.11   Authority and Responsibility

are complements. Treating them as interdependent dimensions and managing their interactions eliminates the need for periodic reorganization when a change in competitive environment necessitates a change of emphasis from one orientation to another—for example, from products to markets or vice versa.

Accelerating change and the periodic shift of emphasis from one concern to another, force large organizations into constant disruptive reorganizations. The cost of reorganizations, as well as the frustrations and tensions associated with them, generate a desire for stability and a resistance to change.

The viability of any organization depends on its ability to actively adapt to the changing requirements of the emerging competitive game. The ability to adapt requires some form of flexibility and responsiveness, which in turn demands that some degree of redundancy be built into the system.

A modular structure embedded in a multidimensional scheme can achieve the required level of flexibility and redundancy and create an adaptive, learning system by shifting its attention from micro-managing the parts (power over) to macro-managing the interactions (power to do).

Power-to-do is what organization is all about. It should not be confused with power-over. Power-to-do is the foundation of organizational potency and duplication of power, while power-over is about domination. Potent organizations are not built on impotent principles. Power-to-do multiplies when it is duplicated in special purpose modules. These modules enjoy considerable freedom as long as they meet the interface and functional requirements of the larger system of which they are a part. In any system, it is differentiation that keeps the system alive and potent. Organizations that differentiate and integrate create real value for themselves and others.

In my experience, multidimensional, modular design is the most practical means of handling complexity and uncertainty. It makes it feasible to implement a complex design without getting lost in the process. Multidimensional, modular structure consists of a set of distinct, but interrelated, platforms. Each platform represents a dimension of the system signifying unique context, mode of operation, and a predefined set of performance criteria and measures. Each platform hosts a set of special-purpose modules with the same set of behavioral characteristics. Relationships and the interfaces among platforms are explicitly defined, integrating them into a concept of the whole. Parts operate as independent systems with the ability to be relatively self-controlling and act as responsible members of a coherent whole with the ability to respond effectively to the requirements of the containing system.

For example, a technology platform provides a friendly environment for "component builders." Component builders are modules that usually host a core technology and, therefore, require a different mode of management and performance criteria and measures than those which are necessary for managing and controlling the marketing modules.

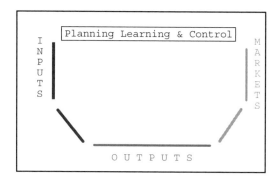

FIGURE 7.12   Multidimensional Modular Design

The organization, so conceived, then becomes capable of expanding or contracting by the addition or deletion of replaceable modules that have the means of vertical and horizontal interactions. The resulting mode of organization is capable of redesigning its structure and redefining its functions, enabling it to exhibit different behavior and produce different outcomes in the same or different environments. This means work can be organized in a variety of ways, and indeed an organizational choice does exist.

Figure 7.12 is an outline of the Multidimensional Modular Design.

Outputs Dimension

Responsibility for achieving an organization's end is vested in the output dimension. The output dimension or platform consists of a series of general purpose, semi-autonomous, and ideally self-sufficient units charged with all of the activities ultimately responsible for achieving an organization's mission and production of its outputs. Note that, for simplicity, the semi-autonomous, self-sufficient, and purposeful units are referred to as modules. Modules are self-sufficient and autonomous to the degree that the integrity of the whole system is not compromised.

Each output module represents a specific level in the hierarchy of multilevel purposeful systems (Figure 7.13). It is a miniature of the whole—the larger system of which it is a part.

Because each module may consume scarce resources of its environment, its outputs should be responsive to the needs of the environment. The lowest-level output module is the smallest unit that can be accountable for producing a tangible, measurable output.

Preferably, the performance of an output module should be as independent of the behavior of other peer output modules as possible; it should have enough authority over its resources—money and people—to be responsible

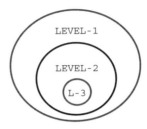

FIGURE 7.13   Multilevel Purposeful Systems

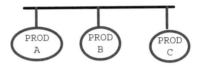

GENERAL PURPOSE OUTPUT MODULES

FIGURE 7.14   Output Dimension

and accountable for its success or failure. It should also be able to retain a percentage of its contributions above a minimum level for incentive and internal development.

Each output module is responsible for making those decisions that affect only its operations. Decisions that impact other units will be made at higher levels with the participation of all affected modules.

An output module is usually conceived as a unit hosting a product, a project, or a program. An effective product module has an entrepreneurial role. It has responsibility for the development, design, marketing, and profitability of the final product. Although they should not be burdened by responsibilities for fixed production facilities, output managers should have the financial authority to select the production facilities and distribution systems.

Including high-capital-intensive production and distribution facilities in a product development module will tie the fates of an organization's major divisions into a single product. The facility-oriented division unwilling to develop any product requiring the use of different facilities will, like the product, experience the cycle of growth, maturity, and inevitable decline. Ideally, the output platform would be a virtual entity with up-to-date information about environmental opportunities and internal competencies. It would have a distinct capability to consider a new set of alternatives and choices that might be available to the organization. Finally, output platform modules should have the ability and the authority to re-engage inputs in a new order.

Inputs Dimension

To create a system that is more than the sum of its parts, the organization must fully use its synergy. Economies of scale, the need for specialization, technological imperative, and development of core technologies are among the reasons why some functions and technologies required by output modules ought to be shared.

These shared services and specialized functions can be provided by groups of special-purpose modules, which together constitute the input dimension of the organization. (Figure 7.15)

For example, designating the manufacturing unit as a profit center in the input dimension not only results in more competitive and flexible facility management, but also provides product managers with the freedom to buy their manufacturing requirements from within or outside the organization without constraint from fixed facilities.

Input modules, in general, are provided with working capital and are expected to earn their operating expenses plus a return on investment by charging the market price for their services.

If insufficiency or unpredictability of demand makes it necessary to provide additional support for an input function, then the general rule is to subsidize the demand instead of the supply. In the early stages of conversion, the operating budget of an input unit may be given to it by means of a purchase contract for its total services.

However, in general, centralization should be avoided unless one or all of the following situations weigh overwhelmingly against decentralization of a particular service.

Uniformity: Some aspects of the system will be centralized when they are common to all or some parts and cannot be decentralized without rendering serious damage to the system's proper functioning. For example, in areas such as measurement systems, where common language and coordination are major concerns, uniformity will serve as a criterion for centralization.

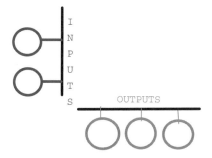

FIGURE 7.15 Input Dimensions

Meanwhile, certain activities that, because of their nature, are deemed indivisible and so require a holistic design can also be centralized. For example, the effectiveness of a comprehensive information system lies in its holism, consistency, real-time access, and proper networking to transfer information as needed to different users. Developing such a system requires cooperation and coordination among all actors in the system.

Economy of Scale: Although economy of scale is generally considered an important factor in creating shared service, the trade-off between centralization and decentralization of each function should be made explicit to ensure that the benefits significantly outweigh the disadvantages before the function is moved to shared services. In this case, it is expected that a service, once centralized, will either generate significant savings for the system as a whole or help those units that would otherwise be unable to afford them on their own.

Core Technologies: Feeling that a certain level of mastery in a given technology will be critical for the enterprise's future success, management may decide to centralize, develop, and make the technology available for all units. Sometimes a technology developed by an output unit has a much greater potential in the marketplace than as a competitive advantage to the product division. In this case, it is management's responsibility to identify it as a core technology and centralize it for full-scale development.

Whatever the justification for centralization, the input units will have to become state-of-the-art and cost-effective providers of choice.

However, a sure way to obstruct the functioning of an input unit is to mix its function with that of control. This practice undermines both the effectiveness of the service function and the legitimacy of the controls.

To protect themselves against the creeping hegemony of service providers and the obvious risks involved in relying on control-driven services, output units resort to duplicating the support services that could otherwise be easily shared and effectively used. Rampant, excessive duplications of services are symptomatic of the natural reaction of operating units to service functions assuming the additional function of control.

On the other hand, disguising a legitimate and necessary control function as a service function transforms the nature of control from learning to a defensive and apologetic act.

Extra care should be taken to ensure that none of the functions of Shared Services undergo a character change and assume control properties. Under the pretext of a need for consistency and uniformity, there is a natural tendency to let the service provider perform the necessary monitoring and auditing function.

This practice has always proved misguided. Providers cannot avoid the slippery slope of wanting, increasingly, to assume a control function. This would obviously scare away users who didn't expect to find a new boss in the guise of a server.

While Shared Services will provide customers with requested services (such as information, benefits, payroll, and billing) it will be the planning and control system that will set the policies and criteria governing these services, as well as conducting the necessary monitoring and enforcing functions to ensure proper implementation of those policies.

Markets Dimension

Market, the third dimension of the organization, is defined as the access mechanism to a class of customers having sufficient purchasing power and an explicitly known need or desire for a given service or product. (Figure 7.16)

The markets dimension is the interface with customers. In most cases, this is where the organization actually happens. Depending on the diversity of the customer base, there might be a need to create a number of costly distribution channels. It then becomes imperative to share these channels with other output units.

Two major functions of the markets dimension are distribution and advocacy. Distribution represents the organization to the outside. Advocacy is responsible for sensing environmental conditions and exploring the expectations of customers. Advocacy serves all those affected by the activities of the organization. Especially important is its role in advocating the consumers' point of view inside the organization.

Distribution and advocacy units may be organized geographically or by market segmentation. However, if one is organized geographically, the other should be based on market segmentation.

Input, Output and Market platforms form an interactive whole engaged in an ongoing process of redesign to create new orders spontaneously as deemed necessary.

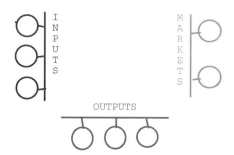

FIGURE 7.16   Inputs, Outputs, and Markets

Because interactions among purposeful actors take many forms (actors may cooperate on one pair of tendencies, compete over others, and be in conflict over a different set, all at the same time), we are dealing with a dynamic structure. In addition, members learn, mature, and change over time. The result is an interactive network of varying members with multiple relationships, recreating itself continuously.

Internal Market Economy

Defining the relationships among input, output, and marketing modules is the most critical task of this conception. Extreme difficulties are encountered when several output units share the vital services of an input or a market unit set up as an overhead center.

The key problem of matrix organizations has also been management of the implicit, ambiguous, and conflicting relationships among the network of input and output units. The "two-boss system" has not only failed to understand the problem, but has also resulted in confusion and frustration.

The answer for this inherent complexity is to create an internal-market environment[1], which converts the relationships among input, output, and market units into the same types of relationships that exist among a supplier, a producer, and a distributor.

While superior-subordinate relationships have traditionally been the only building block for exercising organizational authority, the supplier-customer relationship introduces a new source of influence into the organizational equation. With the supplier-customer relationship emerging only in an internal market environment, the helpless recipient becomes a real customer. Armed with purchasing power, the customer becomes an empowered actor with the ability to influence and interact with his or her supplier in such a way that both parties together can now define the type, cost, time, and quality of the services rendered.

Creation of the internal-market mechanism, and thus a supplier-customer relationship, is contingent upon transforming Shared Services into a performance center. Unlike overhead centers, performance centers do not receive a fixed budget allocated from the top. They have working capital with a variable operating budget. In this model, expenses are proportional to the income generated by the level of services rendered and the revenues received in their exchange. Treating all units as performance centers makes it possible to evaluate every unit at every level in exactly the same way.

These two pairs of horizontal (supplier-customer) and vertical (superior-subordinate) relationships are complementary and reinforce each other. While

---

[1]The idea of *Internal Market* was first advanced by Jay W. Forester (1965), Ackoff (1982). For detail treatment see W. E. Halal, Ali Geranmayeh, John Pourdehnad (1993).

superior-subordinate defines the formal authority dealing with hiring, firing, and promotion, the supplier-customer relationship creates a new source of influence that attempts to rationalize demand.

In the absence of an internal-market environment, there is no built-in mechanism to rationalize demand. An agreeable service provider with a third-party payer creates and fuels an insatiable demand. A disagreeable service provider, on the other hand, triggers prolific duplications of the same services by the potential users. This results in an explosion of overhead expenses in the context of an essentially cost-plus operation. The trend is irrational, and the corrective interventions prove to be ad hoc and ineffective at best.

Creating an internal market not only eliminates growing problems of bureaucratization, but also provides an effective means for dealing with allocation and evaluation problems. Meanwhile, it gives an organization a market orientation by forcing each part to consider the marketing consequences of its actions.

In the internal-market environment, modules ought to have a choice with respect to selling or buying their required services from inside or outside the organization; otherwise, internal buyers or sellers will have a monopolistic advantage. Higher level authority can always override outsourcing by agreeing to pay the cost incurred or the profit lost.

It is useful to review a real life example of converting a traditional organization to one of multidimensional design.

During a design session, a group of executives produced the following organizational chart as the initial structure of their business (Figure 7.17).

When I asked them whether they would mind if I changed their design into the following format (Figure 7.18), they had no objection: "If you like colors [patterns] use as many as you like," one of them said jokingly.

Despite apparent similarities in the two designs, significant differences exist between them.

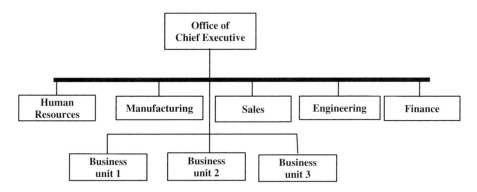

FIGURE 7.17 Traditional Divisional Structure

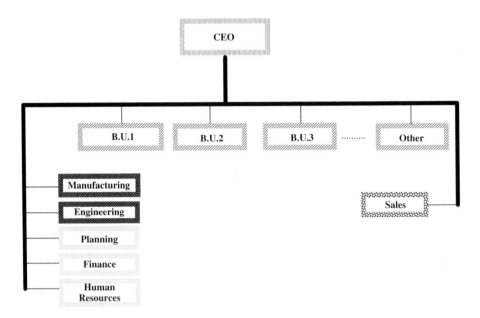

FIGURE 7.18 Multidimensional Representation of the Same Design

Version one represents a design concept concerned only with defining responsibilities and the line of authority. The case at hand is a mix of functional and divisional units all reporting to the CEO. The relationships among peer groups are conveniently ignored, as though the organization were an aggregate of unrelated parts. This is a linear conception of structure in which a single pair of a superior-subordinate relation is used as the building block of the organization. But, to produce the structure that fits our purpose here—that is, to design a business architecture—parts not only have to be differentiated and their roles clearly defined, but the relationships among all peer units must be explicitly known and understood. This is why version two used color to differentiate the parts and group them according to the roles they would play in the organization. In this context, a part can assume the function of input, output, market access, or control.

To demonstrate the flow and relationship in the value chain, the following format was adopted to underline three basic relationships among peer units (Figure 7.19):

1. Output units are in competition with one another to such a degree that animosity among sister organizations is often much higher than it is with outside competitors. To avoid structural conflict, output units should operate virtually independently of one another, with a modular structure and adequate levels of autonomy and self-sufficiency.

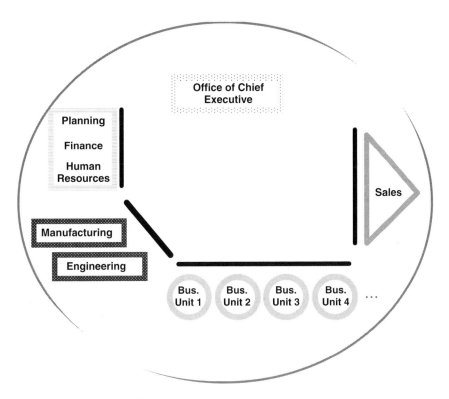

FIGURE 7.19 Value Chain Relationships

2. Relationships between each output unit and the input and market access units are complementary. It is the same relationship that exists between a producer and its suppliers or between a producer and its distributors. An effective interface with all-out cooperation between them is a must to generate a competitive throughput. If the output unit is to be held accountable for the ultimate outcome and proper integration of the operation, it must have some kind of leverage on both input and market access units to influence their behavior. We will revisit this notion when we discuss organizational processes and measurement systems.

3. The relationships between control units and all the input, output, and market access units are one-way, usually bureaucratic and more or less autocratic in nature. This is why combining a service function with a control function in a single unit, which is usually done under the pretext of coordination, is a design for failure. For example, when any one of the service functions, such as HR, Legal, or even Information Services, becomes provider and controller at the same time, both the control and service functions will be undermined.

Finally, the linear framework of version one lends itself to a unidimensional concept of system architecture where product, market, and technology are arranged in sequential order based on their relative importance. The criteria used for determining the order of subordination defines the major differences between alternative designs. The second version attempts to create an interactive relationship among technology (input), product (output), and market (access). This requires a multidimensional structure.

To create a multidimensional structure, we need at least two distinct types of relationships. A single superior-subordinate pair can produce only a unidimensional structure; despite claims to the contrary, a matrix organization is not a multidimensional design. Two-boss systems fail because they create confusion in the power system. Using the superior/subordinate pair in two contexts creates frustration, not interaction.

For interaction among peer units, the interactive paradigm uses two distinct pairs of relationships: 1) superior-subordinate, and 2) customer-provider. This becomes real and meaningful when, and only when, the user of the service has the power of the money and controls the payment to the provider. This requires that providers function with a variable budget paid by the customer in exchange for their services. If a provider of a service has a fixed budget, which is paid directly by the boss, then the boss becomes the customer as well. In this case, the user of the service has no power and customer-provider relations is a meaningless phrase.

Customer-provider relationships can be forged between input, output, and marketing units in the context of an internal market mechanism. If properly operationalized, the customer-provider relationship will effectively supplement the superior-subordinate pair and provide the organization with a much desired market orientation. This means each part of the organization not only understands but also lives with the marketing consequences of its actions.

In this context, the unit of organization is a performance center, a value-adding link in a well-defined value chain. Although each unit has only a single boss (the superior-subordinate relation with its containing system), it can have several customers and suppliers. Customers are the sole source of its operating income.

The measure of each unit's performance includes not only its own operations but also the contribution it makes to the success of its internal suppliers. All units have working capital and operate on a variable budget dependent on the throughput of the system.

PROCESSES

The essential characteristic of a throughput and organizational processes were discussed in Chapter 3 (Dimensions of Social Systems). Recall that throughput processes are those directly concerned with the actual output of the organization. Organizational processes, on the other hand, are concerned with creating integration, alignment, and synergy among the organization's parts. In this context, a Planning, Learning, and Control System is an integral part of designing architecture.

Planning, Learning and Control System

An organization's decision-making process is reflected in its mode of planning. Planning, as traditionally practiced, is either one or a combination of two dominant types: reactive and proactive.

Reactive planning is concerned with identifying deficiencies and designing projects and strategies to remove or suppress them. It deals with parts of an organization independently of each other.

An organization is a system whose major deficiencies arise from the way its parts interact, not from the actions of its parts taken separately. Therefore, it is possible, and even likely, that improving the performance of each part of an organization separately will bring down the organization's performance as a whole.

Proactive planning consists of two major activities: prediction and preparation. The objective is to forecast the future and then prepare the organization as well as possible. Unfortunately, such forecasts are chronically in error, because the social, economic, and political conditions, as well as the behavior of supplier, consumer, and competitor, are affected by what the planned-for organization, and others like it, do. Therefore, it is precisely such plans, taken together, that shape the future.

Systems methodology rests on the interactive type of planning, which assumes that the future is created by what we and others do between now and then. Therefore, the objective is to design a desirable future (idealization) to invent or select ways of bringing it about (realization).

The planning and control system is the executive function of the organization. It oversees the operation of the whole system by managing the interaction among the dimensions. The executive function also has responsibility for creating a vision, generating a shared image of a desired future, and providing the leadership for achieving the organizational mission. It has final responsibility for financial viability, technological ability, and human effectiveness of the organization as a whole.

In the context of designing business architectures, we must deal with two fundamental requirements of idealized design: technological feasibility and operational viability.

Technological Feasibility

Although an ideal conception, idealized design is not science fiction. All of the technologies involved in the design of the throughput processes must be available. At this stage, designers must be sufficiently familiar with the throughput processes to assure themselves of its technological feasibility.

Operational Viability

A system design must be viable in the existing environment. To assess the viability of a business enterprise requires a measurement system. In fact, defining the characteristics of the measurement system is the last connecting piece of the design. Because the members of an organization are purposeful, their patterns of interaction cannot be predefined; therefore, they are not subject to mechanistic concepts of design. Management of multi-minded systems requires that the interests of its purposeful members be aligned. The measurement system is a critical enabler for this process.

Measurement System

To develop an effective measurement system, we need to deal iteratively with two elements: performance criteria and performance measures (Figure 7.20).

Performance Criteria

Performance criteria are the expression of what is to be measured and why (for example, how success is defined). The selection process involves identifying dimensions and/or variables relevant to an enterprise's successful operation.

Relevancy is the most important concern in selecting performance variables. Traditionally, the overriding concern has been with the accuracy of measures. Because we find it difficult to accurately measure what we want, we have chosen to want what we can accurately measure. Unfortunately, the more accurate the measure of the wrong criteria, the faster the road to disaster. We are much better off with an approximation of relevant variables than with precise measurement of the wrong ones.

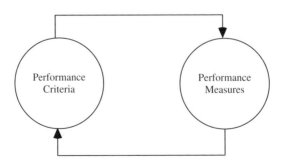

FIGURE 7.20 Relation between Performance Criteria and Performance Measures

Viability of a business enterprise is an emergent property. It is the product of the interactions of various entities. It cannot be measured directly (i.e., by using any of the five senses). We can measure only its manifestation. Growth is the most popular one, but some prefer return on investment, while others like net present value of future cash flows.

Unfortunately, using the single manifestation of a phenomenon as the measure of an emergent property has proved misleading and very costly. For example, if a business is successful, chances are it will grow; however, growth alone does not mean that the business is successful. The same outcome (manifestation) could be produced by different means. Lousy acquisitions can produce high rates of growth but at the same time destroy the company.

Therefore, when we measure an emergent property by means of its manifestation we must do it along several dimensions. For example, concern for people, when combined with the concern for production, has quite a different manifestation from the one without it. Dr. Blake (1968) in his famous work, *The Managerial Grid*, demonstrated how the nature of a variable in a "1.9 orientation" is different from the nature of the same variable in a "9.9 orientation." Freedom without justice leads to chaos, while justice without freedom leads to tyranny.

Performance Measures

Performance measures are the operational definition of each variable—that is, how each variable is to be measured specifically. For example, if we have identified capacity utilization as a performance criterion, then turnover ratio might be designated as its measure. Now we would need a procedure for calculating turnover ratio (e.g., divide sales by assets, divide revenues by assets, or divide output by input).

An important consideration in selecting any measure is its simplicity. The cost of producing a measurement should not exceed the value of the information it generates. Although objective measures are preferable, if the cost of obtaining an objective measure is prohibitive, then use a subjective one. Remember that collective subjectivity is objectivity (provided that collectivity represents a variety of value systems). For example, in evaluating the performance of a gymnast we rely on the collective subjectivity of a number of different judges.

Development of effective performance measures is easier said than done. More often than not, the operational definitions are left vague and ambiguous, even when the underlying concepts are relatively simple, such as minimizing the cost. The usual practice of allocating overhead to various operating units demonstrates how an innocent matter of a convenience produces unintended consequences.

The criteria for allocation of overhead are usually based on conventional wisdom. Factors such as space occupied by a unit, or the labor content of a production process, are among the most popular. Because overhead usually constitutes more than 40 percent of the total cost, we should not be surprised to see that these variables (space and direct labor) are the ones targeted for cost reductions. The fact that allocation rules were only a convention doesn't matter anymore. Once the allocation criteria become a rule, their relation with generation of cost, by default, is assumed to be causal, as demonstrated by the following case.

A large supermarket chain decided to close down 10 of its stores because the accounting system showed they were not covering their allocated overheads. Because the shutdown had no effect in reducing overhead, the remaining stores then had to carry a larger share of the overhead. This in turn put a few more of the stores in the red, and they too were subsequently closed. The company was gradually withdrawing from the market. Then a new design was developed. Each store became responsible for its own operation without having to worry about any artificial overhead allocated to it. The surplus generated by each store was then passed on to the corporation as the income of the executive office. This made the executive office a profit center responsible for managing its operation, or so-called overhead, within the bounds of its income and the profit it needed to generate to meet the cost of its capital.

This situation is by no means atypical. With the prevalence of allocation rules based on labor, pressure is unduly shifted to direct labor. The default reaction is to lay off productive manpower. If the police department is facing deficits, policemen are the first to be fired. If schools are in financial trouble, the number of teachers is reduced. Reduction of operating units does not automatically reduce overhead, as management seems to assume. On the contrary, it increases the burden of the remaining units until the whole system comes to a halt. In the mid-1970s, when per capita income was the conventional measure of development, sudden increases in oil prices produced instantly-developed nations. Because this was not acceptable, a new set of indicators had to be developed. We now have a whole series of indicators that substitute for development, such as per capita steel production, per capita consumption of fuel, etc. It is not surprising, then, to find national development policies aimed at improving these measures, usually at an incredible cost to the society at large. Yes, winning is fun. But to win, one has to keep score. And the way one keeps score defines the game.

Viability Matrix

The following viability matrix (Table 7.1) is a framework for identifying the relevant dimensions—performance variables—for measuring a business's viability or the different aspects of an operation.

TABLE 7.1   Viability Matrix: Identifying Dimensions and Variables

	Structure (Inputs)	*Function (Outputs)*	*Environment (Markets)*	*Process (Know-how)*
Throughput	Capacity Utilization Profitability	Attributes of the Outputs • Cost • Quality • Availability	Access Mechanism Reliability of Demand	Throughput Capability • Waste • Cycle time • Safety • Control
Synergy	Default Values of the Culture	Compatibility of Performance Criteria	Credibility in the Market-place: Relations with: • Suppliers, • Creditors, • Customers	Value Chain Analysis Reward Systems Value-added Ratio
Latency	Bench Strength Core Knowledge	Product Potency	Market Potential Intensity of Competition	Early Warning System Planning Process

The first dimension of this matrix identifies the variables that define the organization as a whole:

- Structure (inputs)
- Function (outputs)
- Environment (markets)
- Process (technology)

The second dimension of the viability matrix identifies processes that define the totality of the management system:

- Throughput (production of the outputs)
- Synergy (management of interactions, adding value)
- Latency (creating the future)

The following definitions clarify some of the variables I have used in developing the scheme.

Capacity Utilization: Turnover ratio is a good indicator of capacity utilization. Compared to industry standards and best in class, it can signal the existence of an excess capacity that can be the major source of malfunctioning and fluctuation in the system.

Profitability: A dynamic and interrelated model of operating income, operating expense, investment (hard and soft), cash flow, and cost of capital.

Attributes of the Outputs: Outputs are defined in terms of a quantifiable delivery of goods or services in time and space. It is measured on three dimensions: price, quality, and availability (time).

Reliability of Demand: Demand for a product is reliable if the amount to be purchased can be predicted reasonably and if actors beyond a firm's influence do not create unexpected fluctuations.

Throughput Capability: The level of integration and effectiveness of activities required for the delivery of goods and services to satisfied customers is measured by cycle time, waste reduction, safety, and competency of critical processes.

Default Value of the Culture: The degree to which members accept responsibility and act with authority; duplication of power, assumptions regarding the source of value, nature of competition, and relationship between equality and competence.

Credibility in the Marketplace: A firm is credible when it can take actions its stakeholders will initially accept on good faith alone, i.e., relationships with customers. This is the reflection of the firm and its sound relationships with customers, suppliers, and creditors.

Value Chain Transaction Index: A model for explicitly measuring the total contributions that a business unit makes to the profitability of the whole organization. The model recognizes not only the unit's own profitability, but also its contribution to the profitability and/or success of other units within the context of a value-chain architecture.

Value-added Ratio: A calculation of the value a unit produces in comparison to the value it consumes. The value a unit consumes is adjusted to reflect the cost of the resources, the amount and kind of inputs (scarce or excess resources) the unit consumes, and whether they are obtained internally or externally. The value a unit produces is also modified to recognize the contribution of each line in its product/market mix. For example, to encourage new product/new market introductions, one might multiply revenues generated by selling a new product in a new market by 1.2.

Reward System: A priority scheme superimposed on the measurement system, which will allow the organization to assign priorities to particular variables (activities) and thus influence the behavior of the actors toward achieving organizational goals.

Product Potency: Defines the degree to which the product meets a variety of customer needs and desires, in absolute terms as well as relative to competitors' and substitute products.

Market Potential: A market has potential when there is a real and sustainable need and sufficient (size) or growing purchasing power to satisfy those needs.

Intensity of Competition: Competition is intense when the supply of a product is greater than the demand, and it is easy to enter but difficult to exit the market.

REALIZATION: SUCCESSIVE APPROXIMATION

Idealized design evolves on the assumption that the system has been destroyed overnight and that the designers have been given the opportunity to recreate the system from a clean slate. The only condition is that the outcome be technologically feasible and operationally viable.

The realization of the design has to take place in a real-world environment. Therefore, we must identify all the constraints that might interfere with proper implementation.

It is crucial to the success of the whole redesign effort that all involved demonstrate the highest degree of candor in identifying any reservations they may have, subjective or otherwise, about the successful realization of the design at this time. If there is one juncture in the entire process of idealized design where nothing, not even an imaginary hang-up or second-guessing, should be spared, this is it. Anything likely to inhibit the implementation is strongly encouraged to be put on the table, shared, and dealt with right then and there.

The constraints to realization usually fall into the following three distinct categories (Figure 7.21).

Type I Constraints

Type I constraints cannot be removed within the existing framework. Such constraints would require revisions and improvisations of the design in order to create a target design capable of being implemented. Target I would be the first approximation of the idealized design. If necessary, subsequent approximations will identify Target II and Target III generations of the idealized design.

REALIZATION : SUCCESSIVE APPROXIMATION

Identify constraints which prevent achievement of the ideal design:

	Type I	Type II	Type III

Behavioral
rational
  • measurement & reward system
  • those responsible for change benefit
    from existing order
emotional
  • fear of unknown/uncertainty
  • mistrust/lack of cooperation
  • apathy (hopelessness)
cultural
  • self-imposed constraint (default value)
	constraints that cannot be removed under existing conditions	constraints whose removal requires extensive preparation	constraints that can be removed now if the designers so desire

Functional
technical
  • inadequate know-how
product
  • deficiency in product mix
market
  • limited market access
operations
  • critical processes not under control
leadership
  • insufficient influence with critical actors
	Create successive approximations of the ideal design, producing a constrained design which improvises for the elements of the ideal design that could not be realized.	Identify preparatory activities which will remove the constraints to achieving the "constrained" design.	Identify all of the immediate decisions and changes to the existing system so the realization process can start.

Structural
legal
  • legal constraints
components
  • missing critical components			

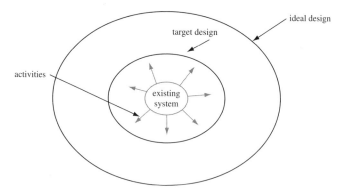

FIGURE 7.21   Realization

It is critical that Type I constraints be continuously monitored so that the target design can further approximate the idealized design as soon as these constraints are removed.

The realization effort, therefore, will not be a one-time proposition. Successive approximations of the idealized state make up the evolutionary process by which the transformation effort is conducted. It may take a number of attempts before the idealized design is reached.

Type II Constraints

Type II constraints are those whose removal will require extensive preparation. They consist of activities that consume considerable time and resources, as well as knowledge and management talent.

These activities usually involve redesign of the products (if necessary), redesign of throughput, and redesign of organizational processes.

Design of the measurement and reward system, with variable budgeting and target costing, seems to be an integral part of all successful realization efforts. This is usually the most resource-intensive part of the change effort. For control purposes, all critical assumptions and expectations about the selected courses of action must be explicitly recorded and continuously monitored.

Type III Constraints

Type III deals essentially with behavioral constraints. These are constraints that can be removed if designers so desire. Selling the idea, removing resistance to change, ensuring acceptance, cultivating support, and providing training are among the efforts targeted at constraints that are basically self-imposed. These constraints, taken together, act as the cultural default of the organization, and their function is to reinforce the status quo. Without a prior foundation of trust and commitment, the system would simply refuse to undergo the planned transformation irreversibly. And in this context, removal of the "second-order machine" is the most critical phase of realizing the idealized design.

DISSOLVING THE SECOND-ORDER MACHINE

Dissolution of the second-order machine consists of two separate, yet interrelated, processes of self-discovery and self-improvement. They involve, first, identifying what is relevant and supportive to our shared vision of a desirable future, and second, diagnosing what turns out to be part of the "mess" and therefore obstructive to our renewal and progress.

Accordingly, successful cultural transformation will involve 1) making the underlying assumptions about corporate life explicit through public discourse and dialogue, and 2) gaining, after critical examination, a shared understanding of what can happen when defaults that are outmoded, misguided, and/or downright fallacious are left unchanged. The process is a high-level social learning and unlearning. Only by the very act of discovering and interpreting our deep-seated assumptions can we see ourselves in a new way. The experience is liberating because it empowers us to reassess the purpose and the course of our lives and, through that, be able to exercise informed choice over our preferred future.

For example, in a design experience with a health-care system, I found that a dominant set of simple organizing assumptions (such as nurses report only to nurses, doctors report only to doctors, or integration is synonymous with uniformity) was at the core of the system's "mess." A candid, open, and in-depth group discussion of the relevance and consequences of these assumptions for the behavior of the heath-care system was the first step toward dismantling the second-order machine and implementing the target design.

Recap

- Idealized design is a process for operationalizing the most exciting vision of the future that the designers are capable of producing. It is the design of the next generation of their system to replace the existing order.
- Although idealizing, we are not dealing with science fiction; our ideal system is designed to be self-sustaining in the current environment. We are not forecasting the future. The ideal design will have sufficient sources of variety to learn and adapt to possible environments.
- Design of a throughput process is essentially technology driven; whereas design of organizational processes depends on the paradigm in use.
- Winning is fun. But to win, one must keep score. And the way one keeps score defines the game.
- The realization effort is not a one-time proposition. Successive approximations of the idealized state make up the evolutionary process by which the transformation effort is conducted.

PART IV

Systems Practice
The Gutsy Few

My phenomenal journey started in the early 1960s. I was studying mechanical engineering at Berkeley when Professor Walter B. Henning, the world's authority in middle-Persian studies, chose me to help him develop a program in middle-Persian culture at U.C. Berkeley. That experience re-formed my understanding of culture and its significance in shaping human systems. After two years of working with Henning, I knew I could not be merely a mechanical engineer anymore. Fortunately, Berkeley was experimenting at the time with systems engineering. After enrolling in an introductory program in cybernetics, information theory, and systems design, I was advised to join IBM if I wanted to pursue this line further.

I was lucky. IBM gave me the opportunity I was hoping for. After five years and 1,400 hours of formal training at IBM education centers, I was on a path to becoming a systems engineer. But it was 20 years of association and finally a partnership with Russ Ackoff—and all that it takes to appreciate his tough, uncompromising standards—that made me a systems designer.

I have practiced iterative design in a variety of contexts and cultures, including Indian tribes in America, Japan, and South Africa. I have even survived a revolution. But in all cases, I have had the luxury of choosing my clients and working only for those I liked. As a result, each case has a special meaning for me and a particular place in shaping my professional life.

Over the years, I have learned more from my clients than I have taught them. Selecting among them has not been easy. For example, eight years with ALCOA (Aluminum Company of America) was a phenomenal learning experience, as challenging as consulting work can be. Material Science Group (MSG), headed by Charlie Ligon, was to create five new startup businesses using technologies developed in ALCOA Lab. Charlie was a demanding, respected leader and a great friend. Ken Blevins (president of ALCOA

Electronic Packaging) and John Star (president of ALCOA Separation Co.) were hard-working, committed, and competent managers. Accepting me as one of their own, they gave me the opportunity to experience firsthand the frustrations, emotional ups and downs, and challenges of creating a high-tech startup business in a conventional, incompatible environment. The experience taught me why the platform for managing a technology business ought to be different from the platform established to manage product businesses.

Working with Clark Equipment Company and Gary Bella, president of the Industrial Truck Division, I learned not to underestimate the value of distribution channels and realized that effective management of the markets requires a distinct platform.

Jerry Goods, president of Super Fresh, and Wendell Young, president of the Clerical Workers Union, with their courage reconfirmed how powerful a shared image of a desired future could be.

I have selected to review in more detail the designs of the Oneida Nation, Butterworth Health Systems, Commonwealth Energy Systems, Marriott Corporation, and Carrier Corporation for the following reasons:

- All five have benefited from the cumulative wisdom of these projects. In all five designs, architecture has been used as a set of distinct but interrelated platforms. Each platform signifies a unique mode of behavior with a predefined set of performance criteria and measures.
- In their diversity, all the designs represent the state of the art. They collectively represent the major areas of concern. Trying times in heath care, tough competition in global manufacturing, deregulation of energy, the collapse of real estate, and the challenges of development seem relevant to the majority of potential readers.

8

The Oneida Nation

The Oneida Nation project has been a beauty. It is probably one of the most emotionally satisfying projects I have worked on. Oneidas certainly have been the kindest, warmest, and most fascinating people to work with. They have treated us as their own and in return we have given them our best.

The members of the Oneida design team who have given their time and ideas generously are Neil Cornelius (general manager, gaming), Debra Doxtator (chairperson), Kathy Hughes (treasurer), and Bruce King (CFO). Artly Skenandore (general manager), with his profound knowledge of the language and the culture and an incredible ability and desire to learn, provided the critical link between past and future.

The members of the work team, without whose commitment, support, and hard work this project would not have been possible, include Jacque Boyle, Elaine Cornelius, Michelle Cornelius, Toni House, Jessica Oudenhoven, Diana Peterson, Terry Pouliquen, and Jackie Smith. Finally, our able project manager, Kathy King, kept us all together with her ample modesty, sincerity, and insight to finish the task.

My old friend and colleague Bijan Khorram has been my partner in three of the four designs selected for this book. That alone should say all that's necessary about his valuable contribution to the outcomes.

This is yet an ongoing project. The version of the design presented here is the outcome of the fifth iteration. The final version is not yet at hand; most probably, it will be significantly enhanced by further iterations.

DESIRED SPECIFICATIONS

The following set of properties represents the desired set of specifications that are expected to guide the development of the intended design.

1. We would learn from our history and combine it with today's emerging values to create a successful way of life that will be a model for other communities to follow.

2. We would like to create a social order that would:

   - Simultaneously encourage social integration and differentiation needed to promote individuality while being mindful of collective identity.
   - Produce goods and services effectively and distribute them equitably while ensuring compatibility among the interests of past, present, and future generations.
   - Identify, develop, and operationalize core competencies that give us distinction and competitive/comparative advantage.
   - Capitalize on the essence of our core values and enable us to evolve them in response to the requirements of present realities and emerging challenges.
   - Encourage the openness of the system to new learning, experimentation, and diversification.
   - Provide us with opportunities to take care of our own and those unable to fend for their basic needs.

3. We would like to see the Nation serve its members and its environment in such a way that:

   - It would project a group identity that will generate internal commitment and external respect.
   - We would be an open culture with a desire to share our rich traditions with others while trying to learn and understand other cultures so we can create mutually beneficial relationships.
   - There would be a complementary educational system to provide each member with opportunities to develop both personally and professionally and aspire to his or her full potential.
   - We would create employment opportunities for each member of our Nation so all can be productively active in generating goods and services that will enhance the quality of our life.
   - There would be a platform for participation and meaningful interaction among our people so that together we can build an integrated Nation with a shared vision of a desired future, in order to empower leaders to effectively pursue and realize our dreams.
   - We would be a sovereign nation with self-determination and self-reliance free from one-sided dependencies.
   - We would be equal partners, of the same height, in every kind of relationship we forge with local, state, and federal authorities.
   - We would be a preferred neighbor in every community we choose to live in, a preferred customer for every provider we choose as our supplier, and a preferred supplier for every customer who chooses to use our products and services.

- We would make the most of our limited resources by outsourcing those services offered more cost-effectively by the environment without imposing undue vulnerability on the Nation.
- We would strike a balance between the material achievement and spiritual fulfillment in our lives.

SYSTEMS ARCHITECTURE

Architecture is a general description of a system. It identifies its vital functions, major elements and their relationships, and the organizational processes that define the nature of the whole. An architecture consists of a set of distinct but interrelated platforms (see Figure 8.1). Each platform represents a dimension of the system signifying a unique context, output, and mode of behavior controlled by a predefined set of performance criteria and measures. These dimensions and their complementary processes are individually necessary and collectively sufficient to give rise to a viable system capable of realizing its desired specifications.

The Oneida Nation's architecture consists of seven dimensions: five operating, one governing, and one judicial. All dimensions of the architecture function under the guidance and leadership of a Business Committee. They are identified as:

- Governance
- Membership Systems
- Learning Systems

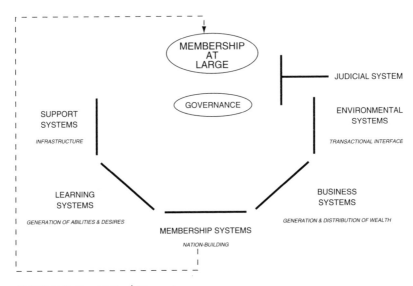

FIGURE 8.1 Critical Dimensions

- Business Systems
- Core Services
- External Environment
- Judicial System

These seven dimensions are identified as necessary and sufficient to create a viable nation capable of realizing its desired specifications.

None of the five operating dimensions should be subordinated to the others. Each one must be treated with the same attention and pursued with the same vigor as the others. However, the performance criteria for these dimensions will not necessarily be the same. For example, whereas units in the Core Services dimension will be performance centers (their budget will be based on a given percentage of total throughput), the units in the Business dimension will all be profit centers. Creation of a new social calculus, in the long term, should facilitate, to the extent that it will be compatible with the interests of the system as a whole, the shift from cost to performance and, eventually, to a profit-centered mode of operation, ultimately maturing them from an input to an output orientation.

GOVERNANCE

For the governance dimension to be effective, the context in which it will be operating should be explicitly specified. According to the Oneida Nation's constitution, all powers, legislative, executive, and judicial, rest with the General Tribal Council (GTC). (See Figure 8.2.) GTC in reality is the meeting of the membership at large. Unfortunately, discharging all three responsibilities directly in a general meeting is a practical impossibility. GTC, therefore, has delegated its authority to an elected body, the Business Committee (BC). Thus, BC, by default, has come to assume all the responsibilities of legislation, executive, and judicial concerns. This was a reasonably practical solution at the time. However, increasing complexities and phenomenal expansion and development of the system in all dimensions have resulted in an unprecedented level of overload for BC. In spite of all efforts for a timely discharge of its responsibilities, BC is faced with an impossible task. Inevitably, it has become the bottleneck.

To reflect the expanded governance responsibility of BC, its name will be changed to the Governing Body. In the new format, the Governing Body will increasingly concentrate on its legislative and policy setting authority and relegate parts of its executive responsibility and judicial function to the relevant platforms of the architecture.

To enhance the monitoring authority of the Governing Body and properly duplicate its power in each platform, a Planning, Learning, and Control Board (PLCB) will be established on each platform. A designated member of the

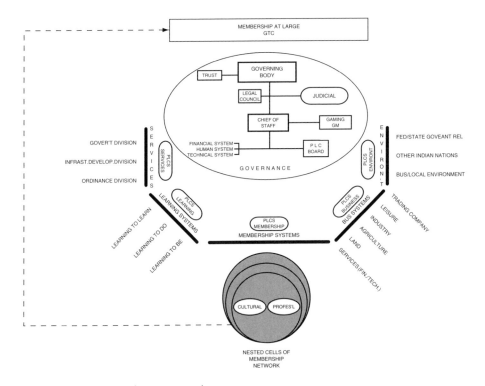

FIGURE 8.2 Oneida Nation Architecture

Governing Body and the Chief of Staff will be on the board of each platform. Creation and composition of the PLC boards will effectively empower the system to be centralized and decentralized at the same time. The focus of Governing Body activities on legislative, policy setting, and oversight, along with the relegation of some of its executive authority to the executive office and operating platforms, will enhance the decisionmaking ability of the system and increase its responsiveness. Delegation of the judicial responsibility to an independent judicial system will also be a welcome move toward proper separation of judicial and executive powers. This separation will also serve as a safety valve. It will channel a major portion of the conflicts to the judicial system where they belong, thus relieving the political system from the untenable situation of being the only channel to absorb the pressures of a polarized nation.

The governance platform will consist of:

- Governing Body
- Chief of Staff
- Planning, Learning, and Control System (PLCS)
- Planning, Learning, and Control Board (PLCB)

Governing Body

The Governing Body is the highest elected authority of the Oneida Nation. On behalf of the membership at large and the General Tribal Council, it acts as the main legislative body and the governing authority of the Nation. It will appoint the Chief of Staff, approve the appointment of the directors of PLCS and general managers, and coordinate and monitor the activities of the operating platforms and judicial system.

Chief of Staff

The Chief of Staff will focus on managing two sets of interactions: 1) internally, dimensions of architecture, and 2) externally, between Oneida and its environment. The Chief of Staff will help define and build consensus around an enduring set of core ideals, purposes, and values that will guide and inspire the organizational culture in relation to itself, its mission, and its community.

The Chief of Staff will also be responsible to:

- Conduct periodic systems analyses and submit Mess Formulation reports to GB and the membership at large.
- Make sure that the needs of the system and its constituent parts are prioritized in terms of their contribution to the national mission.
- Develop and recommend assumptions and policies that will identify the social indicators and set the expected direction and quality of work life of the system.
- Help develop and recommend organizational and departmental standards and measures of performance that are consistent with maintaining a high level of quality of work life.
- Conduct holistic quality assurance audits of the current and contingency game plans of the system.

Planning, Learning, and Control System

To assist the Chief of Staff in carrying out the responsibilities of governance, a Planning, Learning, and Control System will be created. PLCS will consist of a group of experts who are assigned to and operate in three complementary activities: Financial System, Technical System, and Human System.

Director of Financial Systems

The Director of Financial Systems is responsible for making sure that the financial resources of Oneida are safe and their utilization sound. The director will develop financial policies and monitor their implementation, once approved by the Governing Body. To do that, the director will:

- Develop and recommend the criteria, assumptions, and expectations with regard to the operation and management of financial resources.
- Develop and recommend financial policies for resource allocation and management.
- Develop and recommend the standards and measures of performance for resource utilization.
- Identify systemic deviations and initiate corrective action.
- Monitor flows of funds and act as an early warning system.
- Prioritize the investment and divestment needs of the system and its parts.
- Conduct holistic and departmental quality assurance audits of the viability of financial systems and assess their effectiveness.
- Provide the information required by the PLCB to carry out its integrative management function.

The Director of Financial Systems, in addition to managing its core of financial expertise, will supervise the operations of general accounting, grants, and internal audits.

Director of Technical Systems

The Director of Technical Systems, in addition to managing its core of technical experts, will supervise the operations of the information system. Other functions include:

- Help and facilitate development of the system architecture and a detailed design of throughput systems.
- Advocate and coordinate the development and recommendation of the proper standards and measures for assuring organizational effectiveness.
- Monitor and make sure that policies regarding system management and operations, once established, are properly implemented by those involved.
- Develop and recommend policies regarding the collection, operation, integration, dissemination, and management of information.
- Develop and recommend the standards and measures of performance for managing information systems.

Director of Human Systems

Human Systems, in addition to managing its core of human system experts, will supervise the operations of HRD and communications, and will also:

- Define the specifications, directives, and values by which the most qualified, committed, and productive workforce can be attracted, maintained, and motivated to ensure the continued success of the system.
- Monitor significant human systems trends and act as an early warning system.
- Advocate, facilitate, and coordinate the development and recommendation of the human resource policies such as hiring, training, compensation and benefits, career development, and related issues.

Planning, Learning, and Control Board

To create compatibility and manage the interactions among the five operating dimensions of architecture, an integrative function is needed. This integrative function, the critical element of the governance of the system, will include development of master plans and general guidelines concerning the performance of each dimension.

The members of the PLCB will consist of the Chairperson of the Governing Body, Chief of Staff, the Treasurer, the directors of Financial Systems, Technical Systems, and Human Systems, and the five GMs, each representing one of the operating platforms. The PLCB is responsible for 1) defining problems, 2) designing solutions, and 3) making recommendations regarding policies and decision criteria to be approved by the GB. However, the primary function of the PLCB will be to create synergy among the operations of the Membership Systems, Learning Systems, the Business Systems, Core Services Systems, and Environmental Systems.

The nature of control, as intended here, reconceptualizes the traditional notion of control from "supervision" to "learning" and the nature of authority from "power over" to "power to." Effective control involves the duplication of power. Duplication of power will be achieved if the decision process, rather than the individual decisionmaker, is the subject of control. This will happen when decisionmakers collectively develop a shared understanding and ownership of decision criteria in all dimensions.

Learning results from being surprised: detecting a mismatch between what was expected to happen and what actually did happen. If one understands why the mismatch occurred (diagnosis) and is able to avoid a mismatch in the future (prescription), one has learned.

Learning will include an early warning system that will call for corrective action before the problem has occurred. Such a system will monitor, on an ongoing basis, the validity of the assumptions on which the decision was made, the implementation process, and intermediate results.

MEMBERSHIP SYSTEMS

The Membership Systems are about nation building. Membership provides a platform for participation in order to dissolve conflict, create a shared image of a desired future, and empower leaders to act effectively and decisively on behalf of their constituents.

Empowerment

Empowerment is not about sharing of power. Sharing implies a zero-sum relationship and, therefore, abdication of power. Empowerment is duplication of power. It requires a collective understanding of the reasons why we are doing what we are doing. Such a shared understanding not only empowers the members to act in harmony, but also empowers the leaders to act effectively and decisively on behalf of their people.

The role of leadership is as critical here as the role of the people. The leader cannot afford to leave the people behind or fall behind them. The leaders are empowered to the degree of trust and support they generate among their people. The support or trust does not necessarily require conformity or uniformity. It means that members can agree to disagree, providing they understand the decision criteria and are willing to live with the consequences of collective decisions. Development of this political maturity, an ability to convert dichotomy to complementarity, will be the central aim of the Membership Network.

Polarization is, perhaps, the most obstructive feature of a traditional society on the verge of transformation. The march of events, voluntary or not, makes the conventional solutions ineffective, calling into question the efficacy of the traditional leader-follower relationships. Under these circumstances, the seemingly irresolvable dichotomies between tradition versus modernity, collectivity versus individuality, capital formation versus consumption, and openness versus closedness drive the people into opposite camps. The negative consequence of this polarization manifests itself not only in an obvious breakdown of communication, but, most importantly, in the hidden sense of paralysis and widespread inability to act. At a time when the Nation must be in its most proactive mode, it tends to absolve (benign neglect) rather than dissolve the conflicts (seek complementarities). The purpose of the membership dimension is to empower the Nation out of this dilemma.

Nation building is an evolutionary process. It is participative, highly time consuming, and uniquely value driven. Contrary to road building, it is not a one-time proposition. It cannot be brought about by declaration. Dealing with "why" questions, nation building is necessarily an agreement on a set of organizing principles and common objectives.

The Tie that Bonds

The distinction between a system and an aggregate is the bond that ties the otherwise scattered elements together. The strongest bond that holds a nation together is a shared image of a desired future and a set of organizing principles reflecting the essence of the system's unique historical experiences and its value system.

The membership dimension provides structures and processes that deal with political empowerment, participation, legitimacy, consensus building, self-determination, and sovereignty. As such, the membership dimension is the most critical dimension of the architecture. In a sense, it is about the Nation itself. Direct involvement creates a feeling of nationhood; thereby it makes an environment in which members can and will make a difference in the evolution of the system.

The real challenge to building a viable social system is the ability to create unity in diversity, meeting the varying interests of independent members operating in an interdependent whole. Generation of agreement on a series of organizing principles will permit the Nation to act in spite of its diversity. Society's need for integration is as legitimate as an individual's need for differentiation. Integration and differentiation are two sides of the same coin. Alone, they self-destruct. Together, they synergize.

Collectivity at the expense of individuality leads to totalitarianism and suffocation. Individualism at the expense of collectivity leads to chaos and social Darwinism. In the long run, the society and the individual either stand together or fall separately. A win/win relationship is achieved not through zero-sum or even compromise. For both of them to win requires reconceptualization of the nature and the relationship of the whole and the parts. You cannot build a great society with belittled people just as you cannot build a great people in a belittled society. The greatness of each is preconditioned by the other. An environment should be created in which each can help itself by helping the other.

Once again, the question is not a self-imposed choice between the past and the future; that answer would be an easy one, albeit with disastrous consequences. Roots as well as wings are indispensable to a viable nation. None should come at the expense of the other. The need to fly should not mean rootlessness, just as the need to attach should not negate the need for flight.

Membership Network

Design of the Membership Network will consist of a multilevel network of nested Membership Cells. Each cell will have nine members who will engage in a process of deliberation to produce a shared understanding about the realities facing the Nation. Working together, the cell members will try to understand the context (how the environment is evolving), define the problem (formulating the mess), and produce a recommended solution (designing a solution). The outcome of each cell, once agreed upon, will be passed on either to the lower-level cell for further deliberation or higher-level cells for integration with others. The process will continue until all the critical issues facing the Nation are collected, deliberated, resolved, and bought into by all the active members participating in their respective cells at different levels of the Membership Network.

To start the development of the Membership Network, up to nine primary cells will be initially created. A designated member of GB along with a selected member of the Management Team and a designated member of the Work Team will form the initial composition of these primary cells. Each cell will then recruit six primary members from the membership at large (preferably from active participants of the Tribal Council). The primary cell of the Membership Network will therefore consist of 81 members working in nine cells.

Each one of the members of the primary cells, after sufficient deliberation and generation of consensus, will form other nine-member cells operating on the second level of the network. The second level will therefore be made up of 81 cells consisting of 729 members. The third level of the Membership Network will be populated by 6,561 participants working in 729 cells. It seems that a three-level network will provide adequate national coverage. If need be, other successive levels could be added to the Membership Network until every eligible member is included and nobody is left out.

The Interactive Design document will serve as the starting point of the process of deliberation. After the design team provides the first version of the design, the Governing Body will deliberate on it to generate necessary consensus. Then the design will be taken to the primary cells, where 81 active members of the Tribal Council will have their chance to produce the second iteration of the interactive design. The second iteration will then move down to the second level of the Membership Network for the next iteration. Successive iterations will be continued throughout the network until all active members can have a chance to participate in the design process and make a commitment to its implementation.

The realization of this network (Figure 8.3) requires an effective management and support system responsible for such critical complementary services as:

- Collecting and feeding relevant issues and background materials.
- Providing logistics, scheduling meetings, and keeping members informed of upcoming events and agendas.
- Taking, recording, and following up on the minutes of the meetings.
- Facilitating the processes and making sure that participants understand the protocols and implications of their assigned roles.

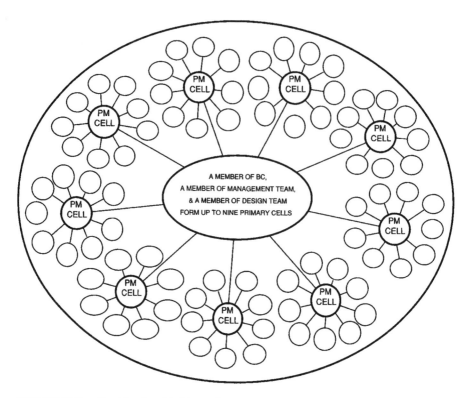

FIGURE 8.3   The Membership Network

Consensus-Building Process

Creation of a platform for participation, although necessary, is not sufficient for proper bonding of the membership. To enhance the bonding process, we strongly recommend that a new approach based on Oneida Nation's traditional means of consensus building, which so serendipitously and beautifully corresponds with the emerging notion of systems thinking, be adopted.

To appreciate the underlying assumptions and organizing principles of systems thinking, it is important to note the following concerns:

1. Appreciate the all-important context. We have a tendency to start with the problem as though it exists in isolation. A phenomenon that can be a problem in one context may not be one in another. Likewise, a solution that may prove effective in a given context may not work in another. In a systems view, neither the problem nor the solution is regarded free of context.

2. There is a need to deal with the problem independent of the solutions at hand. We have a tendency to define the problem in terms of the solution we already have. We fail most often not because we fail to solve the problem

we face, but because we fail to face the right problem. Rather than doing what we should, we do what we can. In the systems view, it is the solution that has to fit the problem, not vice versa.

3. There is a need to redesign as opposed to invoking the same set of predefined solutions. We have a tendency to entertain only the tried and true. If a solution is unprecedented, it is automatically rejected as suspect. The habitual default of so-called problem solving, left to its own devices, can turn into a self-reproducing vicious circle militating against any difference that can make a real difference. Thus, in the name of reinventing the future, we keep on reproducing the past, wondering all along why it is that history repeats itself as though no lesson has ever been learned!

Separation of the three phases of understanding the context, defining the problem, and designing the solution is, therefore, an important element of systems methodology. Viewed in this context, problem solvers and problem formulators exhibit two different sets of characteristics (Figure 8.4). Problem solvers are scientifically oriented. They have a tendency to find similarities in things that are different. They are generalizes. They are concerned with the immediate result as a check on the efficacy of the solution. Problem formulators are artistically oriented. They have a tendency to find differences among things that are similar. They are particularizers. They are concerned with the consequences.

Both aspects are important. They complement each other. The two, however, should not be confused or mixed up. The more the two activities are kept

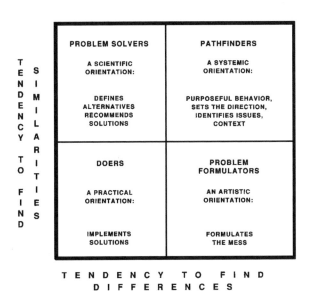

FIGURE 8.4 Complementary Tendencies

separate, the higher the likelihood of effecting a dissolution of the problem as a way of achieving a higher-order synthesis. For a problem to be actually dissolved, two other actors are required: innovators and doers. Innovators are pathfinders. They see the bigger picture. They have a systematic orientation. They exhibit purposeful behavior. They set the direction based on which 1) problems are defined and formulated, and 2) solutions are synthesized and integrated to make sure that they complement each other by getting unified into synergistic wholes.

Doers, however, are practitioners. They are concerned neither with the bigger picture nor the long-term consequences. They enjoy producing, or doing things, using a predefined algorithm. On the other hand, a reflection on the recorded history and the culture of the Oneida Nation points to a similar process of consensus building.

Central to the historical experience, this process was adopted by the Great Law of Peace as an effective means for the great council where governing inter-clan communication, conflict resolution, decision making, and generating agreement was done. It is referred to as "getting to be of the same mind" (Figure 8.5).

Using different attributes and characteristics for each of the three symbols of turtle, wolf, and bear, the culture, to its credit, had identified and separated the three distinct roles of pathfinder, problem formulator, and problem solver. The role played out by the wolves is that of pathfinder/synthesizer. Wolves display purposeful behavior by setting the direction, dealing with "why" questions, identifying relevant issues, and defining the agenda and context before they are presented to the turtles, the problem formulators, to define them. The defined problems are, in turn, passed on by the turtles to the bears, the problem solvers. Bears generate alternatives and recommend solutions. Solutions are returned to the turtles to check on their relevance and potency before referring them back to the wolves to check on their relevance. Wolves are finally responsible for integrating the solutions, keeping the

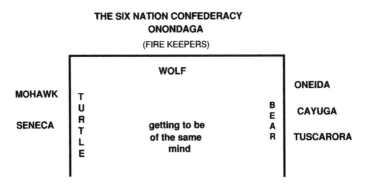

FIGURE 8.5   Getting to Be of the Same Mind

records, and ratifying and communicating the final agreements. Wolves keep the fire alive by motivating and monitoring actions.

Considering that the unit of a social system is not so much the individual but the role one plays in different settings, the wolf/turtle/bear role playing presents an excellent vehicle for group learning and consensus building, the essential ingredients of nation building.

Back to the Future

The design of the Membership Network is intended to approximate and build, as much as possible, on the Oneida's traditional model of forming consensus (Figure 8.6). Symbolism is neither value-free nor inconsequential. There is more to it than meets the eye. We need to appreciate the significance and the implications of what lies hidden at the heart of cultural norms and practices. The insight is indispensable for getting to the bottom of what might otherwise come to pass as a collection of age-old customs. It is by rediscovering the true organizing principles implicit in the culture that people can take stock of their history and know who they are and why they behave the way they do.

This process of consensus building differs from the conventional model of majority rule based on a simple voting routine. The "majority rule," a special feature of the Western model of democracy, presupposes existence of public debate and formation of public opinion aided by mass communication. The voting process is only the means for bringing the process to its ultimate closure. But the cultures that are participative, interactive, and symbolically expressive

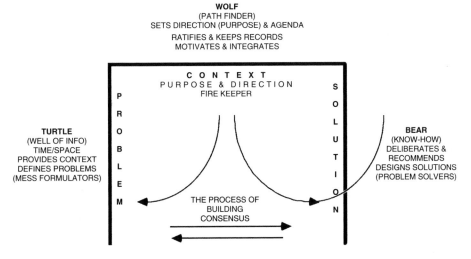

FIGURE 8.6   Consensus-Building Convention

are far more spontaneous. They go through a less rigid process involving both verbal and nonverbal modes of consensus building, referred to as "getting to be of the same mind," before the community arrives at a collectively agreed-upon position. The open, patient, unstructured, and well-drawn-out discussions will continue until an acceptable and practical solution is reached.

This open-ended mode of deliberation transcends majority rule. In fact, majority rule is, in essence, but a special case of consensus building. The limitations imposed by the formal "rules of order," intended to manage time more effectively, therefore prove incompatible with the inherently slow process of consensus building in dealing with critical issues. In such contexts, reaching widely supported agreements cannot afford to compromise the prerequisites of consensus building in the name of majority rule. If it did, the outcome would not only debunk public commitment but would lead to widespread suspicion, if not wholesale alienation.

By capitalizing on the valuable tradition of generating a common understanding, the Nation will benefit from multiple advantages: it is effective because it engages everyone in the development process; it is legitimizing because it resorts to an indigenous device already sanctioned by the culture; and it is exciting because it frees up the richness contained in the past to become an effective vehicle for future progress. The process is liberating because it empowers us to achieve the freedom that we need in order to establish ourselves as the masters of our future rather than prisoners of our past. The future need not be a mere extension of the past. By reinterpreting the underlying drivers of our behavior, we can both preserve and renew our culture in ways that make it consistent with what we are and supportive of what we desire to be.

Performance Criteria and Measures

Creation of the capacity to act is the greatest single function of the membership platform. Although diversity is at the heart of a free society, lack of agreement on a set of organizing principles and operating procedures will rob it of the minimum requirement to act effectively. As such, creation of a capacity to convert the paralyzing dichotomies and structural conflicts to an enabling complementarity will be the basis on which the success of the membership dimension will be measured. The performance system will therefore establish the measures and criteria to determine the degree to which the membership platform has been able to institutionalize the consensus basis for united action in the face of diversity. This should be the outcome of an ongoing and nationwide dialogue, the capacity to listen and empathize, leading to a reduction of the existing levels of tension and frustration while producing a shared understanding and commitment to a set of organizing principles and operating procedures.

To accomplish this purpose, a set of organizing principles, representing the underlying assumptions at the core of the Nation's entrenched polarization, will be identified. For each principle, a pair of pro and con arguments will be developed. Using a predesigned index, the attitude of the membership as a whole with regard to these principles will be periodically measured and tabulated. Successive measurements will yield the pattern of change along the organizing principles. The exercise will not act as a mirror only. It will serve as a medium by which the membership can both understand and influence what makes it behave the way it does. Thus, performance criteria and measures will help the Nation shed its paralyzing "mess" and move voluntarily toward its desired state.

Interdimensional and Interest Group Activities

The membership platform will support and manage all interest group activities requiring voluntarism and participation of active members, such as Pow Wow, Arts, and Aging. The activities and interactions of the membership, learning, and business dimensions will be coordinated at the Planning, Learning, and Control Board (PLCB). It is imperative that each one take the initiative to coordinate itself with the other two. To facilitate this coordination, members in the membership network will be encouraged to join a cultural or professional group. The cultural, professional, and other interest groups will act as advisors for the learning and business dimensions.

LEARNING SYSTEMS

The success of the Oneida Nation will ultimately depend on the competence of its members. Oneidas are both the ends and the means of the system of which they are the parts. Like any other human system, Oneida Nation is as good as its members. The development of Oneidas, the system's human assets, therefore constitutes the second most critical dimension of the architecture.

The function of the learning dimension is the development of human assets. It is about reinvigorating the ability and desire of the members to satisfy their needs and desires both individually and collectively. Ability without desire is impotent, just as desire without ability is sterile.

Cultural development involves desires while professional development involves abilities. Desires are the essential ingredient for creation of an achieving society. Cultural and spiritual mobilization deals with the desire dimension. Abilities, no matter how high, are only the necessary condition for success. To the extent that they are not energized by relevant desires, abilities tend to remain latent. In the absence of desires, abilities would be mere potentials.

The vitality of a culture is in its potency to act as a vehicle for the realization of the societies' shared dreams. A potent culture can rekindle the necessary desires without which dreams degenerate into daydreams. Renaissance requires reinterpretation of the cultural symbols in such a way that new goals can be collectively legitimized and effectively pursued while the continuity of group identity is preserved. Ultimately, cultural vitality is measured by success in getting the traditional symbols and images to support the emerging needs of a progressive society. Respect for culture does not imply regression nor should progress mean a break with the past. Old values themselves were born in response to new needs. In the context of national development, innovation is getting these powerful engines reconnected to the emerging needs that keep replacing the ones that may have outlived the reason for which they were born.

Abilities, on the other hand, involve operationalization of the knowledge required for formulating effective responses to new challenges. They involve a whole set of approaches, know-how, and skills for defining problems and designing solutions. Professional development, therefore, is the vehicle to leverage the ability dimension. It requires a professional-based system of education. The system should be designed so that it can be 1) compatible with the system's special needs and, at the same time, 2) capable of meeting licensing requirements of the external environment (federal and state) of which it is a part. The external requirements are so easily achievable that the educational system of the Oneida Nation should position itself to function as complementary to, rather than a redundant duplication of, the U.S. educational system. The system should therefore avoid producing what it can procure from the outside.

The Learning Systems will be responsible for three basic outputs: Learning to Learn, or formal education; Learning to Do, or professional education; and Learning to Be, or cultural education (Figure 8.7).

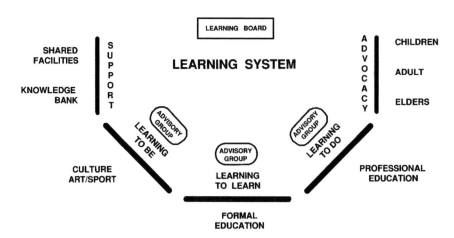

FIGURE 8.7   Learning System Structure

Learning to Learn (Formal Education)

Given the accelerated rate of change that keeps transforming everything, and with it the useful life of learned subject matter, the real responsibility of an educational system is to convert the learners to self-educators. It can achieve this by increasing the students' desire and ability to embark on a never-ending process of learning, unlearning, and relearning, both within and beyond the conventional frameworks. The responsibility for these first- and second-order learnings should be common to all levels of formal education, from elementary to higher education. Formal education, a licensing activity, covers the whole spectrum of K-12, college, and postgraduate studies.

To ensure the quality and availability of formal education, the Learning System will:

- Be responsible for identifying and publicizing the Nation's educational needs and priorities and making sure that there will be sufficient information and resources available to help the members make informed decisions in terms of their educational goals.
- Provide financial support (i.e., scholarships) to eligible students who will otherwise be deprived of pursuing courses of study that are needed/endorsed by the Nation.
- Create a trust fund to offer interest-free loans to eligible students, who will be allowed to write them off by working in the Nation's governance or its business development efforts.
- Generate and continually develop a national database to monitor the educational progress of each member throughout his or her life.
- Consider all Oneidas, regardless of their residence, as its constituency and do its best to 1) keep itself informed about their educational history and progress, and 2) make itself accessible to them when conditions require and justify supporting the members' academic pursuits.

Learning to Be (Cultural Education)

Cultural education covers the whole spectrum of learning experiences that result in both individual and collective development in arts, languages, sports, traditional ceremonies, and other quality-of-life-enhancing activities that involve leisure time. Learning to be is essentially a character building activity. It is about values, worldviews, and identities. It involves desires as opposed to abilities; the capacity rather than the content; the direction rather than the speed; the *whys* rather than the *hows*; the feeling rather than the thinking; the meaning rather than the action; the process of becoming rather than the state of having. It is about doing the right thing rather than doing it right.

Learning to be, in essence, involves aesthetics. If history is a lesson, national declines are preceded by cultural declines. Aesthetics, contrary to popular belief, is not a luxury. Societies that were antithetical to aesthetics invariably proved to be antihuman and antidevelopment as well.

Learning to Do (Professional Education)

Professional education is responsible for creating the marketable competency of the members. In doing this, it will avoid reducing the context of learning to theoretical inputs and rigid classroom formats. Conventional formats, the predominant mode of instruction in higher education, are either incompatible or very expensive. The world does not divide itself the way universities do. Small communities cannot afford the luxury of having a proliferating number of specialists who enjoy knowing more and more about a smaller and smaller set of problems facing Oneida Nation. What the Nation requires is a people capable of performing multiple roles and being able to deal with the totality of a problem.

Professional education should carry out its own survey and draw up its own conclusion about the Nation's professional needs and desires. It can then set out to create plans and programs that will match the nation's business and developmental potentials.

Professional education's best option would be to launch apprentice models of training. To the extent possible, it should recruit its indigenous experts who have proven competence in the needed areas. Such mentors will then be supplied with the necessary resources and trainees to produce the needed technicians (accountants, carpenters, librarians, computer experts, health technicians, etc.). The system can forge alliances or affiliations with known colleges and universities in order to get its programs accredited.

Support Functions

The support arm of the Learning System will consist of Shared Facilities and Knowledge Bank. They will represent those resources commonly utilized by other dimensions of the Learning System.

Shared Services

Shared Services cannot belong to any one output unit acting as supplier to others. Otherwise, the ensuing power imbalance would favor the owning unit at the expense of the other users, rather than letting different units duplicate and diffuse scarce physical resources (buildings, facilities, equipment, etc.).

Knowledge Bank

The Knowledge Bank will host the core competencies of the Nation. Membership in the Knowledge Bank should be considered a privilege. The Bank will consist of full-time and part-time members. Part-time members are those who have parallel responsibilities in other platforms, but their expertise is so much in demand for the system as a whole that their membership will be necessitated by the Bank. This will make it possible for the system to capitalize on these rare expertises. For example, experts serving in the Planning, Learning, and Control Systems will also be part-time members of the Knowledge Bank.

The Knowledge Bank will be the "think tank" of the Nation. It will be involved on a project basis in all three areas of consulting, education, and research, both for internal and external clients. The Bank will be able to recruit specialized and/or complementary talent from internal and external sources on a temporary project basis.

Advocacy Functions

Advocacy will make sure that the learning needs of *all* members, children, adults, and elders, are actively catered to. In order for this to happen, all the members will therefore be registered with one of the three advocacy groups of the Learning System.

Advocacy Services will:

- Interact with the three output dimensions to make sure that members, especially the youth, are receiving the proper education at the right time, in the right amount, and of the right quality.
- Intervene, coordinate, and take whatever action is necessary to make sure that constituencies are properly treated and their individualized needs satisfactorily met.
- Keep in touch with parents and enlist their active support for the success of educational efforts.
- Create special programs for members who are in need of rehabilitation services.

Oneida Multiversity

The educational effort of the Oneida Nation will be leveraged to operate far more effectively by making a fundamental break with the conventional models. Conventional models of education, relevant in the previous era, have outlived their useful life. They are proving to be more of a constraint than instruments of the kind of education needed to create the contemporary citizen. There is a real need for an alternative model grounded in an open learning paradigm. The new learning experience, which can be called Oneida Multiversity, would have the following characteristics:

- It will cover all levels of education from kindergarten to postgraduate.
- It will create a learning society by turning the whole Nation into a school without walls where learning can be freed from time and place restrictions.
- It will provide formal, professional, and cultural education.
- It will use learners as educators and educators as learners in the same course.
- It will remove boundaries between the worlds of work, hobby, and learning.
- It will remove the boundaries between theoretical, vocational, and artistic studies so that members can be learning while earning, and vice versa.
- It will provide opportunities for every member of the Nation to be, potentially, a teacher and a student at all times.
- It will allow sufficient flexibility so that noncompulsory (ages six to sixteen) learners can get in and out of the system at will.
- It will introduce learning cells, research cells, and practice cells that allow the participants to carry out multiple roles in all of them (as educators and/or researchers and/or practitioners) at the same time.
- It will be open to all kinds of pedagogic approaches, formats, methodologies, and curricula in addition to useful conventional ones.
- It will be accessible by all members—anytime, anywhere.

The Learning System employs the following educational vehicles.

Learning Cells

A learning cell is a vehicle for increasing the knowledge and understanding of the participants in a collaborative context. By operationalizing the idea that the best way of learning is teaching, it will make the learners responsible for both teaching to and learning from each other. The success of students assigned to a learner-teacher will then be a measure for evaluating the success of the learner-teacher.

Language dissemination, adult literacy, and vocational education and training, for example, can best be achieved through learning cells, which produce cascade effects by making learning by teaching and training by trainers happen at the same time. Such a system of learning could be made exponentially effective by providing added extrinsic incentives to learner-teachers, whose students could demonstrate proficiency in their subject matter. The students who pass the standard can, in turn, go on teaching other learners and get compensated for it on an output-oriented basis. Thus the motivation of learning to learn is multiplied by learning to teach and learning by teaching.

By taking advantage of what is already available in the environment and concentrating on an internally generated supply of services in the areas unique to the system, the education system can maximize its effectiveness. It does so by capitalizing on the available resources in its environment and complementing them when they are lacking. One such example would be to make the externally-hired contractors commit themselves to the task of training counterparts from the internal pool of personnel as an integral part of their professional responsibilities. They should expect not to receive the balance of their compensation unless the preassigned trainees achieve the requisite level of competence.

This pyramidal structure of group learning requires its own system of organization, management, and support services to take care of such arrangements as assignment of roles, interconnectivity with training cells in the business dimension, and the action plans for future application of learned skills in professional/vocational contexts.

Research Cells

Research cells, like learning cells, have a participant-centered focus. Among other things, they are charged with cultural reinterpretation. Research cells are to find out how the future can be built with the aid of the past. In this regard, a shared vision of the desired future will help them identify and select—from a rich and, at times, quite heterogeneous content of cultural heritage—the values, the symbolism, the meanings, and the rituals that will be relevant to reinventing the future and helpful in the nation-building effort.

Practice Cells

Practice cells will involve all kinds of participatory group activities such as theater, arts festivals, fashion shows, and sporting events. Practice cells will promote those activities that are high in their experiential learning content. They will be instrumental in the cultivation of those tastes that will ultimately result in the creation of an environment promoting ever-increasing generation and consumption of aesthetic creations, artistic values, and cultural commodities. The idea is to erase the conventional boundaries of education, work, and fun and integrate art, sports, and pastime into creative activities that attract and engage all the members, especially the young, wherever they are.

Practice cells, mediums of competency development, will be run by members with proven capabilities in specific activities. These mentors design the projects and are provided with a budget to develop the participants as well as the market for their services. Each cell is typically made up of five to six participants.

Performance Criteria and Measures

The learning system will be a performance center. It will be a throughput-oriented operation with a built-in tendency to keep the consumption in check and not allow it to grow beyond a healthy percentage of value generation. The operating budget will therefore be a percentage of its actual throughput.

Participating learners pay a tuition in the form of vouchers they have obtained. A tuition is considered as income only when the voucher is cashed in. The budget, therefore, is on a per-head basis. The source of vouchers, and ultimately the budget of the learning system, is the education trust fund set up to finance the system as a performance center. The designated fund will only be realized by the system once the participant is actually picked up for processing by the learning system.

The design of the performance measures will be informed by the degree to which the following indicators are realized:

- Cultural, educational, and professional integration.
- Widespread and active interest in learning to be, learning to learn, and learning to do.
- Demand, both internal and external, for the graduates of the system.
- Multidimensionality, as manifested by the participants (being a learner, a teacher, and practitioner at the same time), as well as resource utilization (multiple use of facilities and resources for all kinds of learning activities in the system).
- Cultural vitality through revitalization, adaptation, and adoption of the norms that prove relevant to the preservation and continued development of the Nation.

The measures will be eclectic; they will be both objectively and subjectively devised and applied. Objectivity, after all, is collective subjectivity.

Governance and Intersystems Relationships

Since compatibility among the membership, learning, and business dimensions is of utmost importance to the success of the Nation, their interactions will be coordinated at the Planning, Learning, and Control Board (PLCB). In addition, the learning system will operate under a PLC Learning Board that will be made up of a member of BC, the general manager, the director of the learning platform, and his or her direct reports. Each basic unit of the system will also be assisted by an advisory group whose members will be selected from cultural and professional cells operating in the membership network.

BUSINESS SYSTEMS

To be viable and self-reliant, a nation should be able to generate and disseminate wealth, products, and services effectively. It should be capable of addressing all those factors that affect the standard of living, such as health, food, housing, and other material needs of the membership. Generation and dissemination are two sides of the same coin. Generation without proper distribution breeds alienation, whereas distribution without adequate generation will lead to equitable distribution of poverty. Self-reliance, to be self-sustaining, needs to be grounded in diversity. History has not been kind to societies that relied on a single source of survival.

Business systems is the dimension of architecture responsible for expanding and mobilizing the Nation's capacity for viability. In charge of entrepreneurial and business development, it will be involved in creating business opportunities and supporting the members to successfully detect, seize, manage, and exploit the emerging opportunities.

Ultimately, real wealth is about the competence to convert opportunities into values that are essential for satisfying both one's own needs and desires and those of others. Success in contributing to both collective and individual life-achievement goals is a vital sign of people who have earned the right to be in charge of their destinies. Economic success is, ultimately, about freedom to exercise choice. The ugliest manifestation of poverty is powerlessness.

Perhaps no other mission of the business function is as important as helping communities to prosper while learning to attain higher levels of self-reliance. The Indians have always been proud and resourceful people. Their culture is replete with qualities that are essentially entrepreneurial. Although they valued communitarianism, they have also celebrated rugged individualism, self-reliance, and bravery.

Success is about desires and abilities. Desires and abilities do not have substitutes. They cannot be given nor be imposed from the outside. That is perhaps the reason why trusteeship, no matter how noble the intentions, has the potential of defeating the very purposes for which it was originally set up. Intended to help, it can lead to helplessness. Mandated to create autonomy, it can degenerate into dependency. Meant to preserve ideals, it can end up corrupting them. Experience shows that well-intentioned systems of bureaucratized assistance can prove, counterintuitively, devastating. This trend, however limited, needs to be reversed. The answer is subsidizing demand instead of subsidizing the supply.

To realize its mission in serving the Nation's economic interests, the business system will engage in all of the activities that are primarily designed to:

- Ensure the long-term financial self-sufficiency of the Nation.
- Diversify the sources of revenue.

- Eliminate the Nation's reliance on a single source of income.
- Create employment opportunities.

Business development includes identification of business opportunities, raising capital, infusion of seed money, investment, partnership, management of operation, and provision of management support services. It will actively explore and identify the potential opportunities for Oneida entrepreneurs. It will also support Oneidas about, and encourage them to take advantage of, the available federal provisions for securing special business privileges for specific minorities.

All the units in the business dimension will be profit centers. If and when management finds it necessary, for whatever reason, to subsidize a particular service to a particular user, it will have to do so by subsidizing the demand and never the supply. Such a market-based discipline will protect both the provider and the user of the service from the unhealthy effects of bureaucratized relations leading to providers' arrogance and insensitivity toward the user and the users' helplessness and dependency on its supplier.

In this context, the business system will consist of a series of business units formed as profit centers organized into five dimensions: Services, Industry, Leisure, Land and Agriculture, and Marketing (Figure 8.8).

Services Sector

This platform will consist of businesses in the services sector. The service providers, operating within the government division, will eventually be transformed into a profit center and become a member of this group. However, initially, the service units in this sector will consist of: financial services, such as

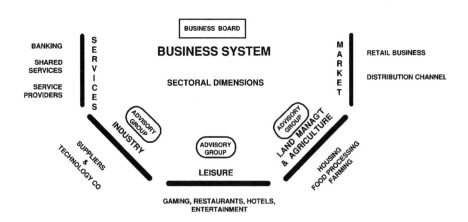

FIGURE 8.8 Business System Structure

investment or commercial banks, and ancillary services, such as engineering and business development.

Industry Sector

This will include suppliers and technology companies whose output will be bought and integrated into the outputs of other platforms or sold directly to external clients.

Leisure Sector

This will include gaming, restaurants, hotels, and entertainment operations. Generically, gaming belongs to the entertainment industry. It is but one of the wide-ranging business activities that capitalizes on the vast opportunities emerging from ever-growing leisure time. Approached from a leisure-based vantage point, gaming can be treated as one link in a long value chain providing a whole array of services in response to the entire spectrum of vacationing families' needs. Hotels, resorts, amusement and/or theme parks, zoos, transportation, and other tourism-related services are promising pieces of the entertainment jigsaw. Other than lodging requirements, adequate land and air accessibility, from as many points as possible, is crucial to the success of a broad leisure-based portfolio. Gaming, in terms of its functional properties, belongs to the leisure dimension. However, because of its sheer size and stage of maturation, it will be managed as a separate entity until such time that other nascent leisure-related businesses reach a level of growth that removes the threat of their being overshadowed by gaming's presence.

Land and Agriculture Sector

This will include housing, food processing, and farming operations. Land is a precious resource. Although it has extrinsic value in terms of national sovereignty, its opportunity cost is too high to let it lie fallow simply as a piece of property. Once the ownership of land is established, it should be managed by this platform in the most effective manner.

Marketing Sector

The marketing arm of the business systems will consist of the Retail Business and Distribution Channel, which will aggressively search and exploit the existing and potential needs of the current and emerging markets in and outside of the United States. They will work closely with all output units and act as their marketing arm.

Each platform is intended to house all three distinct types of ownership as follows.

Collective Ownership

This type of ownership will consist of all the business activities that are collectively owned by the Nation. This type of ownership can be used in all platforms. Collective ownership can be formed in agriculture, services, industry, land management, housing, and leisure/entertainment. For example, because of the significant role that gaming plays in the operation of the Nation, it is only natural that it continue to be collectively owned. However, peripheral activities that are related to gaming but can enhance the leisure dimension could be created by means of individual ownership.

Individual Ownership and Strategic Alliances

Business units created by entrepreneurial members, alone, in groups, or in strategic alliances with outsiders (in all platforms), will be supported by the Nation. These units will be licensed to operate for a minimal fee as long as their activities are compatible with the economic interests of the Nation and provide employment opportunities for its members.

Partnership and Franchise Development

Franchising will be an appropriate format to create partnership between the Nation and the individual members to encourage the proliferation of business activities that can be packaged and duplicated within or outside the reservation.

The franchise model would be a powerful entrepreneurial tool for economic development. Well planned, it can easily create hundreds of outside businesspersons who would otherwise have no chance of ever becoming such for lack of capital, training, access to professional assistance, or all of those factors combined.

Governance and Intersystems Relationships

Activities and interactions among the membership, learning, and business dimensions will be coordinated by the Planning, Learning, and Control Board. However, business systems will be governed by a PLC Business Board that will act as a holding company. Membership of this board will consist of the treasurer, chief of staff, GM of gaming, director of financial systems, director of technical systems, GM of business systems, and his or her direct reports. In addition, each sector of business platform (services, industry, leisure, land and agriculture, retail) may choose to have an Advisory Group selected from the members of the professional cells in the membership network.

CORE SERVICES

Core services will consist of three basic services that are necessary to maintain the physical infrastructure and social stability of the Nation. These services will benefit all the members collectively and indiscriminately.

Government Services Division

Health services and social services are the major function of the government services division.

Health Services

Delivery of all health services, preventive and interventive, including dental and medicinal, will be organized and managed through this department. In addition, the department will have responsibility for all the environmental services such as sanitation, industrial hygiene, safety, and community health.

It is recommended that the department be redesigned in such a way that it will, in general, subsidize the demand instead of the supply of health delivery. Delivery units should be gradually converted to profit centers and moved to the services dimension of the business platform.

Social Services

The social services department will be responsible for three basic outputs:

- Counseling: Relief and treatment of all chemical dependencies, domestic abuse, and other social ills. Provision of paralegal services as well as support of senior citizens and veterans are also the responsibility of this unit.
- Economic Support and Income Maintenance: This unit will support those who are not able to support themselves. However, as much as possible, it is the responsibility of this unit to work closely with the learning and business systems to create meaningful employment opportunities for the ablebodied in the Nation.
- Housing Authority: This unit will make sure that all those who need a home or shelter will get one. It will develop and manage all group homes and shelters and provide assistance to those families that need help in securing housing for themselves. The overriding policy should be aimed at integrating rather than segregating people.

Infrastructure Development Division

This division will be responsible for space planning and engineering as well as public works.

Space Planning and Engineering

This department will plan the space for the Nation. It will deal with all environmental concerns, land use, housing, utilities, and transportation. It will be responsible for project coordination and construction management. Development of zoning, issuing permits, and inspection and enforcement of space plans are the responsibilities of this department.

Public Works

This department will manage the operation of all utilities, wells, septic maintenance of buildings, facilities, grounds, parks, and recreational centers, and automotive and Oneida Transit services.

Ordinance Division

This division will be responsible for compliance and records management.

Compliance

The Compliance Department will be responsible for law enforcement (the police), conservation, preferences, vendor licensing, and collection of any taxes required.

Records Management

This department will house all the national historical documents as well as registry of individual membership, identification records, and land and property titles.

Performance Criteria and Measures

These services will have to be incented to act in a cost-effective manner, doing more with less. They will have to operate on a throughput-oriented basis with a budget that will be kept as a portion of their revenues. The success of these units should never be measured by their size (amount of budget, number of employees, or size of populations served), but by the cost effectiveness of their delivery.

Governance and Oversight

In addition to the PLC Board, which will coordinate the activities of the core services with other platforms, core services will be governed by the PLC Services Board. Members of the PLC Services Board will consist of a designated member of the Governing Body, chief of staff, GM of the platform, and her or his direct reports.

It is imperative that core services act as servers and not, as is often the case, controllers. Since membership at large is the beneficiary of these services, a number of advisory committees, as deemed necessary, may be set up to oversee the operation of these services.

EXTERNAL ENVIRONMENT

The external environment dimension will provide mutual interfaces between the system and its containing environment. This dimension will operate on the assumption that, in order to survive and grow, Oneida Nation, like any viable social system, must remain open and continuously interact with the other actors in its environment. It is, therefore, a means of channeling the scattered energies of the Nation that would otherwise be wasted in nonstrategic, and even conflicting, activities to focus on external opportunities and threats facing the Nation as a whole.

No nation is capable of satisfying all its needs by itself alone. Self-determination and self-reliance should not be confused with self-sufficiency. Interdependence implies that relationships are two-way. It requires giving and taking at the same time. Ultimately, a developed society, given the same level of resources, can do more with less.

Environmental interface, especially where one represents a minority, requires recognition of special burdens and responsibilities that go with it. External perceptions and the group image are crucial. Insofar as minority groups are concerned, an individual's actions tend to receive much greater attention because one is automatically perceived as a typical representative of the group. Thus, the actions of a few, for better or worse, reflect disproportionately on the image of the whole. Minorities, therefore, ought to be that much more sensitive to the image they project. They need to take much greater care of the way their image is received. Minorities can hardly afford to neglect their PR sensitivities. Negligence and complacency can prove too costly.

The external environment dimension will operate at the following three levels:

- Federal and State Government
- Local and Business Environment
- Other Indian Nations

All three levels will make sure that the system is kept adequately informed. By constantly monitoring the environment, it will provide timely inputs on significant trends and developments representing emerging threats and/or opportunities. They will also relentlessly pursue the interests of the Oneida Nation by influencing the events in their respective environments. The idea is to influence where one cannot control and appreciate where one cannot influence.

JUDICIAL SYSTEM

The two basic functions of an Oneida judicial system are as follows:

- Consummation of the national sovereignty: the ability to interpret and modify the constitution and to ensure equal protection of members under the law.
- Creation of an independent and legitimate channel for conflict resolution and redress of grievances, thus relieving the government from becoming diverted by concerns that are basically judicial in nature.

Contextual Analysis

Designing an effective judicial system for the Oneida Nation requires that the unique characteristics of the system in which it is intended to operate be fully understood, explicitly stated, and widely agreed upon. This understanding is essential to clarify such questions as:

- Why a separate judicial system is needed.
- How it will relate to the existing order.
- What the main source and nature of different conflicts are.

That the Oneida Nation is a unique social system should not be so difficult to understand. The relationship between the Oneidas and their government is different from that of nations whose governments play a much smaller role, and a purely noncommercial one at that, in the lives of their people. Therefore, the overriding concern for the Oneida judicial system would involve the relationship between the individual and the collectivity.

Government responsibility for collective ownership of critical resources, while it may serve a useful purpose in special contexts, is fraught with powerful political implications. For nations whose governments are saddled with the responsibility for collective ownership in addition to governance, the way the two functions are arranged and prosecuted impacts their systemic consequences enormously. The following points underline some of the adverse consequences of bundling up the two functions:

- The governance and business management roles would get so mixed up that neither of them, even under the most ideal circumstances, could be achieved and assessed satisfactorily.
- Government becomes responsible, not only for normal governance functions, but also for providing employment as a means of distributing wealth. Loss of clear-cut accountability would then be the first casualty

of such an arrangement. The natural consequence of regarding government employment as a right rather than a privilege eliminates competence as a requirement for employment. The result would be an irresponsible tendency to do less for more, and a burgeoning attitude characterized by hostility and negativity.

- In a single-employer environment, the individual's dependency on the state would take on larger and more complex dimensions. Losing one's job would then be tantamount to permanent unemployment and condemnation to abject poverty. Chronic dependency would breed learned helplessness, frustration, alienation, and a culture of insatiable demand for free services. Natural conflicts arising out of the normal interactions between a manager and his or her subordinate would take on a political tone and be referred to the political system. In this context, development and enforcement of equitable employment contracts (HR policies) will become the most sensitive and vital concern of every member.

- Based on personal interests and even stylistic preferences, dissatisfactions with any decisions could metastasize into disruptive political pressures. Proliferation and increased intransigence of pressure groups would then further strain the citizen-state interdependencies until they reach explosive proportions. The ensuing fragmentation of the majority into several interest groups would give rise to ever-marginalized pressure groups striking volatile coalitions of convenience based on agreements on means rather than on ends. People would abandon their affiliations around the national mandates and, instead, become subdivided around hidden and irrational agendas maliciously intended to threaten, paralyze, and ultimately undermine the system of which they are a part. As a consequence, the administration cannot help but become increasingly bogged down and eventually truncated from its normal functions by a nightmare of ever-proliferating complaints. This overwhelming tendency, if allowed to continue, would force the system to either resort to an authoritarian style intended to silence all opposition or just cave in to total paralysis.

Contextual Challenge

When the state is the only game in town, existence of an effective mechanism to mediate between the individual and the state becomes a must. Otherwise, political pressure would become more pronounced and present itself as the only possible recourse for redressing grievances that are originally nonpolitical.

The success of a judicial system lies in its effectiveness in handling normal conflicts that are the inevitable by-products of human interactions. If, however, the design suffers from structural conflicts (conflicts whose generation is a function of adversarially designed structures rather than clashes of personalities), then no robust judicial system would ever be capable of coping with the conflictual side effects of such an inherently flawed system. The constant tugs-of-war, arising, for example, from a common tendency to commingle governance proper with management of collective ownership, would produce a no-win situation for any judicial system. The usual never-ending contest between conflict generation and conflict resolution, where public sense of fairness would be the ultimate loser, is symptomatic of such a flawed approach.

When particular socioeconomic conditions make it imperative for the government to assume a collective-ownership role, it is best to make sure that the managements of the two functions are kept separate from each other as much as possible. The stewardship of public resources should be treated as a trusteeship undertaken on behalf of the people, who are the real owners of the assets. Insofar as this trusteeship responsibility is concerned, the system would have to be designed to reflect the commercial nature of such an operation.

This concern has been a critical element in designing Oneida's new architecture. The overall design is intended, among other things, to generate a system free from structural conflict. It separates the conduct of governance from the conduct of the business management by assigning them to distinct, though interrelated, platforms with different performance criteria and measures.

To capitalize on the positives and minimize the negatives of combining governance with collective ownership, it is recommended that the learning systems and business systems platforms become additional and independent sources of employment (each with a separate HR department). This move will create a propensity to expand and increase internal sources of variety in the system, instead of creating a single monopoly that reduces the choices of members. Under these conditions, redundancy of some critical functions is, despite the conventional wisdom, the solution rather than the problem. The business platform should provide additional sources of variety by expanding opportunities for private as well as collective ownership.

Democratic Challenge

When creating, within the context of collective ownership, a viable society based on democratic conventions, it is crucial to define the notion and parameters of majority rule. It is imperative to forge a widespread agreement on what constitutes a legitimate majority: its powers, its boundaries, and whether it has a right to override the individual or trample minorities in the name of the whole. It should define the limits of the minority and majority rights so that they may complement, rather than encroach on, the rights of others. If the rule of law finds its legitimacy in the will of the majority, then tyranny of the majority would be a fait accompli unless it transcends, and reigns supreme over, and above the majority itself. The majority, for example, has no right to disown its right to democracy and, thus, democratically undermine democracy itself.

Collective ownership carries a series of responsibilities that saddle it with commensurate powers. By the same token, the individual has certain rights that correspond with commensurate duties. The judicial system should therefore make sure that there exists a four-pronged balance and reciprocity between rights and responsibilities: both within those of the individual and those of the Nation on the one hand, as well as between the individual's and the Nation's on the other. Rights and responsibilities are indivisible; they are two sides of the same coin. Neither could exist without the other.

The system should have a built-in capability to differentiate between entitlements and privileges of the individual on the one hand, and the governance and commercial responsibilities of the government on the other. The individual and the collectivity, which is represented by the government, both have separate, and yet interrelated, rights and responsibilities. Not only are these two sets of rights and responsibilities not exclusive, but they are essentially complementary. In fact, they are so interdependent that one could not be dealt with without touching the other.

Collectivity has distinct rights to security, viability, and sovereignty. It has a right to act; its decision process cannot be taken hostage. It is also responsible for making sure that the individual, even as a minority of one, is provided with enough alternatives to make his or her choices meaningful.

An individual citizen has inalienable rights, such as the right to privacy and the right not to be discriminated against. In addition to the rights, the individual can enjoy certain privileges, which he or she may acquire or lose, provided certain conditions are, or are not, satisfied. The individual, however, stands to lose the privileges that he or she abuses; irresponsible driving would be one obvious example.

A Critical Concern

The existing alternative in the environment has turned out to be too costly. The exorbitant cost of justice has pushed it increasingly out of the reach of the non-wealthy. Insofar as ordinary people are concerned, it has become an unafford-able commodity. The amount of time and money required to sustain almost any litigation makes the pursuit of justice a luxury not many can afford. More often than not, even winning would be illusory. The Oneida judicial system should therefore be designed in such a way that it will be both accessible to and affordable for all Oneidas, and be capable of addressing those concerns of the citizens versus the collectivity that would otherwise remain unmet by the containing system.

9

Butterworth Health Systems

This report summarizes Butterworth's attempt to redesign itself around a concept of care that makes a significant break from the current practice. The report projects a shared vision of Butterworth's desired future. It is produced by active participation of the Design Team. Members representing Butterworth: Katy Black, Sharon Buursma, Priscilla A. Dakin, Roy Eickman, Michael Freed, William G. Gonzalez, Joyce Henry, Jean Hitchcock, Pat Marks, Philip McCorkle, Irma Napoli, Tom Ouellette, Jon Ganz, M.D., Ray Gonzales, M.D., Brian Roelof, M.D., Suzanne Rogers, Joel Sacks, M.D., Carol Sarosik, James F. VanDam, M.D., Fred Vandenberg, and Randy Wagner. Members representing INTERACT: Jamshid Gharajedaghi and Bijan Khorram.

The design represents six iterations directed at generating consensus on the following key points:

- A shared understanding of the issues, concerns, and expectations of those who have a stake in the organization.
- A shared understanding of the emerging health-care environment.
- Identification of the purpose and strategic intent of the system.
- Identification of the specifications of the desired system.
- The development of the systems architecture (major components and their relationships).

To meet the space limitations of this book, 200 pages of design document had to be condensed to 40 pages. To minimize the compromising effect on the design as a whole, the main reductions were focused on the marketing, administration, and governing dimensions of the architecture. Inevitably in the process, some very interesting ideas have been lost or misrepresented. I hope that the design team will accept my apologies for this.

ISSUES, CONCERNS, AND EXPECTATIONS

The present health-care system has its origin in sickness care. It was designed to provide service to those who fall ill and need medical care. The cost-recovery aspect of utilizing sickness-based health care has been associated with three basic conceptions: fee for service, cost-plus operation, and third-party payer, as described below.

- *Fee for service* is an exchange system in which charges are proportional to the level of services rendered.
- *Cost-plus* is a pricing mechanism in which the incurred costs plus a markup designed to cover the overhead and margin are summed up to define the value of the output.
- *Third-party payer* is an institutional arrangement in which the receiver of the service (the consumer) is not the same as the payer (customer). The arrangement transfers the costs to the institutional customer (insurance companies and government), who in turn transfers them, indirectly, to ultimate payers and the public at large.

The current model has no built-in mechanism of self-control to discipline the relationship between the provider and the patient. It has created a positive feedback loop that has fueled an insatiable demand for more services. The demand feeds on itself as long as patients are willing to ask, providers are eager to serve, and third-party payers do not mind picking up the tab and adding a margin before passing it on to the ultimate payer. In such a context, demand cannot be rationalized.

Advances in technology have expanded the possibilities for continuous medical breakthroughs. As a result, life expectancy has increased and the desire to delay the final exit has caused the demand for technology to grow exponentially. However, technology can only delay the final exit at exorbitant costs, and every time it does it further fuels the insatiability of the demand. This exponential growth in demand for postponing the eventuality at all costs cannot be left unchecked—especially if costs are conveniently passed to a third-party payer, leaving the demanding population under the illusion of a continuous free lunch.

The system seems to have hit its upper limit. Alarmed by the long-term consequences of its own irresponsible demand for more, better, and costlier care, the stakeholders of the system have begun to apply the brakes. This has forced the growth curve into an S-shaped form.

The first corrective action against this runaway escalation has been the introduction of HMOs to manage care. To reduce the rising costs of care, one has to begin to manage the care, since 85 percent of the operating expenses were assumed to be the cost of goods (care). The majority of HMOs, however, have not been successful at managing care. Instead, they have relinquished this responsibility by moving into a contractual mode that exchanged volume for wholesale discounts. Thus HMOs have achieved economies of scale by delivering their captive customers to the health-care system. Although this has reduced the rate of growth, the pressures to contain costs have continued and the idea of managing care has resurfaced. HMOs have been forced to use a bureaucratic system and a mechanistic mode of operation to manage the most emotional and sensitive behavior of a human system of health care.

Not surprisingly, the mechanistic management of care has been received with resistance. The idea of a bureaucrat telling the health-care system what to do, or not to do, proved unacceptable for the two critical stakeholders: the patient and the provider. Although some HMOs have developed more elaborate models to manage care, they have retained their bureaucratic character and have operated within a mechanical framework. Structural conflict, compounded by intractability of developing a simple mechanistic solution to what is essentially a complex living phenomenon, has led to the abdication of the problem. The emerging response yielded itself to the concept of capitation (per-head payment), pushing the decision and the financial risk lower in the supply chain to the provider level.

In a parallel development to capitation, the concept of preventive care has emerged as an effective way to control costs. HMOs got into the act by default and broadened the notion of health care to include wellness. The combination of wellness with capitation had promised to be an effective solution to the problem of depersonalization of care by removing the bureaucrat as an intervening agent between the patient and the provider.

This could have proved effective as long as the service was limited to preventive and normal care and was carried out in the context of a generally healthy population with a normal risk distribution that could easily be assessed and managed. However, when the treatment of acute cases is mixed in with the routine practice of health maintenance, the notion of risk management takes on a whole new significance. In the conventional capitation model, the patient population is distributed among the primary care physicians with a fixed payment per member. The smaller the population, the higher the risk. This is contrary to the notion of insurance, which is to reduce risk within a large population. Otherwise, the idea of insurance would be pointless in the first place.

To overcome the problem of risk in subgroups assigned to primary care physicians, some HMOs have provided a special case approval process. As a consequence, in cases that involve life and death decisions, the system once again refers the responsibility back to its mechanistic bureaucracy. Thus the old problem of conflict is renewed not only between the physician and the patient but also between the physician and the insurance company.

To aggravate the situation further, the supposition that the primary physician will pay for the services of specialized care throws the sensitive patient-physician relationship, as well as the general practitioner-specialist relationship, into suspicion and controversy. The mere perception of a conflict of interest, even if unfounded, is not helpful in a relationship that should be based upon unshakable trust. Trust among major stakeholders (primary care physician, medical specialist, and patient) is the most crucial element for the success of any health-care model. Any notion of structural conflict will disrupt the whole system. Until the system comes of age, such suspicions should be preempted. This would imply the need to create enough safeguards to make sure that proper functioning of the system is not compromised.

Major overhaul of sensitive institutions, foremost among them the health-care system, should consider the risks of social experimentation. Interventions into social contexts, once brought into existence, tend to take on a life of their own. When a cause goes away, its effects do not necessarily go away. In social domains, cause and effect are separated in time and space. Consequences of an action may take some time to realize. Therefore, any new design should be kept deliberately open, flexible, and mindful of irreversible consequences of its actions.

The new design should create an opportunity for a well-balanced approach. It should avoid alternating between extreme concerns in one direction followed by subsequent reversals in the opposite direction. The virtues of fee for service, capitation, and other useful concepts should be incorporated into an encompassing system that will allow for choice and adaptive behavior without an endless series of disruptive fluctuations along the way. The system should expand its sources of variety by incorporating different alternatives and evolve through continuous selection and learning.

DESIGN SPECIFICATIONS

The new system should:

- Rationalize the relationship between supply and demand in such a way that the patients receive optimum quality care without fueling an insatiable demand for wasteful services.
- Utilize advanced technology to provide the best possible care without creating unreasonable expectations.
- Dissolve the structural conflict among patients, providers, payers, and administrators of the health-care system in such a way that they complement each other without any of them being compromised.
- Maximize the flexibility and responsiveness of the system and take full advantage of the existing and emerging possibilities in the health-care market.

- Be capable of continuous learning, adaptation, and renewal.
- Represent the state of the art in health delivery management without getting sidetracked into irrevocable social experimentation.
- Contain and dissolve the preexisting conditions (the mess) in the current institutional setup while preventing them from spilling over into the newly created components.

THE ARCHITECTURE

The systems architecture (Figure 9.1) identifies the value chain, the critical dimensions of the health-care system, and the way it relates users to providers in the health-care system. In order to create an architecture that will realize the expectations and desires of Butterworth's stakeholders, the designers recognized the necessity of employing a multidimensional scheme. Such an architecture is intended not only to dissolve the existing "mess" but also to transcend it by developing a vision of the next generation of a health-care system.

The architecture represents a platform from which Butterworth's distinctive value chain will evolve. The value chain identifies all of the elements of the health-care system and their relationships along a market dimension (access and

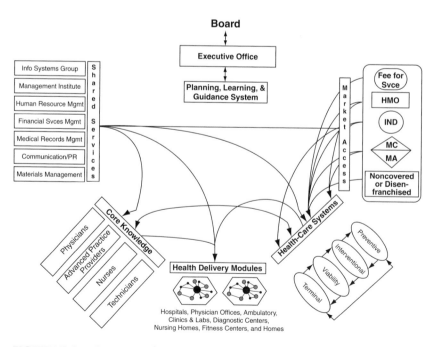

FIGURE 9.1   Systems Architecture

care systems), an output dimension (health delivery modules), and an input dimension (core knowledge and shared services).

This multidimensional framework not only helps the designers understand and differentiate each component of the system, but also establishes the components' relationships in such a way that an integrated and cohesive whole can emerge. Design and incorporation of the missing elements, which can be identified by an analysis of the value chain, will lead to a value-adding system in which the value generated by the whole will be greater than the sum of the values produced by the parts.

MARKET DIMENSION

The market dimension deals with the users of the health-care system. A market is defined in terms of three essential elements: need, access, and purchasing power.

The classification and proper grouping of health-care needs define the nature of products and services rendered. These will be discussed in detail under the following section on the care system. However, the classification of users into various groupings reflects their purchasing power and defines the market access mechanism necessary to reach them.

Market Access

Users of the health-care system are traditionally grouped into the following institutional models.

Fee for Service

The traditional insurance companies such as Blue Cross and Blue Shield usually represent fee-for-service arrangements. Members are free to choose their own providers, who are compensated on a cost-plus basis. Blue Cross/Blue Shield of Michigan has converted to a managed payment system; it pays on a DRG (diagnostic-related group) basis. This arrangement has caused the development of the interventional care system.

HMOs

HMOs were designed as a way to curb the rising costs of health care by managing the members' health-care demand needs. They contract for care on a discounted basis from providers. HMO patients are limited to a preselected group of providers. In evolving HMOs, the providers are given a fixed per-member sum, called capitation, to be drawn against for services rendered. Although originally sick-care oriented, HMOs have begun to build prevention, maintenance, and wellness into their services to curb the treatment costs—hence the term "managed-care plans."

Independents (Self-Insured)

The independents, or self-insured populations, include employers who finance health-related charges for their members based on the plans they design for themselves. They may choose to outsource the management of their system to HMOs, to other insurance companies, or to third-party administrators (TPAs). To serve this group effectively requires a great degree of flexibility because each represents a variety of different designs.

Medicare

Medicare is a federal government health insurance plan for those who have reached a certain age (around 65), have contributed the minimum premiums required to the fund, and thus have qualified for the health-care services that are paid by the Medicare system. Medicare is beginning to move patients toward managed-care plans.

Medicaid

Medicaid is primarily a state government health insurance plan for those who lack the resources to take care of themselves. It also provides nursing home funding for long-term maintenance for the poor. Some state plans are also beginning to move patients toward managed-care plans.

Noncovered Customers

Noncovered customers are disenfranchised individuals who are not members of any insurance plan. The care for these individuals is important to the health system. They ultimately receive care through emergency rooms and inpatient hospitals that receive little or no reimbursement.

Butterworth Health System may take the initiative to design and experiment with a select neighborhood group of noncovered customers and provide them with a Butterworth Health Coverage Card. This program would explicitly address the mission of Butterworth to serve the community, irrespective of ability to pay. The program would be financed by Butterworth and/or the Butterworth Foundation. Later on, the program could be extended to include other underserved populations in the community. Creation of this program would not only make it possible to treat the disenfranchised as any other client, but would also make Butterworth's contribution to the community visible and measurable.

The key responsibilities of the market access function will involve the following: market assessment, packaging, product/market negotiations, customer/consumer satisfaction assessment, and health-system marketing.

CARE SYSTEM

As one of the basic dimensions of the Butterworth architecture, the care system will be responsible for defining and monitoring the virtual output of the system. By doing so, it will bridge the gap between the market and the actual delivery of health-care products and services.

The design of the care system in this format embodies a set of conceptual models, methodologies, and products that represent the operationalization of a distinct system of health delivery management. Such models and methodologies include care management, risk management, quality management (utilization), and referral protocols. The provision of actual care, however, happens at the Health Delivery Modules.

Contextual Background

For the health-care system to deliver its intended goods, it has to deal with both maintenance of health as well as treatment of sickness. The present health-care system is primarily concerned with taking care of the sick. It has evolved into a mature and entrenched system characterized as *sickness care.* The overwhelming success of sickness care has, as financed by historic reimbursement methods, obstructed and even prevented development of other critical aspects for the creation of a well-balanced health-care system.

Despite the fact that health maintenance and preventive care have long been recognized as an effective means of cost control, development of a significant wellness subsystem is practically nonexistent in the health-care system. Few have taken it upon themselves to address the traditional concept of "care" and develop the necessary operational protocols because of lack of adequate funding sources. Development of the care system, as presented here, will fill the chronic void in the health-care environment by introducing a bold, pragmatic dimension.

The conventional approaches of changing the way we pay for health care in and of themselves will not reform the system in the desired direction. Their focus is essentially on payment arrangements. Payment, while important, is but one of the concerns. A comprehensive approach should address the totality of a given care system, including financial as well as operational, technical, and behavioral viewpoints.

Desired Specifications

The care system deals with people when they are most vulnerable. It will involve the most sensitive aspect of people's lives. The design, therefore, should proceed with care because social institutions, once created, cannot be easily undone. The care system should therefore represent a comprehensive frame-work that will:

- Capture the missing dimension in the total management of care—the intervening link that can dissolve possible structural conflicts in the system and create win/win solutions among the patient, provider, and payer.
- Be viable in the current environment, but will also be capable of continuous learning and adaptation in changing environments.
- Allow maximum flexibility for the patient and the payer to exercise choice in terms of required services (selection of care module), access (selection of provider), and payment arrangements (selection of capitation and/or fee for service).
- Center around product differentiation, product development, and product management to enable each of its constituent modules to:
  - Represent a unique category of care; while individually independent, collectively they will create an integrated whole.
  - Follow a model of reimbursement that will best optimize multiple objectives of the care system (cost, quality, simplicity, and, most importantly, avoidance of structural conflict between payer, patient, and provider).
  - Become infrastructure-free, allowing maximum choice in selection and utilization of various care facilities, such as hospitals, homes, clinics, and care centers.
  - Be a decentralized and regionalized community-oriented health delivery system in order to be able to develop rapid and differential responses to its existing and potential communities with different health-related needs.
  - Keep all its options open and remain agile and flexible enough so it can take advantage of the emerging opportunities in the rapidly changing and unpredictable health-care environment.
  - Benchmark its performance against relevant state-of-the-art criteria by making sure that 1) the health-related aspect of the health delivery system (HDS) is targeted at the best performance within the industry, and 2) the support services, such as the administrative services, hospitality and facility management, and information systems, are targeted at the best performance outside the industry.
  - Achieve an order-of-magnitude improvement in the cost effectiveness of operating facilities by redesigning the throughput system.
  - Adopt and operationalize a new social calculus to encourage identification and elimination of waste and value-chain transaction and capacity utilization.

– Replace the dysfunctional matrix organization (two-boss system) with an exchange-based customer-supplier relationship in order to dissolve structural conflicts and create a win/win environment compatible with the systems architecture.

Observation of the above criteria led to the following design and classification of the care system:

- Preventive Care
- Interventional Care
- Viability Care
- Terminal Care

To be effectively cultivated, the care system modules will be initiated and operationalized into separate but interrelated modules. Initially, these modules will be created or redesigned outside of the current environment, under a different set of performance criteria to provide incentive for them to serve the needs of users, providers, and customers (payers) at the same time. Later on, the components can be unified or separated or further differentiated. Unification of the care system's modules, at least at the embryonic stage, will be avoided because it would lead to unbalanced development of one module at the expense of others. For example, the existing size and format of the interventional care module has the potential to obstruct the healthy evolution of the newest modules.

Common Features

The following will be common to all modules of the care system.

- Each care system module will have the requisite flexibility and capability to deal with the capitated model, the fee-for-service model, a combination of the two, or any emerging variation that could prove operationally sound. The care system modules will therefore have mechanisms that will give them the necessary flexibility to deal effectively with the emerging possibilities and make the necessary transitions with ease.
- Each care system module will also enjoy the freedom and responsibility to make its offerings available through the market access dimension to any segment of the market that may promise potential clients. The product (care system module) managers will not, therefore, be limited to a single channel of HMO in their marketing efforts. They can take advantage of different access mechanisms to deal with independent institutions or individuals.
- The care system modules will require the development of an interactive model of operation that will open the system to not only capitation and

fee-for-service populations, but other potential groups such as independent contractors with different interests and requirements.

- Development of the care system is essentially the development of a product line. Each care module will therefore have a product manager operating under a board representing the relevant stakeholders of that dimension, including physicians, nurses, financial and support services, and so on.

- Each care system module will be designed to be a member of an integrated whole while being managed as a stand-alone entity. It will be responsible for its own cash flow and financial performance. If any one module cannot stand alone financially, the system can decide whether to subsidize or redesign the module.

- Each care system module will have a financial model that will preempt structural conflict by aligning the interests of the major players actively involved in the delivery of care: the provider, the patient, and the payer.

- A target costing system will be developed to determine the relative share of each subsystem in the provision and distribution of care. The cost-sharing model will determine the costs of goods, selling, care, shared services, product development and maintenance, and facilities.

- Each and every module will have its own share of indigent patients who will be served in an environment that will promote personal responsibility and self-reliance.

- The health care system will encourage and register the clients to sign up for a total care package: preventive, interventional, viability, and terminal care. However, it will also have an a la carte flexibility that will make it possible for customers to pick and choose among the types of services offered—for example, a school system interested in utilizing the preventive care for its students, a corporation needing the interventional offering, or a selected group requiring the viability package.

- The pricing model should make it cheaper to purchase the product offerings as a total package rather than selectively or on a partial basis. The cost of interventional care, the largest portion of care, will therefore be significantly reduced if the customers are encouraged to buy other pieces as well. Thus, the impact of imposing a disproportional allocation to the rest of the system would be significantly reduced whenever a group of customers happens to opt for partial, rather than total, access.

- Protocols will be formulated to make explicit the predefined sequence of procedures as each type of patient is processed through the system.

- Each care module will have the responsibility of defining its information requirements and working closely with the information system unit to develop an interactive and comprehensive information support system that will not only service all the care system modules, but all the care providers as well. This information system will act as an input to the learning system.

The care system, in essence, will act as a customer of the information system unit and present a major market for information-based products.

- Each care system module will be equipped with an embedded learning system. The system will have explicitly stated assumptions and expected outcomes. It can and will modify itself based on the inputs that come from continuous monitoring of the actual performance and its comparison with the initial assumptions and expectations.
- The reward and evaluation of the care system and its modules will operate on three levels:
  - At the throughput level, the care system rewards will be based on the measure of the volume processed and its effectiveness.
  - At the latency level, the care system module rewards will be based on the measure of outcome, quality, and effectiveness of the care system as manifested in the general health of the population covered.
  - At the synergy level, the care system module rewards will be based on the measure of effective cooperation and collaboration shown toward other parts of the care system in particular and Butterworth system as a whole.

Descriptions of individual care modules follow.

Preventive Care

Preventive care will be responsible for maintaining and improving the health of the covered population as a whole. It will carry out this function by:

- Maximizing the health of anyone who comes into the system.
- Keeping those who are free of illness and injury from developing diseases or having disabilities.
- Detecting at an early stage those who are already sick and limiting further illness episodes through early intervention and other preventive measures.
- Developing protocols that will define recommended sequences of procedures for registering, identifying, and directing target groups of patients to appropriate centers staffed by appropriate providers based on initial assessment results, while respecting and supporting the right of each patient to exercise informed choice.
- Developing a measurement and evaluation system that will reward successful incidents of early detection.
- Maximizing patients' choice by providing them open access to clinical expertise. Based on the screening results, the system will identify and target the patients who will then be advised to follow a preferred course of action under a recommended primary care provider.

- The patient, however, will be allowed to make his or her informed choice of a prevention strategy. The patient will ultimately be free to decide whether his or her primary provider should be a traditional primary care provider or a specialist. Care system protocols will spell out the arrangements of the open approach policy.

Interventional Care

Interventional care is responsible for restoring the health of patients by offering a continuous and/or intense level of care. The Interventional Care will consist of the following levels of care: primary care, secondary care, and tertiary care. While primary care will serve as an access point for ambulatory patients with non–life-threatening problems/symptoms, secondary and tertiary care will involve intensive intervention extending over a relatively short period of time.

The basis for care differentiation will be the degree of need for continuous nursing care and specialty provider(s). These different levels of care can be addressed by the same or different providers/care givers carrying varying costs.

Interventional care will be responsible to:

- Develop a treatment plan defining the involvement of specialists, support staff, facilities, and referrals and/or discharge plans.
- Reimbursement for interventional care will likely be a hybrid. While the primary care can be capitated as a whole, secondary and tertiary care may utilize a version of the fee-for-service arrangement by means of a trust fund. This will provide the flexibility to:
  - Deal with the complexities of a treatment program due to inherent uncertainties and the number and varying degrees of other providers involved.
  - Manage the risks involved when small groups of patients may require treatments that are extremely expensive.
  - Remove the potentials for structural conflict and avoid the suspicion on the part of the patient or a participating provider that the payer may have any ulterior motive in defining the planned prescriptions.
  - Optimize interventional care expenses both at the aggregate and individual levels. The patient's well-being will not be compromised because the risks will be shared between the system and individual providers.

Viability Care

Viability care is responsible for restoring functionality (temporary or permanent) to the maximum extent given the nature of the underlying physical limitations.

Functional limitations may occur due to accidents, sickness, birth defects, or old age. Viability care will provide:

- Prognosis for 1) potential functional improvement, and 2) the prospect of returning to home/community based on medical, psychosocial, and economic resources.
- Assessment, treatment/equipment, infusion therapy, education, psychiatric therapy, monitoring, and hospitality services, if homeless.

Viability care will consist of two levels of care: rehabilitative care and supportive care. While rehabilitative care will involve revitalizing the patients by removing their functional limitations, supportive care will involve keeping the existing levels of irreversible physical limitations from deteriorating further. At the same time, supportive care will also involve keeping the patients from contracting other illnesses while providing them with compensatory supports to help them perform their basic functions. Differentiation between the two levels is based upon the duration of care and the chance of recovery from functional limitations.

Figure 9.2 shows the pattern of interactions both within and between the parts of the care modules.

Terminal Care

Terminal care is responsible for developing humane, dignified, and cost-effective means of taking care of patients who are diagnosed to be irretrievably moribund. The function of terminal care will be to:

- Support patients and families through the death experience (choices).
- Provide education and counseling (psychological and legal) to care givers.
- Build cost effectiveness into managed care.

Historically, the cases of terminally ill patients have presented the health profession with one of its most complicated dilemmas. Health-care providers, whose ultimate duty is to save the patient's life, find themselves in a most awkward position when dealing with death. Faced with such a predicament, some go out of their way to delay the inevitable at all cost, while others abdicate the challenge. Failure to address the totality of the situation professionally would be most unfair to all involved. It would continue to exact an unbearable psychological and social cost from the patient, the family, and the health system. Terminal care here is a deliberate attempt to make the painful termination issues explicit and design an optimal system to resolve them professionally.

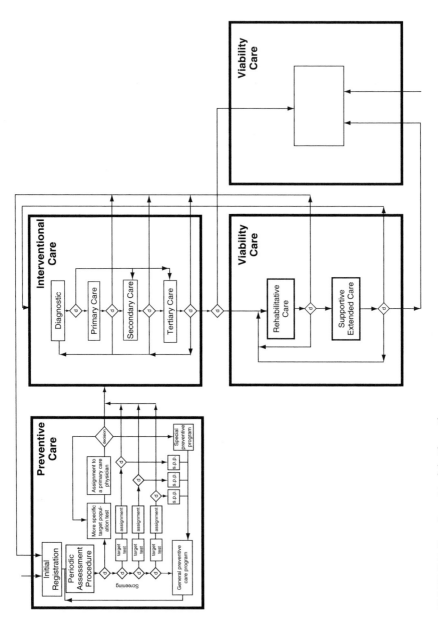

FIGURE 9.2   Care Module Flow Chart

OUTPUT DIMENSION

Care facilities (actual or virtual) will represent the output dimension of the architecture. It provides the interface between patient/client and the provider.

Health delivery is a real-time system, where the provision of the service is contingent upon the interface between the client and the provider. The output dimension will be represented by the location of the interface where care actually occurs. This location is not limited to in-patient, hospital care. Care can occur at other locations, such as ambulatory health facilities, physicians' offices, specialized clinics, labs and diagnostic centers, nursing homes, fitness centers, and the home.

All of these facilities are included in the administration of care in the health delivery modules network. The operational framework for organizing and managing the totality of this network will constitute the basic health delivery module. The module will replicate itself in different degrees and in various regions that will be covered by Butterworth Health System.

The health delivery modules are responsible for the operation and maintenance of the facilities as well as the actual provision of patient care services. The modules will replicate the three-dimensional architecture with their own shared services units, including such services as facilities management and maintenance. However, the model for delivery of each type of care will come from the respective part of the care system.

Some prominent aspects of the health delivery module are as follows:

- The health delivery module will develop a competency in hospitality management. This competency is necessary to redesign the operation so that an order-of-magnitude change in the performance measures, especially cost of operation, can be achieved.
- The providers who are an integral part of a facility, such as operating room, general care unit, specialty care unit, and other ancillary departments, will be permanently assigned to that facility while retaining their membership in the knowledge pool.
- The current model of the "emergency room" operation will be reconceptualized and redesigned. No longer will it be allowed to act as convenient, free access to the care system. Consequently, creation of decentralized regional primary care centers will help take away the incongruent responsibilities that are currently imposed on emergency departments. Such a realignment will make sure that ED units can afford to discharge their legitimate, and highly critical, function without having to get constantly sidetracked by nonemergency referrals that come in through the ED and must be treated in such an intense setting.

- Regional primary care centers will be in charge of services that should rightfully fall into their specialized domain. The decentralized arrangements of the regional primary care centers will have the added advantage of bringing nonemergency services closer to where the patients are.
- The overall cost effectiveness of the care system will be significantly increased by redirecting an enormous amount of expensive nonemergency services, currently seen in ED, to the regional primary care centers.
- So as not to deny access to indigent patients, the creation of the Butterworth Health Care Card for indigent patients will facilitate this rationalization of services.

Output units will have the responsibility of designing the interface among all the facilities and locations dealing with different levels of care in such a way that a seamless flow of patients will be ensured throughout the system.

In developing the HDS structure, two different approaches were initially considered.

Alternative One: Traditional Functional Structure

In a traditional functional structure (Figure 9.3), similar services such as hospitals, VNAs, nursing homes, and clinics, while maintaining their autonomy, will be grouped together. For example, all hospitals will report to a single group leader and will serve all communities. The same will be true for all the clinics, nursing homes, and other functional units. Each function will represent a single organization serving all of the communities.

Alternative Two: Modular Structure

The modular structure (Figure 9.4) would be a community-centered design in which a whole array of complementary activities (hospitals, clinics, nursing

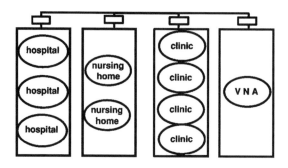

FIGURE 9.3   Functional Arrangement

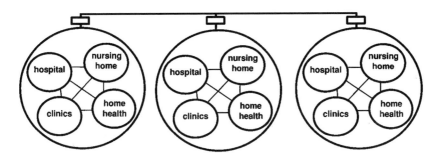

FIGURE 9.4   Modular Arrangement

homes) are grouped together to form an integrated module under single management. This module would have a community focus, and all its units are
supposed to serve a single community to ensure the kind of efficiency and
self-sufficiency needed in responding, on the spot, to the whole range of needs
in a specified community.

The advantage of a functional structure is that it will be easier to implement. There will be no resistance to such a design from the existing system.
However, a functional design will continue to suboptimize and reinforce the
existing disjointed service centers. The modular design, on the other hand,
will face stronger resistance to change and will require stronger resolve to
implement. But it will move the system toward a community-based health-
care system that Butterworth aspires to. The modular design will produce a
well-integrated and cost-efficient health system that is more compatible with
requirements of preventive care, capitation, and decentralized community-
centered health care systems.

However, further iterations led to a synthesis of both alternatives
(Figure 9.5). It was realized that by incorporating the advantages of both
functional and modular design into a single structure, HDS will be able to
avail itself of the flexibility required to strike the right balance between the
two structures rather than make an exclusive choice between the two. In the
new multidimensional structure, all services that are general purpose and community based can be grouped into decentralized modules capable of being
duplicated in each viable community. However, those services that are highly
specialized and capital intensive, requiring critical mass market, can take a centralized form serving the cases beyond the competence of the community-based
modules. Thus the new design can incorporate a learning capacity that will
allow the system to experiment with different ideas in different communities.
Successful experiments will then be disseminated among the communities. This
will provide HDS with opportunities for continuous improvement without sub-
jecting the total system to potentially costly experiments.

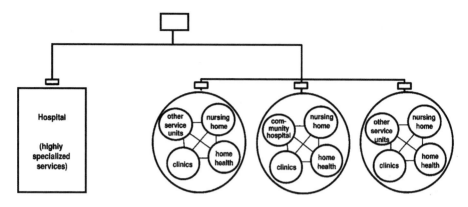

FIGURE 9.5 Mixed Structure

Health Delivery System Design: The Makeup

The HDS design will integrate the advantages of both functional and modular structures into a multidimensional system. It will be made up of five inter-dependent components: community-based health delivery system, specialized health delivery system, shared services, patient relations, and president's office (Figure 9.6).

The existing functions of Butterworth Hospital are reassigned among three platforms. Those functions requiring development of knowledge were housed in core knowledge, those requiring design methodology were housed in care systems, and health delivery activities requiring facility and equipment were housed in HDS.

Community-Based Health Delivery System

The community-based health delivery system will be made up of modular entities offering integrated services to specific communities. It will be driven by a customer focus and be made of regionally dispersed and locally managed networks of delivery modules positioned as closely to the delivery point as possible. (There seems to be a 20-minute time limit that consumers are willing to travel for primary health care unless the area is very rural, in which case the time limit expands to 37 minutes.) Once piloted experiments justify their existence, the networks will offer a whole range of preventative, primary, viability, and terminal types of care. Geographic organization of delivery modules will have the advantage of making it easier for their outcomes to be measured separately.

A network may start as a virtual entity, but it will eventually be organized around a central physical place. The network will be flexible, fluid, and easy to link to. The intention will be to increase the opportunities for expanding and

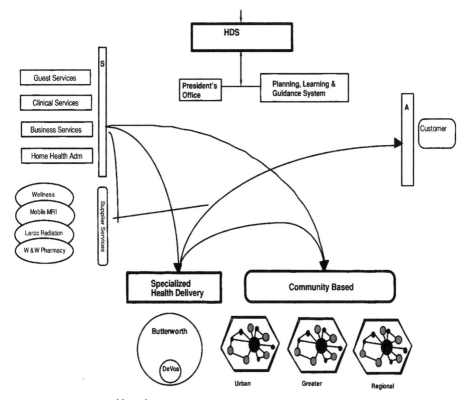

FIGURE 9.6   Health Delivery System Structure

extending outpatient services and, at the same time, push the ancillary services as closely as possible to financially viable core masses of clients.

The community-based HDS will consist, initially, of three integrated modular networks: the Urban Grand Rapids community, the Greater Grand Rapids community, and the regional community. Each community module will report directly to the president of HDS. A typical network will include at least a central community hospital serving the network. The system will include the following services:

- Primary Practices (Physicians' Offices)
- Diagnostics Centers
- Rehabilitation Centers
- Community Clinics
- Urgent Care
- Hospices
- Home Nursing
- Occupational Health Management

Kent Community Hospital will be integrated into the Urban Grand Rapids community, Villa Elizabeth Hospital and Grand Valley Health Center will be integrated into the Greater Grand Rapids community, and United Memorial Hospital, once transferred from the specialized health delivery system to this dimension, will act as the core of the regional community.

HDS can extend its presence into new regions by partnering with existing providers who will have demonstrated that they have workable knowledge of, and access to, a given community. In such cases it will be the nature of the relationship with the supplier unit rather than its ownership that will be of critical importance.

HDS will take advantage of clinical information technology to link all providers in HDS and other parts of Butterworth together.

Specialized Health Delivery System

The specialized health delivery system will represent Butterworth Hospital. It will be a centralized vehicle where capital-intensive, highly specialized health care delivery will actually take place. As such, it will concentrate on those intervention and tertiary cares that will be outside the competence and resources of the community-based health delivery system.

The specialized health delivery system will consist of two interdependent components: patient care and ancillary services. The two units will have their own heads, who will report directly to the president of HDS.

Patient Care

Patient care, as the output dimension of the specialized health delivery system, will consist of the following health-delivery units:

- Children's Care (DeVos Children's Hospital)
- Adult Critical Care
- General Medical Services
- Women's Health Services
- Emergency/Urgent Care
- Specialized Outpatient Care

Ancillary Services

Ancillary services, as the input dimension of the specialized health delivery system, will provide clinical/technical support services to both patient care units as well as the units of the community-based health delivery system. These shared services will have to undergo periodic process redesign in order to remain self sustained and competitively cost effective. Ancillary services will consist of the following units:

- Operating Room
- Rehabilitation Center
- Laboratory
- Cardiology Laboratory
- Radiology
- Respiratory Therapy
- Pharmaceutical
- Aeromed

Patient Relations

Patient relations will perform an advocacy function. It will represent the interests of the patients to the system. It will make sure that patients have a voice in the system and are fairly treated. The unit will act as an ombudsman to help settle grievances and compensatory claims. This will help prevent problems from growing into major litigation. Advocacy will also be responsible for providing social and financial counseling services to the patients who will need them.

Patient relations will also represent HDS to its environment. It will develop operational contacts with the corporate market access platform to receive feedback about the way HDS is perceived by its environment. This will ensure that Butterworth's policy of preserving a close community touch is enforced.

To effectively safeguard the interests of the patients and make sure they enjoy a dependable last resort to settle their grievances, it will be important that this dimension be taken seriously by all units of HDS. The realization of this market/consumer-oriented policy will require that patient relations be represented and directed by a manager who commands organization-wide respect and prestige and has direct access to the HDS president.

Shared Services

As an input dimension, shared services will serve and support the activities of the other units of HDS. The relationship between shared services and the user units will be that of supplier-customer. Although the general architecture of the system will encourage the self-sufficiency of its constituent units, especially the output units, there will still be exceptional services that will have to remain centralized for reasons of ensuring policy conformance, systemwide consistency, economy of scale, and requirement for critical mass and/or large capital expenditures.

Shared services will consist of the following five components. These services could have been assigned to the shared services platform at the corporate level. However, since they will be utilized mainly by HDS units, it was decided that their retention here will help minimize complexity and unnecessary interactions that would otherwise be unavoidable.

Hospitality and Facility Management

Hospitality and facility management will include all those guest services that will contribute to the hospitality aspect of a health delivery system. The idea is to make sure that the patient is treated like a guest at a hotel where his or her satisfaction receives utmost priority and attention. To ensure a total hospitality approach to health-care delivery, hospitality and facility management will be in charge of all activities that will be necessary in creating a hospitable environment. These will include facility planning, construction, management and maintenance, escort and hospitality, and communications.

Clinical Services

Clinical services will function as a centrally managed scheduling and deployment system that interfaces with core knowledge. Clinical services will include infection control, food and nutrition, volunteer services, laboratory, family care services, information technology, and medical services records.

Business Services Function

The business services function will include management consulting, materials management, plant operations, procurement, general financial services (payroll and reimbursements, patient financial services), malpractice claims, risk management, process control, environmental safety, and home health, and hospice administration.

Home Care Management

Home care management at this dimension will only represent the management of home care that will actually take place on a widely dispersed basis throughout the community health modules. It will take advantage of the large economies of scale associated with such a large core mass. Moreover, HDS may partner with other hospitals to manage these services for them. Home care management will therefore consist of general management, oversight, scheduling, standardization, and accreditation.

Occupational Care Management

Like home care management, occupational care management will represent only the management of occupational care that will take place throughout the

HDS's geographical regions. The service will be provided to corporate customers interested in outsourcing to HDS their health-care needs, as well as other health-related issues of their employees, such as workers' compensation. The economies of scale associated with such a potentially large volume of widely dispersed services warrant centralized management and oversight.

CORE KNOWLEDGE

Core knowledge is one of the two components of the input dimension of the architecture. Core knowledge is responsible for ensuring the availability of the appropriate service scope and number of providers to meet the whole spectrum of health-related care in its regions.

Core knowledge will be the system's center of expertise. It hosts and develops the provider resource of the system and helps the care system disseminate the state-of-the-art knowledge throughout the system. It will represent Butterworth's core competencies in medical practice.

Core Knowledge will consist of the following health-care providers:

- Medical staff (primarily consisting of physicians as independent contractors)
- Advanced practice providers
- Nurses
- Technical health workers and other professionals/clinicians
- Other professionals/technicians

The core knowledge network will be designed to accommodate a broad range of relationships. It will define and develop the structure for various types and degrees of membership in the system and the necessary operating procedures for members to interact.

Without an infrastructure for collaborative effort, the scarce provider resource will tend to be defused and wasted. The supportive organization should therefore be flexible enough to enhance maintenance and utilization of provider resources. This would ideally require each member of the provider system to be a high-level learner/educator, practitioner, and a leader of systems development. The absence of any one of these critical and interrelated aspects will undermine the others and eventually compromise the capacity of Butterworth to perform as a fully functioning system. Sustaining such a balanced state of readiness will ensure the comprehensiveness and the flexibility of the system's response to emerging problems and opportunities and at the same time encourage professional pursuits of purposeful networking and results-oriented collaborative initiatives.

To enjoy constant access to a rich resource of expertise representing state-of-the-art health care, the organizational context of core knowledge will constantly welcome maximum flexibility for innovative collaboration and will remain open to existing and emerging inputs of relevance both from within and outside the system.

Membership in the core knowledge system will therefore take a wide variety of forms functioning at multiple levels of involvement. The types of membership will be both full-time and part-time and will include the following:

- Independent practitioners (retainer-based)
- Associates (referral-based)
- Partners
- Nonaffiliates

To assure openness to external inputs of needed competence, the core knowledge system will operate as a confederation. Members of the confederation can be individuals as well as groups of providers. The status of the members of the core knowledge confederation may take the following form:

- Integrated: full-time members of Butterworth Health System
- Part-time: individuals with limited and predefined contributors
- Strategic alliance: organization-based partners operating within an agreed upon framework

Core knowledge members may choose to assume or relinquish different degrees of autonomy in working with Butterworth Health System. The nature and terms of this voluntary association define the areas in which the parties will choose to compete, collaborate, or cooperate. Thus, core knowledge members and Butterworth are codependent parties; their commitment to, and freedom from, each other is mutually reciprocal.

Creation of mutual trust between the Butterworth Health System and the core knowledge dimension will be the keystone to the ultimate success of the system. They should represent a united front to competition. A prerequisite to this loyalty-based success will be an environment that minimizes and dissolves conflict, whether real or perceived. Such an environment will require the following:

- All the members of core knowledge, regardless of their status, will have an equal voice within their panel, in the management of the group.
- All the members of core knowledge, regardless of their status, will have equal access to the shared services, such as billing, which will be provided to them on a marginal cost basis.
- An explicit internal system of conflict resolution will prevent, minimize, and dissolve potential conflicts before they are polarized.

The architecture of the core knowledge dimension will be a clone of the Health System. It therefore has the same input, output, and market dimensions. The output dimension defines the types of contributions of the integrated, part-time, and strategic partners of core knowledge to the care system and health delivery modules. The market dimension defines the access mechanism by which core knowledge services are deployed. The input dimension represents those support services that are core knowledge–specific and cannot, by definition, be provided by the system's shared services. The input dimension will provide its services on a marginal cost basis to its users.

To bring about a productive climate for continuous innovation and improvement of health-care delivery, the professional contributors will have to develop an additional vital dimension: the ability and desire for organization building. Traditionally, the complementary responsibility for designing and managing the contextual environment of health delivery systems has been uncoupled and transferred to administrators who are removed from the actual provision of clinical services. Because of this separation, substantial amounts of energy have been wasted in settling the unnecessary incompatibilities in the structure, function, and process of health-care delivery.

The only way to dissolve the paralyzing effects of the structural conflict is to add the missing dimension of care management leadership to the health-related expertise of the clinical providers. Equipped with leadership and design capability, health-care professionals can properly influence and/or help design the necessary interface between the context and the mode of delivery. The dual capacity would not only remove bureaucratic compartmentalization, but would enhance the effectiveness of care services by tapping the potentials for experimenting with alternative ways of teaming and complementary relations.

Core knowledge will be responsible for the generation and distribution of the knowledge, deployment of expertise, and exercise of leadership. The three functions are described below.

1. Generation and Dissemination of Knowledge (Learner/Educators). The providers system will be responsible for continuous learning and self-renewal of its members. The members will be expected to represent the health profession's state-of-the-art expertise. They will conduct most of this high-level self-education through teaching themselves as well as participating in applied research activities. They will be learning by teaching and learning while earning.

A portion of the provider resource may be engaged in ongoing academic pursuits that are either an integral part of medical schools or activities complementing such faculty engagements.

Members of the provider system may also engage in educating those who have a stake in health-related activities. Those who will be taught will include peers, students, interns, consumers, and the public at large.

The core knowledge dimension, however, will be responsible for creating interfaces and developing active associations with other sources of research and learning, such as universities, research institutions, medical and paramedical education centers, and technological development organizations.

2. Deployment (Practice). As pointed out earlier, core knowledge is responsible for ensuring the adequate availability of and the appropriate scope of and level of providers required to meet the whole spectrum of health-related care in all its regions at all times.

Members of the provider system, operating within the framework and protocols set by the care system, will contribute their knowledge and expertise by participating in different long- or short-term projects/programs that are created and terminated within the care system or the health delivery modules. The practice will take place in inpatient care (hospitals), clinics, labs, local health centers, wellness centers, homes, and long-term-care institutions. Members of core knowledge can choose to function on a permanent or temporary basis on different programs and projects without losing their full-fledged membership, and the privileges that come with it, in the core knowledge group. Each member can work in multiple programs/projects at the same time.

The power of multidimensional architecture, as developed in this design, is that it intentionally avoids the danger of tying the fate of the providers and the programs inseparably together. Once created, there is a tendency for the programs and projects to become a permanent feature of the organizational landscape. Left to their own devices, they develop a life and a mind of their own. Their fate is sealed, however, when their personnel are permanently assigned to them. The seed of the problem is in identifying the product with the provider, as is done in a divisional structure commonly used in academic and industrial settings wherein a program or product, once initiated, can never be discontinued. As long as a program's or project's termination threatens one's job and all the hard-won advantages associated with it, it is only natural that the job holder, whether a manager or a simple worker, does his or her utmost to lengthen the life of the project at all costs. This explains the inner rationality of the seemingly irrational resistance and obsolete relics that somehow manage to survive in corporate life.

Dissolving the problem will require that the life of the programs and projects be uncoupled from the people who are assigned to them. One of the advantages of having a core knowledge dimension in the systems architecture is that it will serve as the permanent home base for the professional resources of Butterworth. Any other relationship and assignment will, by definition, be considered as contingent and temporary no matter how long it is expected to last. The permanence of the core knowledge home base, requiring continuous reassessment and renewal, and the impermanence of programs and projects, allowing continuous innovation and adaptation, remove the obstinate conditions that lead to inflated bureaucracies and entrenched resistance to change.

3. Leadership. Leadership in this context is defined as the ability to influence those over whom one does not have authority. Competency in medical and health technologies, although a crucial necessity, does not by itself guarantee the success of a health-care system. To be sufficiently effective, every professional member of the system should be an influential leader as well. Thus every provider should have the desire and the ability to positively impact the context, structure, and process of Butterworth. To achieve this vital task requires knowledge workers who 1) internally, seek to participate in the design and management of care modules and procedures for doing more with less, and 2) externally, proactively influence the contextual environment of Butterworth in order to remove the obstructions and expand its potentials for doing more and better. Butterworth simply cannot afford the conventional, and dysfunctional, division of labor between clinical and management-related functions.

In the final analysis, a good provider, therefore, is a good learner/educator, a good practitioner, and a good leader. The success of Butterworth and its providers, and by the same token any health-care system, will ultimately depend on whether the members of the provider community have achieved this multifunctionality in addition to being competent practitioners.

Building multifunctionality into the provider community will convert obstruction into opportunities and replace aggregates with systems. Thus individual providers will become purposeful members of a highly interdependent system that will make a difference. They will effectively use their multiple competencies in managing upward and influencing other parts of and stakeholders in the health-care system over whom they do not have direct control but on whom the success of their professional effort will depend.

The multifunctionality will also give providers the capability and the possibility of designing and managing their practice in terms of affordable and user-friendly packages and programs that are both accessible and relevant to the consumers. They will cooperate with the care system in the development and continuous improvement of generic models, protocols, and procedures needed to manage the different aspects of health delivery systems.

While the core knowledge group is responsible for medical research and education, it will replicate the three-dimensional scheme to create its own special shared services. Shared services in this context will include physician's office management and provider recruiting and credentialing.

SHARED SERVICES

Shared services is the other component of the input dimension of the architecture. It will be the provider of specific services required for the proper functioning of the system as a whole. To ensure its proper functioning, shared services will be designed with close attention to the issues surrounding centralization and decentralization, separation of service from control, and customer orientation.

Need for Centralization

Centralization will be avoided unless one or all of the following situations weigh overwhelmingly against decentralization of a particular service.

Uniformity

The aspects of the system that will be centralized are those that are common to all or some of the parts of Butterworth and cannot be left decentralized without rendering serious damage to the proper functioning of the system. In areas such as measurement systems and communications, where common language and coordination are of major importance, uniformity will serve as the criterion for centralization.

Technological Imperatives

Certain technologies, which, because of their nature, are deemed indivisible and therefore require a holistic design, can be centralized. For example, the effectiveness of a comprehensive information system is in its holism, consistency, real-time access, and proper networking to transfer information as needed to different users. Development of such a system requires cooperation and coordination among all the actors in the system.

Economy of Scale

Although economy of scale is generally considered an important factor in the creation of shared services, the tradeoffs between centralization and decentralization of each function should be made explicit to prove that the benefits significantly outweigh the disadvantages before it is moved to shared services. In this case, it is expected that a service, once centralized, will either generate significant savings for the system as a whole or help some of the units that otherwise would not be able to afford the service on their own.

Management may feel that a certain level of specific activities will be critical for future success and therefore decide to centralize, develop, and specialize them. It is management's prerogative to identify the services that should fall under this category either as optional or mandatory. Where only one unit/customer is involved, it is best to decentralize the relevant service.

Whatever the justification of the services shared, the unit will have to become the state-of-the-art and cost-effective provider of choice.

Control versus Service

The combination of a control function with a service function is the most obstructive element to the functioning of shared services. It undermines both the effectiveness of the services and the legitimacy of the controls. To protect themselves against the creeping hegemony of service providers and the obvious risks involved in relying on control-driven services, the operating units resort to duplicating the support services that could otherwise be easily shared and effectively utilized. Rampant and excessive duplications of services leading to paralyzing bureaucracy and unnecessary redundancy are symptomatic of the natural reaction of operating units to service functions developing such dual personalities. On the other hand, disguising legitimate and necessary control function under the pretext of a service function transforms the nature of control from a learning mechanism to a defensive and apologetic act.

Extra care should be taken to make sure that none of the functions of the shared services, as is the usual tendency, undergo a character change and assume control properties. Under the pretext of a need for consistency and uniformity, there is a natural tendency to let the service provider perform the necessary monitoring and auditing function. This has always proved to be misguided. The providers cannot help falling into the slippery slope of wanting, increasingly, to assume a control function. This obviously would scare away the users who did not expect to find a new boss in the guise of a server.

While shared services will provide the customers with requested services (such as information, benefits, payroll, and billing) in accordance the criteria and protocols set by the Planning, Learning, and Guidance (PLG) System, the PLG System will be in charge of setting the policies and the criteria governing these services, as well as conducting the necessary monitoring and enforcing functions to ensure proper implementation of those policies.

Customer Orientation

While superior-subordinate relationships have traditionally been taken as the only building block for the exercise of organizational authority, the supplier-customer relationship introduces a new source of influence into the organizational equation. With the supplier-customer relationship, which emerges only in an internal market environment, the helpless recipient becomes a real customer. Armed with purchasing power, the customer becomes an empowered actor with the ability to influence and interact with his or her supplier in such a way that both parties together can now define the type, cost, time, and quality of the services rendered.

Creation of an internal market mechanism, and thus a supplier-customer relationship, is contingent upon transforming the shared services into a performance center. Performance centers, unlike overhead centers, do not receive a fixed budget allocated from the top. They have working capital with a variable operating budget. In this model, expenses are proportional to the income generated by the level of services rendered and revenues received in their exchange.

These two pairs of horizontal and vertical relationships are complementary, synergizing one another. Whereas superior-subordinate defines the formal authority, dealing with hiring, firing, and promotion, a supplier-customer relationship creates a new source of influence that tries to rationalize demand.

In the absence of an internal market environment, there will be no built-in mechanism to rationalize demand. An agreeable service provider with a third-party payer creates and fuels an insatiable demand. A disagreeable service provider, on the other hand, would trigger a proliferation of duplications of the same services by the potential customers. The result would be an explosion of overhead expenses in the context of an essentially cost-plus operation. The trend would be irrational and the corrective interventions would prove ad hoc and ineffective, at best.

On the basis of these criteria and considerations, the composition of Shared Services is as follows.

Information System Group

- Data Management (clinical data, financial data, and human resource data)
- Information Technology
- Systems Analysis

Management Institute (Education Services)

Implementation of the proposed design will require institutionalization of a whole new set of management capabilities, such as crisis management, conflict resolution, managing decision system, learning system, early warning system, measurement system, and quality. The services of the Management Institute will interface with external centers of relevant expertise and disseminate the required competencies throughout the Butterworth Health System, especially the executive office and core knowledge groups.

Human Resource Management

- Payroll
- Benefit Administration
- Compensation Management
- Recruitment (implementation only)

Financial Systems

- Budget and Cash Flow Management
- Accounting

- Billing
- Collections

Medical Records Management
- Release of Information
- Consistency Standards for Records

Communications
- Public Relations
- Media Interface
- Audio/Visual Equipment and Management
- Corporate Branding
- Advertising

Materials Management
- Purchasing

HEALTH DELIVERY SYSTEM, CORE KNOWLEDGE, AND CARE SYSTEMS INTERACTIONS

The health-care system is a unified process. It has, however, three manifestations representing three aspects of the same thing: generation and dissemination of health-care knowledge; design of health-care products; and practice of health care. Correspondingly, the architecture provides three interrelated platforms to make sure these three aspects are considered prime functions requiring equal attention. To safeguard the integrity of the health-care process, it is therefore critical that the integrative agent of these seemingly different functions be clearly identified (see Figure 9.7).

The integrity of the process of health-care delivery, more than anything else, will be the property on which the system will ultimately stand or fall. This will require that the three activities of generation and dissemination of health-care knowledge, design of health-care products, and practice of health care, while receiving equal attention, be integrated. The importance of the three activities is such that the proposed systems architecture assigned each one of these activities to a different platform under a separate manager.

The contextual requirements for management are basically different for the three activities. Educational activity at the core knowledge level is basically a specialized science-oriented function lending itself to knowledge-based unidisciplinary management of learning. Design activity is basically a methodology-based function lending itself to transdisciplinary management of product development. Practice is basically a line function lending itself to interdisciplinary management

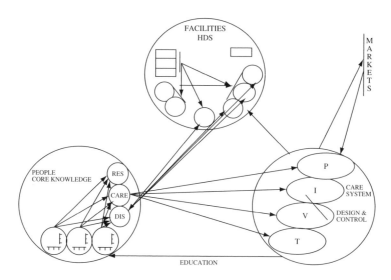

FIGURE 9.7   Interrelationship of HDS, Care Systems, and Core Knowledge

of throughput. Otherwise, using a single manager for all three platforms will lead to (depending on the professional orientation of the manager in charge) serious malfunctions. The ensuing suboptimization would favor one of the three aspects, which would gain ascendancy to a primary position, thus relegating the others to second-class citizens.

On the other hand, these three activities are so interrelated that their integration will be a prime concern. This seems contradictory to the above statement that explicitly assigns the three activities to three separate platforms. The question, therefore, is how the integration of the three platforms is supposed to happen. This brings us back to the core idea of the architecture. A key assumption of this design is that the only way to ensure the integration of the system would be for the knowledge worker to become the integrator.

This means that the integration of the three activities of learning, designing, and practicing health care will be realized by the fact that the designer, the educator, and the practitioner would be one and the same. To preserve the wholeness of the process of providing care, each professional contributor, whether a doctor, nurse, or technician, will be engaged in the three distinct and yet interrelated roles that will feed on and contribute to each other's strength. When in core knowledge, the same provider will help generate and disseminate knowledge by participating in learning cells as a learner/researcher/educator. When in care systems, the same provider will help operationalize his or her knowledge by participating in design cells as a designer/evaluator. When in HDS, the same provider will help utilize new knowledge by participating in practice cells as an implementer/practitioner.

Engagement and ownership of each one of the three complementary and mutually reinforcing roles will prepare, empower, and motivate the provider to succeed in dealing with the other two. Thus a designer/evaluator and at the same time the practitioner of particular products and services will always be most qualified and ready to teach them; a learner/researcher/educator and at the same time the practitioner of particular products and services will always be most qualified and ready to design them; and, finally, a designer/evaluator and at the same time the learner/researcher/educator of particular products and services will always be most qualified and ready to administer them.

In all three contexts, the integrative agent is the doer who has first-hand experience with the problems. Thus the system will become self-correcting, self-educating, and self-integrating. The design will allow the professionals to manage upward and create a "low-archical" approach intimately suited to the idiosyncrasies of a multiminded and professionally driven organization. Thus, the success of the system will depend on the ability and willingness of the professionals in acting out, depending on the context, all the different roles of learner, educator, designer, and practitioner interchangeably. Although this seems to be against the implicit assumptions of health care, it is perfectly compatible with human nature. In real life, individuals perform many different roles. For example, one plays, quite naturally and almost simultaneously, the roles of parent, professional, friend, boss, and subordinate in different contexts without difficulty. As a matter of fact, this happens to be one of the characteristics that distinguishes humans from other species and constitutes the keystone of social existence.

The composite performance profile of each professional will therefore reflect the three aspects of his or her role as an educator, a designer, and a practitioner. The profile will show the value of the individual to the organization based on the quality and diversity of the roles he or she will be called upon to play in the different contexts of the value chain. The higher the competence, the greater the demand; the greater the demand, the higher the value. One point, however, needs to be underscored here: the design will not encourage, but it will certainly respect, the personal preference of those professionals who, for whatever reasons, might elect not to engage in multiple roles.

In the trio of core knowledge, care system, and delivery system, core knowledge will serve as the home base for the system's physicians, nurses, technicians, and other health-based professionals. This will make it possible for the knowledge worker to accept different roles with different durations in all three platforms. When at core knowledge, it will be the providers themselves who will help perform the stewardship function of the human assets. They will be engaged in learning from and teaching each other in order to make sure that the health-care competency of Butterworth represents the cutting edge of the health-care profession at all times. They will constantly monitor the direction and state of the science and practice of health care. They will make sure that the entire professional competence of the system is in a state of readiness to respond rapidly, effectively, and adequately to the changing and growing requirements of the market.

While care systems will be responsible for designing the process and packaging health-care products and services, as well as monitoring and ensuring the quality of their deployment, HDS will be where health care will actually happen. HDS will own the capital-intensive and health-related physical assets and will be responsible for their effective utilization in providing the care deliverables.

The three-dimensionality should not be mistaken for the conventional concept of the division of labor and the three-boss system. The three platforms manage the three different aspects of the system, each with a clear-cut accountability in the process. Their relationships will be governed by all three aspects of authority: legal, knowledge, and financial. Across the three contexts, knowledge is the common denominator and therefore will work as the integrative agent. The relationship of the members and their manager in the core knowledge group is boss-subordinate (legal), while in the context of the care system and delivery system the relationship is customer-provider. The successful operation of the three units will therefore require that the creation of a throughput and measurement system with variable budgeting be an integral part of this design.

The design uniquely matches the exceptional requirements of knowledge-driven organizations. It is based on the fact that role rather than individual is actually the building block of social systems. Owing to this, people can have multiple memberships in a variety of organizations in which they act out very different roles. By taking advantage of this phenomenon, the design will provide the individual contributor with unrestricted possibilities for the kind of continuous development and creativity that come with multirole, total involvement in the whole process of health care. Multirole involvement will safeguard the wholeness of the knowledge worker by saving him or her from compartmentalization. Uncoupling the professional from the trappings of narrowly defined jobs will de-bureaucratize the system and rescue both the people and the organization from insulation, unidimensionality, rigidity, petty turf wars, and inevitable obsolescence in a rapidly changing environment.

Freedom from fixed and permanent job descriptions will provide the care systems and HDS platforms with equal freedom from resistance to change, structural conflicts, and suboptimization. It will provide them with infinite flexibility and capacity for unprecedented experimentation and innovation.

Separation of the knowledge worker from a rigid job description is a means for institutionalizing creative freedom. Such freedom ensures professional excellence and organizational viability through continuous learning and total involvement. Freeing the system to constantly define and redefine its basis for competitive advantage will prevent strategic myopia and those organizational defaults that let the requirements of past success become the source of future failure. The design is intended to promote meritocrity and combat bureaucratic tendencies that, when left unchecked, would lead to mediocrity, promotion to incompetence, and eventual conversion of competence to a disqualification.

Project managers at care systems will be responsible for incorporating the inputs of the practitioners in the design of care products. They will make sure that the product development will reflect the emerging market needs. They will also make sure that the integrity of the design is not compromised. Project managers will provide the content and be responsible for the potency of the deliverables, as well as pay for the services of the practitioners/designers who participate in product development. The actual training and development of the practitioners/designers, however, will take place in core knowledge. Thus the development process will have a dual interface: the market and core knowledge.

The challenge is to realize the potentials of the design for responding to the individual's need for independence and the organization's need for interdependence at the same time. The design is a deliberate attempt to avoid sacrificing the good of the whole for the convenience of the part, and vice versa. Suboptimization is deliberately designed out in order to make it possible for the system to avoid imposition of win/lose solutions that would pit the members against each other in their attempts to win functional battles at the expense of the corporate war. An operation can hardly be qualified as a success if the patient ultimately dies.

The integration of the three platforms, although attractive, should not be considered easy. It will take the total cooperation of these platforms, the full attention of the HDS president, and a real cultural transformation (not to be mistaken with a climate survey) for its enormous potentials to be realized. In the process, the intensity of the resistance associated with the comfort level that comes with prolonged adaptation to single-role performance should never be underestimated.

THE EXECUTIVE OFFICE

As a whole, the executive office will be responsible for ensuring the overall viability and effectiveness of the system. It will be responsible for creating a vision and generating a shared image of a desired future and providing the leadership to help achieve the organization's mission. To do this, the executive office is responsible for creating the following three critical processes.

1. Latency. The essence of creating latency will be a strategic planning process that institutionalizes the continuous search for new opportunities relevant to the value chain. This process will develop and implement activities leading to cultural transformation, business renewal, generation of

innovative ideas, and improved ways of delivering quality care and conducting business.

2. Synergy. The essence of synergy is management of interactions. It is concerned with the development and implementation of processes, systems, and incentives that produce cooperative efforts and alliances that will make the whole of the value chain greater than the sum of its parts. These measures, which include the internal market, target costing, measurement systems, reward systems, early warning systems, and learning systems, are intended to create a win/win environment by dissolving structural conflicts among the internal units, and linking the performance measure of each unit to its contributions to other units.

3. Throughput. Throughput processes will be concerned with the quality and efficiency of operations. They will help the system increase its effectiveness both within and among all the units of the value chain. The system will do so by utilizing continuous improvement methodology. The objective is to enhance operational potency through systems solutions intended to:

- Decrease cycle time
- Eliminate waste
- Improve flexibility
- Increase quality

Throughput happens at two levels. The executive office will set the policies and standards while the operational managers will be responsible for operationalization. The implementation activities concerning the throughput process will be carried out at all levels of the organization. Every member of the system will participate in the continuous improvement activity.

Under the leadership of the president and CEO, a small group of interdisciplinary staff, operating in cross-functional teams, will be responsible for instituting the latency, synergy, and throughput processes in their own area.

Recap

This section is intended to serve as a reminder of the key points of the new design. The design utilizes the three bases of authority at the same time: the legal source (the boss), the knowledge source (competence), and the economic source (assets and money).

While in core knowledge, all doctors report to a doctor, all nurses to a nurse, and all technicians to a technician. Here, the management and interrelationships will be solution oriented and compartmentalized. This arrangement will recognize and satisfy the requirements for specialized knowledge boundaries and establish the environment and rationality for the disciplinary approaches to professional development and peer oversight. In core knowledge, the organization will be input based and therefore functional.

When in care systems or HDS, however, the mode is reversed from functional to modular. The management, the team, and the relationships will be problem oriented and treatment driven. The requirements of patient care, which is usually a multidisciplinary phenomenon, will become the criteria for the composition of the project teams and the application of the design and practice methodology. In care systems and HDS, the organization will therefore be cross-functional and output based. The competence of the manager here is not necessarily a function of a single specialization. The requirements of the totality of the output will determine the most suitable leader, who might happen to be a doctor, a nurse, or a technician.

Taken to its logical conclusion, the widely held misconception that nobody should report to anybody who represents a different discipline will prevent a health delivery system from adopting the interdisciplinary approaches based on real-world problems that are so radically different from the way universities divide themselves. Such compartmentalizations will not only be unidisciplinary and solutions oriented (rather than interdisciplinary and problem oriented), but they will invariably lead to creation of structural conflicts and imposition of win/lose solutions. That is why conflicts based on the traditional division of labor can never be dissolved unless the system is redesigned.

The new design will prevent structural conflicts rather than leaving them for managers to cope with. The prevention is assured by getting basically the same people to engage in learning, designing, and practicing health care. This is the essence of self-management and managing upward.

Pathways that are not the product of cross-functional teams, even if efficient, will not be widely owned or find general acceptance. To be both inherently effective and actually applied, the pathways not only should be collectively coproduced but should leave a certain degree of freedom for the practitioner to improvise. Otherwise, a seemingly perfected procedure will prove suffocating because it will be too rigid for adaptation to the case at hand and too tight for the practitioner to innovate. An inefficient system that would allow choice and experimentation will ultimately prove superior to a perfected straitjacket.

10

The Marriott Corporation

Kathy Dannemiller, a dear friend, had recommended me to the Marriott people. Dean Pat Stocker invited me to make a one-day presentation at the Aspen Institute, where Bill Tiefel, president of Marriott Lodging, and his direct reports were attending a week-long executive seminar.

The Marriott seminar was very exciting. The company faced an incredible challenge. Times were bad. The game had changed drastically. Real estate had collapsed, and hotel owners (Marriott's main customers) needed more cash to survive. Corporate America (Marriott's major source of cash) was involved in so-called "right-sizing" and cutting costs left and right.

A month after our first seminar, in the summer of 1992, the Lodging Executive Committee decided to engage in an ideal-design process to replace the ineffective and costly divisional structure with a noble design. The outcome was a profound transformation of Marriott, which put it right back on the path to its continued success.

Two parallel teams were formed: one for design and the other for "mess" formulation. The design team consisted of 24 members of Bill Tiefel's executive committee. The mess team consisted of six able Marriott Lodging professionals. However, the mess team's report, because of its confidential nature, will not be discussed here.

John Pourdehnad, my colleague and old friend, was my partner in this project. He not only guided the mess team to an outstanding mess formulation, but was also an indispensable participant in the design process.

What follows is a summary of the three iterations by the design team. The design process involved the following steps:

- Developing a collective understanding of the environment—"How is the game evolving?" and "What are the new bases for competition?"
- Identifying the purpose of the system to be designed (specifying the desired properties, core values, and mission).

- Creating a platform, a vision of a desired future for Marriott Lodging and a direction for its development, and a learning system that would be capable of responding continuously to the challenges of a changing environment.

THE ENVIRONMENT: HOW THE GAME IS EVOLVING

The future is not what it used to be. It is becoming increasingly difficult, if not impossible, to predict and prepare. Contemporary organizations, therefore, need to focus on creating their own futures rather than waste their time attempting to predict and prepare.

- The current state of the economy (1992) cannot be explained away only as a cyclical phenomenon. And it does not only imply recession. The economy seems to be restructuring toward a level more compatible with the emerging state of its competitiveness.
- The real estate market has changed. The current weakness of the real estate market is not temporary and is unlikely to change in the foreseeable future. Therefore, the game cannot be played on the assumption that one can win through asset appreciation alone.
- Consumer behavior is changing. Customers are becoming smarter and want more and more for less and less.
- Businesses face cost pressures and are becoming very price-sensitive.
- Demand is shifting from one tier to the next.
- Quality, cost, and time are interdependent and form a complementary whole. None can be compromised at the expense of the others.

Bases for Competition

- Learn to live with uncertainty. Become more flexible and agile—have an early warning capability.
- Reduce the cost of operation by an order of magnitude. Select the right services and improve their quality.
- Adopt price-competitive measures to fill up unused capacity.
- Redesign the product, the process, and the structure to reap a 20 to 30 percent cost reduction.
- Avoid being pushed into an undesirable product/market niche.
- Differentiate and match products in response to the market's emerging needs.
- Write down the assets (reflagging)—be a smart deal maker.
- Factor in the ratio of debt service to asset value. Factor in how the owner perceives value and is motivated to get into this business.

- Develop a strategy directed at the owners and the lenders.
- If the owners are failing, find out who is buying their assets. The asset management advisory group should be charged with developing both a strategy to deal with this situation and a capability to anticipate rather than react.

PURPOSE
Principles and Desired Characteristics

- Our commitment will be to total *guest satisfaction*.
- We will deliver value (benefits/costs) at all levels of the service value chain. We will define value at the end of the chain, "the guest," and work our way back to property, owner, region, brand, division, and corporation.
- We will continuously match the product offerings with changing customer needs (strategic product-market fit).
- We will take responsibility for creating a win/win environment that dissolves conflict among guests, associates, shareholders, owners, and distributors at various levels of the operations.
- We will challenge the industry by becoming the undisputed leaders in hotel management. We will accomplish this by:
  - Fostering a lean, simple, nonbureaucratic, and flexible organization in which formal and informal systems are in synch and easy organization-wide communication is enjoyed.
  - Creating a mutually supportive and interdependent system that takes full advantage of the synergy resulting from the interaction of technology, product/brands, and markets.
  - Being identified with value excellence through knowledge leadership.
  - Dissolving the dilemma between freedom and accountability, ensuring that authority and responsibility are matched at all levels.
  - Designing a throughput-oriented, win/win reward system that helps dissolve structural conflicts.
  - Leveraging technology to deliver value—doing more and more with less and less, resulting in higher resource productivity/yield.
- We will attempt to achieve mutual satisfaction of all stakeholders by understanding the dynamic interaction of their needs. We cannot succeed unless all of our stakeholders—guests, associates, shareholders, owners, and distributors—are successful.
- We recognize our multitier customer base. In addition to our guests, property owners are the other critical customers. And when our customers are in trouble, we are in trouble.

MISSION
We want to be your "FIRST CHOICE."
At Marriott:
Every guest will be eager to return.
Every associate will be able to realize her or his potentials.
Every owner will be supported by superior management services.
Every shareholder will be rewarded by premium returns.

THE ARCHITECTURE

The following architecture (Figure 10.1) was accepted as the basis for building an idealized Marriott Hotels, Resorts, and Suites (MHRS). The architecture, as represented in the following diagram, has four distinct dimensions:

1. Region/market operations: Representing the essence of the system. This is where MHRS ultimately happens—where the properties are located and where services are provided to guests.
2. Products/brands: Representing the output (end products) of the system.
3. Core components: Representing operating subsystems that are shared throughout the system and/or sold to external markets.

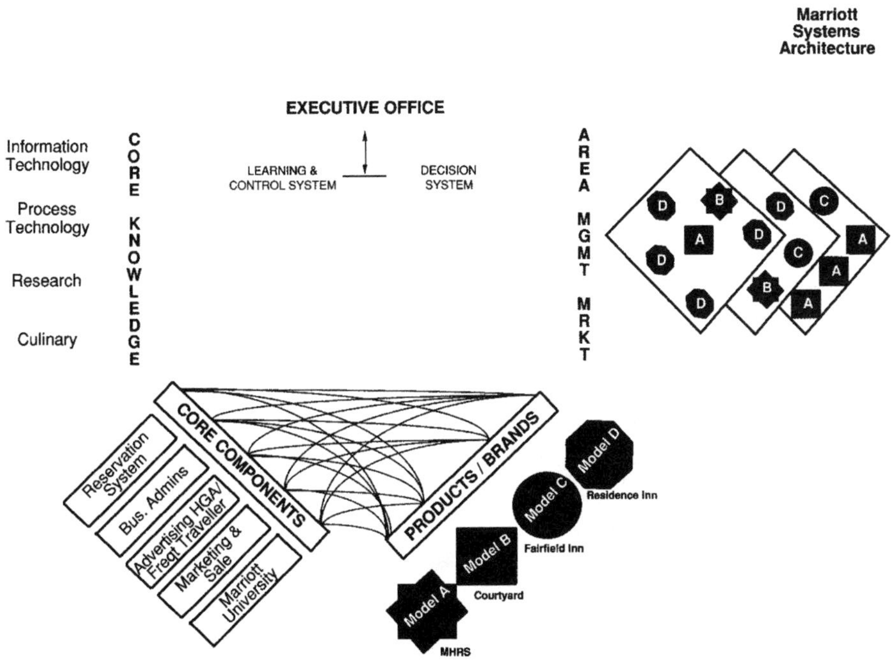

FIGURE 10.1 Systems Architecture

4. Core knowledge: Representing MHRS's unique state-of-the-art know-how to be used across the value chain by any or all of the above dimensions directly.

The architecture recognizes the necessity for achieving competitive advantage in all dimensions of market, product, and technology simultaneously. It therefore seeks to eliminate suboptimization around any one dimension. The objective is to actively generate synergy, latency, and efficiency by creating a win/win relationship among the three dimensions.

This architecture opens up possibilities that are usually closed to traditional approaches by:

- Adding new types of relationships to the superior/subordinate pairs as the fundamental blocks for organization building—(customer/supplier).
- Changing the nature of control from supervision to learning—supervision is considered wasteful.
- Dissolving structural conflicts between the requirements of the marketplace and the diverse interests of competing product groups.
- Reducing complexity by developing integrated solutions instead of patching together a multitude of incompatible and discrete solutions.
- Allowing centralization and decentralization, integration and differentiation, interdependency and autonomy to all be realized simultaneously.

Product/Market Mix

Matching products with markets is not a one-time proposition. It requires continuous research and redesign. Introducing the concept of brand managers as a new dimension in the architecture will institutionalize this function to provide an ongoing response to the challenge. The ideal company will also seek new opportunities for some of its core components and for its core knowledge (for example, reservation/Honored Guest programs and training).

Region/Market Operation

Operations will be organized and managed across all lodging products according to each market's specific characteristics and requirements, taking advantage of the total opportunities presented by the marketplace. The markets will be segmented based on the behavioral characteristics and requirements of customers in any given economic region. This will reduce the structural conflict between competing product divisions and make it possible to create an optimum product mix for each regional operation to realize its maximum potential.

The total world market will be divided into ten regions. Each region will manage 50 to 75 different properties (including all brands). Large properties will have GMs, and smaller properties will be clustered into area management. The major concentration of effort will be to empower properties to do their work on their own and with minimal supervision.

Depending on the extent and diversity of functions, regional managers will have several assistants. These assistants to regional managers will be trained with candidacy for GM posts in mind. Assistant managers will be competent in several functions—to avoid top-heavy bureaucratization and to promote managerial and organizational flexibility under changing environmental conditions.

Within each region, operations will be designed bottom-up, not top-down. First, those functions and services that are desired and can be best operated at the property level will be identified. Then, those functions and services that can be shared at the regional level will be identified before deciding which ones will best be provided at the regional level.

The organization of each geographical region will differ based on the market potential of each area. However, the following functions will be used as a model.

Business Management

This function will include finance, accounting, administrative and human resources services, and any other regional management support operations (including owner relations). This group will be supported by the business services unit of the core component dimension.

Project Management

Project teams will be organized around specific throughput processes, but will all have cross-functional expertise in information technology, TQM, human systems, and design. The objective is proper implementation of the integrated solution (developed by each brand manager) at each site in the region, allowing all of the following critical goals for success to be accomplished simultaneously: reduction of cycle time; elimination of waste; creation of flexibility; and management of total quality. Rollout of any other projects developed by the core knowledge groups or the corporation as a whole will be undertaken by this function.

Maintenance Management

All of the activities directed at the upkeep of the sites and the engineering and maintenance function will be grouped under this function, which will provide services to the regional bases.

Sales

The regional sales effort will include direct sales, pricing, positioning, and sales training.

Brand Management

Brand management will assume total responsibility for product development and product management. It will develop all the necessary operational procedures to operate a given type of lodging operation. Brand management will be the owner of the design and the lodging concept, and it will be a supplier to the region/markets operations.

Initially, brands management will be limited to four models: basic, luxury, group, and convention. However, Courtyards, Fairfield Inn, and Residence Inn might be added later.

Product/brand management will perform the following functions:

- Concept development and concept implementation guidelines.
- Brand marketing and positioning, guidelines, penetration, demand requirements, and competitive intelligence.
- Franchising guidelines, business modeling, system integration, and core deliverables.
- Operating procedures and maintaining brand identity (keeping the brand clean from other niches).
- Determining the appropriate standards for the product, deliveries in service, rooms, restaurant, lounge, catering, services, and amenities.
- Feedback and interaction with advertising, promotion and public relations, price analysis, product criteria refinements/value engineering, emerging trends and market requirements, and adjustments to positioning.

Core Components

Core component groups will make their services available to the internal customers at the lowest available price. Internal purchases might initially be subsidized by the corporation. The services will be sold at the market price to outside customers.

The following will constitute the core components of the lodging operations:

- Reservation System: The reservation system will be designed on a modular basis and offer its services on a differential price base depending on the needs of the user (services will be customized).

- Marketing and Sales
  - Marriott video productions, advertising management, customer database, superior channel access, brand name, and other customer issues that go beyond one particular property.
  - A customer survey system—to measure guest satisfaction.
  - The national sales system—to include a sales deployment and lead referral system.
  - A customer response (off property) system—to be developed for escalation.
  - A national public relations network—to be utilized.
  - Meeting and conference management services—to be available.
- Human Resources: The Associate Opinion Survey System, career planning system, succession planning, employee relations, recruitment, performance evaluation, promotions/transfers, training and development, compensation and benefits, termination, retirement, personnel audit, and quality of work life.
- Business Management: Payroll and benefits administration, procurement, accounting.
- Marriott University: A system will be created to offer continuous training and education as an integral part of the MHRS operation. Every member of the Marriott family will become a teacher and a student.

Core Knowledge

MHRS will develop state-of-the-art capabilities in the following areas:

- Information Technology
- Process Technology
- Culinary Research

The expertise of this group will be utilized by all dimensions of the organization including core components, brand management, and regional and property management.

In MHRS, every unit will be a "performance center." For each unit, a set of specific measures of performance will be developed. Each unit will be expected to add value to MHRS through its operations. Therefore, profitability will be a key factor in performance measurement of each unit. Each unit's revenues will be derived from their "sales" to other units and/or to external customers.

To ensure cost and quality competitiveness, each of the component businesses will be capable of surviving on a stand-alone basis. Therefore, each of the units in this group will be treated as a separate business.

Units within the components dimension will have the option of selling their products and services outside MHRS. Likewise, regional managers will have the option of sourcing their core components from external suppliers.

At the beginning, it might be necessary for the MHRS to subsidize the core components provider before it can offer competitive prices to its internal customers.

Critical Processes

The design team concurred in using planning boards as a vehicle for creating and controlling the decision process in the ideal MHRS. In particular, the planning board concept will be utilized for the following reasons:

- To achieve consistency and empowerment at the same time.
- To eliminate supervision as a bureaucratic waste.
- To match authority with responsibility at all levels of the organization.
- The organization will be flat and decisions will be made at the lowest relevant level.
- Core competencies and values (parameters/customer-based) will be known at every level of the organization.
- A process that is proactive and anticipates the needs of the customer will be used.
- Feedback processes that surface mismatches (e.g., misalignment with customer expectations; mismatches with reality) will be developed so that corrective action can be taken.

Processes that anticipate the future needs and new ideas of our customers, and processes that surface problems that can be incorporated before a program is rolled out will be developed.

Interactive policy teams will be the main vehicle for alignment of policies and plans and for dissolving conflicts among units in MHRS.

Each interactive policy team will have a minimum of three levels of management as members: the manager whose team it is, his/her boss, and his/her direct reports. Other members may be added on a regular basis or on specific issues.

Each policy decision will explicitly specify assumptions under which the decision is made and its expected outcome, specifically on the impact of the decision on:

- Financial Performance
- People
- Output (quality of service)

Interactive policy teams will be responsible for making policies. They will not get involved in operation decisions. Policies will establish the criteria by which managers make decisions. Agreement on decision criteria will be the key to successful decentralization. If no policy exists for a pending decision, the responsible manager will make the decision on his/her own. The appropriate interactive policy team may later decide to make a policy for future situations. Each policy will be made at the lowest level team possible.

Special interactive policy teams will be formed to coordinate policy on specific issues of strategic importance. Examples may be a technology team and area/market teams.

Recap

The design of a new architecture for Marriott is based on the following assumptions:

- Property owners (franchisees) are the real customers of Marriott Corporation; therefore, they have to be recognized and treated as such.
- Troubled customers are the most serious early warning system for any business concern.
- Current weakness in the real estate market is not temporary and is unlikely to change in the foreseeable future. The game can no longer be played on the assumption that asset appreciation generates sufficient return on investment for property owners.
- There is an urgent necessity to reduce costs by an order of magnitude and generate sufficient operating profit to overcome the weakness in the real estate market.
- Divisional structure with all its elegance and simplicity is a luxury that cannot be afforded any longer.
- Competition among various product divisions in Marriott in a given marketplace is much more intense than the conflict between Marriott and its competitors.
- Structural conflict among product divisions needs to be rationalized by optimizing the product mix in a given marketplace.
- Supplier-customer relations should govern the interactions among market management, brand management, and core components.

11

Commonwealth Energy Systems

D_{r.} Thomas Lee of the Center for Quality Management and Professor Gerald Wilson of MIT introduced me to Commonwealth Energy Systems. I had developed a great respect for Dr. Wilson when I worked with him on the redesign of Carrier Corporation. I welcomed the chance to collaborate with him again when he asked me to help develop a new corporate strategy for COM/Energy, where he was a trustee. This was a unique opportunity because three members of the Board of Trustees, the CEO, and all the company's senior executives had joined together to create a compelling vision and new strategic direction that would place COM/Energy among the leaders in the next generation of the energy business.

The Design Team consisted of the following members: officers included Leonard Devanna, Vice President, Systems, Planning (project coordinator); Kenneth Margossian, President, Chief Operating Officer, Commonwealth Gas; William Poist, Chief Executive Officer, Commonwealth Energy Systems; James Rappoli, Vice President, Finance, and Treasurer, COM/Energy; Michael Sullivan, Vice President, Secretary and General Counsel, COM/Energy; Russel Wright, President, Chief Operating Officer, Commonwealth Electric. Trustees included Dr. Sheldon Buckler, Trustee, Polaroid Corporation; Sinclair Weeks, Jr., Chairman of the Board of Trustees, Reed & Barton Corporation; Dr. Gerald Wilson, Trustee, Massachusetts Institute of Technology.

In addition, the following employees formed the "mess team": Rob Bucknell, Director of Sales, COM/Gas; Peter Dimond, Director of Communications, COM/Electric; Robert Fleck, Manager, Gas Procurement; David Gibbons, Sr., Forecast Analyst, COM/Energy; Charles Kiely, Manager, Consumer Service, COM/Electric; Michael Kirkwood, Director, Resource Planning, COM/Electric; Paul Lynch, Director, Treasury Services, COM/Energy; Robert Martin, Manager, Cost Administrator, COM/Electric; Richard Morrison, Sr., Attorney, Assistant Clerk, COM/Energy; Denise Murphy, Sr., Forecast Analyst, COM/Energy; Bernard Peloquin, Manager, Benefits, COM/Energy; and Ronald O'Brien, Manager, Marketing & Conservation, COM/Gas. Their report, because of its confidential nature, is not reproduced here.

270

Consultants were: Jamshid Gharajedaghi and Bijan Korram, Interact; Dr. Thomas Lee and Toby Woll, Center for Quality Management (CQM).

The designers believe that the resulting design, presented here, is an expression of the expectations, aspirations, and preferences of all stakeholders. The design focuses on dissolving the mess and creating a desired future.

STAKEHOLDERS' EXPECTATIONS

A *stakeholder* of a system is an individual or a group that is directly affected by the performance of the system and can have an influence in creating its future. Below is a summary of what the design team feels are the expectations of COM/Energy's stakeholders and some implications of these expectations (Figure 11.1).

Shareholders' Expectations

The expectations of shareholders are changing. Until recently, COM/Energy, like most utilities, had been regarded as a safe investment. However, because of the franchise's limitations and changes in the business environment, COM/Energy's present operation is no longer seen to provide a significant growth opportunity and a minimal investment risk. The basis for many investors' historical preference for utilities in general—a guaranteed return on investment—is being called into question by the changing environment. Under the circumstances, there might be a transformation in shareholder profile indicating a preference for significant growth in earnings or a higher rate of return as compensation for the increased risk associated with this business.

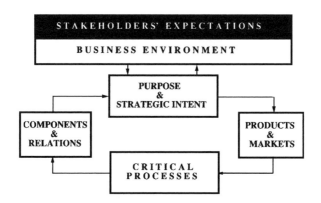

FIGURE 11.1   Stakeholders' Expectations

Regulators' Expectations

Regulators have been caught between two apparently opposing expectations. One is to respond to politicians' and environmentalists' pressures to promote a costly social agenda. This has been accomplished by incorporating social justice issues into rate formulation in order to satisfy public expectations. However, using rate increases as a means of accomplishing these objectives is no longer acceptable; the regulators find themselves under public and political pressures to decrease rates to satisfy customers and promote economic development. The regulators therefore would welcome those who offer innovative solutions to their dilemma.

Employees' Expectations

Employees realize that the game has changed. They would like an environment that assures them continued job security, a quality of work life in which they can develop, empowerment to pursue new ideas, differentiation based on their performance, and the ability to build a productive career. They have regarded COM/Energy as a preferred employer and have responded, in turn, with loyalty to the system.

Recently, however, the employees' sense of job security has been disturbed by the negative impact of emerging national economic and industry trends affecting COM/Energy. They seem willing to go out of their way to help secure the advantages of working for COM/Energy. Under the circumstances, the management has an unprecedented opportunity to gain the cooperation of the employees in introducing positive changes in the company's direction and organization.

Customers' Expectations

Customers are responding to their own economic pressures by demanding that energy services be provided at the lowest possible cost. They believe that the cost-plus monopolistic system is not responsive to their demands. They appreciate the reliability and other benefits that the system has provided, yet find the price for maintaining and improving it unreasonably high. Industrial customers' expectations are fueled by suppliers promising them lower prices if regulations did not keep them out. Customers, therefore, welcome the promises of deregulation that would give them the power of choice.

Some customers are equally frustrated by a limited set of utility services that ignores their emerging needs and problems just because they do not seem to fall into one of the categories of conventional services traditionally provided. Integrated total energy services are value-adding initiatives that customers expect to have in the future.

Suppliers' Expectations

Suppliers have seen major changes in their own business areas. They are aware that the advent of new competition and the existence of chronic oversupply will usher in increased uncertainty and insecurity. They have a considerable level of investment to protect. They need to hedge their enormous vulnerability against an increasingly unpredictable environment. They would like to be considered legitimate members of the family and treated as partners who are equally affected by the system and who have genuine stakes in its success. They therefore expect to be included in companies' strategic planning processes, to make sure they have a chance to contribute to the viability of COM/Energy and ensure the future of their businesses. The suppliers are prepared to enter the entrepreneurial game. However, they expect fairness and equal opportunity to provide their services based on a level playing field. They would welcome participation in alliances that strike a balance between risks and rewards.

Public's Expectations

The public at large, and especially environmentalists, are worried about the environmental threats of energy generation and consumption. They welcome moves toward conservation and away from pollution. They support some form of internalization of external costs associated with pollution and safety, but believe these measures can be taken even at lower prices. The public in general seems resigned to the inevitability of changes in energy's economic equation. Taking some of their cues from European initiatives, they expect utilities to be efficient and reliable, to project a positive public image, and to be generally regarded as a benign "green" operation.

BUSINESS ENVIRONMENT

The redesign process was conducted under the assumption that the system had been destroyed overnight but that its environment remained intact. The general and industry-specific changes in the environment that are likely to impact COM/Energy are identified as follows (see Figure 11.2 for an overview of the environmental dynamics of the energy industry).

The Changing Game: The Energy Industry

- FROM a cost-plus regulated environment in which the regulator sets the rate in order to generate a fair return on investment TO limited regulation in the areas of generation and distribution with rates highly influenced by competitive benchmarking.

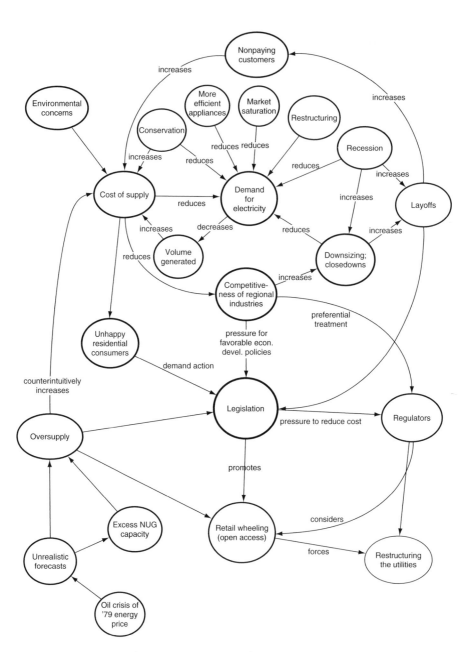

FIGURE 11.2 How the Energy Game is Evolving

- FROM peaceful coexistence among peers and respect for each others' territories TO a zero-sum, competitive environment in which many energy players try to succeed at each others' expense.
- FROM a relatively simple and nondifferentiated business environment TO a field ever more crowded with pressure groups (environmentalists, politicians, consumer activists, suppliers, brokers), each competing for dominance to advance their specific agenda.
- FROM the stability of a publicly regulated environment TO the unpredictability of a competitive market economy in which competition defines the game and customers choose the winners.
- FROM operating in a docile and permissive environment TO one characterized increasingly by hypersensitivity to environmental impacts and natural resource conservation.
- FROM a relatively simple and nondiscriminatory customer base TO a highly differentiated customer base representing an ever increasing variety of criteria.
- FROM the security of a closed and exclusive franchise TO the insecurity of a market open to competition.
- FROM offering discrete solutions to independent problems TO producing integrated solutions to a host of interdependent problems.
- FROM a traditionally capital-intensive industry with heavy reliance on capital cost recovery TO a niche-oriented marketing of services and/or products with a shift of emphasis on core competence and the wealth-creating power of the "knowledge worker."

The Changing Game: COM/Energy

No one knows, with any degree of certainty, what the future of COM/Energy, and all utilities for that matter, will look like. What is certain, however, is that the future of COM/Energy will not be the same as its past. In a small, saturated franchise, growing pressures for further deregulation, inclusion of environmental costs, increasing cost-effectiveness, and intensified competition are among the major forces changing the company's familiar landscape beyond recognition. The only certainty will be uncertainty.

As to what directions the energy industry may take, we identified the following possibilities:

- Insufficient growth within the current franchise area to support the increasing costs associated with providing necessary energy services.
- Differentiation of customer base (each with a unique set of preferences) requires differentiation of products and services. This will further open up opportunities for different providers to compete in the same markets on

the basis of the most effective offerings in order to meet the needs of certain preferred customers (e.g., MIT self-generation).

- Deregulation providing COM/Energy with access to new customers in geographic areas that are less saturated and mature than the existing franchise.
- Emergence of nonregulated entities (e.g., brokers, wholesalers, and retail wheelers) as major players.
- Modification of the cost equation makes the application of alternative technologies feasible (for example, possible imposition of environmental taxes on the generation of pollution).
- Introduction of mergers, acquisitions, strategic alliances, and networks.

Whatever shape it takes, the emerging new reality will be abundant with unprecedented threats and opportunities. In light of its possible impact, different stakeholders have already begun reassessing their expectations. Most importantly, the prospect of limited growth is a source of anxiety not only for the stockholders but for all the stakeholders of the organization. This is so because the viability of the system has been essentially growth based. Insufficient growth produces two disturbing effects: internally, it will upset the built-in cost increase system; and externally, the emerging new game will disrupt the peaceful coexistence of the peer utility companies. The game will turn zero-sum; some will win at the expense of others. While growth opportunities in the franchise area have become limited, promising new opportunities in the unregulated areas are emerging. The implication of these changes is that, in order to preserve the beneficial environment COM/Energy has enjoyed, a new approach to conducting the business is required.

DESIGN

Developed under the assumption that the system has been destroyed overnight but that everything in its environment has survived, the preceding sections outlined COM/Energy's defining context in terms of stakeholders' expectations and business environment. Once this context was established, the design team began the next phase of iterations intended to redesign COM/Energy from a clean slate. The design represents a shared vision of COM/Energy's desired future.

Purpose and Strategic Intent

Although efficient performance in energy distribution is a prerequisite to COM/Energy's viability, this commitment in and of itself will not be sufficient for creating the results the stakeholders truly desire. Facing lack of growth within the existing franchise and emerging uncertainty in the energy industry as a whole, COM/Energy is required to adopt a three-pronged strategy that will in make it possible to explore and exploit the most favorable opportunities that present themselves on all dimensions of the value chain—technology, product, and market. Such a multidimensional strategy will enable COM/Energy to effectively extend its operational reach beyond the existing franchise and regulated framework.

Working from such an advantageous platform, the system as a whole will become greater than the sum of its parts. In the context of an integrated value chain, we will therefore define our strategy in terms of the following three activities.

1. Regulated Businesses: Retaining and creating the most efficient energy distribution businesses. We intend to retain the existing regulated franchises as our mainstay. We believe that the retail distribution of energy will remain regulated, albeit in a different form. We are therefore determined not only to do our utmost to contain the mess and dissolve it within the regulated businesses, but to become one of the most efficient operators in the retail distribution of energy.

Since the prospects for significant growth within the existing franchise are limited and the successful dissolution of the mess in the regulated businesses will require a few years of intensive improvements, COM/Energy will pursue a parallel strategy to explore and exploit the potentials of the nonregulated market.

2. Customer-Oriented Businesses: Creating growth opportunities for integrated services outside the franchise area. We intend to extend our search for order-of-magnitude growth beyond the regulated territory. This parallel strategy will capitalize on COM/Energy's multiple intrinsic advantages: 1) extensive knowledge of the energy businesses; 2) small and potentially agile size; 3) financial strength; and 4) committed personnel. These advantages will help achieve the kind of growth that can come from market-based offerings that incorporate a variety of inputs in response to a wide range of user-specific demands.

The key to a successful customer-oriented dimension is to remove the traditional barriers that have made gas and electricity expertise mutually exclusive. Customer-oriented businesses, by definition, must avoid exclusive standardization designed to meet only those specific offerings that fall comfortably within the narrow confines of an exclusive source of energy (for example, an isolated gas unit and an isolated electricity unit working independently of each other, thus missing the vast opportunities representing real-world, user-oriented, and synthetic needs/problems).

To this end, our utilization of the value chain will involve a deliberate shift toward user-specific integrated systems and services designed to solve unmet and latent customer requirements. We will, therefore, operate from a combined vantage point that opens up opportunities that had been closed to our conventional way of doing business. We will apply a highly concentrated effort to continually developing various integrated energy services and systems that address emerging real-world needs/problems irrespective of the original sources of required inputs.

At a minimum, we intend to establish two business entities. The first will concentrate on residential/commercial energy services, which may include conservation and energy management products and services. The second entity will focus on the industrial sector and provide energy management, cogeneration, brokerage, and other services. Recognizing the need for additional expertise in these areas and access to new market areas, these business entities will pursue appropriate partners in developing these opportunities.

3. Technology (Supply-Oriented) Businesses: Leveraging energy-generating capacities to synergize potentials of the value chain. We intend to retain the energy generation and storage businesses. Through these businesses, COM/Energy is a major purchaser and/or supplier of oil, natural gas, and electrical energy. These markets, which were previously isolated and distinct, are now becoming increasingly integrated. Other companies, operating in only one of these sectors, are forming strategic alliances that simulate, to a lesser degree, the structure of the COM/Energy System. As a system, we will develop opportunities that integrate oil, natural gas, and electrical energy suppliers of energy and energy-related technologies to form mutually beneficial alliances. These relationships will serve not only as new sources of income, but will also enable us to respond to the energy markets' latent and emerging needs for new products and services.

For COM/Energy, deregulation is, in fact, filled with opportunities. Considering the limitations of our franchise, we stand to gain more from deregulation than our competitors. The franchise is land-locked, whereas consumers are everywhere. By capitalizing on the uniqueness of COM/Energy, the three-pronged strategy will allow us to exploit emerging opportunities in energy markets.

Core Values and Desired Specifications

- Remain in the energy business.
- Be a proactive organization capable of reinventing itself.
- Take advantage of opportunities that will add value to the whole and thus create the potential for its members to grow (a win/win relationship).
- Be among the pioneers that will redefine the energy industry of the future, while maintaining organizational stability and minimizing risk.
- Be the preferred investment for our shareholders, assuring them of a secure and rewarding investment.

- Create the norms, performance measures, and incentives that will promote a challenging entrepreneurial culture in which people will enjoy stretching to achieve worthwhile goals that give them both intrinsic and extrinsic satisfaction.
- Be seen by peers as a model organization worthy of emulation.
- Be able to transcend the traditional frameworks of doing business by getting regulators and other stakeholders to buy into different and better ways of doing business.
- Project a positive public image as a "green" company.
- Be able to detect, early on, imminent shifts in the relevant technologies, modes of operation, and customer needs and preferences.
- Make sure that the new businesses enjoy maximum entrepreneurial freedom to achieve competitive advantage immune from the spillover of norms and practices specific to the regulated businesses.
- Be able to constantly overcome the mess (e.g., empire building, alienation, hierarchies, resistance to change, lack of accountability).
- Change the nature of control from supervision to learning and early warning.
- Simultaneously exploit the advantages of both centralization and decentralization, integration and differentiation, interdependency and autonomy.

GENERAL ARCHITECTURE

To realize the expectations of COM/Energy's stakeholders, the designers recognize the necessity of employing an integrated value chain strategy. The architecture will be positioned to freely explore and exploit emerging opportunities along technology, product, and market dimensions. This not only will dissolve the mess, by transcending the traditional separations of gas and electricity operations, but will enable COM/Energy to offer systems solutions that will address unmet and latent needs of preferred customers.

The following describes the basic components of the architecture and the critical relationships among them. It represents the platform from which COM/Energy's value chain will evolve. The value chain will not be limited to these components alone. As the environment evolves, other value-adding units will be created. The identification of the components was aided by the use of the Business Identification Matrix (see Figure 11.3).

The criteria for expansion will include the contribution each additional unit will make to the entire value chain. Thus, the architecture will take advantage of the interrelated dimensions of technology, product, and market by allowing capitalization on opportunities that would otherwise remain inaccessible to a unidimensional strategy. The schematic view of COM/Energy's architecture is shown in Figure 11.4.

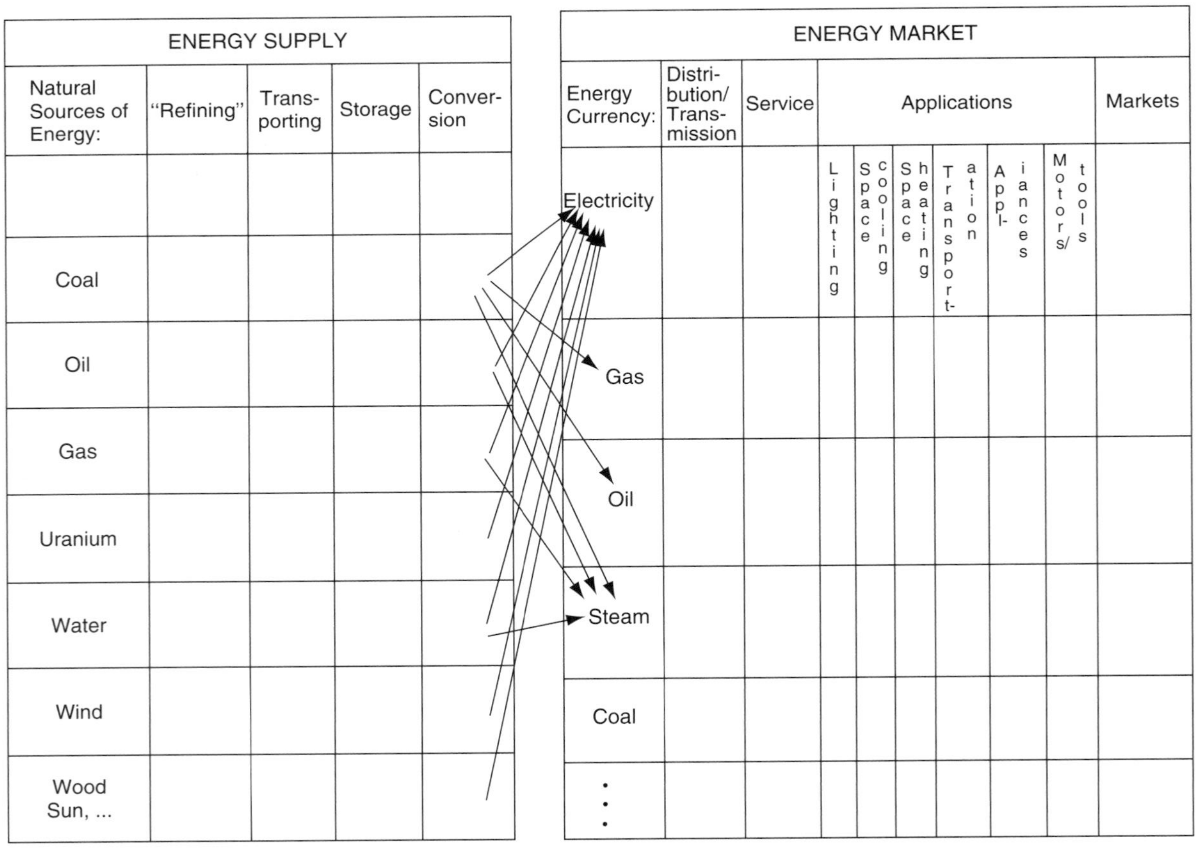

ENERGY SUPPLY

Natural Sources of Energy:	"Refining"	Trans-porting	Storage	Conver-sion
Coal				
Oil				
Gas				
Uranium				
Water				
Wind				
Wood Sun, ...				

ENERGY MARKET

Energy Currency:	Distri-bution/ Trans-mission	Service	Applications (School, Transportation, Space heating, Lighting, Appliances, Motors/tools)	Markets
Electricity				
Gas				
Oil				
Steam				
Coal				
...				

FIGURE 11.3 Business Identification Matrix

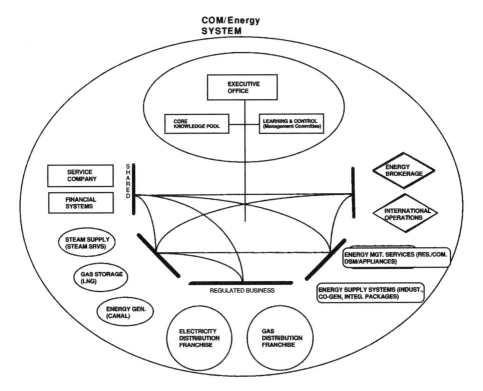

FIGURE 11.4 COM/Energy Architecture

The components of the architecture include an executive office (a CEO supported by a core knowledge pool), regulated business units (gas and electricity distribution), customer-oriented business units (energy services and systems), technology/supply-oriented business units (energy, gas, steam generation, and storage), and shared services (service company and financial systems).

Aside from the regulated businesses, which are bound by state and federal regulations, all other units of the architecture are considered to be performance centers expected to:

- Be self-sufficient units with explicit sources of income.
- Meet and exceed the cost of capital.
- Produce values that are measured against the formula: EVA = I $(r-c)$, where EVA stands for economic value added, I is investment, and r and c represent return and cost of capital correspondingly.
- Operate on target costing. Conventional profit centers operate on *target pricing*. Prices are set by a cost-plus-margin formula. The assumption

is that costs are uncontrollable but prices are not. Therefore, higher profits are achieved by targeting higher price levels. In contrast, performance centers operate on *target costing.* Here, prices are assumed to be uncontrollable and are set by the market on a competitive basis, while costs are assumed to be controllable and are targeted for a profitable operation. Initially, performance centers are given a grace period to learn how to adjust their operations before they are required to meet target costs.

* Be measured not only on the basis of their own profitability but also on the contributions they make to the profitability of other members of the value chain.
* Manage operations at the lowest competitive cost. The relationships among the performance centers are determined, in part, by an internal market mechanism, which makes them conduct transactions on the basis of supplier-customer relationships. If any unit is made to buy from or sell to other internal customers at a comparative disadvantage, that unit's opportunity cost would be compensated by the corporate entity that imposes the constraint.

CORE BUSINESS UNITS: GAS AND ELECTRICITY DISTRIBUTION

The gas and electricity distribution business units will constitute the first output dimension of COM/Energy's value chain. They will continue to operate within the regulated environment. All indications are that, for the foreseeable future, the distribution of natural gas and electricity will remain regulated. Gas and electricity businesses will represent the franchise and contain only those activities that must be managed in the regulated format. They will capitalize on the unrealized potentials within the existing franchise.

These two units will report to an internal board of directors. As core businesses, they will be fully autonomous units. They will have control over all of the activities necessary to help them exploit the full potentials of the franchise. The units will, of course, fully abide with all the laws and requirements pertaining to regulated energy distribution.

The core businesses, gas distribution and electricity distribution, will provide COM/Energy's stability. For the foreseeable future they will be the infrastructure necessary for developing other units of the value chain. These business units will have the responsibility and the challenge of further identifying, containing, and dissolving their mess. Each will become a model of an efficiently managed distribution business in a regulated industry.

Customer-Oriented Business Units: Energy Supply Systems and Management Services

The customer-oriented business units, energy supply systems and energy management services, will constitute the second output dimension of COM/Energy's value chain. They will operate outside the regulated environment.

The experience that COM/Energy has gained as a gas and electric holding company provides it with a unique understanding of customers' needs, which can be met by combinations of energy products and services. With the full support of the gas and electric segments, COM/Energy will develop a wide range of energy products and services to complement its traditional offerings. These services will encompass industrial/commercial cogeneration, packaged cogeneration, operation and maintenance of existing generation, and residential/commercial energy management services.

Cogeneration and Packages of Energy Supply (Industrial and Commercial)

With regulatory reform and rapidly escalating energy prices during the 1980s, the application of cogeneration to meet energy requirements became increasingly common. Throughout the United States, cogeneration now represents nearly 10 percent of total electricity production—in New England, cogeneration represents greater than 10 percent of electricity generation. In recent years, cogeneration activity has been expanding rapidly. From 1988 to 1992, total electricity generation in the United States increased 7.9 percent while cogenerated electricity increased 74 percent. By 1992, the total market for cogeneration had reached roughly $4 billion. Cogeneration applications can provide customers with a payback of one to four years and a return on investment of roughly 15–30 percent.

Although the market for cogeneration is maturing, it has proven its applicability in many energy-intensive industries and is likely to experience continued growth for the foreseeable future. Utilities are experiencing increased difficulties regarding transmission facilities. As a result, providing localized sources of power that obviate the need for transmission facilities will become increasingly necessary. This trend toward distributed generation is only in its infancy, with cogeneration being the first commercial step. However, cogeneration will be the beginning of a greater wave of activity that will ultimately include such technologies as fuel cells and photo voltaic arrays.

To meet the need for distributed energy generation, the energy supply systems business unit will be involved in commercial and industrial consulting, development, service, and financing for cogeneration projects. This subsidiary will:

- Offer consulting services (feasibility studies and evaluations).
- Act as a developer to install equipment.
- Provide service/maintenance contracts.
- Provide financing and leasing services.

These services will be offered both inside and outside the regulated businesses' service territories, with the primary market being driven by where the best opportunities exist. The services will be marketed to industrials, such as manufacturing companies, or large commercial establishments, such as hospitals. Energy-intensive industrial firms, such as pulp and paper producers, chemical plants, and large manufacturing plants, are sites that can benefit most from cogeneration.

Although cogeneration is generally targeted to single-plant sites, it has applicability to multiple associated sites as well. Industrial parks offer a particularly attractive target market. This subsidiary will offer products that meet all the energy-related needs of the companies within an industrial park, including electricity, gas, and/or steam. Similar opportunities exist in large office complexes, universities, and shopping plazas.

A related opportunity exists for the more standardized version of cogeneration, referred to as *packaged cogeneration*. This option will also be offered by the subsidiary to commercial operations such as restaurants, hotels, or multi-family housing units. The value of packaged cogeneration lies in its modularity, low cost, and minimal maintenance. To offer packaged cogeneration, the subsidiary will align itself with vendors of packaged cogeneration technology.

This energy supply systems subsidiary will become a member of the COM/Energy family of diversified energy suppliers (electricity, gas, and steam). Cogeneration will become a service that complements the traditional offerings of the regulated subsidiaries. With this new business opportunity, COM/Energy will achieve synergy between its current product and service offerings. Involvement in the cogeneration market will provide an expertise that can be shared with the system so that the system obtains a better insight into the needs of specific market sectors.

Synergy will also be achieved with COM/Energy's other new business endeavors: an energy management services business unit. As opportunities for applying cogeneration technologies are explored, it is likely that related opportunities for energy efficiency improvements will be uncovered. These opportunities can then be capitalized upon by the energy management services subsidiary. Similarly, the energy management services subsidiary will likely uncover situations where potential customers could benefit from cogeneration technology and pass such information along to the energy supply services subsidiary.

It is also possible that other synergies will arise between proposed subsidiaries. An energy brokerage subsidiary could act as a fuel supplier to potential cogeneration customers by providing natural gas and oil and/or marketing excess electrical energy. Cogeneration plant operation and maintenance will also complement COM/Energy's experience at the Canal plant and steam facilities.

The business structure for the energy supply systems subsidiary will entail acquisitions or joint ventures. Under the latter structure, the subsidiary could act as prime contractor and project manager with the partner generally the supplying its technology.

The shared services unit of COM/Energy will provide accounting, legal, and basic information services to this nonregulated operation. These services will be charged to a separate chart of accounts set up specifically for this operation and will be funded from this operation's profits. The subsidiary may also procure services from outside the system.

Energy Efficiency and Electrotechnologies (Residential and Commercial)

In addition to "before-the-meter" activities of the energy supply systems subsidiary, the company will engage in "after-the-meter" activities offering customers services and products designed to save money on utility services. The electric and gas distribution companies typically have not offered new services to customers; they have merely provided either kilowatt hours or BTUs. However, as deregulation progresses, new services will be created.

These new services are already provided to industrial natural gas customers whereby the transportation and commodity portions of a previously bundled product have been separated with FERC Order 636. This separation has allowed customers to establish futures contracts as a means to hedge energy costs. Similarly, in the electric utility industry, once hourly pricing of electricity takes hold and the appropriate technology becomes available in appliances, customers will be able to regulate usage of appliances in the home based on hourly price signals from the local utility.

Preliminary research indicates that the energy management systems and home automation markets offer great potential. Surveys show that U.S. business spends $7 billion on energy conservation in commercial buildings annually. Studies also report that the home automation market could exceed $3.5 billion by the year 2000. Many sizable utilities, such as American Electric Power and Southern Company, envision great potential for this market niche and have become involved as equity participants and testers of advanced energy management systems. Pilot projects with this equipment have yielded dramatic results in terms of improving load management and increasing customer satisfaction. By pairing with technology players in this marketplace, the company can increase earnings from its nonregulated subsidiaries while preparing itself to face the challenges of more aggressive competition and the growing need for better customer service.

In addition to offering new services, this subsidiary would also offer the following energy management consulting services to customers both inside and outside the electric and gas distribution territories:

- Audits and management programs for commercial and industrial facilities (including public and commercial office facilities, schools, hospitals, etc.).
- Energy accounting methods and investment strategies (including feasibility studies, payback methodology, and use of tax credits and grant programs).
- Assistance with implementing electrotechnologies.

In addition to providing energy management services directly to ultimate customers for a fee, the company may also act as a performance contractor for utility companies. The growth rate for utility DSM budgets shows that the New England market is mature and will not be growing at the rapid rate of recent years. The North Central area of the country is the fastest growing, and the West and Northwest are also growing fairly rapidly.

Because COM/Electric has significant experience in the area of demand-side management, a great deal of knowledge could come from the electric distribution company. The shared services entity would provide accounting, legal, and basic information services to this nonregulated entity. These services would be charged to a separate chart of accounts set up specifically for the nonregulated entity and would be funded from this entity's profits.

By establishing an energy management services subsidiary to promote these energy utilization products and services, COM/Energy will position itself to participate in this newly created industry between the utility and the customer.

TECHNOLOGY/SUPPLY-ORIENTED BUSINESS UNITS: ENERGY GENERATION AND SUPPLY

The technology/supply-oriented business units will constitute the third output dimension of COM/Energy's value chain. To the extent possible, they will operate outside the regulated environment. This dimension will represent all of the components, activities, and businesses that involve the generation, conversion, and storage of energy. Traditionally, Canal, LNG storage, and steam have been part of the regulated franchise. But, in order to exploit their full potential, they will be transferred, where possible, to the nonregulated part of the value chain, where they will be treated as independent businesses. The business units within energy generation/supply will be as follows.

Energy Generation (Canal)

Canal is a wholesale electric company providing power to a number of electric utilities, including COM/Energy subsidiaries. A portion of the electric distribution company's supply comes from investments in a number of utility power facilities, including the Seabrook nuclear station, which are managed investments as part of a portfolio of earnings. Canal also owns and operates Canal Unit 1. This unit sells its power to Boston Edison, New England Power, Montaup Electric, and Cambridge/Commonwealth Electric. The existing contracts to this unit end in 2001, at which time Canal will have a fully depreciated power plant that may offer a significant business opportunity

Recognizing the presence of other fully depreciated facilities and the fact that capital and operating costs are relatively consistent across many units, a newly structured power supplier can be effective only with a lower-priced fuel supply (compared to other units) or an efficiency advantage. Since efficiency advantages cannot be captured with older units, Canal is negotiating a potential business alliance with major fuel suppliers. To prepare for 2001, Canal 1 will pursue a distinct business strategy to continue the life of the unit and market power to existing and new customers. To achieve this, Canal will enter into the necessary business partnerships to produce market-based pricing with a competitively priced fuel supply.

Canal Unit 2 is jointly owned with Montaup Electric Company, and its capacity is split evenly between Montaup and Commonwealth/Cambridge Electric. Canal Unit 2 will continue to supply power under its existing contracts through 2010. With its conversion to natural gas, Unit 2 will not only lower its emissions, but will also have the flexibility to instantaneously switch between oil and natural gas. By utilizing the existing oil storage facilities and securing various natural gas supplies, Canal will have the opportunity to broker significant quantities of natural gas, oil, and electricity as markets develop.

Canal, although currently part of the franchise businesses, will eventually be managed as an autonomous unit with customer and supplier relationships. As an autonomous unit, Canal will be responsible for managing its operations and associated costs to meet market expectations. The first phase of this transition will be to establish a project venture as part of the marketing and reengineering of Unit1 to obtain extended-life customer contracts.

Gas Storage (LNG)

Now known as Hopkinton LNG, this storage facility subsidiary will continue to supply natural gas to the gas distribution company during the coldest winter months. Given the prospect of deregulation, Hopkinton LNG management will be investigating other business opportunities, which include the marketing of liquefaction services, emergency backup services, and peak shaving services. The development of these opportunities depends upon the economics of the gas distribution company's continued usage of LNG for its own purposes.

This subsidiary also owns a satellite vaporization plant in Acushnet, Massachusetts, with additional storage capacity. The Hopkinton facility is operated and maintained by Air Products and Chemicals, Inc. under a long-term contract. The Acushnet plant is operated and maintained by gas distribution personnel.

Steam Services

Steam is currently supplied from two Cambridge Electric plants, Kendall and Blackstone, through a four-mile distribution system of steam supply and return piping. As a nonregulated entity, the steam company will continue to provide steam to commercial and industrial customers in Boston and Cambridge, including a hospital, a museum, two universities, a manufacturer, and a genetic researcher. This subsidiary will be developed as a separate entity with its own marketing and technical staff.

The concept of district heating systems using steam has received the backing of the State of Massachusetts. In its 1993 Energy Plan, the state recommended the support of district energy systems and thermally oriented cogeneration. With this state support and by applying the expertise it has gained in operating its Kendall and Blackstone cogeneration plants, the company will foster the development of other potential district heating systems established through its energy supply systems subsidiary.

Also, through business partnerships with MIT and Boston Thermal (organizations with contiguous steam systems), the company could establish interconnections to existing district heating systems and expand its customer base beyond the current geographic area. The current steam company system is economically more efficient for the customer than the Boston Thermal system because the latter contains no condensate loop. Last, turbine modifications to the Blackstone plant could also offer inexpensive incremental power to be brokered by the energy brokerage subsidiary.

ENERGY BROKERAGE AND INTERNATIONAL OPERATIONS

Two major developments in the industry will likely be networking and access to energy markets (both buying and selling). These activities will be integral to COM/Energy's value chain. To explore these opportunities, other business units, including energy brokerage and international operations, will be developed. Before these units are formed, opportunities in these markets will be evaluated.

Energy Brokerage

Brokerage of energy is a major area of opportunity that is evolving. For many years, oil has been purchased on a commodity basis with associated futures options. With the implementation of Orders 436 and 636, natural gas can also be purchased on a commodity basis. Similarly, with the introduction of self-generation as a major source of power, electricity will be purchased as a commodity in the very near future. With these changes, financial instruments are now being introduced as a means to establish short- and long-term pricing options. The introduction of futures contracts is the result of the markets' need for greater certainty regarding energy prices.

With the utilization of oil, gas, and electricity hedges, new products will be launched to meet customer needs. These products will be required in the marketplace as a way for utilities and customers to minimize price risks. In addition, the coupling of fuel and electricity options will allow for contract innovations that will change the industrial and commercial markets.

COM/Energy is a major purchaser and supplier of oil, natural gas, and electricity. To effectively carry out its business in the future, it will be involved in futures markets. Recognizing the multitude of physical energy options that the system controls (i.e., Canal Unit 2 oil/gas interchangeability, LNG storage, multiple fuel supply contracts, oil storage, natural gas supply and transportation rights) the brokerage of energy represents a significant business opportunity.

Energy brokerage will serve all the units of the value chain. This subsidiary will be engaged in oil, electricity, and natural gas brokerage. The unit will coordinate and manage all activities necessary to develop energy sales opportunities outside of those that must be kept within the regulated entities. In the electricity market, the subsidiary will act as a power marketer of the low-cost power generated from Canal 1 and other units. In the natural gas market, the entity will procure natural gas for cogeneration customers, power generation, and other select customers.

In the oil market, the subsidiary will utilize various oil storage options and contracts to meet power generation requirements. Finally, this business unit will serve as the access mechanism into markets that are speculative, out of normal reach, or unfamiliar to existing business units.

International Operations

Energy markets are becoming increasingly global in nature—events in Europe the Far East, and Latin America have direct consequences for energy markets in the United States. This has been true in the oil industry for years and is becoming more the norm in other energy markets, including gas and electricity Whether in the form of industry restructuring (British electricity markets) or cross-border transactions (Canadian natural gas), events throughout the world are directly affecting, or influencing the future of, domestic energy industries As a result it is increasingly important that COM/Energy not limit its perspective to the United States, but rather keep a watchful eye on events and technologies evolving around the globe.

In this vein, the international operations unit will be responsible for monitoring and evaluating trends in energy markets outside North America. This unit will continually search for ways to leverage new ideas from other parts of the world into the other COM/Energy business units. Additionally, this unit will serve as the stepping stone for future overseas ventures that capitalize on competencies resident within other COM/Energy business units.

Already, COM/Energy has established alliances with organizations based in other countries (Venezuela and Canada). The international operations unit will continue to seek out and create further alliances in global energy markets. Whether leveraging a competency in a market outside the United States or capitalizing on an emerging global trend within the United States, the international operations unit will depend initially upon partnerships in any ventures it undertakes.

SHARED SERVICES (PERFORMANCE CENTERS)

Shared services consists of service company and financial systems business units. The transactions between the shared services and other units will be governed by an internal market mechanism, analogous to the discipline that regulates customer/supplier relations in a free economy. Some practical implications of an internal market interface are as follows:

- If any unit finds that it can buy services cheaper elsewhere, it will be allowed to outsource only after it has given the internal unit a fair chance to make its prices competitive. The shared services will have to become the state-of-the-art and cost-effective provider of choice.
- If the business units, regulated or otherwise, choose to outsource their needs, they will still be bound to pay their proportional share of the corporate office's fixed costs, which would have been allocated to the shared services until these costs can be eliminated. This charge will be levied on them as an internal tax. Therefore, the decision to seek an alternative source of supply will be made if the combination of variable cost and internal tax to cover the proportional fixed cost justifies the tradeoff.

A note of precaution: in dealing with the costs of the shared services, it may be best to use throughput accounting that considers certain elements of the cost as fixed—the costs that will not be reduced when services are eliminated. Therefore, to provide the shared services with a reasonable chance of survival, those fixed costs that have been superimposed on the operation of the shared services should be paid on the basis of a tax, not as throughput. This makes the company's prices more comparable with alternative sources of supply offered externally. Shared services will be driven by target costing measures in order to become competitive enough to retain its internal customers, especially the regulated ones, by helping them reduce their costs. Shared services will be encouraged to attract external clients as well.

Service Company

The service company intends to transform itself from an overhead center, engaged in providing support services to other units operating in a cost-plus environment, to a viable, competitive, and state-of-the-art performance center generating profit while making positive contributions to the success of other members of the value chain. The transformation of the service company is contingent upon the development of the following core competencies:

- Information Know-How: The service company will keep and enhance its existing information-processing capability centered around designing, developing, and operating information systems.
- Industry Know-How: The service company will retain and enhance its accumulated industry know-how unique to the regulatory/utility environment. This competency will spin streams of advantageous professional services off the strengths of COM/Energy.
- Process Redesign Know-How: The service company will create and enhance the process redesign capability as a new competency dimension. This competency involves interrelated capabilities such as interactive design, process technology, continuous improvement, and throughput management.

The strategic intent of the service company is to integrate the above core competencies into customized packages of products and services that will significantly add to the competitive advantage of the value chain. Such multidisciplinary know-how is brought to bear on cross-functional teams of experts assembled to offer energy-specific products/services, turn-key operations, and consulting and education services. To make a clear and lasting break with its past as an overhead center, the service company will use the following guidelines for product offerings:

- By default, all services that the internal customer units are willing to keep or are interested in assuming will be released to them.
- Corporate policy-related activities will be relinquished to the executive office of COM/Energy System.

All preparatory work leading to drafting of proposed corporate policies will be carried out by ad hoc committees chaired by one of the parent company's corporate vice presidents and staffed by nonpermanent members drawn from relevant parts of COM/Energy System and/or its environment. These committees will dissolve once the issues have been resolved.

The service company will divorce all activities that involve providing COM/Energy with corporate control, monitoring, and auditing functions. Like any other customer, however, the corporate office of COM/Energy System may buy services from the service company.

Financial Systems

Financial systems will play a critical role in realizing the value chain. It will act as the system's in-house investment center. It will provide the businesses with the vital seed money and initial leverage that they need to achieve viability. It will effectively serve the capital and the cash-flow needs of all the business units. Leveraging COM/Energy's financial resources, financial systems will continue to develop relations with bankers and other institutions in order to reinforce the system's financial capacity in launching new projects and/or expanding the existing ones in order to further realize the potential of the value chain.

EXECUTIVE OFFICE

Aside from the two core businesses that are already mature and well established, other business units will need a period of careful attention and nurturing before they achieve viability. The executive office's responsibility is to conduct this incubation function while managing the entire value chain. To do this, the executive office is responsible for creating the following three critical processes.

1. Latency: The essence of creating latency will be a strategic planning process that institutionalizes the continuous search for new opportunities relevant to the value chain. This process will develop and implement activities leading to business renewal, generation of innovative ideas, and improved ways of conducting business. Once such opportunities are identified, members of the core knowledge center will conduct the relevant feasibility studies, and, if merited, they will be assigned to the management of the startup phase of such projects. To ensure the continuous renewal of the system through successive approximations, COM/Energy will engage in an interactive planning exercise every three years. The exercise, carried out at the corporate level, will result in either changing or reconfirming the strategic direction of COM/Energy and setting goals, objectives, and policies for realizing the next achievable approximation. The interactive planning exercise will consist of two functions: mess formulation and design.

The bottom-up mess formulation will identify and define the interrelated set of variables, as well as the second-order machine, which, unless dismantled, makes the system behave the way it does and thus frustrates efforts to introduce desirable changes. Mess formulation will move upward, whereupon each level will formulate its mess by taking the higher-level system as its environment.

The top-down design will assume that the system (the unit to be redesigned) has been destroyed but that its environment (the larger system of which it is a part) has remained intact. The design activity will move downward, whereupon each level will redesign itself by taking the higher-level design as its environment.

2. Synergy: Synergy is concerned with developing and implementing processes, systems, and incentives that produce interactions, alliances, and cooperations that will make the whole of the value chain greater than the sum of its parts. These processes, systems, and incentives include the internal market, target costing, throughput-oriented measurement systems, reward systems, early warning systems, and control systems. These measures are intended to create win/win incentives by dissolving structural conflicts among the internal units, and linking the performance measure of each unit to its contributions to other units.

3. Throughput: Throughput processes will be concerned with operational efficiency and quality. They will help the system increase its efficiency and productivity both within and among all the units of the value chain. The system will do so by utilizing TQM and continuous improvement methodology. The objective is to increase operational potency through systems solutions intended to:

- Decrease cycle time
- Eliminate waste
- Improve flexibility
- Increase quality

The activities concerning the throughput process will be carried out at all levels of the organization. Every member of the system will participate in the continuous improvement activity. Members of the mess team will provide the seed talent for developing and implementing these critical, processes and for helping other parts of the organization plan, learn, and control the processes.

Core Knowledge Pool

To discharge the responsibility for latency, synergy, and throughput processes, the executive office will be equipped with a core knowledge pool. The core knowledge pool will be the system's center of expertise that develops and disseminates state-of-the-art knowledge throughout the value chain. All the essential functions of the executive office will be carried out by professionals who operate in pools of expertise and work in an interdisciplinary manner on specific projects. Each member of the pool can be involved in more than one project. The main outputs of these projects include creation of startup businesses, improvement of existing operations' effectiveness, design of measurement, reward, and early warning systems. Generating systemwide "bench strength" and fostering an entrepreneurial culture are among the byproducts of these corporate activities.

The core knowledge pool will be staffed by a select group of top-notch experts who will rotate among all activities. They will be drawn, temporarily or permanently, from internal businesses and recruited or contracted from external sources in order to contribute to the richness and variety of the system's gene pool. Initially, the nucleus of the core knowledge pool will consist of the design team members who will be involved in the development of design details for the new architecture. These activities will provide an environment for learning by designing, learning by doing, and earning while learning. Core knowledge members will offer their expertise in the context of project teams designed to produce integrated solutions.

The core knowledge pool will also be responsible for creating a common language and acting as a center to reinforce organizational learning. Organizational learning will include reciprocal traffic of knowledge and mutual exchange of people. No new professional will enter the system without first being initiated through the core knowledge pool.

Members of the core knowledge pool will have a good insight into environmental trends, technological developments, and changing customer needs. They will operate in modular cross-disciplinary teams and, through the mechanism of project management, may be assigned to other shared services for systems development and/or to line-management roles for carrying out special missions. The core knowledge pool will also be responsible for developing models for the throughput system, target costing, the measurement and reward system, and an internal market mechanism.

Learning and Control System

The following description elaborates on the essence of a learning and control system. The system, which underlines COM/Energy's new concept of empowerment, will be compatible with the design's desired specifications and the preferred style of COM/Energy's management. The system will change the nature of control from "supervision" to "learning" and the nature of authority from "power over" to "power to." Although learning and control are highly interrelated aspects of a single system, each aspect is described separately below to facilitate understanding.

Effective control involves, essentially, duplication of power. Duplication of power will be achieved if the decision process, rather than the individual decisionmakers, is the subject of control. This will happen when decisionmakers collectively develop a shared understanding and ownership of decision criteria.

Decision criteria define the rules of decision making. Decisions themselves are applications of the decision rule to specific situations. What operationally distinguishes decision criteria from decisions per se is the existence of some degree of freedom in decision criteria. The absence of at least one degree of freedom virtually converts the decision criteria to decisions.

Decision criteria can be grouped into two categories: policies and procedures. A *policy* is a decision criterion at a higher level of abstraction. Policy essentially deals with choice dimensions (variables involved), "why" questions, underlying assumptions, and expected outcomes. Policy decisions are value-loaded choices that are explicit about their implications for human, financial, and technical domains. *Procedures*, on the other hand, are derived from policies. They deal with "how" questions. They explicitly specify the method or the model to be used for applying policies to specific situations. Policy making will deal with at least three sets of decision categories:

1. Interaction: These are the policies governing the interactions among the dimensions and components of the organization. They include target costing, value chain, synergy, reward, measurement systems, and internal transactions.
2. Allocation/Selection: These policies normally involve the selection of criteria for allocating resources and capital.
3. Execution: These policies pertain to operating decisions affecting purchasing, contracting, generation, distribution, marketing, personnel, and research and development.

Learning will include an early warning system that will call for corrective action before the problem has occurred. Such a system will monitor, on an ongoing basis, the validity of the assumptions on which the decision was made, the implementation process, and intermediate results.

At the corporate level, the management committee, consisting of the CEO and all direct reports, will be the vehicle for institutionalizing the learning and control system. In this case, the core knowledge pool will provide the technical support for designing and operationalizing the system.

At the business unit level (specifically the two regulated businesses), the operation of the learning and control system will be the responsibility of the internal boards of the business units, collectively referred to as the *nested network*. To maximize the effectiveness of the system, it is recommended that each board, which will consist of members of the executive office and the president of that unit, invite the president's direct reports to participate in the board's deliberations. Later on, the components at the business units, if so desired, may choose to create management committees in their own operation in order to adopt the learning and control system described above. Further evolutions would eventually cover the whole organization by a nested network. As such, the nested network will facilitate COM/Energy's vertical and horizontal integration. The ongoing activity of the nested network will provide integration along the time dimension as well. The vertical, horizontal, and temporal integration brought about by the activity of the nested network will also ensure the compatibility of ends and means at all levels of the organization, making coordination automatic and self-administered. Finally, the new design is expected to usher in a mode of organization that thrives on the following drivers for change:

- Cultivating members' ability and desire to behave entrepreneurially and to achieve competitive advantage free from the norms of the past (i.e., those of an overhead center operating in a cost-plus regulated environment).
- Shifting the character of the organization from management of actions to management of interactions.
- Taking advantage of the emerging opportunities that will add value to the whole, creating the potential for members to grow.
- Creating the norms, performance measures, and incentives that will motivate people to stay the course as a lean, simple, and flexible organization.
- Demonstrating an unfailing customer focus and product/market orientation.
- Fostering empowerment by matching authority with responsibility at all levels of the organization and keeping formal and informal organization "in synch."
- Shifting the nature of control from supervision to learning and early warning.

12

Carrier Corporation

I got the opportunity to work with Carrier Corporation when Professor Tom Lee and Gerald L. Wilson of MIT asked me to make a presentation to Karl J. Krapek, then the CEO of Carrier Corporation. I was told that I would be paid for the full day, but that if Mr. Krapek interrupted me to make a phone call I should assume that the presentation was over. Although this seemed a little awkward, it somehow challenged me. Oddly enough, fifteen minutes into the presentation, Karl wanted to make a phone call. I collected my papers, assuming the session was over, but much to my surprise he asked me if I could give him ten minutes to get a few of his colleagues to join us. He wanted them to hear what I had just said. A full-day presentation led to a contract and a redesign project for Carrier.

The challenge for Carrier was to create a system out of an aggregate of more than 90 autonomous operations. The question was how to integrate and differentiate a global operation so it could be both centralized and decentralized at the same time. Carrier had to revitalize its core technology, manage its interactions with a patchwork of semi-autonomous manufacturing units spread all over the world, and become cost competitive in many highly competitive markets, despite having a huge network of aging distributors who were unwilling to learn the implications of new technology.

This document summarizes the design produced by a fifteen-member design team consisting of Karl J. Krapek and his direct reports in several sessions during the fourth quarter of 1992. Ali Geranmayeh from Interact was my associate in this project.

This is an idealized design. Its content, at this stage, is tentative and subject to change. Implementation of this design requires planning. Because of changes in the corporate environment and a shift in strategy, implementation of this design was not attempted. Nevertheless, it represents a state-of-the-art design based on Carrier's original intent.

EXPECTATIONS, ASSUMPTIONS, AND SPECIFICATIONS

Carrier is not just a manufacturer of equipment. We are designers, producers, and distributors of climate control systems. We own different parts of the value chain in different parts of the world. Regardless of ownership, however, we must understand the desires and needs at various levels of the chain.

From Carrier's perspective, all the actors and participants in the value chain, from the producer to the end user, are considered customers. They may be classified as follows:

- Distributors
- Dealers
- Consulting Engineers
- Contractors
- Retailers
- End Users

We must deliver value (benefits/costs) at all levels of the chain. But we must start defining benefits at the end of the chain (the end user) and work our way backward to the manufacturer. Value comes from the total package:

- Performance
- Price
- Service
- Installation

Significant opportunities for creating value for the end user exist in understanding the latent needs and desires of customers.

The Changing Game: In General

- **FROM** mass production based on economy of scale, and reliability of forecasts **TO** flexible production based on a low break-even point and rapid change of products.
- **FROM** management of independent variables with separate solutions **TO** management of interdependent variables with integrated solutions.
- **FROM** generation of knowledge as the basis of competitive advantage **TO** operationalization of new knowledge as the basis for competitive advantage.
- **FROM** sole reliance on product technology **TO** investment in process technology.
- **FROM** target pricing, taking price as the controllable variable, **TO** target costing with cost as the controllable variable.

- **FROM** regarding labor as a variable cost and considering dispensable cheap labor as a competitive advantage **TO** regarding labor as a fixed asset and considering knowledgeable workers as a sustainable advantage.

The Changing Game: The HVAC Industry

- Emergence of strong (independent) component suppliers—their large scale and focused scope give them the capability to eventually control key components that comprise much of the cost, technology, and basis for differentiation of final products. They also pose a threat as potential competitors in the end-products market.
- Emergence of "no frills" competitors offering very low prices. These are low-technology, low-cost companies with nimble and lean operations.
- Japanese competitors combine operational effectiveness with high-technology products. Their likely strategy will be to:
  - Concentrate on the lower end of the market (a growth sector).
  - Offer easy-to-use, fully engineered packages requiring little maintenance.
  - Sell directly to retailers, bypassing the distributors.
  - Then move up to larger products, relying on engineers and architects to sell.
- Integration of electronic controls is becoming a must.

Drivers for Change

- Environmental concerns
- Maturation of large markets and emergence of new ones
- Increasing discrimination and differentiation by customers
- Globalization of competition
- Miniaturization (size of products, material weight and bulk)
- New technologies (e.g., in heat exchange and transfer)
- Duct-free splits change the traditional structure of the value chain

Bases for Competition

- Delivery
- Cost
- Size
- Time to market
- Service
- Distribution
- World-class manufacturing processes

CORE VALUES

We will create wealth throughout the chain from the supplier to the end user. We take responsibility for creating win/win situations to dissolve conflict among players at various levels of the chain. We take total responsibility for the entire system all the way to the end user. The Carrier name backs the product, guaranteeing it all the way down the chain. Even if we do not own pieces of the chain, and even if the product is a private label, we guarantee proper functioning of what the customer buys (product and service). No excuses.

- Our commitment is to total customer satisfaction.
- We value excellence through knowledge. We promote intolerance of incompetence.
- We are committed to providing clearly communicated rules of the road and expectations of performance.
- We will be undisputed leaders in core technologies.
- We will be a mutually supportive interdependent system.
- We will invest in our employees, distributors, and dealers.
- We will influence the industry.
- No one will lose his or her job at Carrier as a result of circumstance, plant closings, departmental restructuring, or market downturns.

Three main questions are to be answered in this section:

1. Whose problems are we trying to solve?
2. What solutions are we providing to them?
3. How will we deliver the solution to those with the problem?

The first question deals with market segmentation, the second with product line offerings, and the third with access mechanisms. The business can be understood in terms of the cube formed by these three dimensions. Each dimension is considered in more detail below.

Products and Services

We will use the following criteria for deciding whether to participate in a particular segment of the product line:

- Is the product a requirement for global leadership in climate control?
- Will the product help us compete more effectively from a strategic point of view? (Strategic concerns may be defensive, such as helping to keep

our distributors/dealers loyal to us by providing them with a broad line of products; or offensive, such as discouraging competitors from going after our distributors/dealers, utilizing our distribution channel to move products made by others, or reducing costs due to economies of scale and scope.)

- Are there opportunities for utilizing our assets? From time to time we may selectively choose to participate in segments where there is no long-term strategic advantage but opportunities for utilizing our assets. We will not make new investments in such segments.
- Is this an opportunity to broaden the breadth of the line? A wide range of products is important to us because 1) it helps us win and maintain the loyalty of our distribution network and 2) it helps us leverage our technology and reduce our costs. In addition, a broad product line is an important defense against smaller competitors "niche-ing" us out of various market segments, and it helps support dealers and distributors in down cycles. A financially strong and loyal distribution network is a significant barrier to entry for would-be competitors.

The following obstructions in the current state of the industry provide significant opportunities for product/service offerings:

- The basic problem of climate control is not solved very well: people in large buildings are either too hot or too cold and they can't easily manipulate the controls; in residential buildings the draft bothers people and stiff necks are common.
- There is no integration or cooperation between us and other actors controlling major elements of the building that affect the overall performance of the climate control system—insulation, windows, building materials, architects, and so on (in automobiles, climate control people must work very closely with glass, especially windshield, manufacturers).

Core Technology and Know-How

- We must have system design capability in all aspects of our business. In addition, we must have the following core components (in order of importance):
  - Compressors
  - Electronic controls
  - Heat transfer devices
  - Enclosures: shape and configuration; aerodynamic content and capability; and the fan

- Motor
- Diesel engines
- Air cleaning devices

- We must develop technical capabilities to integrate controls and motors (e.g., to generate orbital motion, and use refrigerants to cool the motor and the electronics inside it). United Technologies Corp. (UTC) has a motor supplier company. Can we work with them?
- We must have design capability for electronic control systems (including sensors). We can continue to buy components off the shelf. Partners are desirable to get the best electronic design capability.
- We will develop cross-disciplinary knowledge at every level of the engineering organization. An understanding of environmental trends and changing customer needs (both manifest and latent) will accompany this knowledge to ensure that innovative products reach the marketplace in a timely manner.
- A significant competitive advantage exists in the effective integration of disciplines through modeling. To accomplish this, we will encourage modeling through incentives and mentoring. Time constraints must be balanced with the need to learn by documenting and refining models after the design effort is complete. New engineering talent with disciplinary skills must be trained to think cross-functionally and the build and test culture must be replaced with a scientific predictive modeling culture.

Sales and Distribution System

- Our basic approach is a commitment to customer satisfaction: we will guarantee the satisfaction of the end user with all our products.
- We must develop dealer and distributor agreements such that we create partnerships throughout the value chain. We will need to rely heavily on them to a large extent to help us deliver our guarantee.
- Our guarantee applies to the system as a whole. Therefore, we must be able to:
  - Produce the critical elements of the system (e.g., A/C unit).
  - Specify minimum standards for all other elements to be used by our dealers (our differentiating factor).
  - Buy and distribute noncritical items (e.g., duct works, coils, and thermostats) through our dealer system—but always give them the choice to obtain them elsewhere (so long as they meet standards); we supply through our "trading company."
- We will treat our distributors/dealers "almost as franchisees." We hope to get the cooperation level of a franchisee relationship without the legal hassles.

- Compliance with standards will be a major part of our dealer agreements.
- A loyal and efficient distribution network is essential to our leadership in the marketplace. We will have to create win/win situations in which our dealers and distributors remain financially healthy.
- We will have a hybrid distribution system: some company-owned distributors and some independents. We will own distributors when:
    - We can meet the cost of capital of our investment.
    - Ownership is strategically important to us.
    - We have no other presence in the region.
    - We will actively develop and utilize independent distributors in cases where their strong relationships with local dealers and customers cannot be duplicated by us.
    - Irrespective of whether a distributor is independent or company-owned, we want them to be successful businesses in their own right and to work very closely with Carrier as a partner.
- We must be customer-focused. This implies sensitivity to geographical and national differences: understanding the needs of Latin American residents as well as those of North American residents (homes in Japan and homes in the United States versus roof tops and room A/C).
- Our marketing challenge is to find solutions for specific segments and applications.
- We must continually strive to drive costs out of the chain. We will achieve this through improved logistics, reduction of inventories, and lean manufacturing. These improvements will enable us to reduce the number of steps in the chain over time.

SYSTEMS ARCHITECTURE
Desired Characteristics

- A customer focus.
- Well-understood rules of the road and expectations of performance, with explicit decision criteria.
- Respect for the need for a control system to assure accountability, thereby allowing effective decentralization: supervision is a waste.
- Effective processes for dissolving internal conflicts. There are no conflict-free organizations. Those that can deal with conflicts constructively can use them as the engine for the system's vitality.
- Throughput-oriented rewards (not functionally oriented). Such incentive systems help dissolve structural conflicts while functionally oriented ones create them.

- One integrated solution for problems of reducing cost and waste, compressing time, increasing flexibility, and improving quality (as opposed to different solutions for each one).
- Lean, simple, nonbureaucratic, and flexible organization with easy communication up and down.
- Few written rules and procedures with formal and informal organization "in synch."
- Empowerment at the lowest level (authority matching responsibility).
- Time sensitivity and awareness of the pressures of external competition.

A Multidimensional Framework

A multidimensional architecture employed in the following design recognizes the necessity for achieving competitive advantage in all three dimensions—market, product, and technology—at the same time. It therefore seeks to eliminate suboptimization around any one dimension. The objective is to actively generate synergy, latency, and efficiency by creating a win/win relationship among the three dimensions. A three-dimensional architecture recognizes the need for centralization and decentralization, integration and differentiation, and interdependency and autonomy at the same time.

In a three-dimensional architecture, structural conflicts inside the corporation are dissolved by incorporation of market mechanisms as the basis of interactions among different units wherever possible. The architecture, however, provides only the hardware for the system; business processes provide the software.

Carrier's architecture must be designed to support equal emphasis on markets, products, and technology. The architecture which follows will be used to accomplish this multidimensional focus while creating a market-driven business.

The predominant strategic thrust of Carrier Corporation is a strong market orientation and responsiveness to customers. Organization will be flexible enough to adapt to internal and external changes, stimulate continuous improvements in the quantity and quality of its outputs, and be able to learn rapidly and effectively. The systems architecture described (Figure 12.1) is intended to facilitate the pursuit of this strategy. It will support equal emphasis on markets, products, and technology, while creating a market-driven business.

MARKETS

Marketing functions in Carrier will be carried out in four semi-autonomous areas. Each area in turn will manage a number of regional units.

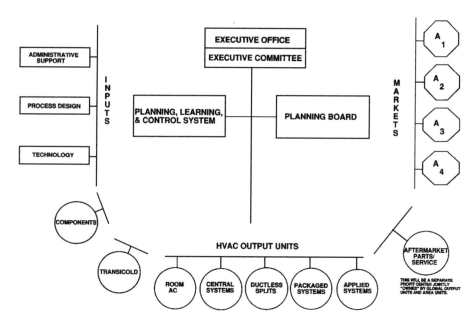

FIGURE 12.1 Carrier Systems Architecture

Regional Units

A region is the basic unit of the market dimension. It is where Carrier actually happens.

- The size and boundaries of a given region are determined by the following considerations:
  - Physical access
  - Climate
  - Construction practices (design and material)
  - Stages of economic development
- As the sole marketing arm of the Carrier Corporation, regional managers are relieved of their manufacturing responsibilities. Exceptions will be for some local factories designed to serve local markets only.
- Regional units will be sales and distribution service organizations. They will be primarily responsible for selling, distributing, installing, and servicing products. They will include application engineering and technical support.
- Regional units will have the responsibility to develop and maintain the distribution system in each region. The distribution system will comprise three main channels: direct, retail, and dealers.

- The sales organization in the field will be connected to plants and product groups by three vital processes:
  - Product design cycle (requirements of the customer communicated to designers)
  - Order payment cycle
  - Logistics support
- Regional units have the primary responsibility for understanding the end user's requirements and helping Carrier provide appropriate solutions to those requirements.
- Regional organizations will be responsible for creating synergy at the local level and reducing unnecessary duplication of services. Since the nature of the problems and opportunities is different in each region, the organizational setup appropriate for each region will also be different in each region.
- Each region will also have a Regional Advocate who will be responsible for the development of new businesses that satisfy the needs of each region.

Figure 12.2 provides an example of how regional units may be organized to optimize market access and user concerns.

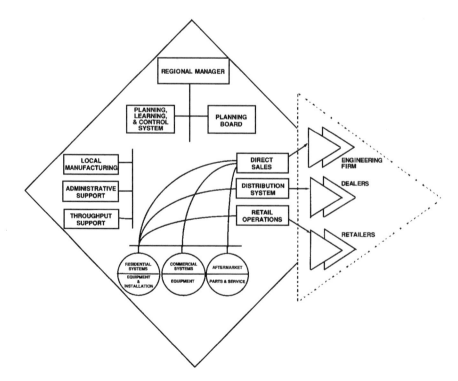

FIGURE 12.2 Structure of a Regional Unit

Area Units

Every area unit will be responsible for designing, engineering, and marketing a system of products and services as solutions to the needs of a given market segment. Initially, there will be three such segments in each area: residential systems, commercial systems, and industrial and institutional systems.

As market-driven units, area units must understand the current and latent climate control problems faced by specific market segments and develop and offer solutions to those problems.

Each unit will be responsible for system development in its specific segment. System designs will be informed by local requirements in different regions. System solutions will be designed on global platforms developed by output units. These platforms provide modular designs that standardize chassis and components while allowing for variations to satisfy different local requirements. Each output unit will have top system engineers on their team for developing global platforms within which local products can be manufactured.

Area units will develop the basic policies and approach for developing and maintaining a distribution system to serve all Carrier units. For example, area units will be expected to develop policies for acquiring and distributing complementary products intended to help increase the business at the dealership level. Implementation of policies will be the responsibility of regional units. Additionally, area managers will be responsible for developing new markets, for liaison between regional units and output units, and for consolidation and administration at the area level.

In general, area units will have no fixed assets. This will ensure that they are not preoccupied with existing facilities and current products. Their total focus should be on delivering the best solution to the customer.

These products and services may or may not be provided by Carrier manufacturing units. This constant examination and reevaluation of the "make or buy" decisions will keep continuous competitive pressure on both the designers and the manufacturers (suppliers).

There will be members of the parts unit in each area to manage the logistics, warehousing, and physical transportation systems at the area level.

Figure 12.3 provides an example of how area units may be organized.

OUTPUT UNITS

Output units will be responsible for the design and production of global end products. Such products are sold in more than one geographic region, have a high level of complexity, and offer significant economies of scale. Output unit managers will have worldwide responsibility for designing manufacturability, functionality, and serviceability, as well as lean production systems, delivery, and costs.

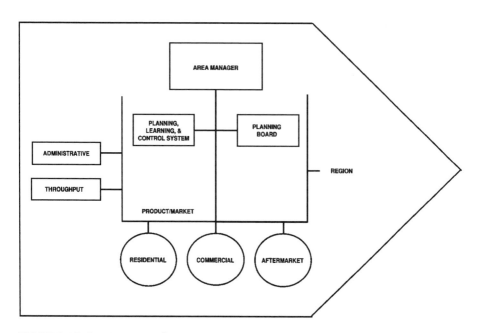

FIGURE 12.3   Structure of Area Management

Global products will be designed on a global platform concept—that is, a modular design that standardizes chassis and components while allowing for variations to satisfy different local requirements. Carrier products must be globally conceived and designed. Carrier technology must be globally applied.

Output managers will be responsible for optimizing manufacturing facilities on a global basis to ensure competitiveness.

In the first approximation to the design, manufacturing resources will be optimized on an area basis. This will not mean, however, that each area will be expected to be self-sufficient from a manufacturing perspective. In fact, each area will be expected to develop at least one facility as a global supplier of products and become the champion of a global product.

Each output unit will be a profit center with the ability to sell and source externally. In addition, there will be two other output units: Transicold and Aftermarket Parts. The unique nature of the transportation product business necessitates treating it as an output unit separate from stationary HVAC (Heating, Ventilation, Air Conditioning) products. Transicold will continue to operate as it currently does; however, it will proactively seek to utilize the services offered by the existing Carrier sales and distribution system.

Aftermarket parts are important elements of our total solution to customer problems and also a big market opportunity. We must aggressively develop these businesses. Aftermarket parts will be a global business unit jointly owned

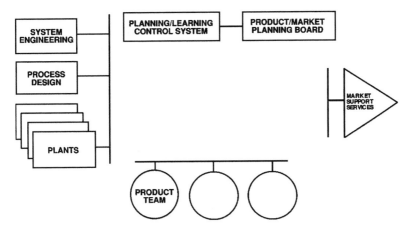

FIGURE 12.4 Organization of Output Units

by area (market) units and output units. It will buy and distribute Carrier and non-Carrier parts and components.

Figure 12.4 provides an example of how an output unit may be organized.

COMPONENTS

The Components Group will be responsible for:

- Developing and maintaining state-of-the-art knowledge (product technology and design) for all of the above categories.
- Manufacturing as many Category 1 products as is economically feasible.
- Seeking and creating partnerships to maintain strategic control over those Category 1 components that it cannot economically produce.
- Creating strategic alliances with producers of Categories 2 and 3 to ensure sufficient influence over the developments and reliable sources of supply.

To ensure worldwide cost and quality competitiveness, each component business should be able to survive on a stand-alone basis. Therefore, each unit in this group will be treated as a separate business. Units within the components group will have the option of selling their products to other original equipment manufacturers (OEMs). Likewise, Carrier product managers will have the option of sourcing their components from external suppliers.

At the start, it might be necessary for the corporation to subsidize the components group until it can provide competitive prices to its internal customers.

Initially, there will be two units in this group: compressors and electronic controls.

INPUTS

The Technology

The technology group will be the research and development arm of Carrier, responsible for identifying and nurturing core technologies required by Carrier businesses. Carrier will continuously assess its technological profile to match the emerging needs of the business. The company's desired position with respect to related technologies and components will be defined using the following three categories:

- Must have knowledge and control in-house.
- Must have knowledge and strategic alliances.
- Must have knowledge to influence independent developers.

Table 12.1 summarizes Carrier's present need for core components and corresponding technologies.

A special group within the technology group will focus on developing service technology (e.g., remote diagnosis capability). This activity will be funded by all the business units.

Operational Support (Process Design)

This unit will focus on increasing throughput of the enterprise. It is organized around modular teams and provides support to all units in Carrier.

Carrier will create centers of expertise that develop and disseminate knowledge throughout the organization. They will be organized into process teams and technology teams. This knowledge is not divided by disciplines, as

TABLE 12.1   Needed Technologies and Components

Core Technology or Component	Knowledge & Control	Knowledge & Alliance	Knowledge & Influence
Compressors	X		
Electronic Controls	X		
Heat Transfer Devices	X		
Enclosures, Fans, & Air Movements	X		
Motors		X	
Air Cleaning Devices		X	
Refrigerants			X
Diesel Engines		X	
Building Software	X		

in universities, but will be cross-disciplinary so it can provide solutions to complex problems.

Process and technology teams will work as internal consultants attacking and improving critical elements of the business. They will educate the rest of the organization on the latest advancements in design and throughput processes. The teams will be expected to market their services to both the executive office and to the operating units. Process teams must recreate themselves in the organization. They are accountable for redesigning, implementing, and handing off systems solutions. Only when the project has been considered a success will the team move on to its next challenge.

Process teams will be organized around specific throughput processes, but all will have cross-functional expertise in information technology, total quality, human systems, and design. Their objective is to produce an integrated solution (a single design) for each of the critical throughput processes so that all of the following critical goals for success can be simultaneously accomplished:

- Reduce the time cycle
- Eliminate waste
- Achieve flexibility
- Achieve total quality

Technology teams will be multidisciplinary, being able to integrate and apply various technologies to solve specific business problems. They are charged with educating everyone in the company, from engineers to the direct sales force, on the potential impact of emerging technologies on Carrier's business. Incentives for team members will be based on the success of the team as a whole. Teams will be composed of very competent professionals and kept together for an extended period to ensure continuous improvement.

Management Support Services

Management support services include financial, accounting, and administrative services, human resource services, MIS, and quality. These units will all provide services. The function of control will be part of the executive office. All input units will be "performance centers." For each unit, a set of specific measures of performance will be developed. Each unit will be expected to add value to Carrier through its operations. Therefore, profitability will be a key factor in each unit's performance measurement. The revenues for each unit will be derived from its "sales" to other Carrier units and/or to external customers.

BUSINESS PROCESSES

Decision System

- Interactive policy teams will be the main vehicle for aligning policies and plans and for dissolving conflicts among units in Carrier.
- Each interactive policy team will have members from a minimum of three levels of management: the manager whose team it is, his or her boss, and his or her direct reports. Other members may be added on a regular basis or on specific issues.
- Interactive policy teams are responsible for making policies. They do not get involved in operation decisions.
- Policies establish the criteria by which managers make decisions. Agreement on decision criteria is the key to successful decentralization.
- If no policy exists for a pending decision, the responsible manager will make the decision on his or her own. The appropriate interactive policy team may later decide to make a policy for future situations.
- Each policy will be made at the lowest-level team possible.
- Special interactive policy teams will be formed to coordinate policy on specific issues of strategic importance.

Performance Measurement and Reward System

- The measurement system will be throughput oriented.
- It will create win/win situations for the units. It will avoid endless fights among internal units over prices.
- It will recognize not only the performance of the unit itself, but also the unit's contribution to other units' performance.
- It will contain incentives for internal cooperation rather than outsourcing. It may, for example, have a differential tax rate for internal and external transactions.

Target Costing and Variable Budgeting System

The following model represents the proposed relationship among the various units in Carrier's value chain. The aim of this system is to align each unit's revenues to the throughput of the system as a whole.

- Each unit will have a variable budget that will be a function of the total throughput.
- Each unit will be a profit center. Revenues for the unit will be a percentage of the throughput of the total system. Costs for each unit will be actual costs.

- The percentage of throughput that will constitute each unit's revenues may be determined by a combination of the following methods:
  - An idealized breakdown derived from corporate strategy and the competitive environment
  - Industry benchmarks
  - Competitive analysis (alternative sources of supply)
  - Historical data
  - Executive committee discussions at the corporate policy team forum

Figure 12.5 illustrates a breakdown of throughput along the value chain.

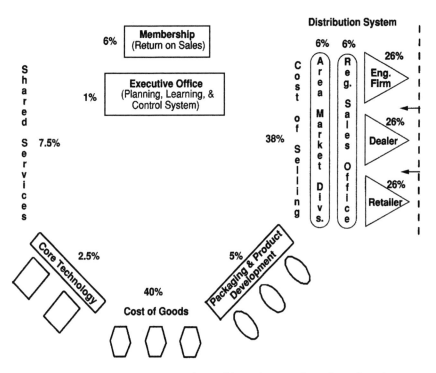

FIGURE 12.5 Target Costing and Variable Budgeting along the Value Chain

Conclusion

Having come this far, you must have gotten the bug already. You may even have realized that there is tremendous power in the idea of holistic iterative thinking. To internalize it, you must make it your own. This means that you should: 1) make notes of the major points that were of interest to you; 2) repeat the main arguments to yourself in your own language; and 3) share them with others. The best way of learning is teaching. If you can excite others and make them listen to you for one hour, you are on your way to becoming an effective systems designer.

Systems thinking is the art of simplifying complexity. It is about seeing through chaos, managing interdependency, and understanding choice. We see the world as increasingly more complex and chaotic because we use inadequate concepts to explain it. When we understand something, we no longer see it as chaotic or complex.

Learning the systems methodology is very much like learning to play chess. The rules are relatively simple, but proficiency comes only with practice. Stay appreciative of the imperatives of the systems dimensions in your life. Apply the systems principles to your daily encounters. These concepts are even more potent and relevant in a personal context. To understand complexity, one needs to discover the underlying rhythm, the order by which things repeat themselves.

The first few tries are not going to be easy, but once you get the hang of it you will enjoy the power of iterative thinking. Seeing things differently and clearly, in their proper perspective results in a new mode of being. You will be able to manage outward; influence those whom you do not control; produce an order-of-magnitude change in the throughput of any system of which you are in charge. Soon, you will discover that the world is full of frustrated heroes waiting to be discovered. Happiness and success, as well as love, must be continuously reproduced. "They lived happily ever after" is a lie. You will learn that excitement, as the essence of beauty, is the most potent instrument of change and social integration. And that power-to-do is a matter of competence. Like knowledge, power is enhanced when it is shared. Last, but not least, people are more likely to implement an idea when they have had a hand in shaping it.

The following tips are to get you started:

Get a good handle on the problem before you try to solve it. Don't accept problems at face value. Remember, neither a problem nor a solution can be entertained free of context. A tendency to define problems in terms of their solutions, and a strong preference for context-free solutions will merely continue regenerating the past, reproducing the same nonsolution all over again. Do not use universal constraints such as time and information or resources to define problems. It implies that you have defined the problem in terms of a known solution. This may be assuming more than what you really want to say. Do not entertain any suggestions for possible solutions while you are still engaged in the process of defining the problem.

Separate the process of defining the problem from the process of producing the solution. Look at the bigger picture; try to see the problems as interactive elements of a mess, the future implicit in the present behavior of the system. To map the mess, generate a snapshot of the system under study. Deal iteratively with function (the output), structure (the major actors), process (how they do what they do), and the purpose (the role the system plays in its containing environment). Try to identify obstructions to proper functioning of wealth, power, beauty, knowledge, and value dimensions of the system. This should point to a web of problems. Finally, you can capture the future implicit in the present order by recognizing that: 1) cause and effect may form circular relations; 2) events may have multiple outcomes, each with a different time lag; 3) if "X" is good, more "X" is not necessarily better; and 4) tenacity in playing the old game converts success to failure. It is seldom a good idea to make people feel defensive about their past. Presenting the mess as the consequence of success will go a long way toward getting it accepted.

To design a solution, start with an exciting vision of the future that you are capable of producing and then work backward to the existing system. There is a logic to this apparent madness. Ask children who like to solve mazes. They will tell you why you should start from the end.

Imagine that the system you were dealing with was destroyed overnight; everything else remained intact, and you are to recreate it anew. There is a twisted logic in this proposition as well. The point is, if you are not able to produce an acceptable design within the existing order, despite the absence of imposing constraints, then there might not be a light at the end of the tunnel at all. This means that real problems may lie in the environment rather than within the design itself. Change your focus; try to influence your immediate environment by managing outward. If this is not at all possible, you may be better off to get the hell out of that impossible situation.

Design is the potential means of controlling, influencing, and appreciating the parameters affecting the system's existence. The parameters that co-produce the future are found in the interactions of five dimensions of a social system. Creating compatibility and reinforcing relations among power, knowledge, wealth, beauty, and value produces a resonance, a 10× force, that, in most situations, will overcome the most stubborn obstacles.

The five systems architectures discussed in the last part of this book were all based on an exciting notion of modular design. Modular design is the most potent and practical means of handling change and implementing complex designs, without getting lost in the process. This notion of modularity is a variation of the powerful concept originally used in the design of complex computers. It is the extension of this design principle to the organization of the computer industry as a whole that is responsible for its remarkable success. It created the ability to build a complex product from smaller subsystems which can be designed independently yet function together as a whole.

Recall that in order to create a modular structure, we first had to design an architecture, a general description of a system in terms of its vital functions, major elements, and critical processes. An architecture consists of a set of distinct, but interrelated, platforms. Each platform hosts a set of special-purpose modules. Relationships and the interfaces among platforms are explicitly defined. Parts operate as independent systems with the ability to be relatively self-controlling and yet act as responsible members of a coherent system with the ability to respond effectively to the requirements of their containing whole. Modular design is a powerful instrument of change. Use it to the best of your ability.

Keep in touch; let me know how this version of Systems Thinking is working out for you. Send your E-mail to: *jghara@earthlink.net*

Bibliography

Ackoff, R. L. *Ackoff's Best: his Classic writings on Management*. New York: John Wiley & Sons, 1999.

——. *Creating the Corporate Future*. New York: John Wiley & Sons, 1981.

——. "The Future of Operational Research Is Past." *Journal of The Operational Reseach Society*, 30 (1979), 93–104.

——. *The Art of Problem Solving*. New York: John Wiley. & Son, 1978.

——. *Redesigning the Future*. New York: John Wiley, & Son, 1974.

Ackoff, R. L., & Emery, Fred E. *On Purposeful Systems*. Aldine-Atherton, Chicago: 1972.

Adler, Mortimer J. *Aristotle For Everybody*. New York: Macmillan Publishing Co., 1978.

Ashby, W. Ross. "*General Systems Theory as a New Discipline*," *General Systems* 3 (1958): 1–6.

Augustine, Norman R. "Reshaping An Industry: Lockheed Martin's Survival Story," *Harvard Business Review* May-June, 1997, pp. 83–94.

Banathy, Bela H. *Designing Social systems in a Changing World*. New York: Plenum Publishing, 1997.

Beer, Stafford, *Brain of the Firm*. Harmondsworth: Penguin Press, 1967.

——. *Platforms of Change*. New York: John Wiley & Sons. 1975.

Beishon, John & Peters, Geoff (eds). *Systems Behaviour*. London: The Open University Press, 1972.

Bertalanffy, Ludwig Von. *General Systems Theory: Foundation, Development, Applications*. Middlesex: Penguin Books, 1968.

Blake, R. R. & Mouton, J. S. *The Managerial Grid*. Houston: Gulf Publishing Company, 1964.

Bogdanov, A. *Essays in Tektology*, Translated by George Gorelik. Seaside: Intersystems Publications, 1980.

Boulding, Kenneth E. *Beyond Economics*. Ann Arbor: The University of Michigan Press, 1968.

———. *Ecodynamics*. Beverly Hills: Sage Publications, 1981.

———. *The Image*. Ann Arbor: University of Michigan Press, 1956a.

———. *The Organizational Revolution*. New York: Harper, 1953.

Buckley, Walter (ed). *Systems Research for the Behavioral Scientist A Source Book*. Chicago: Aldine Publishing Co., 1968.

———. *Sociology and Modern Systems Theory*. Englewood Cliffs: Prentice-Hall, 1967.

Capra Fritjof. *The Hidden Connections*. New York, Doubleday, 2002.

———. *The Turning Point: Science, Society, and the Rising Culture*. Doubleday, 1988.

Checkland, Peter. *Systems Thinking, Systems Practice*. John Wiley, 1981.

Churchman, C. West. *The Systems Approach and Its Enemies*. New York: Basic Books, 1979.

———. *Design of Inquiring Systems*. New York: Basic Books, 1971.

———. *The Systems Approach*. New York: Delacorte Press, 1968.

Cvitanovic, P. *Universality in Chaos*. Bristol, England: Adam Hilger, 1984.

Dewey, John. *Freedom and Culture*. New York: Prometheus Books, Great Books In Philosophy, 1989.

Forrester, Jay W. *World Dynamics*. Cambridge: Productivity Press, 1973.

———. "Counter Intuitive Behavior of Social Systems" *Technology Review, Vol. 73 No. 3 Jan.* 1971, pp. 52–68.

———. "A New Corporate Design," *Industrial Management Review* 7, No. 1. (Fall 1965), pp. 5–17.

———. *Industrial Dynamics*. Cambridge: Productivity Press, 1961.

Fromm, Eric. *The Sane Society*. New York: Rinehart, 1955.

Gharajedaghi, Jamshid. "Making TQM Work for America" *The Total Quality Review*, March/April 1994, pp. 11–18.

——. in collaboration with R. L. Ackoff. *A Prologue to National Development Planning*. Newport CT: Greenwood Press, 1986.

——. *Toward A Systems Theory of Organization*. Seaside, CA: Intersystems Publications, 1985.

——, and Ackoff R. L. "Mechanisms, Organisms and Social Systems." *Strategic Management Journal*, Vol. 5 (1984): pp. 289–300.

——. "Social Dynamics, Dichotomy or Dialectic," *Human Systems Management* 4 (1983): pp. 7–17.

——. *Theory and Management of Systems*. Tehran, Iran: Industrial Management Institute, 1972.

Gleick, James. *CHAOS: Making a New Science*. Viking Penguin Inc: New York, 1987.

Goldratt, Eliyahu M. *Critical Chain*. Great Barrington MA: North River Press, Inc, 1997.

——, and Cox, Jeff. *The GOAL*. Groton-on-Hudson, NY: North River Press, 1986.

Gordon, G. and Colleagues. "A Contingency Model for the Design of Problem Solving Research Program," *Milbank Memorial Fund Quarterly*, 1974, pp. 184–220.

Grove, Andrews. *Only The Paranoid Survive*. New York: Doubleday, 1996.

Halal, W. E., Geranmayeh Ali, Pourdehnad John. *Internal Markets*. New York: John Wiley, 1993.

Hamel, Gary, and Prahalad, C. K. *Competing For The Future*. Harvard Business School Press, 1994.

Hammer, Michael & Champy James. *Reengineering The Corporation: A Manifesto For Business Revolution*. HarperCollins Publishers, 1993.

Holland, John H. *Hidden Order*. Helix Book, Addison-Wesley Publishing Company 1995.

Katsenelinboigen, Aaron. *Evolutionary Change*. The Netherlands: Gordon and Breach Publishers, 1997.

——. *Selected Topics in Indeterministic Systems*. Seaside, CA: Intersystems Publication, 1989.

Lazlo, Ervin. *Systems View of the World*. George Braziller, 1972.

Mandelbrot, Benoit. *Fractal Geometry of Nature*. New York: Freeman, 1977.

McGregor, D. *The Human Side of Enterprise.* New York: McGraw Hill, 1960.

McClelland, David. *The Achieving Society.* New York: Free Press, 1961.

Meadows, D. H., et al. *The Limits to Growth.* London: Potomac Associates, 1972.

Miller, Danny. *The Icarus Paradox.* New York: Harper Business, 1990.

Miller, James. *Living Systems.* New York: McGraw Hill, 1978.

Peters, T. J., Waterman, R. H. *In Search of Excellence.* Harper and Row 1982.

Pine, Joseph B. II. *Mass Customization.* Harvard Business School Press, 1993.

Popper, Karl R. *The Open Society and its Enemies.* Princeton, New Jersey: Princeton University Press, 1966.

Pourdehnad, John. "Interactive Planning," *Ph.D. Dissertation.* 1992, Wharton School, University of Pennsylvania.

Rahmatian, Sassan. *Management Information Systems.* New Jersey: Prentice Hall, 1995.

Rapoport, Anatol, and A. M. Chammah. *Prisoner's Dilemma.* Ann Arbor: University of Michigan Press, 1965.

Richmond, Barry. *An Introduction to Systems Thinking, (ithink software).* High Performance Systems, Inc, 2001.

Senge, Peter, *The Fifth Discipline.* New York: Doubleday, 1990.

Servan-Schreiber, J. J. *American Challenge.* London: Avon Books 1967.

Singer, E. A., Jr. *Experience and Reflection.* C. W. Churchman ed., Philadelphia: University of Pennsylvania Press, 1959.

Shiba, Shoji, Alan Graham, David Walden. *A New American TQM.* Portland, OR: Productivity Press, Center for Quality of Management, 1993.

Thurow, Lester, C. *Zero Sum Society.* New York: Basic Books, 1980.

Wheatley, Margaret J. *Leadership and the New Science: Learning About Organization from an Orderly Universe.* San Francisco: Berrett-Koehler Pub. Reprint 1994.

Wheelwright, S. C., Clark, K. B. *Leading Product Development.* New York: The Free Press, 1995.

Wiener, N. *The Human Use of Human Beings.* New York: Doubleday Anchor, 1954.

Womack, J. P., Jones, D. T., Ross, D. *The Machine That Changed The World.* New York: Macmillan Publishing Co., 1990.

Wolfram Stephen. *New Kind of Science*. Canada: Wolfram Media, Inc., 2002.

Zadeh, Lotfi A., et al. *Fuzzy Sets and Applications*. New York: John Wiley, 1987.

Zeeman, E. C. *"Catastrophe Theory."* Scientific American, 234, (4), 1976, pp. 65–83.

Zeleny, M. (ed). *Autopoiesis*. Amsterdam: North Holland Publishing Company, 1981.

Index

A

ability, 56, 57, 70, 94
Ackoff, R. L., on
circular organization, 72
development vs. growth, 72, 96
ideal-seeking systems, 57
learning processes, 87
management system, 75
operations research and, 21–22
problem definition, 126
purposeful systems, 12, 22–23, 26,
51, 125
on structure and function, 110
systems behavior, 53
advocacy, 169–170, 207, 243
Afghanistan, 101
ALCOA (Aluminum Company of
America), 185
alienation, 26, 66–67, 92, 97–98
American Challenge (Shreiber), 3
analytical thinking
in current society, 25–27
diversity and growth as, 18–20
holistic thinking, shift to, 8–9
independent variables in, 13–15*f*, 13–16
interchangeability of parts and labor
as, 17–18
participative management as, 20–21
systems thinking vs., 15–16, 17*f*, 109
Apple, 158
Aristotle, 57
assumptions, challenging, 87
attractors role in patterns, 52
Autopoiesis, 113, 113*f*

B

beauty, creation and dissemination, 35,
56–59, 315. *See also* excitement
Beer, Stafford, 8, 20, 22, 115–117, 127
behavior
faking, 47–48
goal-seeking, 112–113, 115, 115*f*
purposeful, 36
rational, 33–35
behavior patterns
of attractors, 52
changing, 125
Bella, Gary, 186
Bertalanffy, Ludwig Von, 45
biological systems. *See* unminded
(biological) systems
birth-control project, Ford foundation,
34–35
black Americans, 98
Blake, R. R., 41–42, 177
Blevins, Ken, 185
bonded systems
energy-bonded, 12–13, 83
first-degree agreements, 83
human community, 84–86, 121
information-bonded, 13, 83–84
second-degree agreements,
83–84
Boulding, Kenneth E., 37, 39, 124
Brain of the Firm (Beer), 20
Buckley, Walter, 45, 84
budgeting. *See* target costing; variable
budgeting
Bush, George H. W., 8

business architecture
Butterworth Health Systems
care facilities, 238–245
design specifications, 225–226
design team, 222
desired specifications, 222, 229–231
interrelatedness in, 253–257
multidimensionality in, 238–240,
248, 249
overview, 226–227, 226f
Carrier Corporation, 303–304
Commonwealth Energy Systems,
279–282
executive function in
market-based, 158–159, 159f
Marriott Corporation
brand management, 266
core components, 266–267
core knowledge, 267–269
critical processes, 268–269
dimensions of, 263–264
principles and desired characteristics, 262–263
product/market mix, 264
region/market operation, 264–266
modular. *see* modular design,
multidimensional
multicultural, 160
Oneida Nation
business systems, 211–214
core services, 215–217
external environment, 217
governance, 189–194
judicial system, 218–221
learning systems, 203–210
membership systems, 195–203
product-based, 157–158, 158f
technology-based, 159–160, 159f
unidimensional, 88, 163, 174
business architecture, design process.
See also systems design
dissolution of the second-order
machine, 183–184
examples, 155f, 156f
idealization phase, 175–176
introduction, 152, 152f
measurement system development,
176–181
operating environment, clarifying the,
153–155

operational viability determination, 176
outline, 153f
planning, learning and control
systems development, 175–176
product-market niche selection,
161–163, 162f
realization phase, 181–183, 182f
successive approximations in,
181–183, 182f
summary, 184
systems boundary definition step, 153
technological feasibility
determination, 175–176
understanding purpose in the,
155–161
butterfly effect, 123–124
Butterworth Health Systems
business model, 223–225
customer orientation, 251–253
executive office, 257–258
inputs dimension
business services, 244
clinical services, 244
core knowledge, 245–249
home care management, 244
hospital and facility management,
244
occupational care management,
244–245
shared services, 249–253
learning systems, 247–248, 252
market dimension: access
fee for service, 223, 227
HMOs, 223–224, 227–228
Medicare/Medicaid, 228
noncovered customers, 228
self-insured, 228
markets dimension: care system
common features, 231–233
contextual background, 229
desired specifications, 229–231
interventional, 234, 235f
preventive, 233–234, 235f
terminal, 235, 235f
viability, 234–235
output dimension: care facilities
community-based delivery system,
240–242
introduction, 237–238
shared services, 243–245

specialized delivery system, 242–243
systems design, 238–240
summary, 258–259
systems architecture
    care facilities, 238–245
    design specifications, 225–226
    design team, 222
    desired specifications, 222, 229–231
    interrelatedness in, 253–257
    multidimensionality in, 238–240,
        248, 249
    overview, 226–227, 226*f*

C

Capra, F., 123
Carrier Corporation
    business processes, 312–313
    changing game at, 298–299
    components group, 309
    core technology and know-how,
        301–302
    core values, 300–303
    decision system, 312
    inputs dimension, 310–311
    introduction, 297
    markets dimension, 304–307
    outputs dimension, 307–309
    performance measurement, 312
    products and services, 300–301
    reward system, 312
    sales and distribution system, 302–303
    systems architecture
        desired characteristics, 303–304
        multidimensional framework, 304
    target costing and variable budgeting
        system, 312–313
carrying capacity, 116, 117*f*
catastrophe theory, 54
causality principle, 44–45, 49–50, 110
cause and effect, 49–50, 55, 137
change
    butterfly effect, 123–124
    conflict and, 21
    constraints on, 129–130, 181–183
    dissatisfaction and, 94
    hatred and, 99
    inflection points, 40–42, 53–54, 55
    interactive design for, 125–130
    power and, 37
    qualitative, 40–42, 53–54, 87

resistance to, 5–6, 9–10, 17, 53, 85–86
self-reference in facilitating, 122
shared image role in, 122
state-maintaining systems and, 37
transformational, 9, 85–87, 122
unpredictability and rate of, 22
chaos, 25, 32, 92–93, 92*f. See also*
    feedback systems
chaos theory, 117
Chase econometric model, 22, 30
choice
    ability and, 56
    conflict and, 12
    cultural, 35–36
    emotional, 35
    human development and, 23, 125
    independent behavior and, 9–10
    in mechanistic systems, 10–11, 224
    participative management, 20–22
    power and, 37, 38, 71
    purposefulness and, 12
    rational, 33–35, 55
    in social systems, 12–13
    in unminded systems, 11
Churchman, C. West, 21, 23, 39, 40
circular organization, 72
Clark Equipment Company, 186
Clerical Workers Union, 186
closed loop systems, 114, 114*f*
coalitions, 68
coding, cultural, 32, 84–86, 121–125
cognition, 123–124. *See also* learning
    systems design
Commonwealth Energy Systems
    business units
        brokerage and international
            operations, 288–290
        core units, 285–286
        customer-oriented, 283
        regulated, 277, 282–286
        technology/supply-oriented,
            286–288
    the changing game, 273–275
    consultants, 271
    core values and desired
        specifications, 278–279
    design team, 270
    executive office, 292–296
    financial systems, 292
    learning systems design, 294–296

Commonwealth Energy Systems *cont.*
mess team, 270–271
purpose and strategic intent,
276–278
service company, 291–292
shared services, 290–291
stakeholders expectations, 271–273
systems design, 279–282
value chain strategy, 279, 288–290
compatibility
horizontal, 79–81
temporal, 81–82
vertical, 78–79
competence, 57, 66–67
competition. *See also* games,
competitive; success
the changing game
Carrier Corporation, 298–299
Commonwealth Energy Systems,
273–275
examples, 154, 155–156*f*
HVAC industry, 299
introduction, 6–8
Marriott Corporation, 261–262
multidimensionality as response to,
159–160
paradigm shifts, 16–17, 17*f*
conflict and, 70–71
design and, 131–132
competitive advantage
changing game in, 6–8, 16–17
defined, 161–162
exaggeration as, 6
hierarchy of forces, 4*f*
imitation and, 4–5
inattention, effect on, 6–8
inertia, effect on, 5–6
shift of paradigm in, 8–9
suboptimization in, 6, 52
success and, 5–8
complexity
chaos and, 25, 92–93
iteration in understanding, 112, 112*f*
laws of, 51
organized and chaotic, 92*f*
relative nature of, 114–116
compromise, 38, 71
conflict
change and, 21
choice and, 12

competition vs., 70–71
in opposing tendencies, 38–39
conflict management, 67–71
conflict resolution
compromise in, 38
Oneida Nation judicial system,
218–221
paternalistic systems, 20–21
conformity, 86, 195
consensus, 74–75, 198–202
consistency as decision criteria, 74
constraints, realization phase, 129–130,
181–183, 182*f*
Continental Can Company, 5–6
control, 30–32
Control Data Corporation (CDC), 6
control systems, 75–77, 76*f*, 169,
192–194
cooperation, 67–68
core technologies, 168
Cornelius, Neil, 187
corruption, 99–100
costing
cost-plus, 154, 223
target, 65–66
variable budgeting, 65–66, 129, 174,
183, 312–313
counter-intuitiveness, 49–55, 50*f*,
114–116, 137
creativity, 18, 94
cry for help. *See* terrorism
culture(s)
active adaptation in, 123
cognitive dimension, 123–124
in decision systems, 35, 85
default value of, 85, 180
normative dimension, 122–123
paternalistic, 12, 20–21, 123–124
present day, emergent, 26
role in social systems
development, 124
shared image in creating, 84–86,
121–125
transforming, 85–87
viability elements, 85
customers, 162–163, 170
customer-supplier relationship, 170–174,
243, 251–252, 256, 269
cybernetics, 16, 22
cycle attractors, 52

D
Dannemiller, Kathy, 260
Das Capital (Marx), 128
decision making
    Carrier Corporation, 312
    constraining elements, 35–36
    criteria for, 72–75, 198–202
    decentralized, 72
    decisions vs., 73
    dimensions of, 34*f*
    power and, 37
    working synthesis in, 75
defense industry, 158
delayed response effect, 115–116, 116*f*
democratic process, challenges to, 86,
    220–221
The Design of Inquiring Systems
    (Churchman), 23
desire, 94
determinism, 45
development
    ability and, 94
    growth vs., 95
Dewey, John, 57–58
differentiation, 92–96, 92*f*, 93*f*
Digital Equipment Corporation, 6
diversity management, 18–20
Doxtator, Debra, 187
dynamic behavior mapping, 118–119

E
early warning systems, 77, 127, 140
economic value added, 48
economy of scale, 168, 250
emergent property, 13, 45–48, 46*f*, 177
employees. *See* knowledge workers
empowerment, 71–73, 170, 195
ends and means, 70–71, 100
energy-bonded systems, 12–13, 83–84
energy business' business environment,
    154, 155*f*, 273–275
entropy, 16, 32, 121
environment. *See also* markets
    dimension
    bases for competition, 261–262, 299
    clarifying in systems design, 153–155
    contextual, 31
    defined, 30
    energy business', 154, 155*f*, 273–275
    health-care business', 154, 156*f*, 229

HVAC industry, 299
    in modular design, 163, 169–170, 169*f*
    Oneida Nation, 217
    passive adaptation to, 36, 55
    transactional, 31–32
    uncontrolled, 30
    win/lose, 69–70
equifinality, 45
excitement. *See also* beauty, creation and
    dissemination of
    as decision criteria, 35, 37
    integration and, 66, 82, 97–98, 125–126
executive office
    Butterworth Health Systems, 257–258
    Commonwealth Energy Systems,
        292–296
experience curve, 161
Extend, 60–61

F
failure. *See* success
feedback systems
    carrying capacity impact, 116, 117*f*
    delayed response effect, 115–116, 116*f*
    dynamic behavior mapping, 118–119
    health-care business environment, 223
    linear or nonlinear, 115
    multi-loop nonlinear, 117–118
    open or closed loop, 114, 114*f*
Field Theory, 124
Ford, Henry, 7, 17
Ford Foundation birth-control project,
    34–35
Ford Motor Company, 7, 13–15,
    34–35, 154
Forrester, J. W., 21, 115
freedom, decisionmaking and, 74
Friedman, Milton, 157
frog that boiled to death, 7, 55
frustration, 100
fundamentalism, religious, 94, 101
the future
    changing, 22–23, 37
    parameters co-producing, 56, 94

G
Galinis, E. C., 14
games, competitive. *See also* competition
    analytical thinking in, 17–21
    the design approach, 22–23

games, competitive *cont.*
flexibility and control in, 22
managing growth and diversity, 18–20
self-organizing systems, 20–21
systems thinking in, 21–23
zero-sum, 38, 69, 100
General Motors, 18, 154
Geranmayeh, Ali, 297
globalization, 154
goal-seeking, 12–13, 115, 115*f*
Goods, Jerry, 186
Google, 157
Gordon, Gerald, 42
Grove, Andrew S., 54
growth
development vs., 96
effectiveness vs., 18
managing, 18–20
success vs., 11, 48
Gulf War, 7–8

H
Habermas, Jurgen, 124
Handy, Charles, 99
health-care business environment, 154,
156*f*, 229. *See also* Butterworth
Health Systems
Henning, Walter B., 185
The Hidden Connections (Capra), 123
holistic thinking, 8–9, 59, 61*f*, 108–113,
113*f. See also* systems thinking
Honda, 154
Hughes, Kathy, 187
human beings, characteristics of
abstraction, 84, 121
creativity, 94
image building (worldview creation),
84–86, 94, 121–125
plurality, 44
human development, choice in, 23, 125
HVAC industry. *See* Carrier
Corporation

I
IBM, 33, 157
Icarus Paradox (Miller), 6
identity, shared image in creating, 32,
84–86, 94, 121–125
ideological battles. *See* terrorism
image building. *See* shared image

imitation, failure through, 4–5
India, birth-control project in, 34–35
individuality, 32, 122
industrial age, 10–11
inertia, 5–6
information-bonded systems, 13, 83–84
information vs. understanding, 33. *See
also* knowledge
In Search of Excellence (Peters), 3
innovation typology, 42, 43*f*
inputs dimension
Butterworth Health Systems
business services, 244
clinical services, 244
core knowledge, 245–249
home care management, 244
hospital and facility management,
244
occupational care management,
244–245
shared services, 249–253
Carrier Corporation, 310–311
modular systems design, 163,
167–169, 167*f*, 169*f*
inquiry
iterative process, 112–113, 112*f*,
132–133
obstruction analysis, 132–133
paradigm shift in methods of, 13–16
systems analysis, 132–134
integration, 92–96, 92*f*, 93*f*
Intel, 55
interaction. *See also* relationships
of emergent properties, 45–48
mapping, 135–140
interactive design. *See* systems design,
interactive
interdependence
design approach, 22–23
in emergent properties, 46*f*
flexibility and control and, 22
in independent variables, 14–16, 21
joint optimization, 21–22
of opposing tendencies, 39
paradigm shift, 9–10
in social systems, 94
in systems thinking, 15–16, 21–22
invisible hand (Smith), 119, 119*f*, 120*f*
Iran, 101, 124
Islam, 101, 102*f*, 124

iteration, in
  closed loop systems, 114
  inquiry, 112–113, 112*f*
  pattern recognition, 51–52
  problem definition, 124*t*, 132–133
  systems design, 128–129
iterative thinking, 315
i-think, 60, 62, 63*f*
i-think model, 117–119, 119*f*, 120*f*

J
Japan, 7, 22
Jobs, Steve, 54

K
Katselenenboigen, Aron, 35
Keynes, John Maynard, 89
Khomeini, 101
Khorram, Bijan, 187
King, Bruce, 187
knowledge. *See also* learning
  generation and dissemination of
    Butterworth Health Systems,
      245–249
    Commonwealth Energy Systems,
      293–294
    Marriott Corporation, 267–269
    Oneida Nation, 203–210
    social systems dimensions, 56–58
  success and, 22
  understanding vs., 33
knowledge workers, 5, 154–156,
  255–256
Krapek, Karl J., 297

L
language
  analytical, 25–27
  modeling, 62, 119, 119*f*
  of systems thinking, 26
latency in viable systems, 257, 292, 304
Lazlo, Ervin, 83
leadership, 32, 249
Leadership and New Science (Wheatley),
  124
learning
  experience curve, 161
  first- and second-order, 87
  in social systems, 85–87
  in throughput systems, 65

learning systems design
  Butterworth Health Systems,
    247–248, 252
  Commonwealth Energy Systems,
    294–296
  components of, 75–77, 76*f*
  corrective action in, 77
  Oneida Nation, 203–210
Lee, Tom, 297
Leo, Vic, 14
Lexus, 65
Ligon, Charlie, 185
linear systems, 115, 115*f*
living systems, 11–12, 16, 32, 47, 113,
  121–123
living systems paradigm, 11–12

M
management
  interactive, 22–23, 23*f*
  participative, 20–21
  the transactional environment
    and, 32
  typology, 41–42
The Managerial Grid (Blake), 177
market economy
  counterintuitive behavior in, 54–55
  internal, 170–174, 251–253, 291–292
  rational choice in, 55
markets dimension. *See also*
    environment
  Butterworth Health Systems
    access to care, 227–228
    care system, 229–235
    internal market economy,
      251–253
  Carrier Corporation, 304–307
  distribution and advocacy units,
    169–170
  internal market economy, 170–174,
    251–253, 291–292
  Marriott Corporation, 264–266
  modular systems design, 163,
    169–170, 169*f*, 170–174
Marriott Corporation
  the changing game, 261–262
  design assumptions, 269
  design team, 260
  introduction, 260–261
  mess team, 260

Marriott Corporation   *cont.*
  purpose, 262–263
  systems architecture
    brand management, 266
    core components, 266–267
    core knowledge, 267–269
    critical processes, 268–269
    dimensions of, 263–264
    principles and desired
        characteristics, 262–263
    product/market mix, 264
    region/market operation, 264–266
Marx, Karl, 57, 128
Maturana, Humbertto, 123
measurement
  attributes of the outputs, 180
  capacity utilization, 179
  credibility in the marketplace, 180
  default value of the culture, 180
  of emergent properties, 13, 46–48, 177
  intensity of competition, 181
  market potential, 181
  product potency, 181
  profitability, 180
  reliability of demand, 180
  throughput capability, 180
  value-added ratio, 180
  value chain transaction index, 180
measurement systems. *See also*
        performance criteria;
        performance measures
  learning and control function,
        75–77, 76*f*
  viability matrix, 178–180, 179t
mechanistic systems. *See* mindless
        (mechanistic) organizational
        systems
membership in multiminded systems
  compatibility
    horizontal, 79–81
    Oneida Nation, 210
    over time, 81–82
    vertical, 77–78
  conformity, 86, 195
  integration
    determining levels of, 94
    exchange in, 67
    obstructions to, 97–98
    Oneida Nation, 196, 203
    performance criteria, 66, 77

role and, 66
    sacrifice and, 67
    threat in, 67
  Oneida Nation, 195–203, 207, 210, 214
  shared image and, 32, 84–86, 94,
        121–125
memory
  collective, 32
  read-only, 65
Mercedes-Benz, 65
the Mess, 127, 131. *See also* problem
        definition (formulating the Mess)
Microsoft, 54–55, 157
Miller, Danny, 6
mindless (mechanistic) organizational
        systems
  bonding in, 12–13, 83
  Butterworth Health Systems, 223–224
  interchangeability of parts and labor,
        17–18
  introduction, 10–11
  joint optimization, 21–22
  paradigm shifts, 9*f*, 17*f*
modeling language, 62, 119, 119*f*
modular design, multidimensional. *See
        also* multidimensionality principle
  adaptability of, 164
  inputs (technology) dimension, 163,
        167–169, 167*f*, 169*f*
  introduction, 160
  markets (environment) dimension,
        163, 169–170, 169*f*, 170–174
  outline, 165*f*
  outputs (products) dimension, 163,
        165–166, 166*f*, 169*f*
  power of, 317
  redundancy in, 164
  transition from divisional structure,
        171*f*, 172–174, 172*f*
  value chain in, 172–174, 173*f*
Molavi, Molana Jalaledin (pseud.
        Rumi), 109
Mouton, J. S., 41–42
multidimensionality principle. *See also*
        modular design,
        multidimensional
  cycle attractors in, 52
  defined, 38
  opposing tendencies relationships,
        38–40, 38–43*f*, 52, 62

plurality in, 43–45, 43f
typologies and behavior in, 40–42,
    41–43f
multifinality, 45, 49
multi-loop nonlinear feedback systems,
    50, 117–118, 132
multiminded systems. *See* sociocultural
    (multiminded) systems

N

neg-entropy, 16, 32, 121–122. *See also*
    self-organizing systems
New Kind of Science (Wolfram), 118
Next computers, 54–55
nonlinear systems, 51, 115, 115f

O

obstruction analysis, 132–133, 134t
Ohno, 7, 22
Oneida Nation
    business systems
        governance and intersystems
            relationships, 214
        industry sector, 213
        introduction, 211–212
        land and agriculture sector, 213
        leisure sector, 213
        marketing sector, 213–214
        ownership, collective and
            individual, 214
        partnership and franchise
            development, 214
        services sector, 212–213
        strategic alliances, 214
    core services
        compliance, 216
        governance and oversight,
            216–217
        government services division,
            215–217
        health services, 215
        infrastructure development
            division, 216
        ordinance division, 216
        performance criteria and
            measures, 216
        public works, 216
        records management, 216
        social services, 215
        space planning and engineering, 216

desired specifications, 187–189
external environment, 217
governance
    Chief of Staff, 192
    directors, 192–194
    Governing Body, 192
    overview, 190–191
    Planning, Learning, and Control
        Board, 194
    Planning, Learning, and Control
        System, 192–194
governance and intersystems
    relationships
    business systems, 214
    learning systems, 214
    infrastructure development,
        215–216
    judicial system, 218–221
learning systems
    advocacy functions, 207
    cultural education, 205–206
    formal education, 205
    introduction, 203–204
    Knowledge Bank, 207
    learning, research and practice
        cells, 208–209
    Oneida Multiversity, 207–209
    performance criteria and
        measures, 210
    professional education, 205–206
    Shared Services, 206
    structure, 203–204
    support functions, 206
membership systems
    consensus-building process,
        198–202
    empowerment, 195
    interdimensional and interest
        group activities, 203
    membership network, 196–198
    performance criteria and measures,
        202–203
    tradition in, 201–202
    unity in, 196
systems architecture
    business systems, 211–214
    core services, 215–217
    external environment, 217
    governance, 189–194
    judicial system, 218–221

Oneida Nation *cont.*
learning systems, 203–210
membership systems, 195–203
work team, 187
Only the Paranoid Survive (Grove), 54
On Purposeful Systems (Ackoff), 26
open loop systems, 114, 114*f*
openness, 16, 30–32, 127
operational thinking, 118
operations research, 16, 21–22
organization, circular, 72
organizational processes
conflict management, 67–71
decision systems, 71–75
holistic approach to, 59
learning and control systems, 75–77, 76*f*
membership, 66–67
organizational structure
centralized, 17–18, 71–72, 167–168, 250
circular, 73
divisional, 18–20, 19*f*, 171–172, 171*f*
learning and design cells, 72–75, 73*f*,
196–197, 198*f*, 208–209
modular. *see* modular design,
multidimensional
nested networks, 72–73
participative, 20–21
plurality of, 44
organizational systems. *See also* social
systems development
homeostatic, 11
interdependence in, 9–10, 14–16, 71
living, 11–12, 16, 32, 47, 113, 121–123
mindless, mechanistic. *see* mindless
(mechanistic) organizational
systems
role in success, 8–9
self-organizing, 16, 20–21, 32, 52,
121–124
sociocultural, multiminded. *see*
sociocultural (multiminded)
systems
unminded, biological. *see* unminded
(biological) systems
organizations
change in, 5–6, 9–10, 17–22
culture of corruption, 99–100
effectiveness in, 67
purpose of, 67, 156–161
organizing assumptions, 9–10

outputs (products) dimension
modular design, multidimensional, 163
outputs dimension
Butterworth Health Systems
community-based delivery system,
240–242
introduction, 237–240
specialized delivery system,
242–243
system design, 238–240
Carrier Corporation, 307–309
Commonwealth Energy Systems
customer-oriented businesses,
277–278, 283
gas and electricity distribution
units, 282–285
technology/supply-oriented
business units, 286–288
in modular design, 165–166, 166*f*, 169*f*
Oneida Nation
learning systems, 203–206
social services, 215

P
Pan Am syndrome, 55
paradigm shifts
competitive advantage with, 8–9
elements of, 9*f*
on nature of inquiry, 13–16, 17*f*
on the nature of organizations,
10–13, 17*f*
paternalism, 12, 20–21, 123–124
pattern recognition, 51–52, 119
performance criteria
basics, 176–177
in membership, 66, 77
Oneida Nation, 202–203, 210, 216
selecting, 176–177, 176*f*
performance measures. *See also* rewards
system
basics, 177–178
Butterworth Health Systems, 233
Carrier Corporation, 312
Oneida Nation, 202–203, 210, 216
rewards and, 181, 183, 233, 312
Peters, Tom, 3
planning, learning and control systems,
169, 192–194. *See also* learning
systems design
planning systems, 175, 216

plurality, 44–45, 89–92
point attractors, 52
Polaroid, 6
policy decisions, 73–75
Pourdehnad, John, 260
power
    choice and, 37, 38, 71
    development and duplication of,
        37, 56–57
    duplication of, 71–73, 164
    sharing through compromise, 38, 71
    suffocation vs. chaos with, 71
power-over, 57, 164
power-to-do, 38, 57, 71, 164, 316
predictability, 31, 55
predict and prepare, 18, 22, 31, 175
problem definition (formulating the
        Mess)
    approaches to, 126–128, 316
    introduction, 131–132
    iterative inquiry
        obstruction analysis, 132–133, 134t
        systems analysis, 132–134, 134t
    mapping phase, 135–140, 136f, 139f
    phases of, 132
    real mess formulation example,
        140–151
    real mess mapping examples,
        137–138, 137–139f
    searching phase, 132–133
    telling the story in, 140
problem solutions
    approaches to, 316
    the changing game, 6–8
    idealization phase, 128–129
    knowledge workers role in, 154–156
    realization phase, 129–130
    telling the story, 140
procedures, design criteria, 73–75
Proctor and Gamble, 158
products dimension. *See* outputs
        dimension
*A Prologue to National Development
        Planning* (Gharajedaghi), 23, 97
purposefulness, 33–38, 33f, 34f
On Purposeful Systems (Ackoff), 26
purposeful systems paradigm, 22–23, 26

Q
quality movement, 13–14

R
realization
redesign, type II constraints, 129, 183.
    See also design, interactive
Redesigning the Future (Ackoff), 23
relationships. *See also* interaction
    "and" form, 39, 69
    circular, in interdependent variables,
        111–112
    complimentary, 39, 40f
    continuum in, 39, 39f, 69
    customer-supplier, 170–174, 243,
        251–252, 256, 269
    dichotomy in, 38, 38f, 40, 69, 195
    mapping, 135–140
    multidimensionality in, 39, 69
    of opposing tendencies, 38–40, 52, 195
    "or" form, 38, 69
    plurality in, 44
    superior-subordinate, 145, 170–172,
        174, 252
    types of, 68f
religious fundamentalism, 94, 101
revenge. *See* terrorism
rewards, 181, 183, 233, 312
Richmond, Barry, 117
risk, 35, 37, 224
Rumi (Molana Jalaledin Molavi), 109

S
Santiago Theory, 123
second-order-machine, 118, 122, 137,
    183–184
self-organizing systems, 16, 20–21, 32,
    52, 121–124
self-reference, 122
shared image, 32, 84–86, 94, 121–125
shared services
    Butterworth Health Systems, 243–245,
        249–253
    Commonwealth Energy Systems,
        290–292
    decentralization of, 167–169, 250
    Oneida Nation, 206
Sheldrake, Rupert, 124
Shreiber, Jean-Jacques, 3
simplicity, chaotic, 32, 92
Singer, E. A., 109, 113
singularity, 89–91
Skenandore, Artly, 187

Sloan, Alfred, 7, 18
Smith, Adam, 119, 119f, 120f
smoking, mapping effects of, 49–50, 50f,
    137–138, 138f
social calculus, 77–82
social change, 85–86, 103
social systems, development
    culture, role in, 124
    desire and ability in defining, 94
    differentiation and integration in,
        92–96, 92f, 93f, 98–99
    Field Theory and, 124
    holistic view, 95–96
    knowledge in, 93–94
    learning in, 85–87, 122–123
    modes of transformation, 93, 93f
    obstructions to
        alienation, 97–98
        conflicting value system, 98
        corruption, 99–100
        exploitation, 98
        first- and second-order, 96–97, 97t
        intimidation, 123
        lack of freedom to question, 123
        meaninglessness, 98
        polarization, 98–99, 195
        powerlessness, 97
        rolelessness, 97
        terrorism, 100–102
    summary, 103
social systems, dimensions
    of Aristotle, 57
    beauty, 35, 56–59
    of ideal-seeking systems, 57
    interactions, role in co-producing the
        future, 94
    of John Dewey, 57–58
    knowledge, 56–58, 87, 93–94, 207
    malfunctioning in, 96–97
    obstruction analysis, 132–133
    organizational processes equivalent
        to, 58–59, 58f
    power, 37, 56–57
    values, 56
    wealth, 56, 58
society, global, 101–102
sociocultural (multiminded) systems
    attractors role in, 52
    bonding in. see bonded systems
    changing, 125

counter-intuitive behavior in,
    53, 137
culture in. see culture(s)
design approach (redesign), 22–23, 52
effectiveness measurements, 82
membership in. see membership in
    multiminded systems
paradigm shifts, 9, 9f, 17f
participative management, 20–21
plurality of structure in, 44–45
principles of. see systems principles
self-organizing, 16, 20–21, 32, 52,
    121–124
stakeholder expectations, 153
Star, John, 186
Stocker, Dean Pat, 260
strange attractors, 52
suboptimization, role in failure, 6
success
    defining, 154
    emergent property of, 46–47
    information and, 33
    knowledge and, 22
    measuring, 11, 47–48
    win/win environments, 70
sum of the whole vs. the parts, 47, 48
Super Fresh, 186
synergy in viable systems, 179t, 258,
    284, 293, 304, 306
synthetic thinking, 109
system boundary, 30
system dynamics, 132–133, 135t
systems. See also organizational
    systems
    active, 36
    aggregate vs., 196
    behavioral classifications, 36–37, 36t
    catastrophic, 53–54
    defined, 30, 83
    early warning, 127, 140
    goal-seeking, 36t, 37
    inflection points, 40–42, 53–54
    open. see systems principles:
        openness
    passive, 36, 55
    purposeful, 12, 22–23, 26, 36t, 37,
        51, 125
    reactive, 36
    responsive, 36
    state-maintaining, 36–37, 36t

systems, viable
  adaptability of, 164
  assessment, 176–178
  latency dimension
    Butterworth Health Systems, 257
    Carrier Corporation, 304
    Commonwealth Energy Systems, 292
  synergy dimension
    Butterworth Health Systems, 258
    Carrier Corporation, 304, 306
    Commonwealth Energy Systems,
      284, 293
  throughput dimension
    Butterworth Health Systems, 258
    Commonwealth Energy Systems, 293
systems analysis, 132–134, 134t
systems design. *See also* business
    architecture, design process
  background, 16
  constraints, 129–130, 181–183, 182f
  core elements, 16
  interactive. *see also* emergent properties
    defining problems, 126–128
    idealization phase, 128–129, 175–176
    iteration in, 112–113, 112f, 128–129
    learning and design cells, 72–75,
      196–197, 198f, 208–209
    management model, 22–23, 23f
    mess formulation, 128
    realization phase, 129–130,
      181–183, 182f
    systems architecture, 160
  mental model, 29
  operational viability component, 176
  technological feasibility component,
    175–176
  throughput systems. *see* throughput
    systems
systems development theory
  categories of, 88–89, 88f
  plurality in, 43–45, 89–92
  schematic view, 88–92
  singularity in, 89–91
systems methodology, foundations
  holistic thinking, 108–113, 111f
  interactive design, 125–130
  introduction, 107–108, 108f
  iterative inquiry, 112–113, 112f
  learning, 315–316
  operational thinking, 114–120

self-organization, 121–124
  summary, 130
systems principles
  counter-intuitiveness, 49–55, 50f
  emergent property, 13, 45–48, 46f
  multidimensionality. *see*
    multidimensionality principle
  openness, 30–32, 52
  purposefulness, 12–13, 33–38, 33f, 34f
systems thinking. *See also* holistic
    thinking
  analytical thinking vs., 15–16, 17f
  defined, 315
  design approach (redesign), 22–23
  flexibility and control, 22
  generations of, 16
  joint optimization, 21–22
  language for, 26
  TQM vs., 27

T
target costing, 65–66, 129, 154, 183, 232,
    281–282, 312–313
technology (inputs). *See* inputs
    dimension
terrorism, 100–102, 102f
Theory and Management of Systems
    (Gharajedaghi), 32
thinking. *See also* analytical thinking;
    systems thinking
  defined, 117–118
  holistic, 8–9, 59, 61f, 108–113, 113f
  iterative, 315
  operational, 118
  synthetic, 109
3M Corporation, 159
throughput, defined, 59
throughput systems
  design elements
    critical properties identification,
      63–64
    measurement and diagnostic
      system, 64–65
    overview, 61f
    read-only memory, 65
    simulation process model, 60–63,
      63f, 64t
    target costing, 65–66, 154
  holistic design approach, 59, 61f
  learning system in, 65

throughput systems *cont.*
  management components, 82
  Oneida Nation, 203–210
Tiefel, Bill, 260
time, defining, 52
Torus attractors, 52
Total Quality Management (TQM), 27
Toyota, 7, 22, 65
truth
  generation and dissemination of, 56–58
  Singer on, 109, 113
typologies, 40–42

U
understanding vs.
    information/knowledge, 33
uniformity, 167–168, 250
United States
  corporate corruption in, 99–100
  terrorism and, 100–102
unminded (biological) systems
  diversity and growth, 18–20
  flexibility and control, 22
  introduction, 11–12
  paradigm shifts, 9*f*, 17*f*

V
value chain strategy, 172–174, 173*f*, 279,
    288–290, 298
value-guided systems, 36
values
  corruption of, 99–100
  as decision criteria, 35–36
  ethical, 35–36
  formation and institutionalization of, 56

Varela, Francisco, 123
variable budgeting, 65–66, 129, 174, 183,
    312–313
variables
  controlled vs. influenced, 30–32,
    65, 154
  independent, 13–15*f*, 13–16, 46*f*
  interdependent, 46*f*, 111–112
  performance measures, 177–178
  singularity (inflection) point,
    40–42, 53–54
viability matrix, 178–180, 179t

W
wealth, generation and distribution,
    56, 58
Weber, Max, 57
welfare system dynamics, 49, 50*f*
Wharton econometric model, 22, 31
What is a Business For (Handy), 99
Wheatley, Margaret J., 124
the whole, defining, 111
the whole, defining the, 46
Wilson, Gerald L., 297
Wolfram, Stephen, 112, 118
Woodhaven Stamping Plant, 14, 14*f*
world community, 101–102

Y
Young, Wendell, 186

Z
zero-sum game, 38, 69, 100
Zoroaster, 25

JAMSHID GHARAJEDAGHI, Managing Partner of INTERACT, The Institute for Interactive Management, has more than thirty years of experience with the practice of systems methodology in design and the development of business architecture, planning, learning and control systems. His work has taken him into corporations and government agencies around the world for both private and public concerns.

Mr. Gharajedaghi was formerly the Director of The Busch Center, the research arm of the Social Systems Sciences Department, and Adjunct Professor of Systems Sciences at The Wharton School, University of Pennsylvania (1979–1986). He began his career with IBM's World Trade Corporation where he served as a senior systems engineer (1963–1969). He left IBM to become CEO of the Industrial Management Institute (1969–1979). He has held teaching positions at The Wharton School, University of Pennsylvania (1979–1986); IBM Education Centers (1965–1969); and the University of California, Berkeley (1961–1963).

Mr. Gharajedaghi received his engineering degree from the University of California, Berkeley (1963) and completed more than 1,500 hours of professional training in systems engineering at the IBM Education Centers in the United Kingdom, Germany, and France. From this early training in information systems, his interests led him to operations research, behavioral sciences, and finally, for the last 21 years, to the development and application of interactive design.

He has been a member of: the Research Board of the International Systems Institute, USA (1983–1992); the Governing Body of the Asian

Productivity Organization, Japan (1972–1979); the Board of Trustees for AZAD University, Iran (1976–1979); and Regional Chairman of the Society for General Systems Research—Asia (1975–1979).

He was the project manager for two internationally acclaimed projects: New Economic Order, a United Nations project; and Goals for Mankind, a Club of Rome project.

Mr. Gharajedaghi has been involved with the following sponsoring organizations to redesign businesses, product(s), and/or processes:

Aluminum Company of America (ALCOA)
ANGLOVAAL, Limited (South Africa)
Armco (Latin American Division)
Butterworth Health System
Carrier Corporation
Chrysler Corporation
Clark Equipment Company
Commonwealth Energy Systems
Edgars Stores, Ltd. (South Africa)
Ford Motor Company
Health Care Forum
Marriott Corporation
Martin-Marietta Corporation
Metropolitan Life Insurance Company
NYNEX Science & Technology, Inc.
Oneida Tribe of Indians of Wisconsin
Super Fresh Food Markets
United Food & Commercial Workers' Union

Mr. Gharajedaghi has written several books, including *Prologue to National Development Planning* and *Towards a Systems Theory of Organization*. He is the author of numerous published articles in various international scientific and management journals. Presently, in addition to his consulting activities at Interact, Mr. Gharajedaghi is involved with teaching Systems Thinking at Villanova University, Executive MBA Program.